A CULTURAL HISTORY OF FURNITURE

FURNITURE

VOLUME 2

A Cultural History of Furniture
General Editor: Christina M. Anderson

A CULTURAL HISTORY OF FURNITURE

IN THE MIDDLE AGES AND RENAISSANCE

Edited by
Erin J. Campbell and Stephanie R. Miller

BLOOMSBURY ACADEMIC
LONDON • NEW YORK • OXFORD • NEW DELHI • SYDNEY

BLOOMSBURY ACADEMIC
Bloomsbury Publishing Plc
50 Bedford Square, London, WC1B 3DP, UK
1385 Broadway, New York, NY 10018, USA
29 Earlsfort Terrace, Dublin 2, Ireland

BLOOMSBURY, BLOOMSBURY ACADEMIC and the Diana logo are
trademarks of Bloomsbury Publishing Plc

First published in Great Britain 2022

Series design: Raven Design.
Cover image: Froissart's *Chronicles Banquet*. Fourteenthcentury illuminated manuscript.
Royal MS 14 E IV, f. 244v. London, British Library. (© Photo 12/ UIG via Getty Images)

A catalogue record for this book is available from the British Library.

A catalog record for this book is available from the Library of Congress.

ISBN: Pack: 978-1-4725-7789-4
         HB: 978-1-4725-7780-1

Series: The Cultural Histories Series

Typeset by Integra Software Services Pvt. Ltd.
Printed and bound in Great Britain

To find out more about our authors and books visit www.bloomsbury.com
and sign up for our newsletters.

CONTENTS

LIST OF ILLUSTRATIONS

PLATES

FIGURES

CONTRIBUTORS

Evanthia Baboula is Assistant Professor at the Department of Art History & Visual Studies, University of Victoria, Canada. She received her Ph.D. from Oxford University. Her early work was on the use and exchange of metals in the late Bronze Age of Crete and Cyprus. In recent years her interests have turned to historical periods focusing mainly on the arts of the Eastern Mediterranean from the late antique to the late medieval periods. Her current research is centered on the study of cross-cultural encounters in the crusader and late Byzantine periods and the urban topography of southern Greece during the phase of Ottoman rule.

Caroline Campbell is Director of Collections and Research at the National Gallery, London, UK. She has held curatorial positions at the National Gallery, The Courtauld Gallery, University of London, and the Ashmolean Museum, Oxford. Caroline has published widely in the field of Italian Renaissance painting and its reception. She has curated and cocurated many exhibitions, including *Mantegna and Bellini* (2018–19), *Building the Picture: Architecture in Italian Renaissance Painting* (2014), *Love and Marriage in Renaissance Florence* (2009), and *Bellini and the East* (2005–6).

Erin J. Campbell is Professor of Early Modern European Art in the Department of Art History & Visual Studies, University of Victoria, Canada. Her publications appear in a number of journals and essay collections, including the *Journal of Art Historiography*, *Sixteenth Century Journal*, *Word & Image*, *Renaissance Quarterly*, *The Cultural Aesthetics of Eighteenth-Century Porcelain*, and *To Have and To Hold: Marriage in Premodern Europe 1200–1700*. She is editor and contributing author of *Growing Old in Early Modern Europe: Cultural Representations* (2006), coeditor and contributing author of *The Early Modern*

Italian Domestic Interior: People, Objects, Domesticities (2013), and author of *Old Women and Art in the Early Modern Italian Domestic Interior* (2015).

Leah R. Clark is Senior Lecturer in Art History at the Open University, UK. Her research explores the roles objects play in creating networks in the fifteenth century through their exchange, collection, and replication. She is author of *Collecting Art in the Italian Renaissance Court: Objects and Exchanges* (2018). She is coeditor (with Nancy Um) of a special issue "The Art of Embassy: Objects and Images of Early Modern Diplomacy" of the *Journal of Early Modern History* (2016) and coeditor (with Kathleen Christian) of a textbook on the global Renaissance, *European Art and the Wider World 1350–1550* (2017).

Elizabeth Moore Hunt is an independent scholar. She has published essays on the marginal imagery, heraldry, and material culture of late medieval art. Her book, *Illuminating the Borders of Northern French and Flemish Manuscripts* (2007), examines the expansion of marginal images in devotional books, encyclopedia, and romances during the late thirteenth century. Her forthcoming study, *The Psalter of Guy of Dampierre and Manuscripts Illuminated for the Court of Flanders*, contextualizes a family of devotional and romance manuscripts destined for the family members of the Count of Flanders. The present chapter was supported in part by a grant from the Wyoming Institute for Humanities Research at University of Wyoming.

Ethan Matt Kavaler is Director of the Centre for Reformation and Renaissance Studies and Professor of Art History at the University of Toronto. He is the author of *Renaissance Gothic: Architecture and the Arts in Northern Europe 1470–1540* (2012), *Pieter Bruegel: Parables of Order and Enterprise* (1999), and several essays on ornament, artistic mode, periodization, Netherlandish secular painting, and late Gothic architecture. He is a member of the Royal Academy of Archeology of Belgium and a former member of the managing committee of the Historians of Netherlandish Art.

Stephanie R. Miller is Associate Professor of Art History at Coastal Carolina University, South Carolina, USA. Her research interests include the tin-glazed terra-cotta sculpture of Andrea della Robbia and the material culture of women and children in early modern Italy. Her research has been included in *The Anthology of Chapels* (2010), *Visual Resources*, and *The Sculpture Journal*. She is coeditor and contributing author to *The Early Modern Domestic Italian Interior* (2013). She is editor of *A Cultural History of Interiors in the Renaissance* (forthcoming).

Hollie L.S. Morgan is currently a Research Fellow at the University of Lincoln, working on the Imprint project. She completed her Ph.D. in Medieval Studies at University of York in 2014 and is the author of *Beds and Chambers in Late Medieval England: Readings, Representations and Realities* (2017).

Claudio Paolini is Art Historian for the Ministero italiano per i Beni Culturali (MiBACT), specializing in conservation, restoration, and the history of artistic techniques. He has given courses and seminars at a number of Italian and international universities, and acted as the scientific director of Artis e Plaster Architecture, a project supported by the European Commission to promote knowledge of traditional artistic media and techniques. He is also the project manager of the Argos project, which is building a digital database for standardizing the language in the field of restoration and techniques. He has more than one hundred specialized publications, including many on the history of furniture and woodworking.

Christopher Pickvance is Emeritus Professor of Urban Studies, School of Social Policy, Sociology and Social Research, University of Kent, Canterbury, UK. He has been Chairman of the Regional Furniture Society since 2011. He has a particular interest in pre-1700 furniture in the UK and on the Continent, and in national and regional differences in furniture types, methods of construction, and types of decoration. His research has focused on medieval and later chests now in the UK, including imported chests. His articles have been published in *Antiquaries Journal, Furniture History, Regional Furniture, Archaeologia Cantiana*, and *Sussex Archaeological Collections*.

Matthew M. Reeve is Associate Professor and Queen's National Scholar at Queen's University and a Fellow of the Society of Antiquaries of London. He has published widely on medieval art and architecture and modern medievalisms, including books on Gothic architecture and wall painting. He has published recent essays in *The Art Bulletin, Architectural History, British Art Studies, The Burlington Magazine*, among others, and his monograph *Gothic Architecture and Sexuality in the Circle of Horace Walpole* (2019) is now in press. He is currently working on a number of projects, including a monograph on Welsh Gothic architecture, the intersection of laser scanning technology and the built environment, English Gothic sculpture, and aspects of medievalism in Canadian architecture.

Diane Reilly is Associate Professor and Chair of the Department of Art History at Indiana University, USA. She studies the intersection between art, liturgy, pedagogy, and monastic life in the central Middle Ages. She is the author of *The Art of Reform in Eleventh-Century Flanders: Gerard of Cambrai, Richard of Saint-Vannes and the Saint Vaast Bible* (2006) and *The Cistercian Reform and the Art of the Book in Twelfth-Century France* (2018). With Susan Boynton she edits the journal *Gesta*.

SERIES PREFACE

A Cultural History of Furniture is a six-volume series examining the changing cultural framework within which furniture was designed, produced, and used, as well as the cultural construction of furniture itself, from antiquity through to the present day in the Western tradition. All the volumes follow the same structure: an editorial overview of the historical context of the period under consideration is followed by chapters written by specialists that each correspond to one of the following themes: design and motifs; makers, making, and materials; types and uses; the domestic setting; the public setting; exhibition and display; furniture and architecture; visual representations; and verbal representations. The configuration of the series means that readers can use the material synchronically or diachronically: an individual volume provides a thorough grounding in the furniture of a particular period while following one distinct theme across all volumes presents the reader with the evolution of a specific aspect of furniture over time. The six volumes divide the history of furniture in this way:

Volume 1: A Cultural History of Furniture in Antiquity (From the beginnings to 500 CE)

Volume 2: A Cultural History of Furniture in the Middle Ages and Renaissance (500–1500)

Volume 3: A Cultural History of Furniture in the Age of Exploration (1500–1700)

Volume 4: A Cultural History of Furniture in the Age of Enlightenment (1700–1800)

Volume 5: A Cultural History of Furniture in the Age of Empire and Industry (1800–1900)

Volume 6: A Cultural History of Furniture in the Modern Age (1900–twenty-first century)

Christina M. Anderson
General Editor

EDITORS' ACKNOWLEDGMENTS

We are very grateful to Christina Anderson for her wise and careful supervision of this multivolume project. We also wish to thank all of our contributors: without their impeccable and inspiring scholarship this volume would not have been possible. We appreciate as well the editorial and production team at Bloomsbury. We are thankful to Estelle Kurier for her excellent translation of Chapter 2 in this volume. Nick Humphrey, Curator, Furniture, Textiles and Fashion Department, Victoria & Albert Museum, was generous with his expertise at a very early stage of this project. Christopher Pickvance, author of Chapter 3, also provided wise counsel on various matters relating to medieval furniture. We are indebted to Holly Cecil, who provided invaluable research, which has informed the Introduction.

Introduction

Furniture and Culture

ERIN J. CAMPBELL AND STEPHANIE R. MILLER

Furniture is intimately tied to culture—it is an artifact, namely, "An object made by a human being, typically one of cultural or historical interest" (*Compact Oxford English Dictionary* 1971). The forms and functions of furniture depend on a combination of sociocultural, religious, political, and economic factors. Geography, locality, and cross-cultural exchanges have a determining influence on the development of furniture. Furnishings can reflect cultural transmission, dominance, or collaboration. They depend on the availability of materials, trade routes, alliances, business networks, standards of craft, levels of prosperity, class, and social status. Furniture can express social bonds and create community. It can be an instrument of power and symbolic agency. At the most basic level, human needs condition the evolution of furniture, such as the need for community, for family and connection, for warmth and security. Furnishings evolved to keep foodstuffs safe and to store clothing. Essential human needs and culture shape furniture, and furniture in turn shapes culture.

Furniture is scaled to the human body, adjusted for the human anatomy. The furniture of power and display observes this relationship in the breach, acquiring power by resisting the human scale. Architecture conditions furniture: there is a symbiotic relationship between architectural setting, space, scale, ornamentation, and form and furniture. Furniture forms part of the ecosystem of an architectural environment. It forms sensuous assemblages of textiles, precious vessels, sound, light, food, and scent (Campbell 2014: 15–16). Studying individual examples of furniture extracts them from the meshwork of their ecology, and risks losing the dynamic, living nature of furnishings. Furniture makes culture possible. It provides affordances: that is, furniture enables relationships in the world through its forms and functions. It provides tables for social groups to gather around, chairs to establish social precedence and hierarchies, pulpits to preach from, lecterns to read on, desks to write poetry and literature on, beds to procreate in, and chests, cupboards, and caskets to allow us to accumulate goods, safely store precious items, and to hand down keepsakes and objects imbued with dynastic, familial, or personal memory.

The Arnolfini Portrait by Jan van Eyck (1434), in the National Gallery, London (Plate 1), bears witness to the cultural value of furnishings within late medieval society. In the image, the furnishings occupy as much space as the bourgeois merchant couple. The bed, chair, sideboard, lighting, glazing, and textiles are exquisitely detailed with rapt attention to texture, sheen, design, and craftsmanship. Textiles are crucial to the display. They convey not just the status and wealth of the couple, but the cultural value of domestic warmth and comfort. The carpet under the feet of the couple is a sign of privilege (Eames 1971: 47). The bedcoverings, including canopy, valance, tester at the head of the bed, hanging pendant, curtains, and coverlet distinguish the authority of the merchant within his household (45). The crimson drapery on the chair softens edges, invites the touch, and adds color. The furniture is thus as richly dressed as the couple themselves. The detailed attention to the glazing, chandelier, and mirror demonstrates the importance of light and sheen within this domestic environment of prestige and comfort. In this portrait the furnishings are as important as the people. The people and the furniture are inseparable, inextricably bound together within an ecosystem or habitat.

Similarly, the scene of the Dukes of York, Gloucester, and Ireland dining with Richard II, in the *Anciennes et Nouvelles Chronique d'Angleterre* (Jean de Wavrin, after 1471, before 1483, British Library, Royal MS 14 E IV, f. 265v) (Plate 2) reveals the role of furnishings in creating a highly nuanced social environment. The table, seating, buffet, and textiles are crucial to the display of authority. The benches are carefully orchestrated to convey precedence. The bare, backless bench is contrasted to the comfortable high-backed settle draped with textiles. It is this more exalted seating that holds the king and the most distinguished guests, and separates them from the lesser members of the gathering. The size and shape of the draped table allow the king to be placed symmetrically in a central position of dominance, which is marked by the canopy suspended behind him. The display of plate on the buffet behind the king displays his wealth and underscores his authority. The furniture allows for the transmission of both power and the values of hospitality. Comparable to *The Arnolfini Portrait*, the furnishings in the illumination of Richard II establish status, precedence, privilege, wealth, etiquette, grace, and social relationships.

THE CULTURAL CONTEXT FOR FURNITURE

A major theme in the cultural history of furniture is the role of furnishings in mediating social relationships. The emergence of furniture's ability to play a nuanced role in social life depends on many factors and can be seriously hampered when any one of them founders. The development and refinement of furniture depends on relative economic and political stability, ready availability of materials and skilled craftspeople, and a population with both the need and the means to purchase furniture, as well as places to put it.

The period covered by this book is marked by dramatic social, economic, political, and religious changes. Diverse regional and local conditions, and varied social classes, including peasant, artisan, merchant, clergy, nobility, and rulers, resulted in differing needs for furniture. The earliest phase of the period covered by this volume is marked by migrations and invasions, beginning with the movement of Germanic tribes in the fifth century into western Europe, which disrupted communities, undermined trade, and hampered agriculture. The seventh and eighth centuries, with the blending of Roman, Christian, and Germanic traditions, witnessed constant warfare in some regions of Europe. With the emergence of Charlemagne (r. 768–814) there was a new sense of a shared European cultural identity; however, the medieval world consisted of three separate societies: the Latin West, the Byzantine East, and, the Islamic caliphate, which, by the middle of the eighth century, commanded an expansive empire. Moreover, the period is characterized by extreme divisions of wealth, with impoverished peasants and artisans far outweighing the elite classes.

The political strife, social turmoil, dislocation, poverty, and conditions such as disease and famine, as well as the crusades characteristic of the central Middle Ages (tenth to the twelfth century) all had an effect on the development of furniture, contributing to the emphasis on portable furnishings, which could quickly be moved from place to place in times of strife and social disruption, as ecclesiastical, royal, and noble households became mobile in search of safety and supplies. While the need for mobility conditioned the forms adopted by domestic furnishings, church furniture became more elaborate than household furniture during these periods of relative instability, since church furniture was largely fixed rather than mobile and was closely tied to the architectural environment.

Despite the political and religious upheaval during this period, continental and intercontinental trade was robust. Through trade and travel, greater awareness of goods, peoples, and practices spread. Europe's economic decline in the seventh and eighth centuries began to rebound in the centuries thereafter with active trading with the areas surrounding the Mediterranean, with a variety of goods and materials exchanged in such European ports as Venice, Genoa, and Bruges. Through these points of exchange, Europe exported a variety of goods, especially timber and semiprecious metals, particularly from northern Europe, and imported a wide range of "luxury" objects and materials, such as rugs, glazed ceramics, spices, silks, and ivory, and by the end of the era ebony, bamboo, and lacquered wood begin to be imported (Brotton 2002: 38–9, 173; O'Connell and Dursteler 2016: 131–3), all of which transformed the European environment.

As wealth and stability increased toward the end of our period, with the steady growth of commerce and urban life, secure trade routes, readily available materials, and craftsmen, the need for simple pieces that were easily transported decreased. Furniture design became more sophisticated to meet the needs of a population now attuned to the potential of furniture as a medium of fashion, conspicuous consumption, and social display. Thus, we witness the development of more types of furniture that are designed for specific social purposes. In response to an increased demand for luxury—especially among the courts and the urban elites—techniques of furniture crafting were developed that are associated with the values of luxury, such as metal casting, the mortise-and-tenon joint, and inlay, and there is a new appreciation for imported materials, such as ivory.

Because imported, luxury commodities reflected refinement, status, and worldliness, traders continued to supply the demand for such luxuries to growing European markets. The cross-cultural exchange in port cities led to new manufacturing to also meet this demand and to further profit from it. For instance, as carpets, metalwork, and ceramic objects arrived from Egypt, Syria, and beyond, European craftsmen were inspired to emulate their technique and style and sell them within the European market. As well, the Venetians, who were among the main importers of soda ash from Syria, a necessary ingredient for glassmaking, were exporting this prized glass commodity throughout Europe as well as into the Near East (O'Connell and Dursteler 2016: 133).

Despite religious strife in this period, the Western Church nevertheless provided a unifying force. From its missionary activities in the earliest part of this era to its increasing power throughout Europe, the visibility of the Church in medieval Europe helped spread architectural and furnishing style as well as its message. This is especially true after the eleventh century, when there was a burst of church building activities, which included interior furnishing. Though certain religious orders, such as the Cistercians or the Benedictines, expressed a desire for specific styles, there seems to have been no directive from a centralized authority insisting on particular styles. Nevertheless, church architecture, furnishings, and embellishments are distinctive—not unchanging, but distinct from other domestic or secular forms. As the Church grew in size and in numbers, management and administration became a necessity, as did the need for uniform, liturgical practices. Ecclesiastical rituals became formalized during these centuries, so that even when the papacy itself was weakened, as during the Great Schism between 1378 and 1417 (when there were two popes elected, and at one point three), the ceremonies of the church with its attendant furnishings provided stability.

During this era, the basilica, a longitudinal hall, was the most common church plan. Within it new furnishings began to appear dependent on changes to the liturgy or church protocol. For instance, in the ninth century, desks on either side of the central hall (nave) were used for reading from the Gospels and the Epistles. From the Gospel desk emerged the pulpit, the elevated speaking platform used by church officials to preach to congregants. By the thirteenth century, especially in Italian churches, the pulpit was set to the north side of the hall, not far from the altar (typically at the east end of the church). During this century arose the popular preaching orders of the Franciscans and Dominicans, with especially large churches to accommodate parishioners during their well-attended sermons, making elevated pulpits a necessity.

Church seating was not common at the beginning of the era, but as services and liturgy became longer and more complex, movable and then fixed seating for clergy in the choir (east end of church) developed by the eleventh century. Choir stalls provided rows of sequestered seating for the clergy who sang during service. Misericords also provided standing support to clergy during long services. Misericords, or "mercy-seats," were wooden projections from the undersides of choir stall seats that buttressed the individual when such seats were raised. Despite the increasing intricacies of the Christian liturgy, it might surprise that, until 1215, it was unclear who was allowed to perform the sacrament of the Eucharist, the central element of Christian Mass. In 1215 the Fourth Lateran Council made clear that only the priest could perform the sacrament. At this same council, with new focus on this important ritual, emerged rood screens, barriers of wood or stone in the church separating the chancel or much of the church's east end from the rest of the nave. In essence, this was also a separation of laity from clergy, but with the intention of preserving the Eucharistic host. Squints in the rood screen might be added so laity could "peek through" to witness the Elevation of the Host, the raising of the consecrated bread and wine during Mass (Sauer 2014: 150–69).

DEFINING FURNITURE: 500–1500

The geographical scope of the medieval furniture discussed in this volume encompasses the United Kingdom, Continental Europe, and Scandinavia. The chronological sweep extends from the fall of the Roman Empire through to the early Renaissance. The time period includes a wide array of types, styles, and motifs, including Byzantine, Romanesque, Gothic, and Renaissance. Rural and regional styles of furniture are also considered.

Furniture is typically defined as movable articles within a domestic, civic, or ecclesiastical context, such as chairs, tables, or beds, that make such spaces able to fulfill the functions of living, working, and worship. However, furniture during the time period encompassed by this volume does not fit neatly into this modern definition of furniture. Much medieval furniture challenges the modernist distinction between furniture and room fittings (Mercer 1969: 54). During the medieval period, furniture could be built-in or fixed, such as beds and cupboards built into the wall, or benches that could be built in around the perimeter of a wall (57). Since households tended to be more mobile, especially during the early centuries, built-in furniture was practical since it meant fewer items to carry as families changed residences (Eames 1977: xviii). Furniture made of stone, such as pulpits and bishops' thrones, could not be moved. At the lower end of the social scale, stone used for building could also be used for bed nooks, stone benches, dressers, sideboards, or buffets (Mercer 1969: 55).

Complementing built-in furniture were pieces that were easily folded or carried and could be taken from residence to residence, such as the oak folding table in the Cluny Museum, which has been dated to around 1480 to 1500. The table comes apart, making it easy to store and transport (Eames 1977: 223). Such portable furnishings could be put away for protection when not in use, and could also allow spaces to be used for different purposes (217). Furniture needed to be multifunctional so that rooms and spaces could be used for different activities. Benches could be used as beds, beds and chests could be used as seats, chests and benches could be used as tables and desks (Mercer 1969: 62–4).

Textiles, which could be brought out or stored as needed, are also encompassed within the definition of furniture. Textiles had the ability to transform a room (Eames 1977: xx). Textiles include hangings and carpets, which could be placed on the wall or floor, or textiles that were draped on the furniture itself, such as cushions on chairs and benches, including "bankers" and "dorsers" (textiles draped on the seats [bankers] and behind the backs [dorsers]), as well as bedcoverings, such as coverlets, curtains, canopies, valances, and testers. Tapestries were draped on rough-hewn tables to transform them into items of luxury and display (Mercer 1969: 27–8; Morely 1999: 11), or on buffets to provide a rich backdrop for the sensuous presentation of precious vessels of gold and silver, which were a form of wealth that could be put on show and then locked away for safety (Eames 1977: xx).

The social settings for furniture include official and private residences both grand and humble, churches and monasteries, and civic institutions, including places of governance and learning such as municipal halls, guild halls, and colleges. As social conditions changed over the one thousand years covered in this volume, so too did the architectural settings for furniture, which in turn influenced the evolution of furniture. Thus, by the mid-fourteenth century movable furniture began to replace built-ins. More centralized governments and the increasing importance of urban patriciates and merchants meant that a single prominent residence started to replace the multiple residences of previous centuries, and, along with rising expectations for domestic comfort, put in play by the growing wealth of urban merchants and bankers, we see an increase in the amount of furniture. For example, Florentine records from around 1400, which are thought to still reflect the time of Dante and Giotto, provide evidence that even large homes had few furnishings, which would change dramatically over the course of the fifteenth century, as Florentine homes gradually became full of furnishings (Goldthwaite 1993: 225, 226–7).

Social customs and manners changed and became more formalized throughout this period, witnessed by the increase in texts, poems, and manuals on etiquette, manners, household management, and courtesy. More courtiers by the twelfth century may in part explain the interest in courtesy and the spread of courtly behavior by this time (Whelan 2017: 98). In the centuries thereafter, texts from a variety of perspectives offer guidance on appropriate behavior and social expectations. For example, Daniel of Beccles, believed to be a courtier in Henry II of England's court, is thought to be the author of the early thirteenth-century *Book of the Civilized Man* (*Urbanus magnus*); Robert Grosseteste, bishop of Lincoln wrote his *Rules* (1240) on personal and household governance as advice for the recently widowed Countess Margaret of Lincoln; Leon Battista Alberti, a Florentine humanist and author, wrote *Della famiglia* (1444), whereby through fictional characters Alberti dispenses advice on relationships, household management, and family reputation; Alienor de Poitiers, a member of the Burgundian court, described courtly life, ceremony, and protocol in her *Honors of the Court* (1484–91). Throughout, good manners are associated with good moral behavior as well as meaningful tools to employ for social mobility. Regarding social mobility, in the *Book of the Civilized Man*, the author advises that if he wishes to be distinguished and advance socially, then he ought to "listen, learn the manner of dining" (Whelan 2017: 98). The eyewitness accounts and instruction in this text highlights the sense of personal display while at table. Such advice for table manners and hygiene is significant in the Italian *Ordine et officii de casa de lo Illistrissimo Signor Duca de Urbino* (1482–9), a type of manual for the servants and household manager at the court of the Duke of Urbino. The text paints a picture of a highly ordered and regimented household based on appropriate behavior and expectations, and increased refinement that includes hand washing at the table as genteel behavior suggestive of refined society. Therefore dining, and the preamble of washing before eating, is a visible and social activity in a hall or *sala*, with the appropriate furnishings, tables, and sideboards and buffets, adorned to mark a great celebration. Banquets and dining are given great attention in these texts. Fiona Whelan also notes in her study on the *Urbanus magnus* that courtesy and manners were not superficially only about appropriateness or about social advancement; proper behavior was also seen as morally righteous (2017: 102). Similarly, welcoming guests to one's home was considered hospitable, generous, and an example of Christian charity. Orderliness of home and furnishings also communicated moral overtones in these guidebooks, as it signified diligence and care. Furniture such as tables, buffets, and benches in receiving areas of the home thus demonstrated generosity and morality and one's ability to comport oneself appropriately within this environment became a social necessity during the Middle Ages.

Penelope Eames argues that court culture exerted an influence on furniture development in the later Middle Ages, citing the example of the Duchy of Burgundy. In the courtly context, furniture reflected and shaped court ceremonial (Eames 1977: xvii), which emphasized precedence (xviii). Furniture strengthened the social framework of society, which was still ingrained with feudal concepts of hierarchy and power (xviii–xix). Furniture played an important role in practices of social precedence, which depended on relationships with a chain of power, in which the person of authority in a given social setting is accorded the most prestigious advantage, which is defined through furnishings, such as being seated on a chair on a dais while others are seated below on benches or stools (xix).

During the later Middle Ages in Europe, the courtly display of the Valois dukes in particular exerted influence across France and the Netherlands (Low Countries), and as far away as England, where influence flowed due to the important trade in wool and cloth between these regions (Eames 1977: xvi–xvii). The emphasis on furnishings as integral to the values of court life in turn influenced the ideals of domestic comfort in the bourgeois interiors of Flemish traders in Ghent, Ypres, and Bruges, which are reflected in paintings by Robert Campin, Jan van Eyck, and Roger van der Weyden (xvii). Such images show chambers populated by settles draped with textiles and cushions, tables of various types, chairs, side tables, and beds. For example, the *Annunciation* in the Louvre, by Rogier van der Weyden (*c.* 1435), includes a bench with cushions, a cupboard with doors and a lower shelf, a stool draped in cloth at which the Virgin kneels, and a resplendent bed with a canopy of rich red velvet. The center panel of the *Mérode Altarpiece* by Robert Campin has the Virgin seated on the floor beside an elaborate settle (a wooden bench with arms and a high back), with a round table at her elbow (The Metropolitan Museum of Art, New York, *c.* 1425).

Accompanying such social changes over time, the spaces within residences also changed. The multipurpose medieval hall was the heart of the medieval household. It was in the richly decorated great hall that the entire household and guests would banquet together (Girouard 1978: 30). Such halls were central to hospitality, feasting, and entertainment and judicial courts and meetings of government could be held in them (32). Many halls could exceed 230 square meters (33). Furnishings allowed the lord to demonstrate strength, unity, and generosity. The lord, his family, and important guests would be seated at one long table that from the thirteenth century onward could be placed on a dais. Tables for the rest of the household and guests would be placed at right angles to the high table (Eames 1977: 217), which could be flanked by displays of precious plate. A canopy could be suspended over the dais (Girouard 1978: 34). However, by the end of the medieval period the great hall began to lose some of its functions to the chamber, which introduced new forms of sociability and therefore demanded different kinds of furniture that were less conditioned by the ceremonial routines of the hall. Chambers could be used for sleeping, receiving guests, playing games, and meals (Mercer 1969: 72; Girouard 1978: 40; Goldthwaite 1993: 227–30). Over time, chambers would become the most richly furnished rooms in a house (Goldthwaite 1993: 226).

As the chamber evolved to become the most conspicuous site for the consumption of furnishings, and other spaces in the home slowly began to fill with furniture (Goldthwaite 1993: 226–7), new attitudes toward the value of goods, which favored accumulation as a form of social display and class validation, and a new appreciation of the social nuances of furniture, contributed to a tendency toward fewer built-ins (Mercer 1969: 69–71). At the same time, the organization of interior space into more distinct functions is accompanied by the increasing specialization of types. Specialization is apparent both in the limiting of furniture which had previously enjoyed multifunctions to one function, and in the emergence of new forms (78). For example, the freestanding cupboard now evolved into several specialized types, as in the buffet or dresser, which was a stand of open shelves created to show off precious vessels. However, this form also developed into a type that combined open shelves above a closed cupboard and which had a base stand for less precious vessels (79). By the late fifteenth century, when dining in the chamber was becoming more common, cupboards were devised to hold food in the chamber, and were outfitted with open-work tracery decoration to provide ventilation (79). Tracery is a form of ornament in which panels are divided by ribs into interlacing, delicate patterns in various shapes and sizes. Tables also became more popular and took on more diverse forms. Most early tables consisted of boards placed upon trestles and were used in the medieval hall with benches against the wall. Such tables were usually rectangular and of long and narrow proportions. However, by the late fifteenth to early sixteenth century tables were used for other purposes. We find chess-tables and small, low tables in chambers along with diverse shapes such as octagons and square tables, which could be set on richly carved stands

(80). Ecclesiastical settings such as churches and monasteries demanded special, often elaborate furnishings, such as pulpits, choir stalls, altars, chests, and benches. Monasteries in particular play an important role in the development of specialized types. Within the protected spaces of monastic cells and halls, furniture developed for libraries, including lecterns, cupboards, and furniture for displaying and storing books (Lucie-Smith 1979: 51).

Innovations in building techniques also had an impact on the evolution of furniture. In the later Middle Ages, the increasing presence of wall fireplaces and technical advances in glass manufacture and glazing greatly improved heat, ventilation, and light within rooms (Gloag 1972: 13). As the need for fortifications receded, walls became less thick and window openings became larger. Now that the heat source was transferred from the center of the room to the wall, the arrangement and style of seating was altered. Benches and chests placed against the wall, with a textile hanging (a dorcer or dorcel) placed behind to protect the seat from the cold stone or plaster, were common in the medieval hall. A cloth called a banker could be draped on seats and footboards (15). As seating became lighter, and chairs, benches, and stools easier to move around (24), the wall fireplace could become a focal point in the room, and wainscoting could replace tapestries as the wall covering of choice.

Techniques of furniture manufacture also evolved from the early Middle Ages to the early Renaissance. Furniture of the early medieval period would typically be made of thick timbers cut with an axe, and consequently furniture was very heavy (Mercer 1969: 29, 84). Value was placed on strength and endurance, and the local wood most valued was oak (Eames 1977: 230; Chinnery 1979: 149–50). By the late medieval period, joined construction, which relied on the mortise-and-tenon joint secured by pegs or dowels, was replacing the boarded construction furniture in which split or sawn planks were held in place with iron nails (Gloag 1972: 7). With the advent of joinery, furniture could now be lighter, since it could be made of much thinner panels of wood inserted into a firmly jointed framework (Mercer 1969: 84). The techniques of joinery strengthened and improved the forms of furniture, and facilitated the emancipation of cupboards and beds from the wall, to become freestanding (Gloag 1972: 8). With the adaptation of Gothic ornament to furniture in the late medieval period, carvers and joiners were able to bring a new, more lively definition to Gothic forms since wood was more easily carved than stone. Furniture makers even created new decorative devices to combine with the Gothic ornament, such as the linenfold motif created with more sophisticated hand tools, such as the plough plane, which enabled greater precision (Gloag 1972: 19). The emergence of the sawmill in south Germany by the early fourteenth century was able to support the demand for such furniture (Mercer 1969: 84). Such technical innovation in Europe during the thirteenth and fourteenth centuries, encouraged by the rapid growth of the population, agricultural improvements, and the expansion of trade, was dependent on the establishment of local industries that enjoyed access to regional, national, or international markets. Access to running water that could be used for industry was also a factor (Lucas 2005: 14, 26). The development of technology was joined by the formation of furniture-maker guilds in certain regions of Europe, which marked a nascent differentiation between carpenters and furniture makers. Turners, craftsmen relying on lathes, were among the first to differentiate their skills from other woodworkers; a turners' guild is noted in Cologne by 1180 (Mercer 1969: 46; Sparkes 1980: 11–13). This differentiation facilitated the specialization of craftsmanship, which could support the creation of higher standards of furniture making (Mercer 1969: 85). The emergence of sawn timber also encouraged the proliferation of wooden paneling (85). Because of the high level of craftsmanship made possible by these technical advances, woodwork now attained the level of quality that hitherto had only been apparent in precious materials (86). Metal, such as bronze or gold, was a prestigious material for furniture, which had also allowed for more expressive ornamental work than wood for much of this period. The Throne of Dagobert (Figure 0.1) and the Golden Pulpit from Charlemagne's Palatine Chapel at Aachen (1002–14) are but two notable examples where power and authority are expressed through material and ornament. Once the technology and skill to work wood to the same degree as other materials emerged, fine workmanship in wood could now itself be an item of display, replacing the need to cover rough-hewn timbers with richly woven textiles (Mercer 1969: 86). Rich carving began to replace paint and the application of valuable materials such as metals or precious stones as a choice for rendering ornament, and wooden panels began to replace textiles as a wall covering of choice (86).

Beyond its functional purposes, furniture could carry tremendous symbolic value during the medieval period. For example, the faldstool was symbolic of authority not just for royalty but also for civic and religious leaders. Consisting of an x-frame supporting a seat, which could fold up and was portable, the type has a history with roots in Egypt and ancient Greece. Widely used by Roman commanders during battle, Barbarian leaders adopted the form as a symbol of majesty (Mercer 1969: 33). A much reproduced example is the Throne of Dagobert, mentioned above (Figure 0.1). Once thought to be the seat of a Frankish king, and probably the throne of an early Carolingian ruler, Abbot Suger (1081–1151), the French abbot and adviser to kings Louis VI and VII, who was instrumental in the development of the Gothic style of architecture through his role in the rebuilding of the church of Saint-Denis in Paris, restored and transformed the fold-stool into a throne by adding a back in the early twelfth century (Mercer 1969: 33). Made of gilded bronze with lions' claw feet and lions' heads embellishing the stretchers, the throne is a prime demonstration of how the appropriation of furniture from another

FIGURE 0.1 The Throne of Dagobert, bronze, early twelfth century. Paris, Biblioteque Nationale. Photo: Raphael GAILLARDE/Gamma-Rapho/Getty Images.

period, combined with precious materials and iconographic motifs, amplifies the symbolic value of furnishings. Such was its symbolic value that the Throne of Dagobert was used by Napoleon I to promote his majesty (Morely 1999: 55). The Golden Pulpit from Aachen, mentioned above, is notable not only for its opulent material but also for its integration of ancient ivory plaques, which help to further connect this object to an imperial past. Another example of the symbolic value of furnishings is the casket, which is a small, portable box that was typically decorated with beautiful figural, vegetal, or architectural ornament and often made with precious materials such as ivory, bronze, silver, enamel, or copper. Such heavily decorated boxes were made to hold small valuables, such as jewelry and spices, and could convey a sense of sanctity because they were also used to hold relics.

In addition to its symbolic value, medieval furniture performed important functions with respect to display. Penelope Eames identifies display as the central motivating factor for the creation of furniture, arguing that "The whole scheme of priorities in furnishings in medieval times centers around the necessity of creating significant display" (Eames 1977: 228). Such displays would be created by seigneurial lords through draping furnishings such as beds, benches, and tables with costly textiles figured with coats of arms and other symbolic imagery (229). Tiered buffets adorned with richly woven textiles were used as the backdrop to display precious plate, which could also be marked with dynastic symbols (Mercer 1969: 79). The narrow buffet, with its elaborately carved woodwork and canopy used exquisite craftsmanship itself as an item of display (Eames 1977: 240). Beds and cradles of state (Mercer 1969: 81) were created to convey the authority of the ruler and his progeny. The bed was the most important furnishing for the symbolic expression of power (Eames 1977: 240), to the extent that households kept beds and cradles for the sole purpose of display (241). The cradle of Philip the Fair or Margaret of Austria was a cradle of state in which the form and decoration and its adornment with textiles and furs expressed privilege (241). In the early Renaissance, painted wedding chests or *cassoni* marked with the coats of arms of the groom and bride were intended to display the honor of the family.

SURVIVAL

One of the challenges in studying furniture from the medieval era is that so few examples have survived, especially from the earlier centuries. Tangible evidence is thus insufficient or even nonexistent if scholars were to develop a complete record of furniture on its own, hence the need for auxiliary evidence. Various factors influence survival rates: mobility, social environment, wealth, and material, among other things.

Furnishings throughout these periods are characterized as mobile or immobile. Immobile pieces were considered as fixtures of or attached to the architecture, perhaps, but not necessarily out of stone, or wood that was affixed to the building and thus considered permanent. Stone benches, for instance, might face the exterior of a dwelling or the interior *sala*, wooden choir stalls and stone thrones in churches, and even cupboards and occasionally some storage furnishings were among the furnishings considered permanent and immobile. Despite this sense of permanence, even these furnishings do not survive in healthy numbers. Of mobile furnishings, more chests and cupboards have survived than any other forms (Mercer 1969: 30). Mobile furnishings were not only moved from room to room to clear floor space, but such furniture pieces also moved from household to household. This is particularly necessary for nobility. Because nobility often had several territories under their jurisdiction, which required supervision, there were corresponding residences with those lands among which they would move. The noble's household possessions would move with him, providing not only familiar comfort but also the material projection of wealth and power in each of these locations.

Under these circumstances, mobile furniture was largely dependent on the social class and environment of the owners. For instance, domestic furniture was largely affected by the ebb and flow of family activities; the "peripatetic" nature of secular individuals when compared to the more "sedentary" ecclesiastical life was of consequence to the survival of their furniture (Mercer 1969: 31). If furniture was moved from one residence to another, damage might occur; or if it was left behind, it may have been vulnerable to plunder. Cloistered life was inherently less mobile, its furniture less affected by changing tastes, its "ample accommodations" potentially allowed for more furniture; in fact, laymen were known to deposit at churches and monasteries furnishings and other valuables, including domestic textiles, for the purposes of safeguarding those objects. For these reasons, more ecclesiastical furniture survives than domestic, even if some of the ecclesiastical objects were once domestic, such as chests and textiles that were given to churches (Eames 1971: 55–6). Genuinely ecclesiastical chests were generally not intended for transportation or for generic storage, but were of a truly religious nature, like caskets to hold holy relics, and may have been made out of relatively rare materials, such as ivory, valued as an exotic import from Africa.

Ivory, of course, is not a typical material for furnishings. Wood was the most common material for furniture, but it is prone to the ravages of time and destruction. Wood is susceptible to warping, cracking, and infestation; simply put, it is not a permanent material. However, oak was a popular building material for furniture in these periods, especially in England, which actually faced oak shortages, necessitating oak imports from abroad (Sparkes 1980: 17). An oak shortage in England, noted as early as 1233, was created by the demand for timber construction and for fuel, which outpaced oak's supply due to its slow growth rate (16–17). Imported Baltic oak was a popular substitute in England, as was Norwegian pine. Although softwoods, like pine, were less prestigious than oak, they were commonly used for interior paneling and for the construction of chests (Eames 1976: 104). The use of softwoods for furniture when oak was unavailable might contribute to their diminished survival rates when compared with oak. Beech and elm, both hardwoods, were also used for furniture in this period, but as these materials are subject to warping, the furniture itself may not have stood the test of time. Although oak was difficult to work because of its textures, as a hardwood, it was valued for its durability. Oak was also "easy to split" and ideal for ornamental work, thus the majority of medieval furniture was made of this material. By the end of the period under discussion here, walnut became a popular material for furniture, valued for its aesthetic qualities (Sparkes 1980: 17).

The increased demand for (and supply of) more furniture during the Renaissance period has contributed to more extant pieces from this later era when compared to the earlier Middle Ages, yet the surviving pieces themselves are still few when compared to the quantities produced and documented in contemporary inventories.

SOURCES

For the period covered by this volume, as discussed above, scholars are hindered by very weak survival rates of furniture. In fact, beds from fifteenth-century Italy do not survive at all. Despite a lack of numerous surviving examples, there are other sources of information on furniture types to help augment the physical losses of furnishings. Various textual and visual sources supplement our knowledge. Textual sources range from literary sources, to prescriptive texts such as etiquette books, to letters, wills, and inventories. Images of furniture from the Middle Ages are found in manuscript illuminations or paintings, but rarely as isolated examples. Rather such objects are integrated into scenes, environments, or narratives, such as of biblical subjects. The desire to rely on paintings as source material is hard to deny. This is especially true when it comes to northern Renaissance painting with its nearly obsessive interest in details; viewers tend to believe in the validity of the created illusion. In other words, the viewer takes the painted object as a true representation of reality due to the expert rendering of detail. The appearance of reality is perhaps best represented in the paintings by Jan van Eyck. In his *Madonna in the Church* (*c.* 1438–40; Berlin) the impulse is to believe in the visual and therefore believe in the divine. The architecture of the church in which the Virgin Mary stands is apparently a faithful rendering, as is the altar and carved rood screen behind her. But it is all an illusion, as one author reminds students, "the quests for topographical identities in van Eyck's paintings are misguided games at best" (Snyder, Silver, and Luttikhuizen 2005: 96). Jan van Eyck's now iconic *Arnolfini Portrait*, discussed above (Plate 1), is a full-length portrait of the couple in a fashionably outfitted and modern Netherlandish interior bedroom. The bed and its textiles, the shoes, the *prie-dieu*, the mirror and chandelier all complement the couple in the room. Scholars continue to be challenged by issues of the couple's identity, the purpose of the painting, and the significance of the furnishings and the space. But no one can ignore the room's rich furnishings, so painstakingly rendered as to convince the viewer of the reality of this fifteenth-century interior. Paralleling the thoroughness of the painted interior is Lorne Campbell's description of the room (Campbell 1998: 186–91). Despite, or perhaps because of, the detail, Campbell also warns not to be "seduced" into seeing the interior as a literal space, and rightly highlights the contrivances of scale and perspective, which should remind the viewer that the scene is imagined (202–4). Though certainly such images can be informative, a painted narrative of the Annunciation can also problematize our inquiries into furnishings of chambers, especially when certain types, such as fifteenth-century beds, are no longer extant. Are those visual sources complete enough to offset such physical absence or missing documentation? How much does one weigh that visual evidence? In the case of the *Arnolfini* painting, other documents record the existence of beds similar to van Eyck's painted version, so that despite warnings against paintings as literal depictions, we can isolate furniture within paintings, and when supported by other documentation, we can begin to piece together classes of furniture and their environments.

But that is the question. What weight to give the varied sources? Are they equal? How are they useful? Keeping the prejudicial nature of certain documentation or limited documentation and limited sources in mind, scholars can determine the probative value of those sources. Without abundant auxiliary sources, a diversity of judiciously used sources can richly illuminate form and context. For instance, inventories provide multifaceted details of material, sometimes visual appearance, location, or ownership. But, as outlined by Penelope Eames (1973), not all inventories were created equally. Some inventories recorded financial value, others documented ownership, or were initiated for wills to identify moveable property, or initiated prior to transporting goods between locations. Of the latter, the inventory may not help with contextualizing an object in a secure location, but helps to illuminate the concept of mobility and transportation of furniture. For instance, Eames cites a 1466 inventory to document the goods of a "travelling chest" for the Duchess of Suffolk, whose goods were traveling between two of her estates (1973: 37). Sometimes inferences must be made when inventories neglect to include furniture, yet by all other accounts it must have existed. This is true in the case of John Fastolfe's 1459 inventory, which was drawn up in accordance with his will

(37). In this inventory, wooden furniture was not always considered worthy of documentation. Specifically, wooden furniture used for storage was apparently considered nontransferable property and, therefore, was not included in the inventory. However, given other items in the same inventory, such wardrobes certainly existed at his estate.

Other inventories cross boundaries between civic and domestic, such as those inventories drawn up in the fifteenth century by Florence's Ufficio dei Pupilli. This Office of Wards registered the contents of homes of intestate deceased residents who also left behind minors. These records have been a virtual treasure trove for scholars as they record the goods of families of various social and financial standing (Lydecker 1987: 24–5; Lindow 2007: 5). From the hundreds of inventories made between the fifteenth and seventeenth centuries, a pattern emerged to later scholars, which suggested the layout of homes as well as an apparent priority of goods within rooms. In other words, in bedrooms, bed furniture was always listed first, followed by the room's next major piece of furniture. So, while beds, for example, from fifteenth-century Florence have not survived, these inventories provide information on value, and sometimes size, that corroborate other information, such as pictorial evidence. But the utility of inventories can only go so far. Lydecker and other scholars have rightly noted that those inventories are but a snapshot of an interior at a given moment in time, and in many of these cases, such times are of familial and emotional upheaval, and therefore, we should not treat that space as static (Ajmar-Wollheim and Dennis 2006a: 17). Objects move and are as transient as the people who can carry them or rely on them. The value of inventories is enhanced when used in conjunction with other sources (actual furniture, ideally) such as letters, diaries, and etiquette manuals.

One of the most famous inventories is the 1492 domestic inventory taken at the death of Lorenzo de' Medici, and its copy made in 1512. The room-by-room inventory shows his city palace stuffed with goods, the accumulation of various collections, finery, furniture, textiles, armament, and more, acquired by the four generations of Medici who once lived in that home (Stapleford 2013: 1–2). Because the Medici were expelled from Florence by 1494 and the contents of their home dispersed, when the Medici were restored in 1512, the inventory (or its copy) was used to restitute those items back to the family heirs. A diary entry by Luca Landucci in October of that year further states how the threat of the "gallows" encouraged the restitution of that property, and thereby the restoration of the Medici in the governmental life of Florence (Landucci 1927: 263; Stapleford 2013: 2). In other words, the inventory alone lists the goods, the 1512 copy together with an account demanding the return of the listed items ties the household furnishings to the legitimacy of the Medici family's standing among the citizens of Florence.

In the introduction to the *At Home* exhibition catalog, Ajmar-Wollheim and Dennis present other considerations about premodern furniture and its fluctuating value in the modern era. For instance, they noted while connoisseurship was the preferred analytical approach to studying Renaissance decorative arts and furnishings, furniture studies were fueled by the nineteenth-century art market demands for such objects (Ajmar-Wollheim and Dennis 2006a: 18). In the wake of such demand, the analytical rigor was at times lax, allowing for less authentic Renaissance pieces to be accepted as such, which not only undermined the value for authenticity but also undermined the credibility of this discipline of study. When the fraudulent pieces were ultimately revealed as inauthentic, scholars, curators, and collectors were forced to reconsider accepted pieces, reevaluate "married" pieces that were joined perhaps anachronistically, and apply a variety of approaches to better authenticate and contextualize furniture. Although market demands created "a general suspicion around the history of Renaissance furniture," the discipline's recovery is perhaps due to the renewed scrutiny not only into original pieces of furniture, but also into a broad host of documents and sources and how they can be applied to such studies.

Our own contemporary biases and values can also mislead. Even extant, authentic pieces, for instance, can mislead on their own (or with our help) in providing a complete picture of furniture from the Middle Ages. The survival rates of certain furnishings, such as beds, are poor compared to chests, whether at church or at home. Materials, utility, or how something was safeguarded (or not) can lead to uneven survival rates and, therefore, paint a distorted picture of furniture, contextualized or not. The lacunae can be addressed albeit incompletely with contemporary documents, letters, treatises, indirectly through commentaries on social or religious rituals, as well as with visual descriptions in manuscript paintings, frescoes, and in literature. All contributions help to build out a framework by which we can assess, study, and understand furniture, its forms and styles, and modes of production within a cultural context.

At times, our own value systems have obscured the history and preservation of historical furniture. For instance, many pieces of furniture were painted and as the prestige of painting grew, together with that of the individual artist, scholarly attention focused on the painting often divorced it metaphorically, if not literally, from its associated furnishing and function. Ashley Elston explores such a scenario in which a painted reliquary cupboard (1367) from the Cathedral of Padua was dismantled in the nineteenth and early twentieth centuries, with the ensuing discussion focusing on the cupboard's paintings by Niccolò Semitecolo, rather than the ritual life of the object (Elston 2012: 111–12). Indirect information on furniture provided in other textual sources prove helpful to an object such as this. For instance, church processions were regular activities throughout the liturgical calendar, and such processions often involved processing with relics; or visits to the relics by ranking individuals as well as important visitors to a church or community, who would expect to have a special viewing of significant holy relics, as was the case when Emperor Charles IV visited Padua in1368 (121, n. 65). During these activities, the relic cupboard is clearly accessed, fundamental in the act of enclosure and revelation, accessed at the outset and at the end of such important events. By extension, the cupboard is known to be "a significant component of the church's liturgical outfittings," even if it is not stated so directly (121).

Penelope Eames's (1973) discussion on English wills and inventories notes that it is sometimes what is not included that is significant. Despite great variety in will inventories, Eames mentions one as a fairly typical estate inventory, that of John Fastolfe's largest residence of Caister Castle in 1459, noted above (1973: 37). The will stipulated an inventory and it is relatively detailed. But an interesting absence in the list of moveable objects and furniture becomes apparent—a notable lack of wooden furniture, specifically wardrobes. So, in some instances wooden furniture was not included in inventories even when other items make clear that they must have existed in specific locations to store the itemized list of textiles, for instance. As it turns out at Caister, "all storage furniture" was considered nontransferable, even when they were not built into the residence (38).

CONCLUSION

Medieval furniture is shaped by cultural forces and in turn is itself a shaping cultural force. Its evolution and use is tied to economics, trade, social customs, status, wealth, level of craft, industry, technology, workshop organization, and the availability of raw materials. It operates in distinct social contexts: urban, rural, ecclesiastical, courtly, domestic, and civic. It is created in dialogue with architecture, which is dominated by the medieval hall, the emergence of the chamber, the Byzantine, Romanesque, or Gothic church, and the monastery. Over time, the amount and types of furniture increase with the intensification of urbanism, the rise of the urban patriciate, and the growing wealth of merchants, combined with a growing desire for domestic comfort and new forms of sociability (Mercer 1969: 67–71).

The following chapters elaborate on this brief introduction to medieval furniture in ways that bring depth and dimension to pieces long gone or pieces long removed from their original contexts. Style, form, and types of furniture are discussed together with the cultural and social forces that helped to define their forms and functions. The chapters will also demonstrate that while the furniture discussed herein responded to the period's cultural and social needs, the pieces themselves, in turn, fulfilled significant cultural roles in various environments.

CHAPTER ONE

Design and Motifs

EVANTHIA BABOULA

INTRODUCTION

This chapter considers design and motifs from the perspectives of iconographic consistency and wider contextual themes. In doing so the chapter does not cover the topic comprehensively, but instead draws comparisons between objects from Byzantium, medieval Europe, and the Islamic world. Despite the fragmentary and dispersed nature of surviving material, these cultural worlds have much that was shared, from the use of particular types of furnishings for presentation purposes to affinities in the decoration of furniture. Since decoration and motifs are not isolated from the types or symbolism of the furniture on which they appear, the chapter also foregrounds several themes that will be reinforced in later chapters.

FROM ANTIQUITY TO THE MIDDLE AGES

Sources for medieval furniture are much rarer than for ancient furniture, for which there is relatively plenty of written, visual, and archaeological evidence. For example, it is largely due to the uniquely preserved settlement of Herculaneum, and to the extraordinarily rich funerary assemblages of the tomb of Tutankhamun, that we owe much of our knowledge about ancient furniture, including the materials used as well as typological and decorative aspects. Images of furniture in the art of Egypt, Greece, Rome, and beyond are also known. These images can date from as late as the sixth century CE as in the case of stone couches depicted in a series of Sogdian tombs along the Silk Road.[1] The tomb walls additionally include representations of banquets and their paraphernalia, suggesting that the stone couches were modeled on prototypes made of wood and fabric (Cheng 2010). Although the Middle Ages is a term that is mostly applied to European history, the fourth to seventh centuries can be seen as a transitional phase between antiquity and the medieval period in a much wider geographic base, as in this example. In a similar manner, the types and decoration of medieval furniture do not change abruptly. Rather, both abstract and figural motifs familiar from the classical and Roman world may continue to be used in real and depicted items. This continuity will be evident especially for furniture with symbolic connotations that persist through time, such as thrones.

Amidst the proliferation of monotheistic religions during this transitional phase, an overall shift in funerary practice occurred in Europe and the Middle East: Christianity, Islam, and Judaism all stipulated simplicity in burial. For medieval furniture, then, this means fewer opportunities for researchers to reconstruct what it looked like and how it was used based on funerary contexts, which have proven valuable sources for earlier times. Instead, some of the best surviving furniture of the Middle Ages comes from churches and mosques. This is true especially for the end of the medieval period, from about 1300 to 1500. Domestic contexts comprise less plentiful sources than ritual spaces because, unless occupied by socioeconomic elites, households utilized simple furniture designs in nondurable materials.

A persistent question is the degree to which depictions of furniture correspond to actual furnishings. In fact, where decoration is concerned, motifs on furniture might either imitate actual pieces or be distant from real life. They may also be imbued with symbolic meaning as most furniture appears in images that relate to authority and social status. There are moreover narrative scenes that require the presence of some furniture types, such as the miracle of the healing of the paralytic (bed), the Last Supper (table), and the Nativity of the Virgin (bed). In these and other scenes household furnishings may indicate that the narrative is taking place in an interior space and they thus act as spatial shorthand. It may not be possible to tell how close to reality or fantasy such examples are. Presumably, some actual furniture provided models for illustrations seen in manuscripts, which are fruitful sources of information. Because manuscripts could be highly portable, depictions of individual pieces and how they were ornamented played an important role in the dissemination of ideas about what furniture looked like and what it symbolized. It was perhaps primarily the ideal and symbolic perceptions of furniture, rather than the strictly functional ones, that were of greatest import for what was depicted across geographic and cultural boundaries.

SOURCES AND SCHOLARSHIP

Any analysis of extant medieval furniture has to be combined with iconographic and textual sources to give some sense of what furniture and its decoration looked like, how pieces were made, and what roles they played. Even so, much of what we know is based on the usage of furniture in elite spaces. One of the few synthetic works to deal with the topic of design and motifs in this period, Penelope Eames's *Furniture in England, France and the Netherlands from the Twelfth to the Fifteenth Century* (1977), includes a discussion of decorative techniques in a study that focuses on late medieval armoires, chests, beds, and seats. Eames notes that much medieval furniture is relatively plain in appearance and asks the important question: "why simplicity in furniture when textiles and plate were outstandingly expensive and elaborate?" (1977: xix). She then argues that one of the priorities in the design of furniture was adaptability for practical and socially defined purposes, with furniture acting as a supporting canvas on which diverse social identities and relationships were clarified and refined (xx and *passim*). This contrast will become evident as we move through the present chapter, and it is worth considering whether Eames's question is valid for the furniture we see from different medieval cultures.

Although representations of furniture can be found in secular works of art, especially toward the end of the medieval period, in Europe and Byzantium it is mostly in Christian ecclesiastical art, including architectural decoration and portable media, where we find rich visual information about form and decoration. For example, in *Reconstructing the Reality of Images*, a work that is concerned with the material culture of Byzantium, and which builds on the foundational work of Phaidon Koukoules on the life and culture of Byzantium (1948–57: vol. 2.2: 67–96), Maria Parani (2003) found that the most abundant sources for examining Byzantine furniture between the eleventh and fifteenth centuries are its depictions in art; specifically, religious decoration. Information on the furniture design and motifs of the Islamic world, on the other hand, benefits from the survival of illustrated manuscripts with a secular focus such as the medieval Arabic copies of Dioscorides's *Materia Medica* and the *Maqamat* (Assemblies) of Al-Hariri, several of which date to the first half of the thirteenth century. Furthermore, Persian manuscripts of the fourteenth and fifteenth centuries are markedly rich in the visual documentation of domestic interiors as well as furniture appearing in formal garden settings. Scholarship on Islamic furniture is often incorporated within studies of the larger topic of Islamic ornament (cf. Golombek 1988).

Primary textual sources provide a wealth of material. They are especially useful for identifying connections between the furniture designs of Europe, the Islamic world, and Byzantium. The thousands of documents discovered in the medieval Ben Ezra Synagogue in Cairo, known as the Cairo Genizah archives, for example, contain accounts of furniture, such as chests, cupboards, and beds that moved to and from Egypt, including imports from Byzantium. In particular, testaments and inventories, many of which can be found among the Genizah documents, are fruitful for examining the role of furniture in the domestic context, although fuller studies are needed. Wills from Islamic Jerusalem and Byzantium, as well as inventories, hagiographies, and accounts of ceremonies all inform our knowledge about furniture (Goitein 1967–93; for an overview of the wills from medieval Jerusalem contained in what is known as the Haram documents, see Little 1984).

It is often difficult to date medieval furniture with certainty. Together with a religious slant of the evidence due to the objects often originating from ritual spaces, the uncertainty surrounding the function of surviving pieces and the physical arrangement of their component parts affect how much is known about motifs and their meanings. In the case of the sixth-century ivory-clad throne of Maximian (see below), the panels covering the surface of the throne have biblical figures and narrative scenes, but several panels are missing, so the original appearance might be significantly different from what we see today.

DECORATION, SYMBOLISM, AND MATERIALS

The decoration of furniture was socially significant, and elaborate pieces seem to have been a privilege of the wealthy. Also noticeable is the contrast between the limited repertoire of basic shapes of medieval furniture and its elaborate decoration as depicted in art. The latter is not only a reflection of what furniture looked like, but also denotes points of intersection of the private and public spheres of life. Furnishings we associate with everyday life were not coupled with buildings but people; or rather with the offices they represented and their socioeconomic status relative to others. Depictions suggest that furniture in ecclesiastic and secular art functioned as a symbol of status, especially when accompanying elite personages such as kings, emperors, church administrators, or Christ and the Virgin. Furniture represented its "owners" in their claims as rulers or members of the elite. Significantly, the furniture associated with Christ and the Virgin seems to borrow from actual pieces and rituals of presentation, but also influencing on occasion the symbolism attached to the depiction of figures holding royal or priestly authority (e.g., Breckenridge 1980–1). In art, furniture did not act on its own as an exclusive sign of authority, of course: a throne or a stool, along with body posture and the presence or absence of other figures, could signify the different types of authority or moments in presentation rituals that a single person could embrace. For example, the fourteenth-century Byzantine Emperor John VI Kantakouzenos is shown seated among clergy in one illustration, while standing in his double portrait as emperor and monk in another illumination within the same manuscript (Bibliothèque nationale de France, MS Gr. 1242, ff. 5v and 123v, respectively).

Judging by the presence and decoration of thrones and stools in formal depictions of Byzantine emperors and officials with Christ or the Virgin, on the one hand, or writing desks and thrones in lavish religious manuscripts, on the other, the symbolism of status seems to have permeated the inclusion of furniture in art; but the contrast between simplicity and elaboration of form is clearly not to be understood in a linear fashion. What is more, as the medieval world was characterized by a "textile mentality" (Golombek 1988: 34), the textiles that furnished beds, cradles, and buffets provided important social nuances. For instance, in a late fifteenth-century treatise on court etiquette written by an aristocrat, Aliénor de Poitiers (d.1509), there is a distinction between the trims that are suitable for decorating a baby's cradle. The miniver (white fur) trim of the cradle of a countess should not touch the floor, unlike that of a baby princess, which was made of ermine (including the black tails of the animals) and could indeed touch the floor (Eames 1977: 94).

The use of luxury materials such as ivory, gold, and silver for making and decorating furniture showcases the elite role of specialized objects both in a material and symbolic sense. Precious materials employed in furniture are already attested in early Byzantine treasures, namely, hoards made of precious metals that occasionally include furniture fragments. The Lampsakos treasure, found in the Dardanelles area, comprises objects made in the sixth and seventh centuries, and includes silver fragments that would have embellished furniture, probably a table and a folding stool. Moreover, the gold used in imperial furniture would have expressed the elevated status of the emperor and his association with divinely guided rule. In general, the gold used to highlight items of furniture in Byzantine manuscripts especially from the tenth century onward is part of the overall rendition of divine spaces, which are themselves often shown in a gold background. Even simple pieces of furniture could be imbued with symbolism. This is true for pieces that functioned as indivisible parts of veneration practices. A case in point is a decorated stand that was used to support icons which were known for performing miracles. For example, a famous icon of the Restoration of Orthodoxy (British Museum, accession no. 1988, 0411.1) from around 1400 depicts a stand on which another famous icon has been set. Although the stand itself is not visible, the red cloth covering it is meant to be luxurious and is decorated with alternating gold-woven zones of interlacing design, repeated geometric motifs, and fleur-de-lis. The stand itself is probably meant to be of a very simple type. But the richness of its cover accentuates the miracle-performing icon of the Virgin that it supports.

DESIGN: SOCIABILITY AND AUTHORITY

The form and decoration of seats, including thrones, stools, chairs, and benches, provides a good introduction to the social role of the design and motifs of medieval furniture, and the significance of materials. As the examples discussed below demonstrate, design elements, ornament, and materials varied widely, depending on social function and context.

Marquetry and intarsia (types of inlay decoration, see also Chapter 2 in this volume), which created patterns or images with pieces of bone, wood, or metal could decorate the frame of a seat, for example. Carving was also popular. Carving was used to produce cornice moulding (decorative "ledges" with intricate profiles) as well as paneling. The latter was often decorated in the fifteenth century with variations of linenfold motifs, such as on a French high-backed seat at the Metropolitan Museum, New York (accession no. 47:145). The linenfold motif also appears on other types of furniture, such as in the representation of a bed in the Wedding at Cana scene mentioned later (Hand 2004: 70–1, no. 51). Here there is clear correspondence between art and the ornamentation of actual furniture.

Additional, specific motifs, such as the arcade design (comprising series of blind or open arches) found on thirteenth-century choir stalls from Ely Cathedral in England, on the fourteenth-century throne from Hereford Cathedral (Eames 1977: plate 54, cat. no. 49), as well as in several other objects mentioned in this chapter, confirm that decorative shapes were borrowed across different types of furniture. This popular motif between the thirteenth and fifteenth centuries speaks to the wide reach of Gothic architectural elements. Moreover, this type of motif is seen in furniture from diverse cultural contexts (see the description of the *minbar* of the Kutubiyya Mosque in Marrakesh, and Figure 1.1 below), further indicating that there was cross-cultural sharing of forms across regions as well as between the secular and ritual environments. Clearly, though, decoration was also subject to changing tastes. Later replacements of the Ely stalls dating from the fourteenth century are much more elaborate, including carvings of human and animal shapes, as well as detailed superstructures, and point to the growing trend for integration of lavish furniture into the architectural design of a grand ecclesiastical space (Fearn 1997). Some high-backed chairs that were probably associated with ecclesiastical usage survive from late in the period. In these chairs, a generally austere form may be complemented by elaborate carved paneling on the backrest, including scrolling motifs, arches, and the occasional coat of arms (e.g., Wixom 1999: 210, no. 257, for an example dating from 1450–1500).

The social role of materials in the design of furniture is especially evident in seats associated with authority, including various types of thrones. These came in different forms. The most elaborate thrones were made of marble, while wood was reserved for cheaper furniture or to serve as the support for elaborate ivory paneling. Unfortunately, few medieval thrones have survived.

Among the earliest extant medieval thrones are those made of stone in Italy such as the fourth-century throne of St. Ambrose in Milan and a slightly later one at Santa Maria della Sanità in Naples; and a sixth-century throne at Nôtre Dame-de-Nazareth at Vaison in France. Several early thrones dating to the sixth century show that materials mattered. Ivory paneling and decoration

FIGURE 1.1 Kutubiyya *minbar*, Marrakesh, twelfth century. Photo: © Erich Lessing/ Art Resource, NY.

were probably not uncommon. For example, Maximian's throne at Ravenna is a liturgical rather than a functional item, originally made of thirty-nine ivory panels, some of which have not survived. The panels are arranged in a tight-fitting design and may have dressed a wooden core. The decoration of the panels constitutes one complete iconographic program that includes scenes of

John the Baptist, the infancy of Christ, and the life of Joseph (famously studied in Schapiro 1952). A sixth-century throne-cum-reliquary made of alabaster and known as "the seat of St. Mark" survives in Venice. It may have been a symbolic rather than practical piece of furniture due to its narrow width, inclusion of niches for relics in its lower section, and apocalyptic references in its depiction of trumpeting angels and the winged figures of a lion, a bull, an eagle, and a human. These are often associated with biblical prophetic visions or the Four Evangelists (Grabar 1954). Carved palm trees, the four rivers of paradise underneath the Lamb of God, and a fruiting tree, as well as abstract zigzag and lattice motifs, human figures, and a cross complete the design of this throne, which, atypically, also has armrests. Valuable materials continued to be used in later centuries as in the case of what may be a leg from a throne that was hollowed out of a walrus tusk and decorated with carved vine scrolls. This object originates in twelfth-century Scandinavia and is in the British Museum (inventory no. 1959, 1202.1; Robinson 2008: 92).

Later episcopal thrones include several that are preserved from medieval Britain: the famous early thirteenth-century marble throne from Christ Church, Canterbury, and the thrones from Exeter, St. Davids and Hereford cathedrals, which are all made of timber and date from the fourteenth century. There are also the thrones from Wells and Durham Cathedrals (both made of stone) and from Lincoln Cathedral (Tracy and Budge 2015). Due to the unusually large size of some of the thrones or their prominent placement in the church, as well as their decoration with painted or carved figural images, including those of bishops and saints, these thrones seem to have been meant to augment the status and visibility of bishops. Although not many survive, episcopal thrones with similar decorative patterns, both abstract and figural, are scattered throughout Europe and may indicate some transference of iconographic ideas not only within Europe but also between this region and the Islamic world (see below for thrones from southern Italy).

The frequent appearance of seats in images related to authority, something observed in other historical periods as well, should be noted. The very allocation of a seat to an individual holds social, political, or ritual significance in both medieval texts and art. The form and decoration of the seats of the Four Evangelists in a single manuscript can provide a sense of the variety of formal seating possibilities. For example, a middle Byzantine Gospel in the British Library that dates to the twelfth century (Burney MS 19), has Matthew sitting on an elaborate throne with back, armrests, and a balustrade-motif (f. 1v); Mark on a chair with a lattice design on its back and golden curved armrests (f. 63v); and Luke on a stool that derives from the Roman *sella curulis* (a backless chair with legs that form an X, cf. Wanscher 1980) but combines diagonal and vertical legs (f. 101v). All three seats are represented with a red cushion. The fourth seat, belonging to the scene of John and his assistant

(f. 165r), is a less comfortable, but perhaps much more common, simple wooden stool without a cushion. Depictions of similar seating furniture can be found in other manuscripts as well, but were not necessarily the accoutrements of specific Evangelists; instead, any of the Evangelists could be seated on any of these chairs. This can be seen, for instance, in another Greek manuscript from the twelfth century held in the British Library (Add. MS 5112, f. 134r), in which John is depicted on a latticed-back chair, similar to the one mentioned for Mark above. In yet another example, the famous late tenth-century Lindisfarne Gospels from the North of England (in the British Museum), the Four Evangelists are seated on stools and benches: Matthew on a long bench with what appears to be embossed decoration of repeated circles and a red cushion; Mark on a relatively simple stool with a blue cushion; Luke on a stool with similar decoration to Matthew's seat and a brown cushion; and John on a slightly more elaborate rectangular bench with a blue cushion (Brown 2003). While these images may reflect the diversity of seating furniture in real life, they also draw attention to the illustrative traditions that transferred models across geographic areas and reworked them, without necessarily leaving us concrete clues about the degree of representation of medieval realities. In some cases, nevertheless, we can detect similarities between representations and actual furniture, similar to the case of the linenfold motif. For example, several icons and paintings of the Virgin and Child that date from the thirteenth century (when most of the Byzantine Empire was dismantled into crusader states), exhibit a combination of Italian and Byzantine stylistic elements (e.g., a painting in the National Gallery of Art, Washington, 1937.1.1; Evans 2004: 476–7). The thrones on which the Virgin is seated have similar features to chairs that have survived from this period, such as the arcading design mentioned above. The paintings also show finials (ornaments crowning vertical components) adorning the throne of the Virgin, similar in design to those that have survived on extant benches (Eames 1977: plate 69).

Images of the Virgin throughout medieval Europe depict her seated on a variety of thrones, with or without a back and often bejeweled. The depiction of furniture related to Jesus and the Virgin, as well as that of royal figures, is similarly characterized by a variety of types and decorative patterns. One of the most elaborate thrones, though, appears on the ivory Harbaville triptych, a Byzantine work of art. On the carved surface of this item Christ is seated on a throne that has a backrest and is curved at the top (Durand 1992: 233–6) (Figure 1.2). This type of throne had already been present in sixth- and seventh-century images, as in the case of a famous icon of the Virgin with saints George and Theodore at Saint Catherine's Monastery, Sinai. The Harbaville throne lacks armrests, as is usual for most medieval depictions of thrones, but is replete with horizontally arranged abstract vegetal motifs, strings of pearls, an elongated cushion, and a footrest with architecturally inspired ornament. A similarly

FIGURE 1.2 Harbaville triptych, tenth century. Photo: © Erich Lessing/Art Resource, NY.

elaborate throne, with gold arcading at the back and rows of wavy ornament along the front, can be seen in richly illuminated Byzantine manuscripts such as in the Homilies of John Chrysostom, where the seat is occupied by Emperor Nikephoros III Botaneiates (Bibliothèque nationale de France, MS Coislin Gr. 79, f. 2r).

The Madrid Skylitzes, a richly illustrated manuscript of Byzantine history covering the years 811 to 1057, but likely executed in twelfth-century Sicily, and the product of several artists with different cultural backgrounds and training, includes emperors seated on thrones, both with and without a back. Nevertheless, authority was not necessarily signified through elaborate decoration. Indeed, the seat of a ruler or a divine figure could look quite simple. For example, in the Theodore Psalter, another Byzantine illuminated manuscript (dated 1066), the Babylonian king Nebuchadnezzar is depicted in the guise of a Byzantine emperor, seated on a stool similar to the simple seats that the Four Evangelists occupy in illustrated versions of the Gospels (e.g., British Library Add. MS 19352, f. 202r).

Significantly, the form and decoration of medieval thrones made use of elements that harked back to earlier times through the continuation of manufacturing traditions or the re-creation of symbolic forms that were associated with the past. One of these trends recalls Roman traditions of the presentation of authority figures (Nees 1993; Reeve 2003: 137). A surviving throne that demonstrates this is known as the throne of Dagobert and is now in the National Library of France (Weinberger 1964) (Figure 0.1). It is made of bronze, has a back, and is a composite item dating from the seventh to the twelfth century. Deriving its folding stool form from the *sella curulis* of the Romans, the throne of Dagobert has four legs shaped with lions' or leopards' heads, and slender animal bodies with textured hides along the main part of each leg, which turns into the animal's foot. The addition of animal forms appears symbolic, inviting associations of the seat user with strength and courage. There may also be connections with the biblical ideal that King Solomon embodied (discussed below; Reeve 2003). This tradition of referring to earlier typological and decorative models extended into the Islamic world. We can see this in a thirteenth-century manuscript that depicts sultan Badr al-Din Lu'lu' (d.1259) seated amidst his court on a Roman-derived type of stool similar to the throne of Dagobert (Kitab al-Aghani [The Book of Songs]; Istanbul, Millet Library, Feyzullah Efendi 1566). Deliberate antique references also occur in documented twelfth-century furniture such as the Archbishop's throne at Canterbury Cathedral or the throne at Santa Maria in Cosmedin and the one at San Clemente in Rome (Reeve 2003). On such occurrences, austere decoration, such as plain panel-shaped slabs that remind us of ancient coffered ceilings or inscriptions carved on the throne may allude to a perceived or real origin of the seat, or parts of it, in early Christian times. That there was value in maintaining some continuity of form and decoration through time also becomes evident in the case of elaborate folding chairs that survive from the thirteenth to the fifteenth centuries in western Europe. Among them are instances where the chairs look like they could be folded, but the "folding" was an ornamental rather than functional element (Wanscher 1980).

Other surviving seats show that motifs coming from diverse cultural traditions could be combined in a single piece of furniture. Four chairs of the *sella curulis* type, in this case known as "hip-joint," date from the fifteenth century and are located at the Metropolitan Museum in New York. These were probably all made at the end of the period of Islamic rule in Granada, Spain (Kisluk-Grosheide, Koeppe, and Rieder 2006: 12–14, cat. no. 3). Their frames are inlaid with marquetry that utilizes Gothic arch-like openings, which are also reminiscent of Islamic ornament (Ferrandis Torres 1940). Missing fragments of inlay have also revealed details of the manufacturing process behind the motifs: in one of the chairs, the spaces carved out of the wood meant to hold the inlaid material were first covered with pieces of reused parchment (Koeppe et al.

2012: 229–31; image of the parchment: Kisluk-Grosheide, Koeppe, and Rieder 2006: fig. 5). Similarly, furniture made for explicitly Christian usage sometimes includes Islamic references, as occurs in a series of medieval episcopal thrones from southern Italy. These include thrones at Bari and Canosa cathedrals. The latter has elephants sculpted at the base of the throne. Such cross-cultural references could sprout from diverse causes such as the Islamic history of southern Italy, or the desire to appeal to Christian triumphalist sentiment over Islam, as in the case of the depiction of Muslim slaves on the Bari throne (Dorin 2008) (Figure 5.5).

Thrones, including those made for bishops, are the pieces of furniture par excellence connected to symbolic ideas about authority, especially because their appearance and function could invoke associations with King Solomon's legendary virtue and architectural achievements as the builder of the Temple through comparison of certain visual features with the description of Solomon's throne in the Bible. In the Hebrew Bible, his throne is made of ivory and gold, has six steps, an arched back, and lions on either side of the seat as well as pairs of lions down the steps (1 Kings 10:18–20). Frequently decorated with animals and incorporating steps, medieval thrones provided a distinct opportunity to refer to Solomon's wisdom and promote their users as the epitome of virtuous rule. Such references seem to be typical and were transmitted from the early Christian world to Byzantium and from there to western Europe (Reeve 2003). Figures of lions were included in the otherwise simply designed "throne of Charlemagne" at Aachen, probably a tenth-century creation (Figure 1.3). These connotations are evident even in a work that includes several different seats of importance, such as the Bayeux Tapestry. This depicts a variety of thrones with and without backs, with King Edward seated on a stool in the form of a lion's body and Duke William on a throne possibly ornamented with lions' heads.

Although women are rarely shown enthroned, the earliest image of a female donor in a manuscript presents the Byzantine princess Anicia Juliana (462–527/528) on an imperial *sella curulis* seat in the early sixth-century copy of Dioscorides's *Materia Medica* in Vienna (MS Med. Gr. 1, f. 6v). The *sella curulis* seat was at that time still used as the throne of the Byzantine emperor (Wanscher 1980: 121–90). Anicia's seat is gold and has animal forms, perhaps eagles or griffins, down its legs. In this case the seat has symbolic connotations not only because of its individual decorative motifs, but because although this princess was never an empress, she and her contemporaries compared her achievements as a patron of architecture to Solomon's deeds.

Alternatively, slight variations in the shape of seats and their decoration may be linked to significant symbolic concepts. In an article entitled "Christ on the Lyre-Backed Throne," James Breckenridge (1980–1) discussed the genealogy and meaning of a throne with curved sides on its backrest, different from the throne that is depicted in the Harbaville ivory triptych mainly in that it is the top

FIGURE 1.3 Throne of Charlemagne, Aachen, tenth(?) century. Photograph courtesy of the Author.

of the latter's backrest that is curved, instead. The "lyre-backed" type famously appears in a tenth-century mosaic in the Hagia Sophia in Istanbul. This type may ultimately have been modeled on a specific throne in the Byzantine imperial palace. Breckenridge analyzed the varied curve of the back of this throne as seen especially in coins and argued that there was a change of function of the actual throne type that inspired the images: up to the eighth century the "lyre-backed" throne was mainly associated with the occasions when two emperors ruled concurrently (*synthronos*). After the end of the iconoclastic period (730–843), a time when the depiction of religious figures was banned, the throne became associated with a single emperor. This symbolism probably extended to images of religious figures in Byzantium. That is, in an analogy to the scenes of two simultaneous emperors, showing Jesus on his own on this type of throne before the iconoclastic age could strongly indicate the presence of the Father and Son in one, unified figure, thus connecting the form of the throne to theological principles. This correlation seems to have been abandoned after Iconoclasm, when the Virgin and Child are also shown often using the same type of throne (Breckenridge 1980–1: 259).

Thrones were also connected with representations of scholars, blending elements of the Evangelist portraits with depictions of respected authors of secular or other religious works. Copies of Dioscorides's *De Materia Medica*, for example, a pharmacopeia that had first been illustrated in sixth-century Byzantium and then repeatedly in the medieval Islamic world, developed their own internal tradition of depicting a person of authority. This figure is sometimes clearly labeled "Dioscorides," as in the Anicia Juliana codex from the sixth century. In later manuscripts written in Arabic, this authority figure becomes a teacher in dialogue with a student (e.g., Topkapı Saray Museum Ahmet III, 2127, f. 2v and 2r). The seats used to represent these power relationships share much with images of the Evangelists as well as late Byzantine images of historical figures. Telling examples include the figure of Hippocrates in a fourteenth-century manuscript of his works. He is seated on a throne with a highly curved back and a stool for resting his feet. On the facing page is the figure of the wealthy aristocrat and scholar, Alexios Apokaukos, complete with a lectern and a seat with a rectangular backrest (Bibliothèque nationale de France, MS Par. Gr. 2144, ff. 10v and 11r). The image of the scholar-emperor, John VI Kantakouzenos (1292–1383), enthroned amidst an ecclesiastical council over which he presided, is also from the fourteenth century (Bibliothèque nationale de France, MS Par. Gr. 1242, f. 5v).

Simple stools as opposed to thrones also appear in depictions of authority figures, including those of Byzantine emperors and the Evangelists. Simple folding stools that seem to continue the tradition of the Roman *sella curulis* appear occasionally, including the seat of Caliph al-Ma'mun in the Madrid Skylitzes manuscript (Biblioteca Nacional de España, MS Vitr. 26–2, f. 47r). This image is part of a narrative of the ninth-century exchange of embassies between the courts of Constantinople and Baghdad. In this instance, the Caliph's stool is visually juxtaposed with the elaborate, wide throne of the Byzantine Emperor. Sometimes decorated with terminals in the shape of eagles, the folding stool appears in several other images of emperors and kings on military expeditions.

DESIGN: FORM AND FUNCTION

The famous legend of King Arthur's Round Table conveys the medieval sense of ceremony and protocol for which such furniture was very important. For example, what seems to have been the most luxurious and symbolically important Byzantine table was one used at the center of the ceremonial Chrysotriklinos (Golden Chamber) at the imperial palace in Constantinople. Although it does not survive, it was made of gold or gilded silver and was used by high officials, with lesser administrators arranged on secondary tables, while the emperor seated separately.

Fragmentary evidence of tables from excavations can provide exciting information regarding the decorum of furniture design and motifs. Such is the case with semicircular tables, called "sigma-shaped" from the Greek letter C, which have been excavated in Byzantine Corinth, where they were in use already by the sixth century (Scranton 1957: 139–40). These were made of white and red marble, and were associated with spaces that may have accommodated travelers or other groups of people. Tables of this type were later reused in the walls of the Bimaristan (hospital) of Nur al-Din in Damascus in the twelfth century. In their later use as *spolia*, they have changed into important remnants not of furniture but of the architectural patronage of the Seljuq elites that ruled Syria in the twelfth century (Flood 2001) (Figure 1.4). Monastic refectories have also preserved rectangular and oval-shaped built-in tables from the late medieval period. These tables conform to the needs of communal life in monasteries and are of shapes suitable for eating together and listening to prayer readings. Outside the monastic and elite secular context, however, eating may not have occurred on tables dedicated for that purpose; rather, any flat surface or even the floor may have been used (Goitein 1967–93, 4: 144–50; Oikonomides 1990; cf. Sadān 1976: 81).

Tables depicted in ecclesiastical art are of varied shapes, including round or semicircular, with rectangular tables appearing especially in the art of the latter phase of the medieval period. Banquet scenes in religious and secular contexts alike include tables, which seem to be of very simple design, but may be wholly covered with textiles and the plate to be used for dining or display (Helfenstein 2013). Since they are important components in the depictions of specific biblical stories, tables often represent elements of contemporary life inserted into established narratives. In Byzantine and Western medieval art, tables are commonly included in representations of the Last Supper, as well as of the Hospitality of Abraham and the Wedding at Cana. In a fifteenth-century painting of the Wedding at Cana by an unidentified Spanish artist in the National Gallery of Art in Washington, for example, tables with elaborately carved legs are shown with architecturally derived elements such as a door and Gothic-inspired turrets with spires (Samuel H. Kress Collection 1952.5.42; Hand 2004: 70–1, no. 51).

Writing tables with lecterns are the type of furniture that appears most frequently in representations of the Four Evangelists. A single Gospel manuscript, though, may include diverse tables, as an example in the British Library shows (Burney MS 19, ff. 1v, 63v, 101v; Anderson 1991). Illustrated in the twelfth century, the Burney Gospels include three similar but not identical writing tables with lecterns for three of the four Evangelists. The tables have room for implements underneath the writing surface in the form of cabinets with rectangular or arched doors. Lecterns themselves may have belonged in the church setting and function here as symbolic attributes. The mid-fourteenth-century miniature, mentioned earlier, of the aristocratic official Alexios Apokaukos (d.1345) nonetheless suggests that wealthy readers may have had lecterns in their houses (Bibl. Nat. Paris, Gr. 2144, f. 11r). Such furniture is represented in some

FIGURE 1.4 Marble sigma-table, Bimaristan of Nur al-Din, Damascus, twelfth century. Photograph by Marcus Milwright.

detail, including a revolving spiral support attached to a marble or wooden base for the lectern, as in the late eleventh-century Homilies of John Chrysostom in Paris (Bibliothèque nationale de France, MS Coislin Gr. 79, f. 2r).

Like other items of furniture, the representation of tables frequently straddles cultural divides. One telling example is the sigma-shaped table of the Last Supper shown in the twelfth-century Melisende Psalter in the British Library (Egerton MS 1139, f. 6r). This appears in a manuscript that is a cultural product of crusader Jerusalem, but amalgamates Byzantine and Western features because different artists who were trained in these traditions collaborated to make the book.

In Europe and the Byzantine world, beds are depicted in biblical stories, such as the healing of the daughter of Jairus (Matthew 9:18–26; Mark 5:21–43) or the healing of the paralytic (Matthew 9:1–8; Mark 2:1–12). The birth of the Virgin and occasionally that of John the Baptist are other relevant scenes in which beds are shown, including examples of frescoes among Giotto's early fourteenth-century work in the Arena Chapel in Padua, Italy. These narratives gave artists the opportunity to depict the domestic environment, which does not otherwise often appear in medieval religious art before the latter part of this period. In a mosaic executed in a lunette at the late eleventh-century monastery of the Dormition at Daphni (a suburb of Athens), for example, the bed on which Elizabeth rests after the birth of the Virgin has turned legs and a backrest, but is otherwise largely hidden underneath a white sheet and an additional, elaborate gold cover that almost touches the ground (Plate 3). With a design of a repeated series of spades, diamonds, and circles, the cover points to the prominent status of luxury textiles often associated with a reclining human body. These textiles appear in scenes that include an element of public presentation. Images of the birth of Jesus and the Virgin, as well as of the Dormition of the Virgin, must have been influenced by ceremonial activities that were built around elite births and funerals and involved beds.

Judging from what we see in Western medieval art, in the twelfth and thirteenth centuries the form and decoration of beds used by the privileged became more elaborate, and this is paralleled in the art of the last centuries of Byzantium. Inlay and painted decoration were also frequently featured. Hung beds, in particular, seem to have been favored by elites as they offered the opportunity for the display of rich textiles. These beds were often not meant for sleeping; nevertheless, Eames has remarked that the elite bed was considered an important piece of furniture rather than a mere support for the textiles that covered it (1977: 74; cf. a figure lying in bed in the Madrid Skylitzes manuscript, Biblioteca Nacional de España, MS Vitr. 26–2, f. 163r).

Just as beds had an important role in representing status, so too did cradles. Luxury textiles adorned aristocratic cradles, which could also be painted and gilded (Eames 1977: 93–107; Parani 2003: 192–3). An elaborate example is a crib for Jesus at the Metropolitan Museum in New York. Although this item is of a ritual nature and associated with a medieval convent (the Grand Béguinage of Louvain, Belgium), it allows glimpses into cradles used in real life. The crib is southern Netherlandish, sculpted with a series of architectural arches and angels, and heavily painted. It includes carved images of the Nativity (Forsyth 1989: 124, fig. 8) (Plate 4). Cribs were also represented in art, such as the cradle of John the Baptist in a twelfth-century Byzantine Gospel book in the Vatican (MS Urb. Gr. 2, f. 167v).

Wooden chests, armoires (cupboards with doors), elite buffets, and utilitarian dressers were used for the storage of many portable items, including coins, jewelry, clothes, bed linen, reliquaries, and food (for distinctions in the terminology of storage, see Eames 1977: 55–6; for a fuller discussion of chest types, see Chapter 3 in this volume). The forms and decoration of such storage furniture are characterized by diversity and some are even associated with particular regions. Decorated credenzas, for instance, are a feature of Italian interiors of the fifteenth century (The Metropolitan Museum of Art, accession number 53.95; discussed in Barnet and Wu 2012: 120). Buffets were used for the display of plate, but they were not decorated elaborately. Stepped dressers sometimes show up in late medieval paintings and prints, and act as supports for the valuables that represent a ruler's or nobleman's status (Helfenstein 2013). The major decoration of buffets and dressers came from the textiles that often covered them (Eames 1977: 56, n. 139). An interesting parallel is known from Byzantium, where written sources record a ninth-century luxury cabinet resembling a tower. This was located in the Chrysotriklinos of the imperial palace in Constantinople and contained precious display objects, including crowns, vessels, and other luxuries (Angar 2015).

In representational art, armoires can appear with learned people, as in the image of the biblical scribe Ezra on the frontispiece of the Codex Amiatinus, an early eighth-century Bible from England. The prophet's accoutrements are complete with bench, stool, and writing table (Florence Biblioteca Laurenziana, Codex Amiatinus I, f. 5r; Ramirez 2009: 1–18). The depicted piece has a gabled roof with crosses, peacocks, vases, and geometric motifs in white decorating its exterior. The identification of this manuscript as a product of cross-cultural connections, that is as an Anglo-Saxon work that makes reference to earlier, antique manuscript models (Weitzmann 1966), may also lead us to consider it and other illuminated manuscripts as a medium of communicating ideas about what people thought items linked to biblical narrative looked like.

Depictions of chests show how these could be used as seats, beds, or flat surfaces for any suitable activity. In a scene of Christ washing the Apostles' feet from the Melisende Psalter, which dates to the Crusades period (British Library, Egerton MS 1139, f. 6v), the group is seated on a piece of furniture that may be a chest decorated with stepped borders and vertical molding. Surviving chests show that they could be entirely painted in a single color. They could have carved paneling or blind arcading (Eames 1977: 144), especially on the front side, and carved feet with tracery or columnar forms. In western Europe specialized craftsmen called *imagiers* were responsible for carving and gilding (discussed in Eames 1977: 10–11). Toward the end of the medieval period, carving and painting as well as embellishment of chests with iron became more elaborate in religious and secular settings alike. Examples of ornament in iron include vegetal motifs, such as leaves, animals, and intricate scrolling. Locks with elaborate iron fittings make it evident that safety was an important practical consideration in the manufacture of chests and armoires. For example, an extant chest made for the Guildhall in London was constructed entirely of iron and contained three sets of outer and three sets of inner locks (Eames 1974: 1–4). The design of such chests provided maximum security for the valuables held inside, which in the Guildhall case were associated with the administration of the City of London. We, therefore, find that locks and the decoration of chests and armoires were parts of an integral design. Some of the armoires surviving from England and France retain rectangular lock plates and bars used for locking, which ended in decorative elements such as fleur-de-lis finials.

The front panels of chests provided a field for carved and painted narrative scenes that often had didactic value, such as a (*c.* 1450) panel with a scene of the defense of Rome against the Etruscans in the Victoria & Albert Museum (accession no. 7897–1863; Kauffmann 1973: 107–8, cat. no. 122). A trend for secular iconography can be detected in the fourteenth and fifteenth centuries: a chest at the Museum of London (accession no. 75.2) with a set of narrative relief panels (99 × 49 cm) depicts a short story by Chaucer and conveys the desire to visualize literature and themes of everyday life. At the same time this imagery served as social commentary; it warned viewers against the moral misdemeanor of people wearing rich textiles in spite of sumptuary laws (Whitaker 1999: 174–89). From the end of the medieval period the names of the artists who worked on such scenes begin to survive, as happens with some *cassoni* from Florence. In addition, religious narratives seem to have decorated furniture used in ritual and domestic contexts, and they were not abandoned when secular scenes became popular. Front panels of wooden coffers depict the Annunciation or the Visitation of the Magi (e.g., Eames 1977: 109, 145, fig. 17; V&A accession no. W.15–1920), or Saint George and the Dragon in the case of items from England and France (e.g., a chest in York Minster; Eames 1977: plates 36A–37C). Narrative scenes often ornamented furniture without accompanying text. This suggests that their medieval viewers were meant to understand the narratives by visual recognition alone.

DECORATIVE ACCESSORIES AND FURNITURE

The functionality and overall visual effect of medieval furniture was often complemented by other items. Elite medieval households and ritual spaces, such as churches or mosques, featured accessories such as lamps, braziers, and mirrors that augmented the spaces and its furniture. Looms, too, must have had a regular presence, catering to one of the basic household activities of women. Looms are often seen in illuminated manuscripts of the book of Job, on the occasion of reference to women weaving in 38.36. Woven textiles, which must have been ubiquitous, satisfied a variety of needs from seating to eating, praying to sleeping, and, when not needed, could be rolled away. In the dowry lists of its Jewish brides, the Cairo Genizah affords much more attention to furnishings and household utensils than furniture items, which are nevertheless often inferred by mention of the valuable textiles that covered them (Goitein 1977). Textiles satisfied needs for adjustable seating arrangements when guests were expected and there was a need for their status to be considered in relation to the host (Golombek 1988: 32). The functions of textiles extended to their usage as room dividers and thus as integral items of the "personality" of interior spaces. This includes various floor coverings despite the relative absence of such artifacts in art (Parani 2003: 184–5).

Accounts of diplomatic embassies communicate the fundamental role that textiles played in the composition of elite spaces. In the case of the visit of a Byzantine embassy to caliph al-Muqtadir (r.908–32) in Baghdad we read that: "Then the envoys were ushered into the palace known as 'al-Firdaws' (Paradise), which contained innumerable and priceless quantities of equipment and richly-colored fabrics (*washy*). Five thousand gilded coats of mail (*jawshan*) were hung in the vestibules of al-Firdaws" (translated in Qaddumi 1996: 152, no. 162). In the palaces of the Abbasid caliphs such as this one then, thousands of portable luxury objects combined with the overall opulence of interiors and courtyards to induce a sense of awe and splendor, even if we don't learn specifically about what we would conventionally call "furniture." This emphasis on luxury had a very wide reach in the medieval world. Indeed, one of the most famous scenes depicting a banquet is of the month of January in the *Très Riches Heures* of the Duc de Berry (Musée Condé, Chantilly, MS 65, f. 1v, by the Limbourg Brothers). In this image, rich textiles cover every surface, including the rectangular table and the walls behind the feast.

DESIGN: RITUAL AND WONDER

Some specialized furniture also needs to be mentioned: ritual furniture for reading prayers existed in the form of pulpits in churches and *bimot* (sing. *bimah*) in synagogues, and was made of wood or stone. Analogous wooden items, called *minbars* (stepped platforms for addressing the congregation) have occasionally survived from medieval mosques. A well-preserved example is the elaborate, three-stepped *minbar* of the Kutubiyya Mosque in Marrakesh (Figure 1.1). Such items included inscriptions as well as geometric interlace designs, and could be imported from elsewhere in the Islamic world; this *minbar*, for example, was made in Cordoba, Spain. Made in 1137, the Kutubiyya *minbar* incorporates extensive inlay using wood and bone. Series of horseshoe-shaped and multifoil arches point to the crossover of architectural ornament between Christian and Islamic art that often includes vegetal motifs with interlocking rosettes and vine scrolls. This decoration also allows us to look for cultural distinctions in the symbolism of motifs behind the formal similarities of design with items from different parts of the medieval world. For instance, the repeated arcading is not far removed from Gothic ornamentation on other pieces of furniture mentioned here but ultimately derives from late antique artistic models in painting and other media. Additionally, the decoration of the Kutubiyya *minbar* may be more connected with architectural arcades in the mosques of Spain or even the repeated arcading that appears in the frontispieces of two eighth-century Qurans found in Sana'a in Yemen but probably painted in Damascus (Codex Sana DAM 20–33.1), thus documenting a specifically Islamic concern with repeated, structured motifs.

Clearly, many portable objects could be rearranged to suit the occasion and did not necessarily form permanent fixtures of a room or palace. The discussed *minbar* is composite and portable through a mechanism that allowed it to move in one piece (Bloom et al. 1998). This feature recalls the use of *automata* in the Byzantine and Islamic royal courts. *Automata* were large mechanical contraptions set in imperial audience halls. They were not functional, but were highly important in ceremonies of presentation, especially when viewed by visiting embassies that sometimes left accounts of their visits. Furniture therefore fitted within the larger theme of paradise that opulent spaces invoked through usage of luxury carpets, *automata* and painted or stuccoed wall decoration.

The invocation of wonder ran through the design of thrones and *automata*. The Byzantine imperial palace had a throne that could be lifted in the air and was compared to the throne of Solomon (Brett 1954). Nevertheless, we are also told that precious items could be sacrificed at times when imperial coffers were empty, as in the case of the *automaton* throne in the court of Emperor Michael III (840–867) (Breckenridge 1980–1: 260, with bibliography). Similar associations characterized the arrangement of presentation items in the Islamic world: we are told that the palace of al-Burj in Abbasid Samarra north of Baghdad had a throne of gold, a golden tree with singing birds and a pool with sides that were lined with silver plates (translated in Northedge 2005: 284). Similar features are present in the Islamic Umayyad palace of Madinat al-Zahra' in Spain. Such traditions of opulence in the Islamic and Byzantine world, and deriving from the late Roman world, owe much to the Sasanid (third to seventh century) courts of Persia, where: "When the envoys stood before the king, they were ordered to sit, and the doorkeepers hastened to bring gold and silver chairs for them to sit on; [then] they conveyed their message and departed" (translated in Qaddumi 1996: 147, no. 159). In the court of Harun al-Rashid (763–809) in Baghdad, we hear of ebony seats instead (Qaddumi 1996: 147–8, no. 160). Furniture is an indispensable part of these connections.

CONCLUSION

This chapter has shown that aspects of continuity in the appearance and decoration of furniture display the reverence for antique values, which can be seen in other spheres of material and literary culture. This referencing of older forms is accentuated as we move closer to the tenth and eleventh centuries, as in the case of Romanesque art in Europe or the art of the Macedonian emperors in Byzantium. Such reverence is highlighted by particular design elements of seats of authority that are included in extant or depicted items on coinage and icons among other media, in which the curved sides of the lyre-backed throne, for instance, may be more reminiscent of the antiquity of the shape itself than of the theological concepts they supported earlier (Breckenridge 1980–1; Reeve 2003). Arcade designs and repeated balusters, as well as the representation of animal forms on the legs of seats are typical elements that may hark back to early Christian or earlier, biblical times. The extension of these features to the Islamic world shows the degree to which the Roman heritage of Europe and the Mediterranean was foundational for the forms and motifs of a very large part of the medieval world. In turn, the Roman Empire and its descendant medieval states were heirs of strong Eastern influences, including the importance of furniture in presentation rituals and the (physical and metaphorical) elevation of the ruler on his throne, as well as the setting of a heavenly paradise created around that symbol of rulership. These features were adopted in Byzantium and medieval Europe and persisted for many centuries.

The examination of objects displayed on top of furniture at the turn of the sixteenth century has suggested a redirection of taste in Europe from the appreciation of the preciosity of portable items toward additional or especial note of the technical skill of the makers (Helfenstein 2013: 436–7). This may mean that the items arrayed on shelves, tables, and beds started to be experienced differently from the medieval period. Could we be witnessing also a change in how the supporting furniture of these portable items functioned? And could this relate to the elaboration of designs and motifs that become more evident as we get closer to 1500 and the early modern period?

We can further distinguish several themes that derive from emphasizing cross-references in the design and use of furniture across the medieval cultures of

Europe, the Mediterranean, and the Middle East. These include the transfer of motifs between furniture and other media, including architecture, the expression of connections with antiquity through visual means, and the proliferation of textiles covering items such as beds and seats. From the dowry lists of the Cairo Genizah archive to Byzantine art and European inventories such as those of the court of Burgundy that include the estate of the Duc de Berry mentioned earlier, furniture can therefore be seen as part of a cultural continuum. Ideas, furniture design, and motifs influenced each other and crossed borders, brought about not only by encounters between royals but by interregional trade and the movement of luxury materials such as textiles, ivory, and illuminated manuscripts (cf. Hoffman 2001; Brubaker 2004). More than anything, though, the chapter highlights the "ephemeral sensibility" characterizing medieval furniture: reminding us that before the fixed, modern concepts of design, the appearance and decoration of furniture, and its arrangement in spaces, was not haphazard, but appealed to complex, long-standing cultural memories of the past and relationships of social status (Hollis 2004: 112). It is these relationships that allowed for the fluidity and continuity of shapes and motifs across geographical and temporal boundaries.

CHAPTER TWO

Makers, Making, and Materials

Materials, Tools, Techniques, and Organization of the Trade

CLAUDIO PAOLINI

The vast historical period and size of the area taken into consideration in this volume, with its many and diverse traditions, only allow this chapter to highlight some themes and fundamental moments in the evolution of furniture making in relation to materials, tools, techniques, and the organization of the craft. In particular, it is useful to think of this period in two parts: the first, until around 1300, for which the scholar has to rely on scarce representations of the construction of furniture in paintings and illuminations; and the second, from 1300 to 1500, when written and visual sources increase in number and accuracy (in parallel with the greater attention paid to the social role of manual activities and those who practice them), and for which we have direct evidence, namely, furniture still found in churches and palaces, and held in our museums. In particular, there are examples from the Mediterranean, and specifically Italy, which played a central role in recovering ancient styles and construction techniques that had been, in part, forgotten.

AT THE HEART OF THE MATTER: THE CARPENTER

With the fall of the Roman Empire there is a substantial and progressive impoverishment of the technological heritage accumulated in the previous centuries, which, in the furniture industry, had given life to a highly specialized workforce capable of rather sophisticated creations (Symonds 1962: 243–4).[1] Meanwhile, it is precisely between the sixth and fourteenth centuries that wood became the main material used on building sites, leading to the upholding of high professional standards of carpenters, who were called upon to work out the fundamental issue of giving stability to a structure with the use of wooden elements assembled in different ways. Although elite buildings made in stone and brick have survived until the present day, these grand structures represent only a small part of the building heritage of those centuries. The use of wood was facilitated by the expansion of forests in the early Middle Ages, thus making available an extensive and varied resource of timber to meet the demands of construction. With regard to the building of fortifications in the twelfth century, wood combined with sand or soil was used for defensive architecture, such as the motte-and-bailey castle, documented from the tenth century in the regions of the Rhine and the Loire, and from the twelfth century, widespread through a good part of Europe (in England one thinks of the castle of Restormel in Cornwall, the fort in Dover, and Windsor Castle).[2] Furthermore, while from the fourteenth century on stone and brick progressively replaced wood on building sites in the Mediterranean area, in the northern regions, the presence of large forests with trees possessing thick, weather-resistant trunks ensured that the majority of buildings would continue to be built with wood, which was readily available and easy to work with. The city of London, before the disastrous fire of 1666, was evidence of the prowess of local carpenters, whose role and importance began to decline following the law for the reconstruction of 1667, which dictated the use of stone and brick precisely to avoid repetition of similar tragedies.

The carpenter can also be identified as the main furniture maker of the time based on the type of furniture present in dwellings. Up until the fourteenth century, we have clear evidence that most household furniture was designed and created at building sites, at the same time as the construction of the house. Most types of furniture (with some exceptions, such as trunks and chests, which were made more for the need of moving the goods of the family from one place to another) appear to be brickwork structures, equipped with simple wooden doors.[3] We also have information on beds made with brick, with the use of wood limited to making a flat surface for mattresses, although this was more often achieved with the use of ropes or rods. The construction of furniture used to support objects, such as tables, benches, and stools, falls entirely within the technical expertise of the carpenter. This involves simple furniture, constructed with thick wooden planks, supported by shafts nailed down or inserted in recesses going through the board of the support surface or of the seating surface. In relation to tables, we also know of the widespread presence of drop-leaf tables attached to the walls of a house, to be used with the simple help of trestles and sawhorses (Paolini 2004b: 26–38).[4] In essence, the various construction methods of furniture of the time can be attributed to two main methods used at medieval building sites that, using the terminology adopted by German scholars, we know as *Fachwerk* and *Blockbau*. The first is based on the creation of half-timbered bearings, and the second characterizes the use of wide panels of solid wood. The very simple character of this (for the most part with visible joints and surfaces left in a rough stage of work) should not however make us think that the furniture of wealthy families was lacking or unadorned. One must keep in mind that the appeal that we now have for natural wood, for its grain and for its patina, is an utterly modern taste and was absolutely unknown in those centuries. The furniture and furnishings that were assembled only when needed, such as large tables covered with rugs and tablecloths for banquets, were in fact painted (because this better preserves them, however, the colors were usually garish). The walls of rooms and the backrests of benches were usually made fancier, when necessary, with fabrics and tapestries (Paolini 2004b: 27–8).

These observations not only place building sites as the setting for furniture making in these early centuries, but also show the carpenter as an active figure in close collaboration with the mason and the blacksmith, who, besides being a central figure in the production of tools used in woodworking, creates nails, metal bands of support, locks, and hinges. However, it is important to avoid identifying the carpenter as a worker of low social standing, able to manage only rough work, and it is suggested instead that the joiner and the cabinetmaker will establish themselves in the following centuries as not only highly specialized figures but as products of the evolution of the craft. In reality, the carpenter not only fully carries out the demands of the time, but being a builder, he also, in many cases, possesses characteristics decidedly close to those of the architect and the engineer. The fact that the emblem of the master carpenters of London displays three compasses tells us that during the Middle Ages they wanted to highlight the carpenters' contribution to building sites in terms of their planning ability, more than that of their manual ability, almost wanting to imply that the craft of carpentry shares aspects of the liberal arts and not of mechanical activities (Symonds 1962: 244–8).

The emergence of some figures and the quality of their achievements tends to be attributed to the various abilities of individuals, as well as to the different economic and social contexts in which they work. In one of the frescoes of Agnolo Gaddi in the apse of the Basilica of Santa Croce in Florence narrating *The Legend of the Cross*, we see that the artist relegates the carpenters, focused on sawing the arms of the cross, to a decidedly secondary role: dressed in rather wretched tunics, they appear as simple executors of a laborious and thankless job. Conversely, in the fresco of Piero di Puccio that depicts *The Construction of Noah's Ark* on the Camposanto of Pisa (bear in mind that we are at the end of the fourteenth century in a city where the construction of watercrafts is still a source of local pride), the many carpenters are well-dressed and aware of the importance of their work, showing us the variety of jobs of which they are capable (sawing, planing, building, and progressing with the construction of the ark) (Figure 2.1).

In addition, a clear parallel can be made between the figure of the carpenter with that which later commentators will identify with the term of "woodworker" (*legnaiolo*), essentially making reference to the workshops of central Italy. It is important to highlight that from them emerges the figure of the "woodworker–architect." This refers to a professional who, having been trained in the field of carpentry, is responsible for extremely complex projects and building sites.

Among the main designers of fortifications in the second half of the fifteenth century are the architect and woodworker (carpenter, carver, and inlayer)

FIGURE 2.1 Piero di Puccio, *The Construction of Noah's Ark*, end of the fourteenth century, Pisa, Camposanto. Print: G. Rossi da G. Rosini, *Storia della pittura italiana. Epoca prima* (Pisa, 1839).

Francesco di Giovanni, known as il Francione (1428–95), and Baccio Pontelli (*c.* 1450–*c.* 1494), his student active in the field of architecture and an extremely skilled inlayer. There is also the woodworker and architect Giuliano da Maiano (1432–90) who, together with his brother Benedetto, was introduced to the craft by their father Nardo d'Antonio, himself enrolled in the guild of the woodworkers of Florence in 1439. Da Maiano was capable of carving many kinds of works, building furniture, furnishings and liturgical objects, as well as creating complex wooden structures, machines, and mechanical devices (Raggio and Wilmering 1999: 2:103–21).

In the sixteenth century, the role of the woodworker is still central in the sphere of the history of Italian and, in particular, Florentine architecture. For example, it was the woodworker, "*il legnaiolo*," Mariotto di Zanobi Folfi, known as l'Ammogliato, who directed the building site of Palazzo Uguccioni in the Piazza della Signoria in Florence (1549), based on a project perhaps attributable to Raphael. In the same years (1547–51), it is the "*legnaiolo*" Giovanni Battista del Tasso who planned and constructed the loggia of the Mercato Nuovo, desired by the grand Duke Cosimo de' Medici in the center of Florence.

THE ART OF CONNECTIONS AND JOINTS

The carpenter and the joiner have in common the knowledge of techniques to assemble boards and other elements to ensure the stability of a structure, whether it be a house or a chest. In many cases one would think that the use of a natural glue in the creation of a piece of furniture would be the most simple method to join two elements. Although the manner of producing mastics and glues of different features (ranging from strong glues obtained from animal substances to light glues produced from vegetable substances) was already well known in the medieval period, in the case of furniture, these mastics and glues were only widely used from the sixteenth century on. The lack of these substances in the construction of furniture is not only because natural glues are extremely sensitive to water and humidity, making their durability questionable, but also because of experience gained by carpenters on construction sites. In this context, iron nails are mainly used (which once again reminds us of the close relationship of our masters with the blacksmiths), and large wooden nails or dowels, hammered on the inside of an opening made with an auger. The portrayal of a carpenter carrying an auger, so as to make this his distinctive attribute (particularly in French examples), demonstrates how important and widespread the technique was (Plate 5).

In the construction of furniture, we see a comparable and widespread use of iron and wooden nails, as well as dowels, in the panels of many paintings of the fifteenth century. In some areas (in particular Italy), it furthermore appears that the experience gained in the craft of joinery over an extended period of time, from the Egyptian age to the Roman age, has not been completely lost.[5]

To create large surfaces, one can join boards using tongue-and-groove joints (as can be noted in the case of the backing support of a painting and therefore in the construction of panels). Tongue-and-groove joints involve making a linear groove in the thickness of a board, and making a linear protrusion, called a tongue, in the thickness of the board to join. To save on materials, one can also make a groove on both boards and use a strip of wood of identical thickness and depth for the joint, in place of a tongue. For the creation of a loom, one instead uses the half lap joint or (as we can see in an antique miniature) the widespread joint system of mortise and tenon. In this case, one uses a chisel to hollow out a rectangular cut (the mortise) in one of the pieces to be joined, and in the other piece, one makes a protrusion of identical size (the tenon).

Some evidence also appears to document that in the Italian setting, the ability to construct drawers with sides connected with dovetail joints was in fact preserved. This is an ideal joint to connect two planks at a right angle, reflecting the mortise-and-tenon system, but in this case the sides are cut according to a distinctive design, known as a dovetail. This is very effective and will find wide use, for example, in the construction of the sides of chests of the fifteenth century.

In essence, albeit with the given distinctions from region to region, one notices that all of the main techniques of joinery that we still use today in the construction of high-quality handcrafted furniture were already present in the last centuries of the period considered here, and in some cases the techniques were relatively widespread.

THE WOODCARVER

The appearance of another specialized figure in woodworking within the sphere of medieval construction should be identified: the woodcarver. It is difficult to determine how much the craft shares with the activities of the carpenter, the sculptor, and the more generic stonemason, just as it is challenging to establish if the early Middle Ages appreciated it as a specific expertise or as an aspect of activities that would be part of different trades at different times.[6]

There is no doubt that the figurative and decorative inventory of the time, characterized, for example, by the carving of wooden choirs in monasteries, finds clear correspondence in the shapes that we see sculpted on the capitals and portals within those same monasteries. It is clear, however, that the different materials (stone, with a granular texture, and wood, with a fibrous and grained structure) require extremely different approaches of technique when working with them. This can lead us to consider carving as one of the initial specializations of the carpenter, who would use chisels to dig and carve to create moldings and joints, thus acquiring valuable skills for sculpting brackets to support wooden frames. This would allow the carpenter to later diversify his work to include making sculptural and decorative aspects triumph over structural aspects, as is the case with the wooden choirs previously mentioned. The fact that some documents in the Middle Ages in France already distinguish between the carpenter "of the large axe" and he of the "small axe" would seem to indicate that one differentiates specializations within the trade, or at least makes a distinction between the structural and engineering work and the more purely artistic work intended to embellish the work (Symonds 1962: 248–51).

It is also noteworthy that the carving of wood statuary continued without interruption throughout the Middle Ages (due to the ready availability of raw materials, as we have mentioned). There was vast production of crucifixes, statues of the Virgin and anthropomorphic reliquaries, as well as large, carved wooden doors for the portals of cathedrals, which are perhaps the closest reference points to what is being investigated in this chapter.

Although we cannot generalize, it is useful to mention the story of another Tuscan artist, Ventura Vitoni. Active between the second half of the fifteenth century and the first decades of the sixteenth century in the city of Pistoia (a center of some importance), Vitoni needed a workforce that was not specialized in one specific area, but one that was able to manage many techniques. Ventura Vitoni is a *legnaiolo*, a woodworker (but as Giorgio Vasari points out, one gifted with a "very good talent" and capable of designing "rather beautifully" (Vasari 1906: 4:165 "Life of Bramante"), and with experience in architecture). Documents allow us to trace a rather varied series of works to Vitoni: this includes the construction of fir roofs, lofts, pergolas, staircases, shelving, and window fixtures (the activities of a carpenter), along with wardrobes, benches, and chests (more of the work of a joiner), and even carved shelves, adorned panels for doors, and carvings for choirs and residences (typical of a carver). Lastly, Vitoni was also responsible for intense activities as a designer and director of building sites, which connects him in particular with the construction of the Basilica of the Madonna dell'Umiltà, a symbol of the Renaissance in Pistoia, elevating him, as Giorgio Vasari points out, to the role of architect (Paolini 2004a: 138–9, 143–4).

All of this is to highlight that an investigation that wishes to demonstrate that the crafts connected with the various methods of woodworking diversified and produced specializations, and to interpret this in the sense of an evolution from the "dark" early Middle Ages to the glorious times of the Renaissance, is a modern perspective rather than the understanding of the time that everything was connected to the collective work at building sites and workshops.

CENTERS, OUTSKIRTS, AND REGIONAL TRADITIONS

To understand the evolution of the organization of the craft, we will begin by distinguishing between the carpenter and the woodworker, the carver, the inlayer, the cabinetmaker, and so on. Although the workforce becomes increasingly specialized as we gradually continue through the centuries, the phenomenon was not perceptible in equal measure in all European areas. Beyond the active role held by some great artistic centers (as, for example, for Florence between the fourteenth and fifteenth centuries), there always remain strong variations in the organization of the craft between cities and outskirts, and between populated centers and country villages.

It is clear that where we see a high concentration of the population (it is estimated that around the year 1300 Florence was one of the most populated cities of the West and housed around 100,000 inhabitants inside its walls), there is an equal concentration of workers that tend to specialize in specific kinds of workmanship because of a large and varied market demand. In smaller cities, on the other hand, it is necessary to have workforces that are capable of performing tasks—with a minimal level of knowledge—in many areas of work. The woodworker (we will use this term for an artisan engaged in woodworking) must be equally capable of constructing carts and agricultural tools, resolving carpentry problems connected with building residences, and producing window frames and furniture for the basic needs of residences, as we have seen in the case of Ventura Vitoni (Paolini 2004a: 138–9, 143–4). The refinement of woodworking in the production of furniture occurs primarily in cities, which expanded due to the slow migration of the population from the surrounding countryside from the year 1000.

Another fundamental difference between the various European areas is the kinds of materials used in the construction of furniture, which is closely connected to the type of wood available in an area, in the case of furniture of the time. Although there is material evidence of original furniture from the fifteenth century, we cannot rely on this to establish the main types of wood used at the time. What are in fact preserved (as we said in reference to architectural evidence) are the artifacts of greater importance, which are typically made with premium materials. For example, the assumption that walnut is the most prevalent wood for Renaissance furniture in Italy is in part contradicted by archival documentation and by the many inventories that indicate poplar—which is light, easily workable, and available in great quantity—as the more widespread material of construction. On the other hand, we have fewer extant examples of poplar because it is more perishable, although evidence of poplar panels for painting confirms its prevalence.[7]

The same can be said for the use of oak in England and the region of Flanders. In general, we can show that present at both construction sites and woodworking workshops were woods used in the plains and hills, mostly broad-leafed trees (oak, beech, chestnut, ash, and indeed poplar), and an obvious tendency to use conifers in mountainous areas (pine, fir, larch) (Meiggs 1982; Borghini and Massafra 2002).

In addition, it is clear that each region offers its own specific technical traditions, which in some cases take on a social and cultural value that has a direct influence on furniture, and therefore on the manner of living. Contributing to the complexity of the subject are the variety of contexts for furniture, the range of uses and diverse traditions, and the implications of multiple climactic zones. With respect to techniques of furniture construction, an important factor is the varying abilities of different regions to maintain connections with the heritage of the Roman world. Although we have already noted that there is a general loss of knowledge from antiquity during the early Middle Ages, this is less perceptible in the Italian region as compared to northern Europe.

In Italy, although material examples are not preserved, it appears that the ability to construct drawers with built-in sides using dovetail joints or wooden pins was not completely lost (using techniques developed in ancient Egypt and later documented in both the Greek and Roman worlds). Conversely, in northern Europe, there is no evidence of drawers handed down from the distant past, and it is believed that the drawer appears north of the Alps only in the late Middle Ages. In any event, the drawer reached France, Germany, and the Netherlands along the Rhine valley, a route along which many inventions spread from the south to the north of Europe. It was only in the fifteenth century that the drawer made its appearance in England, where it was called "*till,*" a drawer for money, or a "drawing box" (Symonds 1962: 244).

THE RELATIONSHIP BETWEEN STRUCTURE AND DECORATION

With respect to the history of techniques and the organization of the craft, we must bear in mind another issue. We typically ascribe the creation of complex works to one individual who possesses diverse technical abilities. However, the creation of furniture depends on teams of workers or those who are present at a building site, and in the best examples, the figure of the designer will often play a fundamental role.

On the one hand, there are creations that for their size cannot clearly be produced by a single artisan. One thinks of the choirs in churches, which are closely connected with the architecture, and whose creation may depend on the carpenter and the blacksmith for the adornment of carved parts (the armrests, cornices and moldings, pilasters, and so on), as well as for the works of tarsia (on the panels of individual seats) and of pictorial elements. On the other hand, we have furniture of limited size whose structure and decoration make reference to very distinct techniques. In this case, one thinks of painted chests produced between the fourteenth and fifteenth centuries or, making a brief foray in the centuries after those considered in this chapter, of the effect that leather and upholstery had on the production of chairs and armchairs. The issue is not if the creator of the furnishings is to be identified as a woodworker, painter, gilder, or upholsterer: we must in fact recognize this as evidence of a society in which the true protagonist is the workshop, where various workers collaborate, trade experiences, and contribute to the creation of collective works.

However, to avoid generalizations, in the following section we distinguish between the structure of the furniture and its decoration, dealing with the aspects most closely connected to the construction of furniture, starting with the tools of the woodworker.

THE TOOLS OF THE WOODWORKER

It can be said that there was a substantial uniformity in the basic kinds of tools used for working with wood in all of the West, already established in the preceding centuries, and not very dissimilar from tools already present in ancient Egypt and those that we continue to observe until the nineteenth century.[8] The adz, the axe, the hammer, the saw, and the chisel remained the fundamental tools and independent from specific specializations. Used for millennia, these tools evolved with the ability to better temper iron, thus allowing these now sharper tools to cut with greater ease and precision (Saverio Lomartire in Crivello 2006: 252). The increasingly elaborate carvings seem to show a steady stylistic evolution over the centuries, perhaps due in part to improvements in the production of the blades.

The modest reduction in the kinds of tools known in the Roman age appears to be offset by medieval craftsmen taking maximum advantage of the possibilities of the tools available for constructive and decorative needs, in a constant test of the boundaries of basic methods. The emblem of the blacksmiths' guild of London presenting three hammers with the motto "By hammer and hand all arts do stand" (Symonds 1962: 246) appears to highlight not so much the role of the tool, as much as the ability of the master to use the tool for all of its inherent potentiality.

Among the tools seemingly forgotten in the early Middle Ages is the plane, well documented in ancient Roman times. The fact that it apparently ceased to be used is probably due to the extraordinary expertise of the masters of the adz, who were capable of reducing a board to such perfection as to render the contribution of the plane as barely significant. The plane, however, certainly reappeared in the course of the thirteenth century and was soon documented in relation to specific jobs, as we will have the opportunity to see below.

In contrast, the lathe, a complex machine, would appear to have survived without interruption for the entire medieval period.[9] This is demonstrated by figurative evidence illustrating thrones, small tables, and stools, all equipped with variously shaped ground supports and, for the most part, painted. Furthermore, we know that by 1180 there was a guild of lathe turners in Cologne, distinct from the guild of the woodworkers. Moreover, there is evidence that attests to the presence of various machines designed in relation to different types of manufacturing: the figurative documents in fact show pole lathes (particularly used to turn legs of chairs), lathes known as "lathes with a large wheel," moved by one or two cranks (to work pieces of greater size and weight), and foot lathes, used for works of high quality. The fact that this type of work tends to become rare between the fifteenth and sixteenth centuries is therefore to be attributed more to a change of taste than to limited techniques.

There are also some specific medieval rediscoveries, such as the water saw. Although its appearance is traditionally dated to 1322 when it is documented as adopted in Augsburg, in Bavaria, it is found described in the *Livre de portraiture* of Villard de Honnecourt, composed between 1225 and 1250 (Bibliothèque nationale de France, MS fr. 19093, f. 22v). Here a camshaft is rotated by a gear that transmits a reciprocating movement to the saw, which is capable of cutting a tree trunk (Figure 2.2).

As for the carpentry tools that one would expect to be present at a building site of the fourteenth century, the Master of Bedford presents a wide sample in the exquisite illuminated codex known as the *Bedford Hours*, held at the British Library (Add. MS 18850, f. 15v). In the illumination, the workers are intent on building a complex wooden construction (specifically Noah's Ark). We see twelve carpenters focusing on twelve activities, which allows the artist to illustrate the many tools of the trade, at times shown all over the place, leaning against piles of timber, and at other times in the hands or the ample work belts of the master builders (Plate 6). Visible with the adz and straight-edge axes are a rip saw, a frame saw, a long plane, some bench planes, many augers and various chisels, wooden mallets, a belly brace, and naturally, various nail hammers, typically used by carpenters, with a flat head and a forked claw, used to strike and hammer nails, as well as to extract nails or hoist planks and disassemble boards. The illumination is also of notable interest because of the constructive techniques of the vast structure: that of timber framing/*Fachwerk* architecture, with individual elements held together by visible wooden dowels hammered with a mallet into holes made with an auger. The wooden planks used to close the wall panels of the frame are fixed with nails hammered in by force, thanks to the iron hammer of the carpenter. The techniques are therefore not very dissimilar from those of the construction of a piece of furniture intended to hold items, such as a chest.

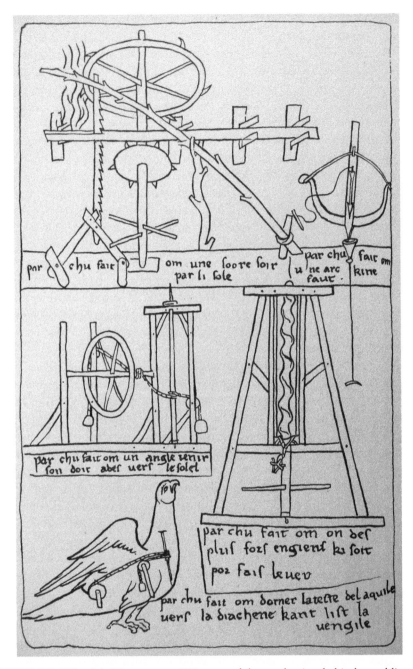

FIGURE 2.2 Villard de Honnecourt, "Diagram of the mechanism behind a nodding eagle," *Livre de portraiture* (1225–50). Bibliothèque nationale de France, MS fr. 19093, f. 22v. Photo: Photo12/Universal Images Group/Getty Images.

In contrast, a well-equipped and well-organized woodworking workshop around the year 1500 is accurately described in the noted illumination of Jean Bourdichon from the series *Les quatre états de la société* (Paris, École Nationale Supérieure des Beaux-Arts). In this case we are in France, in Tours, and the artisan is portrayed while he is focusing on smoothing a board to perfection with a jack plane (Figure 2.3). The tools of the trade are arranged in the foreground (the absence of adzes, axes, and other tools relevant to the carpenter is to be noted): visible are a wooden mallet, a bench plane, a small hatchet, several chisels, among which a mortise chisel seems to be distinguishable, and perhaps a gouge. Beside these are tools for the all-important measurements: a square and a divider. Behind the woodworker, there is a frame saw lying on the ground, together with, arranged on a rack, other scalpels and mallets of various shapes, a rasp, perhaps a round rasp, a hammer, a gimlet, some pincers, a belly brace, and perhaps a marking gauge, an instrument used to draw on wooden surfaces (and also on stone and other materials). Here it is being used to draw lines on the edges of the wood parallel to the edges of the part being worked on (width and thicknesses). Demonstrating what is produced in this workshop are a chest with fretwork, wood with carved spires, and planks that show mortise and tenon, highlighting that construction (indicated by the mortise technique) and embellishment (indicated by the refined carving) are the specialties of the workshop. Lending a note of domestic intimacy is the presence of the woodworker's wife, focused on spinning, and their son, bending down to collect the shavings produced from the jack plane to use as a starter for fires in the kitchen.

Other figurative documents of the period do little more than confirm what we have seen inside of these workshops,[10] but it is worth noting the famous image of Saint Joseph the woodworker on the side panel of Robert Campin's triptych, the Mérode Altarpiece. Held at the Metropolitan Museum of New York, this image shows a saw lying on the ground with an extremely long and thin blade, very much like what we refer to as a compass saw, used to make curved cuts or cross-section holes.

Things do not appear to change over a century, based on the engraving, which serves as the frontispiece for Hieronymus Wierix's *Jesu Christi Dei Domini Salvatoris nostra Infantia*. The image, which dates to the end of the sixteenth century in Antwerp, in Flanders, is for the most part composed of tools of the carpenter (the adz, the straight-edge axe, and the rip saw) and of the woodworker (Figure 2.4). The individual tools appear in a variety not previously documented. There are no less than nine types of planes, including a long plane and some rebate planes. Also visible are mortise chisels, carving chisels, and a marking gauge. There is also a carpenter's bench, very similar to current ones, equipped with a clamp and other elements suitable for securing and holding down boards to be planed and worked.

FIGURE 2.3 Jean Bourdichon, "The Workshop of the Woodworker," *Les quatre états de la société* (*c*. 1500). Paris, Ecole Nationale Supérieure des Beaux-Arts, MS fr. 2374. The illustration is a graphic rendering from Singer et al. 1956. Photo: RMN-Grand Palais/Art Resource, NY.

FIGURE 2.4 Hieronymus Wierix, "Composition with the tools of the woodworker and carpenter," frontispiece, *Iesu Christi Dei Domini Salvatoris nostri Infantia* (Antwerp, 1580). British Museum. Photo: © The Trustees of the British Museum.

These images confirm the ensemble of tools at the end of the time period taken into consideration (and not only the basic types of tools), which remained essential for the construction of furniture, until the emergence, in a time close to ours, of the industrial processes of production.

THE GUILDS

We have already noted that an evolution and diversification of construction and decoration techniques took place when cities once again become populated after the decline of urban centers of the Western Empire in late antiquity. This repopulation occurred in conjunction with the flourishing of trade and the so-called revival of the year 1000. As a result of this phenomenon and the ensuing concentration of mercantile and artisanal activity, guilds were formed between the eleventh and thirteenth centuries to safeguard the rights of various trades, secure their setting of operations, and monitor the quality of production in growing competitive markets. Among these associations (called *arti*, guilds, societies, companies, brotherhoods, universities, and *credenze*, depending on location), some were developed in connection with the various methods of woodworking. Their activities were outlined within well-defined boundaries, albeit different from region to region, established by statutes and laws that in the majority of cases would remain in force until the eighteenth century (for an overview of the topic, see Black 1984).

The impact of the birth of the guilds on the development of trades appears to be a generated phenomenon, with the main preoccupation of these guilds being to maintain the monopoly of the masters affiliated with the different types of work. They were concerned with limiting, if not prohibiting, access of foreign workers to the guild, declaring bans on exportation of raw materials, controlling the inheritance of assets of the workshop in case of the master's death, to avoid the dispersion of the knowledge and abilities acquired, and so on. The challenges that an apprentice encountered in his path to becoming a "master," and to therefore carry out the activity independently, directly impacted the quality of his training. Workers achieved certain powers and stability only after a long period of apprenticeship, first as an apprentice and then as an assistant at a successful workshop. The process concluded with the completion of a "masterpiece," to be judged by consuls and advisers of the guild.

As for the guilds connected with woodworking, the panorama appears rather varied. In some cases, the various stages of production were the prerogative of specific guilds, and in other cases, grouped together in the same guild are carpenters, woodworkers, carvers, decorators, and wainwrights (builders of carts, and it is worth noting that the term carpenter derives from the Latin *carpentarius*, and this in turn from *carpentum*, which specifically indicates a cart).

A guild of carpenters was already established in London by 1333, and in Paris certain areas of the city seemed to be characterized by the various guilds, according to the arrangement of neighborhoods of the various trades. This was typical of medieval times and is still well documented today by the names of places in Paris.

Some examples in the Italian context demonstrate the complexity of the topic.[11] Information on structured artisan societies in Genoa dates as far back as the twelfth century, and it is clear that in the fourteenth century specific groups were formed: *bancalari* (woodworkers) and *caseleri* (a local term to indicate builders of chests).

In Milan, until the end of the fourteenth century, the guild was indiscriminately open to carpenters or "magistri a lignamine," while later charters of the guild (from the middle of the sixteenth century) began to distinguish various specializations within the guild until, for example, the carvers separated themselves from the guild, establishing their own specific society in 1728.

From the guild of the *marangoni* (woodworkers) of Padua, charters exist from as early as 1257. The society welcomed all those who work with wood, but within the guild there appears to be a distinction made between carpenters, woodworkers, and wainwrights.

In Venice, likely by the eleventh century, there was a guild of *casseleri*, builders of nuptial chests. In the fourteenth century, workers seemingly assembled in the more wide and generic group of *marangoni* (woodworkers). Only during the eighteenth century was the core of the guild clearly organized in four distinct sections: the *marangon de fabrica* (a carpenter who worked on a building site), the *marangon de nogherea* (a woodworker skilled in creating furniture with solid wood, identifiable with builders of chairs), the *remesseri* (specialized in veneers and inlay), and the *marangon de soaze* (who did cornices and framing, and in Venice, also collaborated with gondola builders). Also operating in Venice were decorative artists and woodcarvers distinguished in designing (specialized in illustrations made in bas-relief and high relief), but it is not clear what their relationship was with the *marangoni*.

A guild of woodworkers in Florence from 1218 brought together more varied jobs, but ones that were more substantially attributed to four main groups: chest makers, coopers, generic woodworkers, and saw workers. Carpenters were not included in these groups due to the formation of the masters of stone and wood guild in 1358, which brought together all those who were active on construction sites, from dredgers to kilnsmen to bricklayers, and so on (for the birth of wood corporations in Florence, see Cecchi 1998).

Particularly significant is the emblem that the woodworkers' guild gave itself. It is composed of an uprooted tree in front of which stands an unpainted chest in its basic framework. This highlights the prestige that builders of chests enjoyed in Florence at the time (to whom it was due, like the coopers, as a holder of one of the four posts of consul in the guild), and emphasizes that these workers engaged themselves in the construction of furniture, but not the decoration, which was executed by other experts.

THE TECHNICAL EVOLUTION THROUGH AN EXEMPLARY TYPE OF FURNITURE: THE CHEST

To better document the technical evolution in the sphere of furniture making in the last part of the period considered here, it is useful to draw attention to the transformations incurred by a quintessential type of furniture of these centuries: the chest.[12]

Chests and coffers are certainly to be considered among the oldest and most widespread examples of furniture between the fourteenth and sixteenth centuries. Despite the extreme simplicity of their basic shape, they in fact lend themselves to serve unlimited needs. Used to store and above all protect one's assets, they are also useful for sitting on, and they can be placed side by side to prepare an emergency bed. They also appear to be ideal for transporting because they can be straddled in pairs on the sides of animals or hoisted onto carts.

The chest also exhibits many variations in its shape and size. Today we use the word "chest" in a specific manner, but archival documents appear to distinguish "chest" (*cassone* and *cassa*) from *forziere* (coffer) and *cofano* (trunk). Scholars debate the correct meaning to attribute to the various terms, although there is a certain preference to identify the *forziere* with a nuptial chest. This writer believes that *forziere* indicates, regardless of its shape, a chest fitted with a lock (as is often the case with nuptial chests), a feature that is absent in other kind of chests.

If we examine the structure of a chest (which is distinct and separate from the decoration that is added to it), we can see that the oldest examples would clearly be constructed by a carpenter, while chests of the fifteenth and sixteenth centuries would involve workers with different specializations.

With the oldest form of a chest thought of as a simple hollowed-out tree trunk, the basic form from the thirteenth century is easily constructed by assembling five panels (which can also be individual boards) with an appropriate nailing pattern: the individual elements take on the role of front, side panels, back, and bottom. The cover can be made by hinging a last board to the body of the structure (to obtain a flat surface), or by mounting a system of slats to a casting (to obtain a lightly curved cover). To create a system of support on the ground to elevate the bottom from the floor and preserve it from damp, one can nail four legs corresponding to the corners of the chest or, even more simply, have the good sense to make the sides of a greater height than the panels of the front and back, to secure the bottom panel at an appropriate height in relation to the level of the floor of the room. The possible variations of the system (however limited) have been widely documented in the studies of Penelope Eames (1977), pertaining to a good part of the European region. If we instead examine Italian chests of the fifteenth century, we not only see greater care in the construction of the body, which takes a curved and more jointed form, but we confirm that the system of support on the ground was thought of as a separate element from the assembly of the body of the chest by the use of suitable joints. The inside of the chest also begins to change (to better organize the contents and therefore more easily retrieve them), with dividing panels, shelves, and boxes fitted with locks. In the late sixteenth century, the appearance of two drawers in the lower part of the body (to better separate and retain one's belongings) is a sign of the birth of a new kind of chest: a chest of drawers (*cassettone*), which will be used alongside the chest in the seventeenth century.

The techniques aimed at distinguishing the exterior appearance of chests also vary through time. In the fifteenth century, mainly inlaid decoration or pictorial works dominated the front of chests. The pictorial works come to us today as isolated panels, at the expense of intact chests, and are of such high quality that they represent a good part of what museums display to document the painting of the time. In the sixteenth century, the use of the painted coffer (*forziere*) quickly disappears. Giorgio Vasari, in his *Vite*, informs us that in the Florence of his time, only "some relics" remained as evidence of the painted *forziere* (Vasari 1906: 2:148–9 "Life of Dello Delli"). The inventories of the residences of the Medici family around the middle of the sixteenth century document that these painted chests had been relegated to the "rooms of women and nursemaids," while new carved chests occupied the official environments (Trionfi Honorati 1980: 205). At this time, the box-like structure is completely abandoned, and new, high-quality chests assume the shape of a sarcophagus. These new shapes allow room for carving work, particularly widespread in mannerist culture, and transform the chest into a structure with wavy backgrounds, reminiscent of ancient Roman sarcophagi in marble.

All of this implies the involvement of workers with different specialized skills, or at least indicates a real evolution of the craft.

MASTERS OF TARSIA AND MASTERS OF PERSPECTIVE

The art of tarsia and inlay represents one of the highest achievements in the field of woodworking in the fifteenth century, and artists active in the sector achieved high social regard, often referred to as "masters of perspective."[13]

The inlay of wood has very old origins, practiced in ancient Egypt from the time of the first dynasty, as documented by some small chests with geometric motifs in ivory and wood. Although other important examples of this craft have been preserved, attributable to the Cretan world, the Mycenaean civilization, and Greek production, it is in ancient Rome that inlay knew one of its moments of greatest splendor, although in this case connected to architecture and therefore achieved with marble or stones of various colors. While marble continued to be inlaid, in the fourteenth century the technique is once again applied to wood, which has its own distinctive traits. Wood is not as durable as stone, but it is clearly a lot easier to work with. Although the variety of colors of wood seems to be more limited than that of marble and stone, one can still have a large palette at one's disposal, even with only local types of wood. There are colors that range from dark brown to black (as is the case with oak and jujube woods), to shades of intermediate brown (walnut), to reddish tones (strawberry tree, mulberry, yew), to yellowish shades (cherry, boxwood), and to rather pale white shades (cypress, holly, maple, dogwood, spindle tree, lemon, hazelnut, service tree), each with their own texture and hues.

Examples of inlay from the fourteenth century and the beginning of the fifteenth century still preserved today show us that the city of Siena held a clear supremacy in this art. Among the many examples are what remains of the stalls of the choir of the Duomo of Orvieto, the work of Sienese Vanni dell'Ammannato, and the choir stalls of the chapel of the Palazzo Pubblico of Siena, made by an artist called Domenico di Nicolò de' Cori, due to his ability in the art of inlaying the choirs (cori) (Raggio and Wilmering 1999: 2:86–96). In the second half of the fifteenth century, however, the Florentine workshops appear to intrude on the supremacy of the Sienese workshops, distinguishing themselves with their ability to relate inlay to the pursuit of the time, which was Florentine painting.

Occurring at that time in Florence is the invention of linear perspective, a method devised to reproduce the effect of depth on a flat surface. The first depictions of perspective amazed spectators with views of the city. Images of buildings, streets, and other simple geometric shapes favor the rendering of the effect of depth, creating the illusion that one does not find oneself in front of a flat surface, but in front of actual small three-dimensional theaters. Since it is easy to cut wood along straight lines, the masters of tarsia very quickly transformed themselves into "masters of perspective." They created images reproducing areas of the city with hundreds of pieces of wood, and (intensifying the illusion even more) they also made illustrated panels depicting wardrobe doors and semi-open doors, along with panels displaying shelves with objects and books, or open windows with a view. Giorgio Vasari notes that "this work had its origin in perspective, with its aim of *canti vivi*; putting together the pieces would create the perspective, and it would look like one flat piece, even though it was more than a thousand pieces" (Vasari 1906: 1:202–3 "Del musaico di legname, cioè delle tarsie").

In addition to Florentine furniture with inlaid panels is the Sacristy of the Masses in Santa Maria del Fiore in Florence (Haines 1983). Started in 1436 with panels of perspective created by Agnolo di Lazzero and Antonio Manetti, it was finished around 1468 with the insertion of illustrated compositions by Giuliano da Maiano, based on designs supplied by artists such as Maso Finiguerra, Alesso Baldovinetti, and perhaps Antonio del Pollaio.

This is the golden age of Florentine inlay. Benedetto Dei, a chronicler of the time, notes the presence of eighty-four inlay workshops in Florence, citing the most famous: those of the da Maiano family and of Francesco di Giovanni, known as il Francione (Romby 1976: 73). The Duke of Urbino always turned to the Florentine masters for the decoration of small offices (*studioli*) in his palaces in Urbino and Gubbio (the latter held at the Metropolitan Museum of art in New York) (Raggio and Wilmering 1999), to be considered among the highest achievements of this art. Other Florentine masters worked in Perugia, whose churches have many works of this period.

Meanwhile, other great artists of the northern provinces dedicated themselves exclusively to the work of tarsia. Particularly noteworthy are the very skilled Lorenzo and Cristoforo da Lendinara, who created works in the cathedrals of Modena and Parma (Bagatin 1987, 2004). Also of note is the monk Giovanni da Verona, who created at least fifty-two commissioned panels for the choir of Monte Oliveto Maggiore in Tuscany between 1503 and 1505 (Raggio and Wilmering 1999: 2:123–7; Bagatin 2000) (Plate 7).

With these individuals, tarsia reaches its moment of maximum splendor, seeing woodworking fuse inextricably with the art of perspective, and therefore with painting, connecting these great examples, although made with wood, to a wider context, that of the workshop and of artistic Renaissance culture. Unfortunately tarsia's moment of splendor coincides with its decline, at least in the themes and methods that we have presented.

In addition to *tarsia prospettica* (inlay perspective), the fifteenth century also sees the refinement of various techniques of inlay. Purely decorative, we often perceive inlay as created with the same methods as tarsia (with the combination of shaped elements on a flat surface forming the frame of the work while hiding it), but they are in fact defined differently.[14] In contrast with tarsia, hidden inlay involves a sunken, hollowed recess on a flat surface, inside of which is inserted a wooden component created in an array of different colors. In this case, the flat background (which is often a structural part of the furniture) fully contributes to the appearance of the piece.

Other inlay techniques aim to make the work less laborious or structure it to involve more workers, therefore saving time thanks to the specialization of each worker. Likely developed in Florence during the fifteenth century, one technique that produces works of great beauty while significantly reducing the amount of labor is *intarsio a toppo*, used for creating framing of a repetitive geometric pattern that will later be incorporated into a solid wood base. Slats of different types of wood are attached together to create a small block (*toppo*) presenting a specific geometric design when placed upright. The *toppo* is then cut into thin strips, which are the basic form of what will be part of a more intricate design. The many identical strips can then easily be inserted into a recess to produce a repetitive geometric pattern creating a band, frame, or baseboard on a piece of furniture (Raggio and Wilmering 1999: 2:64–73, with explanatory drawings of techniques).

Another technique that considerably simplifies labor and produces results very similar to those of hidden inlay is marquetry (*foro e controforo*), which was likely already in use at the end of the fifteenth century, but only became common in the following centuries. With marquetry, instead of creating a recess within the solid wood of the furniture, one uses two or more wood strips (of a thickness of around 3 millimeters) made of different substances and colors. The strips will be cut according to a specific design to use the various pieces to entirely cover a panel or a frame of the furniture, using one color for the background and another for the decorative motif. Every empty space created by the cut of a strip will always correspond with a usable protrusion on the other strip. Various phrases indicate this technique based on the reciprocal complementarity of the parts (male and female, part and counterpart, empty and full).

This technique will receive a remarkable boost when it becomes possible to produce wood veneer of very slender thickness that is easy to cut, even with complex designs. This will not occur until modern times, no earlier than the last quarter of the nineteenth century, with the invention of peeling lathe machines that are capable of producing sheets of a few tenths of a millimeter.

To conclude, at the end of time period under consideration, the great ancient tradition that appeared to have been forgotten during the "Dark Ages" of the early medieval period has been completely recovered, in many cases advancing well beyond its roots, and consolidating a heritage of techniques and models that, until times very near our own, have accompanied the highest expressions of Western art and culture.

CHAPTER THREE

Types and Uses

Medieval Furniture in Social Context

CHRISTOPHER PICKVANCE

This chapter discusses furniture of varied quality rather than elite furniture alone and focuses on less well-known and dendro-dated examples where possible. It also gives special attention to chests, which are the main surviving type of medieval furniture. It refers to examples from all over Europe but with a focus on the United Kingdom. The earliest pieces included here date from the late twelfth century and the latest vary in date between countries depending on when the Renaissance started to influence furniture: the fifteenth century in Italy; the early sixteenth century in France, Spain, the Low Countries, the Alpine countries, and southern Germany; and the mid-sixteenth century in northern Germany, England, and Sweden.

WHAT IS MEDIEVAL FURNITURE?

Any discussion of medieval furniture has to acknowledge the limited evidential base. There are three starting points: extant medieval furniture, historical images and documents, and later literature relating to medieval furniture.

Extant medieval furniture

Fortunately, a number of pieces of medieval furniture have survived in churches, monasteries, ancient universities, and other places where their age has been valued and there has been little pressure to replace them. The unknowable rate of loss of medieval furniture makes it difficult to judge their representativeness. Very few pieces survive from the thirteenth century, more do so from the fourteenth and even more from the fifteenth. It has been argued that ecclesiastical furniture is more likely to survive than secular (Mercer 1969: 31). However, it does not follow that all pieces in such institutions are as old as they seem. Some items were made for these institutions, such as the *c.* 1176 armoire at Obazine (Aubazine) Abbey in France, the Coronation Chair of *c.* 1300 in Westminster Abbey, the thirteenth- to fifteenth-century chests at Valère basilica in Switzerland, and the fifteenth-century chests at Hôtel-Dieu, Beaune in Burgundy (Eames 1977: 21–5; Conseil General de la Haute-Marne [CGHM] 2003; Charles and Veuillet 2012; Rodwell 2013).

Other furniture has a less clear association with the place where it is currently located. Chests found in churches today were not necessarily commissioned by them; they may have been deposited there by their owners for safe keeping or have been donated or left as bequests. Moreover, as the words *meuble, mueble, mobile,* and *möbel* suggest, furniture is movable and this is particularly true of chests. In his 1533 will Henry Hatch, a Faversham businessman who had moved there from London, left "To the [St Mary of Charity, Faversham] church my chest bound with iron, the which I bought of Henrey Estey of London, to put in the towels and plate of the church" (Lewer and Wall 1913: 54). Not only was the chest a bequest, it also turns out to belong to a group of early fifteenth-century imports from Danzig, as discussed below. This example shows the potential mobility of objects between countries and religious and secular contexts; in fact, the chest has recently been transferred from the church to the town museum. Today, churches are expected to be appreciative recipients of unwanted furniture of all periods, meaning knowledge of their original context can often be lost.

There is also a large volume of "medieval furniture" on the art market whose age and origins are unknown. Some are medieval in style but made at a later date. Some pieces consist of old pieces carved to make them look earlier than they actually are, while still other pieces incorporate genuine early fragments. In particular, wall paneling, especially with linenfold carving, was readily converted into "medieval" cupboards, chests, and tables. In these ways supply expanded to meet demand in the "Gothic revival" from the eighteenth century onwards. Some such "medieval furniture" has passed into notable twentieth-century collections and thereby acquired a deceptive authenticity. The Metropolitan Museum's recent disposal of early furniture, for example, included a wall cupboard from a well-known collection cataloged as "early twentieth century possibly incorporating seventeenth century elements," which appears in the *Dictionary of English Furniture* as a food cupboard "circa 1600" (Christie's 2015. Lot 198; Macquoid and Edwards 1954: 2:186). All early furniture can be expected to have undergone repair but the line between honest restoration and fakery is a blurred one. Furthermore, while the numerous large format furniture books of the early twentieth century, such as the first edition of the *Dictionary of English Furniture* (1924–7) and Macquoid's *Age of Oak* (1925), full of photos of items in famous collections and in the museums of the major European capitals, served as bibles to define what medieval furniture was, they also contained fakes and served as guides to fakers. This was demonstrated by Herbert Cescinsky—a trained cabinetmaker and coauthor, with Ernest R. Gribble, of *Early English Furniture and Woodwork* (1922), one of the best early twentieth-century works on the subject—in his book on *The Gentle Art of Faking Furniture* (1931).

In recent years, there has been a growing awareness of the extent to which so-called medieval furniture is a later creation. The best museums are critically reexamining their collections. Already in 1984 the Gruuthuse Museum in Bruges, Belgium, was adding a question mark to the sixteenth-century dates of two large linenfold cupboards (accession no. 0.7.VII and 0. 8.VII); and the Victoria & Albert Museum has recently demoted two parchemin-paneled chests (panels with opposed ribs) and a narrow-backed, trapezoid-seated *caquetoire* chair (accession nos. W.11–1928, 1750: 1, 2–1869; W.45–1925): the former have sixteenth-century panels in a later structure, while in the latter the "romayne" panel (a head in a lozenge, based on Roman architecture) is considered to be nineteenth century. The Cluny museum's once-praised fifteenth-century chest carved with rows of warriors on the façade and sides is now considered a fake (Roe 1902: 25–8; Schmitz 1956: 39). Lastly, the Metropolitan Museum has a Gothic cupboard (accession no. 09.202.4), now cataloged as twentieth century, which appears in Macquoid's *The Age of Oak* as an "oak double hutch" (1925: fig. 39). In brief, the identification of medieval furniture poses very serious problems, thereby complicating our attempts to understand its creation and context.

Historical documents

A second source of information is historical documents such as inventories, wills, churchwardens' accounts, and port records. These often refer to furniture but only occasionally with sufficient detail to allow precise identification. Penelope Eames, in her book-length essay "Furniture in England, France and the Netherlands from the twelfth to the fifteenth century," notes that "chests were the most indispensable single article of furniture during [this] period" (1977: 108) but the referents of terms such as chest and coffer remain debated. It has been suggested that chests are joined while coffers are boarded (i.e., made of planks held together by nails and iron strapwork) and that coffers are smaller than chests. It has been argued that chests in ships are actually cargo containers and it has been noted that by the sixteenth century the word coffer was still in use in some parts of England in inventories but had died out in others (Tracy 2001: 15; Sleep 2004; Pickvance 2012). In brief, these terms were not used consistently, which poses real problems. Turning to a more specific term,

"Flanders chest," Eames notes that of the "many references to imported chests ... by far the greatest number ... refer to those from Flanders" (1977: 137). Other chests were "Spruse" or "Danske"—from Prussia or Danzig (Chinnery 1979: 355). But what is meant by "Flanders chests" is uncertain: suggestions include light, paneled chests; iron-bound chests; and chests carved with tracery and animals (Eames 1977: 137). The term may even refer to all chests from Flanders whatever their construction and appearance and its meaning could thus have changed over time.

A potentially useful point of departure in studying chests is the royal and papal orders to English cathedrals and churches requiring them to have chests. These go back to Henry II, who in 1166 issued an order for chests to collect money for crusades; Pope Innocent, who in 1199 required "a hollow chest fastened with three keys" for the collection of alms; and Pope Clement, who in 1308 stipulated "a strong and firm chest or trunk" for "alms, emoluments and other things arising in each of your cities" with three locks "having as many diverse keys and all different" to be held by the rector, the proctor, and a trustworthy and devout parishioner (Lewer and Wall: 1913: 39–45; Sherlock 2008: 3–5). The problem is to match these orders with actual chests. Paradoxically, the most often described feature, the presence of three locks, is contradicted by the single locks frequently found on thirteenth- to fourteenth-century chests in churches in England, a point made by Roe (1902: 16–19) and borne out by the author's current research in southern England. In brief, the identification problem reduces the scope for drawing on historical documents.

Images

Paintings in the fourteenth and fifteenth centuries show numerous images of furniture: beds, (dismountable) trestle tables, turned chairs (whose elements were whittled or made on a lathe), (round-backed) tub chairs, thrones, fixed and folding stools, benches, cupboards of various types, chests for storage and traveling, settles (i.e., high-backed wooden seats for several people), desks, and reading and writing slopes (see Von Falke 1924: vii–lix; Wright 1976; Blanc 1999; Bartlett 2001; Oledzka 2016; Medieval & Renaissance Material Culture n.d.). These images are useful to the extent that a date can be attached to them and that one can assume artists are accurately depicting furniture at the time rather than being imaginative or trying to recreate the past. The interiors shown in paintings, manuscripts, and stained glass are generally of high-status buildings but the images of everyday life and occupations allow one to see types of furniture that were of low value. It is striking that some such paintings show relatively lightly built small tables and folding X-frame stools, as well as the familiar heavily built pieces, suggesting that the survival rate of the former has been less than of the latter (Blanc 1999) because many fewer examples of the former are known today.

DATING MEDIEVAL FURNITURE

Stylistic dating

Knowledge of the development of medieval furniture depends on accurate dating. In the fifteenth and sixteenth centuries one can sometimes find incised, carved, or inlaid dates, for example, 1449 on a Swiss chest and 1468 on a Piedmont chest (Windisch-Grätz 1982: 262; Chatelain 2006: 28). Occasionally coats of arms have been used to date furniture, as in the case of the mid-fourteenth-century de Bury boarded chest from Durham Cathedral; but coats of arms were reused by later generations, rather than by the individual they originally belonged to, to give the family an illustrious past. Styles of dress have also been used for dating (V&A accession no. 317–1894). Images can be dated by the style of the artist but attributions are always open to reassessment.

Most often, early furniture is dated by assuming that it follows the styles of church woodwork and architecture. Styles, however, often lasted for very many decades so a single object with a specific date can only be used as a rough guide for dating others, and, as is often observed, furniture design lags behind the latest styles (Roe 1902: 36–40; Schmitz 1956: 22–5; Charles and Veuillet 2012: 1:91–2). For example, in northern Germany carved Romanesque mythical animals have been found on fourteenth-century chests, in Brittany Gothic tracery carving was utilized on chests until the 1660s (Janneau 1973: 6–7), while in England Renaissance influence on furniture did not appear until the mid-sixteenth century. This is because furniture is influenced by local traditions and, therefore, has a degree of autonomy from the latest style. There are many reasons for this: furniture responds to both ecclesiastical and secular needs, the domestic sphere has its own rhythms, "remote" areas are detached from metropolitan trends, new ideas travel through different channels, guilds' resistance to new styles may only be overcome by foreign craftsmen, commissioners of furniture can express their choices (e.g., choosing new furniture to match an old décor), new styles require social groups that appreciate them, different income groups have different preferences and experience different constraints, and furniture has a low status compared with church woodwork and textiles (Mercer 1962: 6–10; 1969: 42–50; Forman 1971; Fligny 1990: 128–9; Charles and Veuillet 2012: 1:91–2). All of these factors make it difficult to date medieval furniture simply based on style. One tendency has been to "other" such deviations from church style, as in Roe's (1920: 277) comment on the "degenerate work" in Brittany, or Eames's (1977: 159) comments on "decadent" style that ignores architectural principles. As a counterpoint to this, Richard Bebb (2007: 2:379–96) has argued that Welsh furniture is not backward but embodies a distinct tradition which is not to be judged in relation to the latest London style. Ideas about what furniture should look like which abstract from the social context in which it is produced are of limited value.

Dendrochronology

Given these limitations, the development of dendrochronology in recent decades has been of great help in identifying and dating medieval furniture and separating it from later productions. This has been especially true since the mid-1980s when it was realized that Baltic oak as well as domestic oak was in use in fixed woodwork and furniture found in England (Bonde, Tyers, and Wazny 1997: Bridge and Miles 2011). Unfortunately, this technique's use for dating furniture has been limited: few of the pieces discussed here have been dendro-dated. Dendrochronology allows date ranges and regional provenances to be attached to individual timber samples based on the similarity of their growth patterns to chronologies established for previous samples (Figure 3.1). It leads to a (tree-)felling date range if the sample contains sapwood (i.e., recent, outer growth) as well as heartwood (i.e., older, inner, growth), and a *terminus post quem* (or earliest felling date) if it contains only heartwood. Nevertheless, matching is always probabilistic as it depends on the availability and quality of chronologies; also abnormal local growth conditions can produce misleading matches. Dendrochronology only dates timber and so questions such as when the timber was made into furniture, whether the dendro-dated timbers are original, whether carving is original, and whether undateable timbers would yield a different dendro-date are always a matter of judgment.

The Boughton Monchelsea chest, a Flemish clamped chest with an all-over carved scene was dendro-dated as mid-fifteenth century, some seventy years later than a date it had previously been assigned based on similarities

FIGURE 3.1 A surface prepared for dendrochronological ring counting, Brandenberg Cathedral. Photograph by the Author.

in the style of clothes and armor depicted to those on the St. George and the Dragon chest in York Minster (Eames 1977: 147; Christie's 1999). However, controversy surrounds the dating of the "Courtrai Chest," now at the Ashmolean Museum, Oxford, which consists of a pair of boards carved with bands showing scenes from the Battle of Courtrai of 1302 placed in a later structure. The boards have been dendro-dated as after 1275 but it has been argued that the scenes are inspired by nineteenth-century sources and that the use of old boards is a deliberate deception (Roe 1920; Didier 1990; Bridge and Miles 2011).

In sum, medieval furniture is a social product resulting from changing tastes or fashions in collecting; the availability of fragments of wood, carvings, or furniture from the medieval period, and later production using these fragments to meet new demand. As a result, all attempts to develop systematic knowledge of it face serious constraints. It follows that any comments on pieces of furniture based on photographs and descriptions are subject to future revision.

THE SOCIAL CONTEXT OF MEDIEVAL FURNITURE: SOCIETY, BUILDINGS, HOUSEHOLDS, LIFESTYLES

In *Furniture 700–1700* (1969), Eric Mercer puts forward a useful conceptual framework for understanding the development of early furniture, its types and forms of decoration, and the differential trends among and within countries. He focuses on changes in institutional structure (court, state, church), socioeconomic groupings (wealth, households, position of women, lifestyles, values), the development of the house, the occupations involved in making and decorating furniture, the supply of timber, the development of architectural styles and the lags in their application to furniture. Unlike Eames who states that "our interest must lie with those sections of society capable of influencing design," the nobility and middle classes, and that "the furniture historian's first task must be to analyse furniture in its most sophisticated context" (1977: xxii–xxiii), Mercer pays equal attention to groups outside the elite and emphasizes the process of making furniture.

Any generalizations about medieval furniture over the period 1200–1500 across Europe and across social classes are bound to be misleading. The arguments below therefore refer to some places more than others. Mercer (1969: 31) emphasizes that cathedral and monastic clergy had the means to commission furniture and that before 1300 furniture was disproportionately ecclesiastical. Until the fourteenth century the European institutional structure included the court and the church, but the state was not concentrated and nobles took on official functions that meant their houses were places of administration, work, armories, and garrisons as well as being residences. Security was a prime consideration. The domestic hall was a multifunctional environment and furniture was limited in quantity and in types. It was heavily made and was likely to be fixed to the floor (e.g., tables), or to be attached to or built into the walls (e.g., beds, settles, and cupboards). Chests were used for safe storage and transport. Only the wealthiest had houses with multiple rooms with more specialized activities and less multiuse furniture.

Mercer sees the fourteenth century as a watershed since by then the expansion of trade had created an urban merchant class and a new sphere of activity for feudal lords, while state functions were starting to be separated from the domestic sphere. He suggests that the slowdown in trade in the late fourteenth century made urban land and building a focus of investment, and nobles and merchants started to spend more on the contents of their homes. The Italian city-states led the way in this. The first types of furniture to be detached from the fabric of the house were the chest, the table (a board on trestles), and the bench. There was also a considerable amount of dual-use furniture: benches and settles could serve as beds; chests could serve as seats and tables; and settles, chairs, and benches could have storage bases. There was a gradual diversification of types of furniture from the fourteenth century: tables acquired fixed tops, small tables supplemented large, armchairs supplemented stools, cupboards supplemented chests, bedsteads developed, cupboards allowed objects to be displayed, and wooden as well as metal and ivory caskets or small boxes were used for valuables such as jewelry and books. Many of these attached, built-in and dual forms of furniture continued for centuries among peasant and poorer groups, a reminder of the class differential in furniture ownership at all periods. The fifteenth and sixteenth centuries saw an increase in the number of specialized rooms in larger homes for eating, sleeping, reading, playing games, keeping curiosities, etc. and consequently a specialized set of furniture.

Mercer (1969: 18–31, 42–52) argues that the development of joinery and carving lagged behind that of work on metal, ivory, and textiles because furniture had low status and was crudely made; houses had little room for it and paint and textiles were used to cover walls, floors, and furniture in houses that had any.[1] This argument is not entirely convincing. High-quality joinery and carving were current in church woodwork and, from the thirteenth century, also on clamped chests in England and northern Germany, so it is not that these skills were lacking. Why they were applied only gradually to furniture is unclear. The nature of the labor market would seem critical: church woodwork may have been in stronger demand and better paid than furniture making, and there may have been prohibitions on church carvers working on furniture. Mercer (1969: 90–1) also suggests that timber type influenced carving, creating a division between the high relief carving of oak-based areas such as northern Germany and the low relief work of softwood areas extending from southern Germany to northern Italy. However, judging by the high relief softwood carved furniture illustrated by Kreisel and Himmelheber (1981), who helpfully describe the woods used in all the furniture they illustrate, and the softwood Norwegian stave church carving (Hohler 1999), this contrast appears exaggerated.

What is not in doubt is that framed and (lightweight) paneled furniture only arrived with the Renaissance, suggesting that a more secure society and the house becoming purely residential were preconditions for its development. In the United Kingdom, Renaissance style appears to have been taken up in fixed woodwork from the 1530s and 1540s, before it influenced furniture after 1560 (Wells-Cole 1997; Pickvance 2015). Elite taste and the arrival of immigrants with skills in carving, marquetry and inlay, and joinery were critical. Forman (1971) shows that the arrival of large numbers of (mainly) Flemish immigrant woodworkers in London in the 1560s and 1570s led to conflict with native woodworkers. The 1570 date of the first charter of the London joiners' guild is therefore significant (Chinnery 1979: 41). Nevertheless, cheaper, heavier, boarded furniture (often with paintwork) continued to be produced until the nineteenth century in rural and Alpine Europe. In the Netherlands today this is more likely to be found in "open air" museums than in major museums such as the Rijksmuseum.

TYPES AND USES

Beds

In medieval times beds understood as pieces of furniture, namely, as bedsteads, were quite exceptional. For all but a miniscule minority the bed referred to bedclothes and whatever else was placed on the hard surface underneath. Sleeping did not justify a separate space. Beds could be made in alcoves, walls, cupboards, drawers, boxes, and truckle (wheeled) beds could be stored out of sight when not in use. The separation of rooms for sleeping happened slowly and at different speeds for different social groups.

Knowledge of bedsteads before the late fifteenth century is dependent on images. The earliest known form of bedstead, dating from the twelfth and thirteenth centuries, had a wooden base with four low posts and railings; any curtains to provide privacy were detached from it (Eames 1977: 74). A turned bed of this type with Romanesque decoration, which may be painted, gilded, or metal-covered, appears in an early thirteenth-century stained glass window in Canterbury Cathedral (Plate 8).

Later in the thirteenth century the canopy becomes more important and throughout the fourteenth and fifteenth centuries the "hung bed" with a suspended rectangular or conical cloth canopy was the main form of state bed. This type of bed could also be found in wealthy middle-class households. Drapes gave warmth and privacy. Van Eyck's *Arnolfini Portrait* of 1434 shows an example. The quality and color of the textiles and the size and the height of the canopy and headboard allowed the expression of subtle social distinctions

(Eames 1977: 76–86; Thirion 1998: 55–61). By the end of the fourteenth century feather mattresses were introduced. Bedsteads with wooden testers were not unknown but were poorly adapted to the mobile lifestyles of wealthy households, and only emerge in noticeable numbers in the late fifteenth century. Narrower beds known as couchettes were also in use, as were folding beds.

The state bed of Duc Antoine of Lorraine of around 1517 at the Musée de Nancy is an early French bedstead and has four plain posts, a large headboard with wreathed triumphs, and low sides with heraldic framed panels carved in the solid (Thirion et al. 2002; Pickvance 2015). Franz Windisch-Grätz, in *Möbel Europas* (1982: 310–13), shows some plain or flat-carved, softwood Tirolese beds of more modest scale with high sides and a more enclosed feel dating from the mid-fifteenth to the mid-sixteenth century. In England, as suggested by Percy Macquoid and Ralph Edwards in *The Dictionary of English Furniture* (1954: 1:36–47), the bedstead as a distinct piece of furniture with headboard and wooden tester developed in the later sixteenth century as houses became larger and more comfortable for the upper social groups and as some of the functions of the multipurpose hall moved into separate rooms. Surviving English bedsteads from 1540 still show a Gothic influence in the carving of the bedposts and in the paneled headboards (Chinnery 1979: 385–93). Inventories refer to bed staves that may have been used to hold the bed in place. Later in the century, Renaissance decoration can be seen on the celour and testers. Bedsteads purporting to be from before 1600 are generally made up of panels and carved friezes from diverse sources, demonstrating again how demand for medieval furniture outstripped supply.

In addition to bedsteads, cradles were also in use in the medieval period. Eames distinguishes between state cradles (for display) and night cradles (for use) among the highest social groups. She shows a paneled, low Burgundian state cradle of 1478–9 for Philip the Fair or Marguerite of Austria, with painted inscriptions (Eames 1977: 101–4). In contrast to this she also presents an English night cradle and stand of *c.* 1500 with sides made of ribbed boards (104–7). Robert Bartlett shows a painted, boarded German cradle and stand of 1320 and a floor-level, fifteenth-century, turned French cradle (2001: 162–3). These are, of course, exclusive items.

Chests and table boxes

In the past there has been a tendency to date chests by the technology of their construction. The four pure types distinguished here might suggest four periods: dug-out chests, boarded chests, clamped chests, and framed and paneled chests.[2] The construction of these four types shows different levels of skill. Dug-out chests are simplest. Boarded chests involve cleft or sawn boards but are also simple given that they are held together by nails or wooden pegs. Clamped chests, which involve mortise-and-tenon joints, constitute a major advance on the previous two types. Framed and paneled chests involve further skills in cutting thinner panels to fit into frames and use the more sophisticated "true miter" joint (where molded frame edges meet on a 45 degree line). In fact, despite the temptation to see a chronological development from one construction method to the next, the first three types of construction were all present around 1200. A boarded chest at Kloster Ebstorf near Uelzen, Germany, and the 4 meter, clamped "Long Chest" at Westminster Abbey are both dendro-dated to the late twelfth century (Von Stülpnagel 2000: 31–2; Bridge and Miles 2011). Dug-out chests are known to have been made until the late seventeenth century in England. Clamped chests died out in England around 1500, but in parts of Wales they continued to be made until the late seventeenth century. In rural and Alpine France, Switzerland, Germany, and Italy clamped chests continued to be created until the eighteenth or nineteenth centuries and in eastern Europe even until the twentieth century. Boarded chests also continued to be a cheap alternative to the other forms. On the other hand, framed and paneled chests arrived with the Renaissance, starting with single (heavy) panel chests and moving on to lighter multi-paneled chests.[3] This shows that technology does not determine chest construction but that cost considerations, aesthetic preferences, and use all also play a part.

The main purpose of chests was storage with regular access and in this role they were gradually displaced by chests of drawers and cupboards, and in the case of valuables and documents by solid iron (e.g., Nuremberg) chests, safes, banks, and solicitors' offices. Eames (1977: 111–34) has classified the main uses of chests based on inventories; they include transporting baggage and storing coin, plate, personal jewels, textiles, vestments, chapel ornaments, muniments, books, arms and armor, candles, grain and bread. (For a fourteenth-century English abbot with his book chest, see Bartlett 2001: 214.) The often cited "muniments" and "evidences" refer to the deeds of land and buildings owned by churches or university colleges on which their wealth was founded. There was a tradition that in churches every chapel or altar had to have a chest to store the altar furnishings (Lewer and Wall 1913: 48).[4] However, over time, chests in churches became places to store valuables of all kinds, for example, money, documents, vestments, altar cloths, church plate, and books. The oldest English dendro-dated piece of furniture (1111–43) is in fact a "cope chest," for the flat storage of ornate vestments, at Wells Cathedral (Bridge and Miles 2011).

Iron strapwork was a common form of added security especially on boarded chests whose pegged or nailed joints are inherently weak. Strapwork ranged from a few front to back hinged straps to grids of straps on each face, to complete armoring. Locks ranged from single padlocks to multiple flap locks. Chests with iron strapwork could be of various sizes and shapes. Some were tall and deep, others were long and narrow. Apart from those intended for transport, chests typically had flat lids. Arks were a variety of chest with shallow gabled lids, some of which were detachable and could be used as troughs for making dough; they existed in sizes from small to very large. Arks rarely had iron strapwork, suggesting that they were more for storing grain and staples in areas which could not afford iron (Windisch-Grätz 1982: 172–3). In rural areas grain storage was a continuing function for the more basic forms of chest. A Norwegian study of clamped grain chests with very narrow stiles and simple arcaded grounded decoration shows the same form in use from *c.* 1300 to *c.* 1800 (Thun and Alsvik 2009). The collection of 127 arks in Bradeni (formerly Henndorf) in Transylvania (now Romania), dendro-dated to 1466–1799, gained extra security from their location in a fortified church tower (Maierbacher-Legl 2012) (Figure 3.2). Some of these arks are painted very decoratively and it has been suggested that a late fifteenth-century example is, in fact, a marriage chest (Kovalovszki 1981).

Overall, therefore, there is a limited correlation between the construction types of chests and their uses; most chests were, in fact, multipurpose. Indeed, all furniture was used for different purposes over its life as needs changed and alternative forms of furniture developed. In the case of chests there were now alternative forms of storage for valuable objects. The author's research on chests in churches has only revealed two that are used for storing documents.

FIGURE 3.2 Arks in the church tower at Bradeni, Romania, beech, fifteenth to seventeenth century. Photograph by Jeremy Bate.

A few were in regular use, for example, for catering equipment, flower arranging materials, children's toys and games, and a few were in occasional use, for example, for storing flags, kneelers, and wedding cushions. But a good proportion were used for long-term storage and were probably never opened; they contain hymn boards, crosses, wall ornaments, old curtains, angels' wings, candles, old candlesticks, old light bulbs, old light shades, and mirrors, among other things. Lastly, a fair proportion were simply empty (sometimes because broken hinges made them unusable) or else locked and the key lost.

A major problem with chests is that their undivided volume makes it difficult to access stored items. A variety of solutions have been found. The commonest is the lidded "till" at the side of the chest, a box allowing small items such as keys or candles to be kept accessible. As early as *c.* 1300 tills were sometimes provided with a lower secret compartment, accessed by tilting or sliding the bottom of the upper box. A high shelf along the back of the chest also provided storage for small items. Pegs, likewise, were sometimes used to suspend small items tied in bags (Steane 2001: 246). Order was further provided by partitions in the body of the chest (a chest at Salisbury Cathedral is divided into "City leases" and "[Cathedral] Close leases") or by removable vertical "drawers." Larger lockers were sometimes added, displacing a till.

Chests were also used for transport. Medieval paintings show (generally small) chests strapped to horses, chests open for al fresco meals, and chests being used to save goods from floods. Eames proposes a division between chests that have feet and flat lids, which were used for storage, and those that lack feet and have domed or gabled lids, which were used for transport (1977: 108). English documents refer to "trussing coffers," but how far these are coterminous with traveling chests is unknown.

There is a debate about whether the presence of handles implies that a chest was used for transport. Mercer (1969: 40–2) argues that given the weight of many chests when empty, let alone when fully laden, it is likely that handles were needed for dragging chests around within a house. However, even if handles or another type of hand grip are not sufficient evidence of a chest being used for transport, they are nonetheless a necessary feature. There is, for example, a group of iron-bound, domed chests with dug-out domed lids and pine boxes, considered to be imports from what is now northern Poland. They have been dendro-dated to the early fifteenth century, the period of the Teutonic Knights, and were almost certainly used for transport as well as storage (Sherlock 2008; Pickvance 2012) (Figure 3.3). They are typically 1.3 × 0.6 × 0.5 meters and would have been suspended from large rings linked by iron bars to small rings at the ends of the chest.[5] The bars could have been held by two people or suspended from a stout pole.

Mercer (1969: 41) suggests that chests used for transport are unlikely to have survived as they are more likely to have become damaged, be too small to

FIGURE 3.3 An iron-bound chest, Ramsgate, red stain under later paint, pine and lime, early fifteenth century. Photograph by the Author.

be useful for storage, and be less likely to be decorative. The surviving domed chests are well made and while their ironwork can be crude they undoubtedly served for storage as well as transport, as the Faversham example mentioned above shows. A later, more lightly made type of leather-covered (softwood) traveling chest, on the other hand, is more vulnerable to destruction and few survive, for example, the "Lady Margaret Beaufort chest" discussed by Eames (1977: 177). It has been suggested that the shape of the sides of some ark lids and the holes in them are to tie the ark down when being transported, but other types of chest could also be used for transport using straps.

The extent of decoration on chests varies greatly. The thirteenth- and fourteenth-century chests in the Luneberg Heath monasteries in northern Germany have single locks and little or no decoration. This is compatible with their being for the storage of the clothes of the daughters of wealthy families who entered the monastery, rather than for display (Von Stülpnagel 2000[6]) (Figures 3.4 and 3.5). The thirteenth- and fourteenth-century archive chests at Westminster Abbey are also plain, except for their carved feet. There is a very large pine chest dendro-dated to 1270 with applied Romanesque arcading at Valère (MV82; Charles and Veuillet 2012: 2:48–56) (3.31 × 1.04 × 0.90 meters) and a chest of similar size from Poissy in the Cluny Museum dendro-dated to *c.* 1300 considered to be a grain chest (accession no. 21545, 2.84 × 0.95 × 1.16 meters; Pousset 2004) (Figure 3.6). The latter is of local oak except for the applied Gothic arcading in Baltic oak. Both have a central partition. The earliest carved chests, from the late thirteenth century, had a limited carving

FIGURE 3.4 A clamped chest (KW49), Kloster Wienhausen, oak, 1269. Photograph by the Author.

FIGURE 3.5 A corridor of thirteenth- and fourteenth-century chests at Kloster Wienhausen. Photograph by the Author.

repertoire consisting of rosettes, roundels, and blind arcading. The Chichester Cathedral chest (dendro-dated 1256–88) has polychrome roundels. Chests that bear a great deal of ironwork are generally plain but the ironwork itself can be decorative as on chests from Voxtorp and Rydaholm in Sweden where the ironwork is pictorial and those from Noyon in France and Icklingham in

FIGURE 3.6 A clamped chest with Romanesque applied arcading, pine, *c.* 1270.
Photograph courtesy of Musées cantonaux du Valais, Jean-Yves Glassey.

England, where it takes the form of scrollwork (Swedish History Museum,
inventory no. 115693; Geddes 1999) (Plate 9).

The fourteenth century saw a great upsurge in carved decoration on chests
in northern Germany although German sources show nothing comparable
in southern Germany. Images of carved mythical beasts in medallions and/
or Gothic arcading and tracery could extend over the whole of the chest's
façade (Von Stülpnagel 2000: 147–77). These would have been very costly
objects and were probably for use in churches and very wealthy households.
There is a group of Baltic oak chests with deeply carved Gothic tracery
arcading that is generally dated to 1330–1400 in Kent and East Anglia (which
Roe [1905: 118] labeled "Kentish Gothic") and in Oxford (Pickvance 2007,
2014, 2017). These chests have many distinctively German features and
given the strong Hanseatic trade carried out through ports in the east of
England, and English port records mentioning chests in cargos from Danzig,
it is likely that they were imported rather than that they were made by
German craftsmen in England.

In the fifteenth century, biblical and mythical scenes such as Saint George
and the Dragon were frequently carved on clamped chests in northern Germany
and Flanders. Examples are at York Minster, Boughton Monchelsea, and Harty
in England, and in Ypres and Bruges in Belgium (Roe 1902; Christie's 1999:
Lot 807; Von Stülpnagel 2000: 191–202) (Figure 3.7). From around 1470

FIGURE 3.7 A Flemish clamped chest, formerly at Boughton Monchelsea, oak, mid-fifteenth century. Photograph courtesy of Christie's Images Ltd.

there was a large production of Westphalian clamped chests with a revival of iron strapwork, many of which survive (Baumeier 2012). In southern Germany and the Alpine countries carved softwood chests were typical; Kreisel and Himmelheber (1981: figs. 122–3) show two mid-fifteenth-century examples from Austria. Rural furniture (*bauernmöbel*) was more likely to be painted. The Bradeni arks belong to this tradition. Their painted scrolling, geometric and figural decoration was no doubt brought by "Saxon" immigrants encouraged to settle in the periphery of the Austro-Hungarian Empire (Maierbacher-Legl 2012). Renaissance motifs, such as "Romayne" heads, appear on north German chests and cupboards after 1550.

In Italy *cassoni* were associated with high-status weddings and contained the bride's trousseau; they were often made in pairs. In the fourteenth and fifteenth century they displayed painted or stucco decoration. In the late fifteenth century the early Renaissance brought frame and paneled construction, marquetry, round-headed arcading, and exquisite painted scenes of mythical stories (V&A accession nos. 317–1894, 8974–1863; Kreisel and Himmelheber 1981: fig. 134c; Simmonneau, Benoît, and Bergbauer 2010). From the late fifteenth to the seventeenth century there is a group of Renaissance cypress chests with distinctive pyrographic (wood decorated with burn marks), penwork, and punchwork decoration attributed to Crete or northern Italy, which is widely distributed; collections of similar juniper chests exist in Portugal (Ferrão 1990: 4:3–67).

By the later fifteenth century, French boarded, usually dovetailed, chests showed fine Gothic arcading and tracery, and by the early sixteenth century, expansive "first Renaissance" carving had developed (Boccador 1988: 24–40, 92–8; Thirion 1998: 36–9, 64–73). This term refers to the motifs such as ("Romayne") profile heads in roundels, vases, fantastic animals, masks, interlace, and scrolling plants. In Flanders linenfold, parchemin, and Gothic tracery paneled chests were made from the mid- or late fifteenth century, earlier than in France. A small, late fifteenth-century boarded chest with heraldic and tracery decoration in Kortrijk 1302 museum has been dendro-dated by Haneca (2010). At the Hôtel-Dieu, Beaune, multi-paneled parchemin chests have been dendro-dated to c. 1450, the earliest date in Europe for chests with panels (Figure 3.8).

England appears to have missed out on the creation of Gothic tracery chests, and the making of multi-paneled chests began only after about 1560. (However, imported chests and chests with earlier Gothic and Renaissance panels can be found.) The earliest chest in England with Renaissance carving is a boarded chest dated 1519 and named for Thomas Silkstede, Prior of Winchester 1498–1524. It has been argued, though, that it was made by French craftsmen employed in Winchester and, therefore, to lie outside the evolution

FIGURE 3.8 A parchemin paneled chest, Hôtel-Dieu, Beaune, oak, mid-fifteenth century. Photograph by David Dewing.

FIGURE 3.9 A dated boarded chest inscribed "Thomas Silkstede," Shanklin, oak, early sixteenth century. Photograph by the Author.

of English chests (Pickvance 2015) (Figure 3.9). Chests in northern Germany were likewise late in showing Renaissance influence. German craftsmen are believed to be responsible for the architectural marquetry chest at Southwark Cathedral in London, which Roe dates to 1588 when Hugh Offley ("H.H.O.") became Sheriff (Roe 1905: 150–3). Similar chests were made in Germany into the seventeenth century.

Medieval paintings and sculpture frequently show scribes, monks, and scholars seated at various types of desk, sometimes with built-in seats (Von Falke 1924: xi–lix). These pieces of furniture can be highly elaborate, reflecting their users' status. In fifteenth-century Venice, writing boxes developed often with fine *certosina* inlay, using a light-colored material such as bone, ivory, a light-colored wood, or metal against a dark-colored material, in which a hinged lid gave access to small cupboards and drawers around a central space. This led to writing boxes, which could be placed on the table and hence allowed the writer or reader some flexibility of location. The Victoria & Albert Museum has a combined desk and small cupboard in oak with Gothic arcading on the sides, dendro-dated to 1425–50 (accession no. 143–1898), believed to be English and to have been a lectern used in a monastery. The museum also holds a Renaissance writing box from *c.* 1525 in walnut, oak, and painted and gilded leather believed to have been owned by Henry VIII (accession no. W.29:1 to 9–1932). The country most associated with table boxes is Spain, where the sixteenth century witnessed an explosion of types: top-opening or fall-front, large or small, with many or few drawers, and with marquetry or carved decoration (Aguiló Alonso 1993: 224–319; V&A accession no. 294–1870).

Cupboards

The terminology for different types of cupboard has always been confused. Eames (1977: 1–2, 55–6) distinguishes between armoires (storage space behind doors, with or without shelves), buffets (used in hall and chamber for display), and dressoirs (used in serving quarters), but admits the latter two may not differ in form. Chinnery (1979: 315–27) distinguishes "court cupboards" (with three open shelves for display—described in medieval times as "cup boards"), livery cupboards (with a closed upper section, associated with food storage), and press cupboards (with closed sections at both levels). The oldest extant cupboard is the plain boarded armoire with applied Romanesque arcading at the sides at Obazine dated c. 1176 by Eames (1977: 21–5). There are also built-in cupboards there. Another entirely boarded armoire with remains of painted figural decoration at Bayeux Cathedral in France is dated c. 1240 by Eames (1977: 25–7). There is a freestanding cupboard at Chester Cathedral in England with two thirteenth-century doors with iron scrollwork (Eames 1977: 44–6, Geddes 1999: 159 and 312) and a similar fourteenth-century French example (Eames 1977: 46–9; Blanc 1999: 29).

In northern Germany there is a distinctive group of gabled oak cupboards (*giebelschranken*) as well as plain flat-topped cupboards, the earliest dating from around 1300 (Kreisel and Himmelheber 1981: figs. 25–39), all of which have one or two central doors. They were used for storing a range of items from documents to reliquaries. The Luneberg Heath monasteries house many smaller, plain, domestic cupboards. Cescinsky (1934) documents how one of the latter type was "improved" by the insertion of openwork Gothic roundels and is now in the Victoria & Albert Museum (accession no. W41–1918). There is a rare fifteenth-century cupboard with apparently original paintwork at Brandenberg Cathedral in Germany (Kreisel and Himmelheber 1981: fig. 66) (Figure 3.10).

From the late fourteenth and fifteenth centuries there is a series of cathedral armoires, some built-in, some freestanding, such as those at Salisbury and Winchester Cathedrals and York Minster in England, with plain doors and narrow iron hinges with rosette decoration (Geddes 1999: 345, 367, 384, 392). The Westminster Abbey example has white stars on a red ground (Eames 1977: 30–3). These exemplify ecclesiastical uses such as document storage. In the softwood cupboards of southern Germany, the Alpine countries and Translyvania, plain or crenellated (battlemented) cornices with deep carving below flat surfaces were the norm. Some were of exceptional dimensions and carving quality and must have been for display in domestic contexts (see Kreisel and Himmelheber 1981: fig. 121). Italian craftsmen were recruited to decorate church furniture with marquetry in the early sixteenth century in Translyvania, which was then part of Hungary (Kovalovszki 1981).

FIGURE 3.10 A painted cupboard, Brandenberg Cathedral, pine, fifteenth century.
Photograph by the Author.

In France and Flanders a different tradition of cupboards developed that was closely related to increased wealth and its deployment in the domestic setting. Here, from the fifteenth century, cupboards diversified to include surfaces for display as well as cupboards and drawers for storage, and existed in many different sizes (Boccador 1988: 50–86, 109–15; Thirion 1998: 40–3, 80–3). They ranged from high sets of shelves over a cupboard base, to small cupboards with drawers below over an open boarded base that could be used for display (Blanc 1999: 34–42). The cupboard section often had Gothic tracery carving. At Plougrescant in Brittany the lower part of a cupboard is entirely devoted to storage and the doors are carved with figures, while above there is a curved canopy over the display area (Eames 1977: 70–2; Blanc 1999: 30). Such pieces were placed in the hall or chamber. Frame and paneled cupboards started in France in the later fifteenth century, coexisting with boarded cupboards. Very large two-door storage cupboards with linenfold, parchemin (and, later, Romayne) panels emerged especially in Flanders. These were also reproduced at later dates with period panels. Small cupboards for food storage often had holes pierced in the sides.

In Britain, there are several cupboards attributed to the period 1500–50: an armoire with carved foliage panels at the University of St Andrews in Scotland and some large cupboards with elaborately carved Gothic panels including the Wynne cupboard (now in the Burrell collection in Glasgow; Jones 1990). The Cotehele cupboard front in Cornwall, the only one to have been studied by dendrochronology, remains a puzzle as the panels dated 1524–50, with musicians and huntsmen, may be coeval with, or up to forty years earlier than, the frame (Riall 2012). The preservation of well-carved panels, showing the instruments of the passion, in a later gabled "chest" structure that has no openings can be seen at Coity in Wales (Bebb 2007: 1:159). Later sixteenth-century cupboards show Renaissance influence in the form of marquetry introduced by Continental craftsmen from the 1560s and floral inlay.

Seating

Eames's analysis of medieval seating distinguishes between three types of "seats of authority" (X-frame, post, and boarded) and lower status benches, forms, and stools (1977: 181–209). This may be too neat a division since turned (post) and boarded construction can be found in seating of various levels of sophistication of design. High-status seating at this time was often made of, or encrusted with, jewels, inlay, metal, ivory, and/or was carved (Mercer 1969: 44–9; Eames 1977: 184–5). The medieval seating that survives is mostly exceptional and hence untypical.

An idea of the range of seating can be gained from a stained glass window in Canterbury Cathedral of 1178, which shows Methuselah/Lamech seated in a turned chair possibly with ivory decoration, and from surviving examples (Plate 10). Eames (1977: 210–11) discusses the substantial twelfth- to thirteenth-century turned chair in Hereford Cathedral in England. The Swedish History Museum has a turned oak chair (inventory no. 116321), with matching bench and desk, dated stylistically to 1250–1350 (Windisch-Grätz 1982: 159; Bartlett 2001: 170) (Plate 11). In southern Germany there is a pair of very long thirteenth-century turned oak and pine benches (Von Falke 1924: 1). There is a rare, long, heavy, joined rather than turned bench in Winchester Cathedral, which Eames (1977: 209) suggests is twelfth century. Turned chairs have too few growth rings to date by dendrochronology. Their simple technology and unchanging style is deceptive; they continue to be made well beyond the medieval period, especially in Germany (Ryder 1975, 1976).

The Coronation Chair of 1300 is unusual in being boarded. Its construction might be explained by the fact that it replaced a gilded bronze chair, which was not completed due to its excessive weight. The Coronation Chair has applied Gothic arcading on the back and sides enhanced by cloisonné-type glasswork, openwork carving in the base, carved lion feet and gilding on the inside with a punchwork lattice and flower pattern (Rodwell 2013).

As noted earlier, the folding stools shown in medieval images seem surprisingly fragile objects in a period associated with heavy construction. Mercer describes their history as going back to dynastic Egypt and suggests the "aura of kingship" clung to the folding stool (1969: 34). This could explain their exceptionally fine construction and decoration. Folding stools have X-frames but not all X-frame seats are folding or of fine construction. Windisch-Grätz shows a folding stool of 1242 from Germany or Austria with bone inlay (1982: 167) and X-framed chairs can be seen in illuminated manuscripts, for example, from 1372, 1410, and 1418 (Blanc 1999: 36–7; Bartlett 2001: 222; see also Eames 1977: 182–91). The surviving fifteenth-century northern Italian folding chairs and stools in walnut and beech of narrow timbers look easily portable (Windisch-Grätz 1982: 245). Some southern German fifteenth-century softwood benches with flat carving exist (Von Falke 1924: 98–9) but early seating from this region seems not to have survived.

Built-in benches and separate stools and forms of lower status with whittled, turned, or sawn splayed feet were the most common types of medieval seating. They can be seen in paintings of both indoor and outdoor scenes from the fourteenth and fifteenth centuries, for example the turned three-legged stool (or low table) in a Jan van Eyck illumination of 1420–5 and a fifteenth-century painting of a young witch (Bartlett 2001: 203; Blanc 1999: 34). It is not surprising that they have not survived. However, this way of making stools and chairs continued until the nineteenth century, good examples being Welsh "stick" chairs in which turned legs and back uprights are fixed into sockets or holes in the solid seat (Bebb 2007: 2:45–52).

It was not until the mid-fifteenth century that the first high-quality boarded and joined seating outside exceptional examples appeared in Flanders and

France. These include stools of more elaborate boarded construction, and an open-backed joined bench with a movable backrest with openwork arcading in the sides that can be seen in a French painting of 1438 (Blanc 1999: 32, 38; Bartlett 2001: 173). There is a heavily built fifteenth-century closed armchair at the Alfàbia in Mallorca with five panels carved with the Tristan and Isolde story and a series of stopped chamfers around the panels (these are canted edges that stop before the corner of the panel) (Aguiló 1987: 84–5) (Figure 3.11). The carving style recalls the Boughton Monchelsea chest, which has similar chamfers underneath the lid, suggesting the armchair too may be Flemish or Flemish-influenced. The Rijksmuseum has a bench-chest with linenfold panels (accession no. BK-NM-1971). Single, joined, closed armchairs of very high quality appear in France and Flanders with linenfold or tracery back, side, and front panels (Boccador 1988: 1–13, 40–9). Some are of throne-like height and recall the choir stalls that may have inspired them. These carry on into the sixteenth century with early Renaissance design (87–90, 105–8).

There are a few tub chairs, which combine post and boarded construction, dating from the fifteenth century. They include walnut examples with tracery panels in the backs and below the seat from France and Spain (Metropolitan Museum of Art, accession no. 41.100.125; IVDJ, Madrid in Bartlett 2001: 171). Simpler northern Italian tub chairs with tracery carving on the front and open backs between curved rails in walnut/pine/lime and oak are also known (Metropolitan Museum of Art, accession nos. 30.93.1 and 40.100.124).

Around 1500 a new form of folding chair with a boarded seat and twin slats in the back originated in Venice (Schmitz 1956: 80). By the later sixteenth century it had spread to England and in the nineteenth century fixed-back versions, known as Glastonbury chairs, found popularity in English churches. In Italy the highly carved boarded *sgabello* was a post-1500 Renaissance form of seating. The *cassone* was also used for seating. In the sixteenth century the fixed X-frame chair became increasingly popular in Italy and Spain, then spread throughout Europe as a "seat of authority," for example, for bishops (Aguiló Alonso 1993: 348–50). In France chairs of lighter construction only arrived after 1550 some of which were designed for women, reflecting their changed position in the household. Was there a degree of domestic comfort in wealthy homes in France and Flanders lacking in the rest of Europe? For the majority, benches, forms, and stools remained the norm.

In England there are built-in and freestanding settles with linenfold panels in the West Country, those with rounded corner moldings around the panels possibly made by French immigrant craftsmen (Eames 1977: 213–14) and the V&A has a box armchair with linenfold and Renaissance panels dating from 1520–40 (accession no. W.39-1920). Boarded stools date from the early sixteenth century and joined stools are mentioned in inventories from the 1560s. The Sizergh Castle carved, panel-back armchairs and forms, dated to 1562–72,

FIGURE 3.11 A Flemish or Flemish-influenced closed armchair with Tristan and Isolde carved panels, oak, fifteenth century. Photograph courtesy of Alfàbia Gardens, Mallorca.

are the first reliably dated Renaissance English seats (inventory no. 997990; Pickvance 2015).

Tables

It is usually argued that boards loosely placed on trestles and easily disassembled were the predecessor of the joined table. As in the case of seating, the evidence from thirteenth- to fifteenth-century paintings is more complex than this. It shows a variety of small tables that have not survived and a variety of forms of construction: trestle tables, splayed stick-leg tables, small stool-like tables with three turned legs and crudely joined supports for boards. These paintings show tables in use for a variety of purposes, for example, serving and eating food, playing cards and other games, reading and writing, holding paint pots, carpentry, making candlesticks and selling objects in a goldsmith's shop, and holding armor (Blanc 1999: 30–55; Bartlett 2001: 109, 123, 127, 155, 175, 203). In the first two cases they were generally covered with cloths.

In the fifteenth and early sixteenth centuries there was a diversification in types of (especially smaller) tables as larger houses with specialized rooms emerged. Monique Blanc's *Le mobilier français: moyen age et renaissance* shows a polygonal table with a shaped, boarded, central support of 1438 (1999: 44). It looks similar in size to the heavy folding octagonal table at Cluny Museum with Gothic tracery supports dendro-dated to *c.* 1500 (accession no. 22795; Blanc 1999: 45). The very similar one-sided Gothic tracery trestles of the table at the Musée des Arts Décoratifs, Paris, have been dendro-dated to the late fifteenth century (Figure 3.12). The Cluny Museum also has a very long, lightweight, painted fifteenth-century German board, 4.5 × 0.75 meters, whose ends fold in to 2.25

FIGURE 3.12 A table with tracery trestles, French, Musée des Arts Décoratifs, oak and chestnut, *c.* 1475. Photograph by the Author.

meters and which must have been supported on trestles (accession no. 7725). This looks very portable and was no doubt for outdoor use.

In Germany two main types of table have survived from this period. One has fixed, shaped, boarded ends with two stretchers with through tenons and face pegs—a reminder of their dismountable predecessors—and a plain board top with or without an enclosed compartment below (Von Falke 1924: 130–9; Bartlett 2001: 173). The other is the "counter table," popular in southern Germany and Alpine countries (Windisch-Grätz 1982: 304–7). This was rather square and had a top which slid to and fro giving access to a "safe" box. This form continued into the nineteenth century in rural areas and was made with traceried, flat carved, inlaid, or painted decoration according to period and cost.

In Italy and later in Flanders Renaissance tables with carved, shaped, solid end supports and a long stretcher, sometimes with supporting columns, became popular. Simpler versions had cross-ended stretchers supporting a row of columnar supports. In Italy long rectangular joined tables with bulbous legs also appeared in the sixteenth century (Schmitz 1956: 90) and were followed in Flanders and England. Smaller Flemish counter tables in the sixteenth century were rectangular and had fixed, often linenfold, panels in their sides. In Spain early Renaissance tables had top boards dovetailed to splayed open trestles attached underneath the top with S-shaped iron supports (Aguiló Alonso 1993: 341–2).

In England the transition from the trestle table can be seen in long, plain, heavy tables with fixed trestles themselves fixed to the floor as in the kitchens at Hampton Court Palace and Rockingham Castle and in the Church House at Sampford Courtenay, Devon (Figure 3.13). Penshurst Place has two very long

FIGURE 3.13 A table with fixed supports, Church House, Sampford Courtenay, Devon, oak, sixteenth century. Photograph by the Author.

fifteenth-century tables with three cruciform pedestals (Windisch-Grätz 1982: 226). As well as the long joined "refectory" table, smaller tables with fixed T-shape trestles also developed (Chinnery 1979: 282–6).

CONCLUSION

This chapter has tried to sketch the types of furniture and their uses over time across several parts of Europe and relate them to changes in society, the house, and the household. Inevitably, it has only skimmed the surface. The difficulty of knowing what extant medieval furniture consists of has been mentioned. As more individual pieces are examined closely further reassessments will undoubtedly follow. Another limit is that dendrochronology has been little used to date furniture outside the United Kingdom, France, and Germany.

On the "uses" side, there has recently been an upsurge of work in sociology, anthropology, and art history on "material culture." Furniture is an object of production, design, cooperation between trades, domestic use, memory, consumption, display, movement, inheritance, collection, investment, commerce (and subject to de- and revaluation), and an expression of status, identity, and values. These aspects mark out a wide research agenda. Court records, diaries, and literature allow for some progress in understanding furniture of the medieval and early modern period (Hamling and Richardson 2016). Given the scope and confines of this chapter, very few of these aspects have been addressed but some are tackled elsewhere in this volume.

ACKNOWLEDGMENTS

For help in supplying information and photos: Jeremy Bate, Pia Bengtsson Melin, John Boram, Adam Bowett, Martin Bridge, Stephan Baumeier, Erin Campbell, Jan Chinnery, David Dewing, Kristof Haneca, Hans Linderson, Léonie Seliger, Didier Pousset, Nicholas Riall, Sofia Rodriguez, David Sherlock, Charles Tracy, Karl Heinrich von Stülpnagel, and Cristina Zaforteza. For also commenting on the whole chapter, my particular thanks to Nick Humphrey.

CHAPTER FOUR

The Domestic Setting

STEPHANIE R. MILLER

The domestic setting was an active force on the furnishings of the multipurposed spaces of the evolving home between 500 and 1500. Domestic customs (from childbirth, to wedding celebrations, to death) contributed to the appreciation of specific types of furniture, both movable and immovable. By considering furniture as agents of social action/interaction for residents and their guests, the cultural life of furniture from specific rooms of the household is revealed. The acquisition and use of household furniture responded to family rituals both prosaic and profound. Tables, chairs, desks, benches, *credenze*, beds, *cassone*, and more—all functioned in the daily life of the family as well as memorialized people and events on more seminal occasions. Throughout this chapter, the central role of furniture in family rituals will be considered.

During the era under consideration, homes could be quasi public and a measure of permeability between public and private domestic spaces existed, often depending on degrees of familiarity or other hierarchies. This chapter examines how furniture produced for these spaces responded to such social requirements. The frequent presence of nonresidential family members was a consideration to homeowners when acquiring furniture. With this varied audience in mind, examples of furniture, such as beds and buffets, are herein explored as objects that highlighted and communicated family identity, honor, and longevity to people within and beyond the immediate family, while at the same time served ostensibly ordinary functions.

There are few surviving examples from the early period, a fact demonstrated in other chapters and notably Chapter 3 in this volume. However, when approaching 1300, there is a demonstrable surge in the consumption of material goods intended for new forms of domestic architecture. This is particularly well documented in Italy, where its strong economy led to surplus wealth among merchants and elite families (Goldthwaite 1993). This helped lead to new consuming habits including new homes or *palazzi*, which moved away from defensive, tower structures to more open and receptive residences with rooms having more specified functions, for instance studies. Because of this documentation—of surviving pieces as well as recorded evidence—Italy is a good comparative reference point to consider changes and continuity in furniture throughout Europe during this long era. During the later part of the era, individuals across the social spectrum, influenced by the revived interest in ancient authors, increasingly sought to express personal fame and family honor. To this end, homes became multifaceted reflections of esteem, a type of self-promotion, which was further articulated through the home's furnishings and customs. Often the furnishings—a room's furniture, fittings, and accessories, were extensions and elaborations of types and pieces from earlier generations. Like the home itself, they communicated to fellow citizens and visitors the respect, magnificence, and splendor of that family.

The critical furnishings and spaces of the Italian domestic interior highlight numerous enduring forms from earlier times and from around Europe, and demonstrate the longevity and geographic spread of types of pieces, which are also tethered to family life. Beds, seats, chests, tables, and buffets are among the core pieces of furniture that persist in the home throughout this era. This chapter explores these pieces and how and where their uses were predicated upon family needs and rituals.

THE HOME

It is worthwhile to provide an overview of the types of domestic environments during these centuries. The most common, and the one figuring most prominently in this chapter, was a home in which people ate, slept, and where ritualized family behaviors took place. However, throughout Europe monasteries and convents also provided a domestic setting for religious men and women, hospitals for the poor and sick, and by the beginning of the fifteenth century in Italy orphanages had been established for abandoned children. Though these places certainly fulfilled a domestic function with necessary furnishings such as beds, they were communal and institutional with differing priorities than a family residence and may be considered here only for comparative value.

Family honor was a defining characteristic of the social and political fabric at this time, and the home became a visible, public expression of it. Honor and respectability could be achieved in Florence, for example, through palace building, which expressed wealth and status. The house was a "symbol … [and] repository of a family's wealth" (Crum 2001: 45), and the domestic environment was the setting for "ritual expressions of honor" (Strocchia 1989: 120). Florence, like other capitalist, mercantile societies at this time, seemingly borrowed aristocratic, courtly elements to promote individual worth and reputation. Aristocratic families were defined by noble lineage, which secured to them an elite social standing, among other things. These families employed strategic marriages and inheritance systems to consolidate wealth and power and to promote the continuation of their noble lineages and were further defined by their customs and culture. Scholars define courtly culture as a self-conscious code of behavior intended to reflect positively on oneself by promoting good manners, courtesy, sociability, and generosity (Barton 2009: 502–15). Such behaviors could be demonstrated at a variety of venues with social interactions, including the domestic. Furnished rooms staged these customs. By borrowing from established courtly customs, and despite lacking an aristocratic pedigree, successful merchant families promoted themselves. These customs and venues proved useful to these families in shaping public opinion (Strocchia 1989: 121).

Regardless of owner wealth or home type, common residential spaces included a hall (often, but not always, with a fireplace) and a chamber, which were used similarly by their inhabitants. For instance, the *domus* or dwelling at Caen Castle in France (begun in the eleventh century), like others of this period and later, included a hall and chamber. If the castle's tower was an externally visible sign of seigniorial power, the hall was an internal emblem of power; the hall (or *sala*) with suitable furnishings, adornment, and guests was the more "public" of the two spaces, and was a suitable space for banquets. The French medieval aristocratic chamber (bedroom) may have been contiguous with the hall, perhaps separated only by a textile (Duby 1988: 60), thus highlighting the flexibility and fluidity of domestic spaces making it difficult to sustain a strictly public–private space dichotomy. The chamber–hall spatial emphasis is a constant refrain of this chapter as it contextualizes the furniture and rituals of the domestic setting throughout this period. In the fourteenth and fifteenth centuries when home spaces became more numerous and specialized, these two rooms remained with similar, albeit nuanced functions. The consistency of these two rooms of the home are paralleled by a few persistent furniture pieces throughout this span of time and found in several centers throughout Europe.

In Italian centers such as Florence, a capitalist republic without the same feudal history of northern European centers, the domestic habits and behavior of its elite classes often mimicked those of the northern aristocratic past. In the French aristocratic model, homes had "areas for ostentation and areas for retreat" (Duby 1988: 57), spaces arguably considered domestic public and domestic private spaces. It was once argued that the fifteenth-century Italian palace was notable for its newly private emphasis (Goldthwaite 1993). However, the seemingly private spaces of the palazzo were often communal—accessible to those outside the family, but with some familiarity with it—and used for a wide range of purposes. Throughout this long period, versatility and a lack of privacy are common features of medieval European homes, regardless of social class and rank. The notion of private at this time does not mean alone or isolated, but cloistered and sheltered—within one's home, with one's things, furnishings, and with one's family and friends.

A well-organized home was a virtuous reflection of social order in the family unit (Ajmar-Wollheim and Dennis 2006a: 15). By the end of this period, inventories and household journals confirm a wide variety of ostensibly utilitarian objects and furniture, but which were profoundly social, defining the "palace environment" through honorific display (Crum 2001: 45; Lindow 2005: 634). Leon Battista Alberti used the term *masserizia* to refer to household possessions and furnishings; these possessions and furnishings connoted strong moral qualities and "represented family solidarity and honor" (Crum 2001: 44). Thus, the furniture types explored below were not merely utilitarian, but were possessions laden with familial and social significance (Goldthwaite 1993: 230). Certainly furniture, both mobile and immobile, was also intended to meet basic needs of living. This is especially true for mobile, noble, aristocratic families, where built-in furniture is useful as it negates the need to move all furniture from one household to the next (Eames 1977: xviii). Medieval records and inventories included core pieces of furniture: beds, seating, tables, chests—utilitarian and display objects, which provide insights into the medieval household. The longevity of certain furniture forms also endowed them with meaning beyond pure utility.

Not surprisingly, the home and family wealth determined the quality and quantity of furniture (Mercer 1969: 18). With the exception of the most aristocratic and elite in medieval society, the majority of homes had limited furniture (20). Being wealthy did not necessarily imply a sprawling residence. For instance, Eric Mercer noted that at the beginning of the fourteenth century, even the wealthiest homes in Colchester, England, did not have more than three rooms, and usually just two (the hall and chamber), to fulfill the personal, familial, and social needs. Thus by necessity, these multifunctional rooms were free of unnecessary furniture to allow for maximum adaptability (21). Although families with limited means had limited furniture, aristocratic families might also have limited furniture that would travel with them from residence to residence (22). Additionally, in a great feudal home and for sociopolitical reasons, wealth was expected to be shown through "expansive generosity," so one's status was aided not just by the possessions, but how they were shared, perhaps in the form of a great banquet (Duby 1988: 69). Later in this long era, even though more rooms existed in a fifteenth-century Italian palazzo, those same core rooms (chamber and hall) continued to serve the same multifunctional purpose as prior centuries.

A HOUSE AWAITS ITS GUESTS:
BENCHES AND SEATING

Façades were literally the public face of the family and certain external features revealed the "inner" life, furnishings, and *splendore* of the palace (Crum and Paoletti 2008: 275). Most obviously, family *imprese*, coats of arms, and even portrait busts on the home's borders publicly promoted the citizen who lived within. Ancient to Renaissance commentators from Cicero to Giovanni Rucellai to Niccolo Machiavelli, wrote how the number of waiting visitors at a man's home reflected the esteem of that owner (Kent 1987: 60; Elet 2002: 459; Linghor 2008: 262), and façade benches were intended to attract visitors to the home by offering a place to sit, talk, and wait (Figure 4.1). Façade benches, a sign of perpetual welcome, led privileged guests all the way through the home, as they are found leading from the façade, through the *androne* (ground-floor passageway), to the courtyard, to the upstairs *sala*, and to the bedroom or *camera*, where even the bed was often surrounded by similar benches. Thus, even bed furniture reflected the rather public function of the bedroom when a patrician was there, such as Giovanni de' Medici who negotiated from his own room (Elet 2002: 449). In grand medieval homes, "windows were crowded with seated ladies," with benches here, too, built into the fabric of the building at windows and balconies; they were ideal areas for "intimate conversations" (Bumke 1991: 112).

The typical fifteenth-century Italian courtyard with its interior loggia lined with benches, created a space that Brenda Preyer described as a "theater for social interaction" (Preyer 1998: 358). Certainly, the courtyard with its embellishments and garden view, as at the Palazzo Medici, offered respite from the city streets, where visitors were received in a dignified manner worthy of the owner (Preyer 1998: 364; Welch 2002: 216). With a preference for business conducted directly through face-to-face interaction and discussion, visiting was a key ingredient to harmonious social interactions, and the courtyard with its internal loggia on one side could be used for formal events, but more commonly was filled with people for routine interactions; in fact, one 1490 source estimated upward of forty people waiting in the Medici courtyard eager to speak with Lorenzo (Preyer 1998: 359).

The courtyard provided new, ideal places for "public" deliberation and private trials and judgments, just as advocated by Vitruvius (Linghor 2008: 256). For instance, Lorenzo de' Medici's secretary, Niccolò Micelozzi, noted that Lorenzo arbitrated between parties in his room and, on one occasion, two parties waited in the courtyard for Lorenzo's counsel upon his return home that evening; his decision was given to them in the courtyard (Kent 1987: 62).

FIGURE 4.1 Façade, Palazzo Rucellai, Florence. Photograph courtesy of Wikimedia Creative Commons.

It was through doorways that increasing familiarity with the family or patrician was implied as the visitor moved into the home, with the most privileged guests moving into the inner most sanctum of the home, the chamber and its associated rooms.

THE CHAMBER

John Kent Lydecker's *The Domestic Setting of the Arts in Renaissance Florence* analyzes the types and locations of objects and furniture in the Renaissance palace by exploring various archival sources. Based on these sources, and confirmed in texts by Renaissance humanists, the main bedchamber "was a complete decorative environment of considerable complexity" (Lydecker 1987: 171). If a home had paintings, including and especially religious ones, they were found in the bedroom along with the home's other finest works, chests, daybeds, decorative wall panels, and of course the marital bed. Much of the furniture was commissioned on the occasion of a couple's wedding to properly furnish this room (Crum 2001: 43), as the space and its goods were testimony to the status, honor, and histories of the newly joined families. Even in modest dwellings, the *camera* was the home's focal point where most material goods were stored, treasured, and on occasion displayed for family and guests.[1] The sanctity of this room is supported by the oft-cited reference to Alberti's conversations in his book on the family, where the new husband is advised to introduce his new wife to her new home, and ultimately to the bedchamber, where the secrets of the household are kept (Alberti 1969: 208–9).

Beds

The social-domestic importance of beds cannot be overstated. The bedchamber with its huge bed surrounded by many of the household's other furnishings and objects (Plate 12)[2] was not isolated from the social role of the rest of the home, but rather participated in that function with guests and esteemed visitors to this room. The impression intended by bedroom furniture, in particular the bed, is suggested by Matteo di Ricci's 1420 inventory, which included a bed (*lettiera*) of 5½ braccia (over 3 meters) (Lindow 2007: 126).

Nuptial beds were very large and certainly the most substantial piece of furniture in the bedchamber. Despite the marital bed being one of the most significant pieces of furniture in the entire home, none survive from Renaissance Italy. The famous Davanzati bed (Figure 4.2), once thought a prime example of this type of furniture from the fifteenth century, has actually been shown to be a marriage of parts from later centuries; however, if contemporary paintings are accurate records, the reconstructed form may be correct (Ajmar-Wollheim and Dennis 2006a: 20). Beds were among the husband's contributions to the chamber; in fact, should the bride become a widow, the bed might not be considered hers unless specified in the husband's will (Bellavitis and Chabot 2006: 79). However, in fifteenth-century Venice, if the bed was the wife's property, she might bequeath it, for instance, to a grandchild (78–9), bestowing on the bed connotations of life, death, and the continuity between families and generations. Specifically, because they were often commissioned around

FIGURE 4.2 Davanzati Bed, Metropolitan Museum of Art, New York (65.221.1). Walnut. Photograph courtesy of Metropolitan Museum of Art.

weddings, one must acknowledge the "symbolic overtones" of nuptial beds (Preyer 2006b: 40)—for sleeping or for sex, beds connoted family, unity, procreation, abundance, and the family's stability. Medieval practice provides precedence for such symbolism, whereby feudal nuptial ceremonies would include a benediction *thalami*, or blessing of the bed, and the newlyweds would be witnessed in bed together (Duby 1988: 133).

From major castles to minor dwellings with meager furnishings, a bed was typical, though in some lower ranking households it may have been nothing more than a mattress on the floor and, thus, lacked the same social overtones as at grander or later residences (Mercer 1969: 24). Furthermore, neither the medieval chamber or bedroom nor its bed furniture denoted privacy. Family members as well as guests commonly shared beds in medieval Europe. The virtues of a shared bed ranged from providing "warmth and security" to solidifying trust or political accord (Classen 2012: 3–4). The sharing of one's bed was a gesture of magnanimity and "munificence" found at the highest levels of medieval society, for instance, a chronicler wrote in 1187 how Richard the Lionheart of England shared his bed with his ally King Philip II of France (Heng 2003: 91). Mercer also noted that French queens, when not with their husbands, shared their beds with their ladies. Warriors might share beds with captured enemies, and two to three medieval scholars could be found per bed in dormitories at Eton or Wells (Mercer 1969: 25). Graciousness and seigniorial honor was communicated by sharing one's bed with guests. Medieval audiences, accustomed to this arrangement, would appreciate depictions at Autun Cathedral, France, of the Three Kings sleeping together, sharing a bed on their way to Bethlehem (Classen 2012: 3). Added to this list of bed-sharing and noble generosity is Chancellor Nicholas Rolin's (1376–1462) establishment of the Hôtel-Dieu (1443) in Beaune, France, a public hospice. While it was not a domestic residence, this institution took in the sick, most of whom would stay until their death (Lane 1989: 170). Rolin was the patron of the hospital and much of its furnishings, including beds, curtains, and notably, the famous *Last Judgment* altarpiece (1445–8; Musée de L'Hôtel Dieu) by Rogier van der Weyden. This public residence for the sick consisted of a long hall, along the sides of which were thirty four-poster beds with curtains, large enough for two patients per bed, a relatively sumptuous arrangement when compared with other contemporary French hospitals, which held many more patients per bed, even up to fifteen (Lane 1989: 170).

One of the earliest hospitals in Italy offers another picture of temporary residential sleeping arrangements, the Ospedale di Santa Maria della Scala, Siena, which opened its doors as early as the tenth century. However, a 1090 document is the earliest mention of it as a "hostel and hospital," as a place for those in need, including orphans, the poor and the sick, and a place for travelers and pilgrims (Baron 1990: 1449–51). Its 1305 statues described beds as necessary remedies for neglect. Beds for the sick were seemingly instrumental in patient treatment, in that they were intended for individual use (an uncommon practice during this period), made of iron rather than wood, and with sheets that were changed as needed.

Households might also provide their guests with their own beds of various forms and character. Temporary, overnight guests were clearly anticipated in fifteenth-century Italy. Collapsible, camp beds (*letti da campo*) could be found in a Genoese main hall and, when beds are found in this customarily more public home space, devotional images were also an expected accoutrement (Cavallo 2006: 74–5). However, devotional images are found in Genoese halls usually only when a bed is present, whereas religious images are regularly found in the main *camera* with its permanent bed, as elsewhere in Italy. Thus, the bed, regardless of its room, helped create a space intended for domestic, personal devotion. Nonetheless, not all guest beds were as temporary or in the main hall. Maria DePrano's study of the Tornabuoni inventory (1497) of the ground-floor chamber near the entrance to their palace revealed a lovely, well-appointed room with a substantial bed with intarsia decoration, among other things (DePrano 2013: 128–9). Further, to honor the guest, not to mention the homeowner, this bed was ornamented with a "curtained canopy."

Returning to the main *camera*, this bedchamber and its furniture, such as a bed, benches, or chests (to be covered later) were intended to impress visitors, a fact highlighted by the abundance of textiles that must be considered as requisite accessories of beds, and indeed most furniture of this long era. Beds in the main chamber often included curtains or canopies of some sort, such as a canopy suspended from the ceiling (a *padiglione*), or curtains surrounding a bed that could be opened or closed depending on need, with fabric that could also be changed depending on occasion or season (Preyer 2006b: 40). Textiles themselves were considered necessary luxuries, which defined the owner's wealth and status. Even in more humble dwellings, textiles and bed accessories were considered essential assets, an important element of "public display" (Cavallo 2006: 73). Not only were beds surrounded with fabric to frame, shelter, or enclose the space, the doorway also might have a hung fabric door, one that was flexible and opulent, which, depending on the pattern of the fabric, brought visual unity to the space.[3]

Medieval aristocrats, who commonly accessorized their beds with fabrics, furs, and textiles to convey the owner's status, honor, and rank, established a taste for bedroom textiles. These accessories, too, suggest an expectation of an audience to achieve the desired significance. So although drawn bed curtains allowed for a modicum of privacy and warmth, when they were parted it was an act of revelation, framing the worthy occupant (or implied occupant). Various means of suspending curtains were used throughout the Middle Ages (as noted in Chapter 3 in this volume), but the bed canopy became popular during the thirteenth century and soon after a requirement of bed furniture for the "seigniorial classes" (Eames 1977: 74). By the thirteenth century, the state bed as a status item was more symbolically important than it was functional, and in this context it influenced later generations of royal and aspirational classes. The public nature of state beds is also discussed in Chapter 5 in this volume. Although state beds ultimately were not for sleeping, their association with dynasty and family continuity fits within the spectrum of domestic furniture and family life.

Curtains and canopies were not exclusive to the royal classes, but they became expected features of their bed accessories. King Henry III's (r.1216–72) four-poster bed in England with a gold star embellished canopy is one of the earliest documented examples of the canopy as an official feature of a state bed (Eames 1977: 75). For royals and their beds of state, the size and sumptuousness of the posted bed, canopy, and curtains represented precedence (Morley 1999: 76). For instance, though canopies extended across the widths of these beds, the length of the canopy depended on one's rank—the higher the rank, the greater the length of the canopy (Eames 1977: 77). A bed with stately trappings (canopies or curtains) reflects official ceremony, rather than exclusively family ceremony. The social and dynastic value of state beds and their accessories was also evident when newborns were presented on such beds after baptism (85). Elaborate state wedding beds created for royal marriages were also intended for display rather than sleeping, explaining their sometimes-curious location in a reception room. A smaller room with a more modest bed for sleeping contrasted with the purpose of the bed in the receiving room. For example, these two bed types were created on the occasion of the 1468 marriage in Damme (near Bruges) between Charles the Bold and Margaret of York (85).

Beds were also given as gifts and precious heirlooms among royal family members. Or, beds of state could be bequeathed as with King Richard II of England's (r.1377–99) beds from his father, Edward Prince of Wales (1376), some of which were embellished with ostrich feathers arranged in the prince's heraldic badge (Stratford 2012: 50). Richard II's mother, Joan of Kent, likewise bequeathed to her son her "new bed of red velvet embroidered with ostrich feathers of silver and leopards' heads of gold" (51). The same King Richard II also gave a different sumptuous bed with a canopy, textiles, and fur to the Duke of Burgundy in 1396 (Morley 1999: 77).

Given the bed's ritual significance and the intention of its owners to display or present in medieval households, especially in the later Middle Ages, it is no surprise that after the birth of a child, extended family members and visitors arrived to greet the newborn and mother in the bed chamber (Cavallo 2006: 73). In fifteenth-century Italy, the confinement room was where pregnant women and new mothers at home, in bed, would receive visitors, putting the mother and the room's furnishings on display (Musacchio 1999: 44–5 and 185, n. 68).[4] High infant mortality and maternal death in this and earlier eras were more common than safe pregnancies and childbirth. While bed furniture might not change, the accessories adorning it and other objects in the confinement room were intended to reassure the pregnant woman (15, 28). Renaissance paintings of holy births seem representative of contemporary confinement rooms with the women in attendance, beds and daybeds, benches, and cradles. How accurately paintings depicted actual spaces and objects is debatable (Syson 2006a, b; Introduction in this volume), but given the dearth of surviving beds, such images are illustrative when weighed with other supporting evidence.

Children embodied the union of two families and were a much-desired security for the continuation of the families' lineages. By extension, cradles supported and protected not only the baby but also the families' longevity. In both rural and noble households, plainly to elaborately carved wooden cradles with rockers are found (Klapisch-Zuber 1985: 148–9; Miller 2013: 70–1). Sleeping in cradles was also considered more protective than having infants sleep in caregivers' beds. Cradles reflected contemporary concerns about infants being crushed by adults in their beds, or being suffocated by overlaid blankets (which happened with enough frequency that such sleeping arrangements were declared a crime by the church) (Klapisch-Zuber 1985: 148–9). Remedying this concern were boxes in beds for infants and protective ribs on cradles to support blankets.

Cradles for royal infants paralleled the intention of a state bed, and thus two cradles were necessary for royal babies—one to display the newborn (and family lineage and succession) and one practical cradle for the baby and caregiver to use. The two cradles, commonly known as day and night cradles, were each of a particular form. The day cradle displayed the baby to adults and was necessarily higher, "suspended between two uprights," for ideal viewing, but not caregiving (Eames 1977: 95–6). The night cradle was commonly lower to the ground and suitable to the needs of a seated caregiver (96). Regarding the forms of the cradles, Eames relies on inventories and treatises, in particular Alienor de Poitiers's book on courtly etiquette, *Honors of the Court* (1484–91) that described the day or state cradle as being in two parts—the cradle and the stand that elevated and suspended it (99). Further, this treatise confirms that state cradles, like state beds, required appropriate textiles and fabrics not just to keep the newborn warm, but also to honor the baby and family. The only surviving fifteenth-century state cradle also adhered to this two-part structure; it was made in the Netherlands in 1478 or 1479 for the birth of Mary of Burgundy and Maximilian I's child, either Philip the Fair or Margaret of Austria (Eames 1977: 100; Morley 1999: 77). Night cradles, described in inventories, are much simpler affairs, still with rockers, but lower and therefore more suited to infant care. They are represented in medieval illustrations of infant death, such as *The Friar and the Child* woodcut print in Guy Marchant's *Danse Macabre* (1485). Sophie Oosterwijk cites several visual and textual depictions of swaddled infants in their cribs being summoned by death (Oosterwijk 2006: esp. 148–54). The cradles, with side-to-side rockers, had protective straps across the tops to keep the infant safe from overly zealous rocking, but clearly, such devices could not protect the infant from death when it arrives. Like adult beds, cradles were associated with both birth and death.

A fifteenth-century relief sculpture by Andrea della Verrocchio's workshop for Francesca Pitti Tornabuoni's tomb depicts birth and death in the Renaissance. Francesca, who died during childbirth in 1477, is shown on what was both a birth- and deathbed (Musacchio 1999: 30). The bed was at once hopeful and symbolic of future offspring and the continuity of family, while at the same time foreshadowed death. In addition to difficult pregnancies, plague, disease, and death were real and constant threats. Records describe visitors who called on ailing friends at their bedsides or the bedside dictation of wills with patients surrounded by "a large turnout of witnesses, a priest [or] ..., a medical practitioner" (Cavallo 2006: 73).[5] Given such circumstances, beds could be "ceremonial buffers" (Strocchia 1992: 64), objects that mediated and contextualized life's most intimate and profound moments.

Daybeds

Renaissance paintings illustrate what inventories record: the commanding presence that beds and *lettucci* (daybeds) enjoyed in the Italian chamber (Preyer 2006b: 42). The impression of wealth, comfort, and status in the *camera* or chamber was solidified by the daybed (*lettucio* or *couchette*; see examples in Plate 12 and Figure 6.4). *Lettucci* could be adorned by sculptures (for example, heads or busts) or paintings; such adornment could be found above headboards (Preyer 2006b: 41). Assuming that listing order in inventories implies importance, the fact that beds were generally listed first in inventories, then *lettucci* or chests, demonstrates their standing in the hierarchy of domestic furniture. Daybeds were useful for storing various items (keeping in mind that the room itself was a repository of valued items). It was also useful, of course, as seating for visitors in the chamber. Like beds, *lettucci* were usually commissioned at the time of one's marriage and thus were associated with seminal family moments, including childbirth, with all the attendant symbolism. While furniture was often kept to a minimum in a confinement room, the room itself might nevertheless have a daybed, possibly a large bed, and chests to seat the numerous female visitors who called on the new mother (Musacchio 1999: 47). The *lettuccio* thus was used for seating, storage, temporary or short-term rest, and perhaps, because of its versatility, is also associated with tending to the ill. Brucia Witthoft notes, furthermore, an example where the daybed was used by an invalid who described himself as "living between letto and lettuccio" or "from bed to sofa" (1982: 55, n. 22).

Medieval French aristocratic chambers might also include a daybed or *couchette*. Like a medieval hung bed, a *couchette* was similarly accessorized with fabric or other accoutrements of state, depending on one's rank. For instance, sources describe the sumptuous hangings and ermine covering of Isabel of Bourbon's *couchette* at the Burgundian court in 1456 (Eames 1977: 87). When in the same room as a bed, however, the *couchette* was less significant, and, in fact, the word is not well understood; in some situations it seems a *couchette* was simply a "low bed" or one that was stored underneath another bed or couch (Eames 1977: 87; Lezotte 2004: 87).

Seating/Chests

While chairs were found in chambers, they were not common forms of seating and, like a bed, their use and style were determined by rank and precedence. By the fifteenth century, wealthy merchants were using domestic chairs with high backs, folding chairs, or especially, chairs with footstools. Like other fifteenth-century furnishings, the social-domestic appreciation of seating was also influenced by earlier courtly customs (Morley 1999: 75–6). The use of X-chairs, for instance, denoted authority, especially in halls or in public spaces such as a church. So, when such chairs are emulated in the fifteenth century and used in chambers, echoes of that prestige still resonated within the more intimate, domestic environment (Eames 1977: 198). Armchairs in the home varied in size, with the largest one accorded to the most important person of the household, though on special occasions this chair could be given to guests of honor as a sign of esteem and graciousness (Thornton 1991: 174). To communicate comfort and wealth, chairs in chambers could also be cushioned and upholstered with leather and cloth, as indicated in fourteenth-century French and Burgundian inventories (Eames 1977: 202). However, benches were the most common seating form at home, and for additional seating in the *camera* or chamber, chests were the other frequent alternative. They were not, however, merely utilitarian: large chests also contributed to the grandeur of the *camera*.

Chests fulfilled dual functions of use and display and were numerous in any home (Plate 13; see also the related examples in Chapters 3 and 6 in this volume). The 1471 inventory of the Florentine Inghirrami home lists a large number of chests in the *camera* with many of them placed around the bed and room, as was commonly noted in inventories and rendered in contemporary depictions of Italian chambers, such as the bedrooms of Polia and Polifilo in the 1499 woodcuts from the *Hypnerotomachia Poliphili*; grouping the chests around the bed and the wall had the dual benefit of "highlighting the bed and providing extra seating" (Lindow 2005: 635). Though chests were certainly found in other spaces, they were most commonly found in the bedroom where the majority of household valuables were also kept, and specifically kept in the chests, some of which had locks, as did Matteo de Ricci's chest (1420 inventory; Lindow 2007: 126).

During the Middle Ages, chests of various forms, domed or with flat lids, footed or not, supported domestic needs of "mobility and security for household possessions" and important documents (Eames 1977: 108). Such functionality continued to the end of this long era, but with more profound connotations. A number of chapters in this volume discuss chests (*cassoni* or *forzieri* in Italian) from various perspectives. It was a furniture type that remained useful and increased in symbolic value, as it often held sentimental significance through generations. For instance, Italian *forzieri* were certainly associated with marriage and its rituals in the fourteenth and fifteenth centuries. Marriage chests were originally a major commission by the bride's family. Then, grooms assumed this responsibility. By the mid-fifteenth century, they were typically commissioned in pairs to highlight the distinction of two families' gifts to the bride (Witthoft 1982: 52; Lindow 2005: 638).

Family identity was associated with such chests. Given to the new teenage bride, the object represented paternal family honor as well as the joining of families. At this pivotal moment in the lives of two families, the bride brought the chest with her family's possessions, her trousseau, from her natal home to her new home as a wife (Bellavitis and Chabot 2006: 78). Often embellished with family heraldry, fifteenth-century *forzieri* were massive pieces of furniture, creating a visual impact in the bedroom, and through that visual effect, the symbolic significance of the piece resonated: the bridging of one's old life with the new and the bonding of two families (Lindow 2005: 640–1).

In Italian marriage rituals of the fourteenth and fifteenth centuries, *cassoni* and *forzieri* were among the most publicly visible pieces of domestic furniture. In Florence and other Tuscan towns, with their lids closed, they were carried through the streets, but onlookers were nevertheless aware of the associated costs of such chests and their contents; this journey of domestic furniture through the towns' streets ultimately ended at the groom's house (Witthoft 1982: 46). Brucia Witthoft's study cited a 1337 Lucca statute, which ordered processional chests to be carried through town with closed lids to keep the contents discrete; arguably, the procession with the chest was a "substitution for display of the dowry itself" (51). Despite the public display of the chests during the marriage ritual, the chests and their exterior adornments (perhaps paintings of virtuous historical or moral subjects) were intended for domestic appreciation once in the chamber. Painted narratives often included biblical or mythological subjects to ancient histories, such as the meeting of Solomon and Sheeba or the marriage of Aeneas and Lavinia. The subjects demonstrated the families' erudition and simultaneously instructed the new couple on their relative duties and virtues (see Apollonio di Giovanni's *Death of Camilia and the Wedding of Aeneas cassone* painting, *c.* 1460; Musée de la Renaissance, Écouen). Not only would guests to the room see the painted chests, so, too, would the couple's future babies, who might learn their first lessons from these eye-level images. However, Witthoft notes that "about half" of the surviving wedding chests include paintings on the inside lids of "intimate" subjects associated with marriage and procreation, images intended for the newlyweds themselves in their *camera* (1982: 52).

As a container of goods and valuables, even a closed chest implied abundance. A 1448 Florentine inventory described a locked chest in a ground-floor room that included several pieces of maiolica. A 1495 inventory of a small chest in a study (usually a small room close to the *camera*) included a collection of valuable glasses and salt-cellars—novelties in the fifteenth century and valuable for both use and display (Lindow 2005: 641, 643).[6] Chests as containers of valuables and documents (whether during travel or meant to remain stationary in the home) were nothing new in the fifteenth century. Though most surviving medieval chests were ecclesiastical, wooden chests, some worked with leather, others banded with iron, and still others with wicker, were suitable containers for safeguarding valuables in a household or from weather while in transit. Eric Mercer cites a chest of "worked leather banded with iron" containing silver, which was portable, mentioned in the 1265 Household Roll for the Countess of Leicester (1969: 40). It also appears that traveling chests were certainly smaller for easier transport, while chests intended for a home were larger, and may have had legs to keep them and their contents off damp floors. By the fifteenth century, most chests were not intended for transportation (40–1).

The valuables kept in chests or wardrobes were not intended to stay permanently hidden from view. Shelves in chambers, usually of simple boards attached to a wall, could hold and display goods, as could a hat-rack with a board over it (*cappellinaio*), small tables, or headboards. A special wall-mounted shelving unit emerged in fifteenth-century Italian *camere*, the *restello*, which held personal grooming objects, or suspended clothing or other items from its pegs. Though they could be entirely plain and utilitarian, these objects apparently became so lavish that a Venetian 1489 sumptuary prohibition was placed on gilded *restelli* (Thornton 1990: 174–5; Fortini-Brown 2006: 188).

Fifteenth-century Renaissance paintings, especially of the Annunciation, confirm that furniture in domestic spaces, especially the bedroom, sparked devotion. Artists from this century around Europe often depicted the Annunciation in a contemporary bedchamber for the purposes of making the holy accessible and to promote private devotion, the *devotio moderna*. So whether or not Rogier van der Weyden's painting of the Virgin's bedroom or thalamus in his *Annunciation* (Figure 4.3) is a true reflection of an actual Renaissance chamber, Luke Syson argued that the individual objects, the bed, the chandelier, the bench, were "visual prompts" depicted with such accuracy to remind viewers of the "spiritual truth," so that when these objects were "encountered in real life" they became devotional prompts in and of themselves (Syson 2006a: 46–7). Thus in addition to their practical and social purposes, bedroom or chamber furniture also had the potential to provoke religious contemplation.

LIFE AND FURNISHINGS IN THE *SALA*/HALL

Throughout the period under discussion here, European homes consistently had one large communal space known by various names: hall, *sala*, solar, *portego*. Eric Mercer quoted from Bede's *History of the English People* (731) to explain the consistency of the medieval hall. According to Bede (672–735), this room "was the heart of the little community which used it" (Mercer 1969: 19). As the heart of the household, the hall hosted residents and visitors of

FIGURE 4.3 Rogier van der Weyden, *Annunciation*. Louvre, Paris. Oil on panel.
Photograph courtesy of Wikimedia Creative Commons.

various classes and was used for occasions great and small. By necessity, this
room needed to be adaptable and by extension this flexibility included furniture
considerations. To maintain the social utility of the hall or *sala*, the amount
of furniture was restricted to keep floor space as open as possible. Immobile
fixtures, such as fireplaces, were often in this room, and toward the end of
this era, one could find *acquaii* or fixed water basins; stone benches could line
the *sala*'s perimeter, mimicking and mirroring the permanent stone outdoor
benches in the courtyard or on the palazzo's façade. Fixed seating on the hall's
perimeter on the second floor allowed for looking out the window as much
as sitting. The Italian *sala*, though lined with windows, did not offer easy or
passing views in or out; rather, windows were elevated, so standing on the
benches allowed for a good look at street activity below. In Florence, where
women were more cloistered than in other Italian localities, this must have

been extremely advantageous as it allowed them to see, but not easily be seen (Thomas 2008: 314, 318).

Room-by-room inventories of fifteenth-century palazzi often list this room at the top of the stairs, at the beginning of a succession of rooms on the *piano nobile* (the main living floor, usually the first, but not ground, floor) that suggest it was more "public" than the spaces beyond it. The room allowed for social permeability as well as a measure of "crowd control" by limiting immediate access to rooms beyond it, such as the *camera* or *anticamera* (Lindow 2007: 125–7). The *sala* was a connecting room, a receiving room, a banquet and dining hall, a multipurpose room whose function changed depending on who was present and for what event. Routine dining occurred in various locations, including the *camera* or *anticamera* (Lydecker 1987: 40), outdoors in a courtyard or loggia (weather permitting), or in the case to be discussed here, the *sala* (McIver 2013: 166). In Venice, this space was called the *portego*, a long space in the middle of a narrow Venetian home on the *piano nobile*, and which culminates at the home's façade, was the ideal location for dining with numerous guests.[7] Men and women seem to have sat together while dining, but perhaps they were also segregated on occasion, such as at the wedding of Lorenzo de' Medici in 1469 when women dined in the upstairs *sala* and men celebrated in the palazzo's ground-floor spaces (Preyer 1998: 362). While daily dining could take place anywhere, it was the number of people and occasion that transformed a meal to a banquet necessitating the use of larger domestic spaces and a more elaborate arrangement of furniture.

Tables and seating

All meals were socially significant because, regardless of location, meals bound a household to the table. The domestic significance of the activity, as well as the table, is one that was long and enduring. Roy Strong in *Feast* (2002), articulates the various historical and biblical precedents to medieval and Renaissance meals, which imparted to meals and their accessories a sense of the sacred or the historic. For instance, with medieval meals, a gathering around a table might intentionally recall the Last Supper or the Wedding at Cana, whereby the dining itself was an "expression of love, communion, and fellowship" (Strong 2002: 55). Similarly, but dependent on who was present, the meal might recall heroic Nordic or Anglo-Saxon legendary gatherings in great halls with long tables, which commemorated community and "social bonds" (55). Fifteenth-century Renaissance humanists were also lured by biblical and historical, especially Roman, precedents for dining rituals. Although monastic dining, recalling the Last Supper, helped to establish domestic etiquette at the table (from appropriately passing food to companions to eating in moderation [51–5]) the silence that often accompanied monastic meals was abandoned in secular Renaissance homes in favor of lively conversation, emulating the Feast of the

Gods. In fact, good conversation at the table became an expected and desirable feature of dining entertainment.

The dominant movable feature for dining in the hall or *sala* was the table. Although round tables were used from the early medieval period through the fifteenth century, rectangular tables, typically trestle or knock-down tables, were the norm and seemingly preferred for several reasons (Eames 1977: 217; Thornton 1991: 205; Strong 2002: 62). Trestle tables had practical advantages because they could be placed anywhere and their arrangement could create symbolic overtones. For instance, echoing monastic dining in a refectory, trestle tables in halls might be placed along the walls, not in the center of the room, and with benches also between the walls and the tables. Movable tables, like trestles, were preferred for the halls as they could be put up for meals and quickly dismantled (and easily stored) to free floor space for post-dining socializing and other activities. For elite classes with more than one home, such portable tables could be easily transported and reassembled anywhere.

Tables of such adaptability were useful to great and small houses alike. For humble homes with little space and few rooms, knock-down tables kept floor space clear when tables were not needed; for great homes with more space, but many more constant guests, the same was true. Further, a number of trestle tables could be set together; therefore, without difficulty, this form accommodated great numbers of people on special occasions. Penelope Eames, for instance, cites a 1377 inventory with fourteen tables requiring fifty-one trestles and a pair of forty-foot-long French tables from 1373 from the hall of Argilly castle in France, belonging to the Dukes of Burgundy (Eames 1977: 217). Both examples demonstrate the potential sizes of trestle tables and how many people could be seated at them. Although tables could be quite large for grand events, guests only sat on one side of them.

Benches and stools were the most common seating forms throughout the period and, as noted by Eames, were often associated with trestle tables (1977: 202). Because of the sizes of tables at weddings, banquets, and feasts, benches were the most logical. At these events, guests sat according to rank, and certainly courtly homes would include comfortable cushions covered with colorful fine fabrics (Bumke 1991: 183). Such a hierarchical seating arrangement worked in concert with the long room and table shape to communicate desired social conventions to the audience in attendance. Banquets and feasts for coronations, for weddings, or to honor esteemed visitors were all about "putting on a good show" (McIver 2013: 168). And to put on a good show in this long era, a series of rules and rituals about seating and table arrangement, food presentation, and etiquette allowed the dining event to be choreographed in such a way that it communicated a multitude of messages about power, community, sociability, wealth, and munificence (Taylor 2005: 621; McIver 2013: 168). Furthermore, while the host displayed power and hospitality, among other things, the guests were on display to each other and the host. The arrangement of tables facilitated social function through the hierarchy of "public" dining. For instance, in French feudal households, ritualized hall celebrations highlighted the host's ability to display and maintain order (Duby 1988: 75). The Italian *sala* and hall celebrations continued this medieval practice and the prestige it guaranteed.

On grand dining occasions, tables were arranged along three walls in a large U-shape, allowing servers to enter and attend to guests from within the table-framed central space (Eames 1977: 217; McIver 2015: 126). The host and esteemed guests were at the "head" of the room as much as at the head of the table—the short end of the room or bottom of the U. The middle table itself was likely elevated on a dais to highlight and display the privileged guest. Also demonstrating wealth and prestige was the use of cloth. Trestle tables were never bare, but always covered with textiles; a cloth of honor might even hang behind diners and esteemed guests, as depicted in a 1460 manuscript illumination by Jean Vauquelin (Plate 14). A good example of formal elements of dining rituals used to promote a royal individual is demonstrated by a 1428 banquet where the King of Portugal was both host and highest ranked. The king's table was at the end of the hall "taking up most of its width" and raised by "several steps," and in the middle the king sat another six inches higher with a gold cloth canopy (Strong 2002: 125–56).

The festivities for the 1468 wedding of Charles the Bold and Margaret of York in Bruges were recorded by the Burgundian courtier and chronicler Olivier de la Marche (*c.* 1425–1502) in a letter to the steward for the Duke of Brittany, Giles du Mas, and included with la Marche's *Mémoires* (Brown and Small 2007: 58–85). Many banquets and jousts were held between July 3–14, to celebrate their marriage and la Marche described them in rich detail, including banquets held in the tennis court because the hall of the ducal residence was not large enough for all the guests. The tennis court for one banquet held in honor of the bride was described as lavishly decorated with tapestries, colored cloth, and chandeliers. Regarding this banquet, la Marche noted the arrangement of the table of honor, which was placed at the end of this long space, the other tables, and the sideboard (buffet):

> It was higher than the others, reached by steps, and along its length, made of very costly cloth-of-gold, was a costly tester and a hanging so large that it made a cloth covering the seat. Along both lengths of the room ran the other two laid tables, both beautiful and very long, and in the middle of the room was a tall and costly lozenge-shaped sideboard. Its lower section was closed up like a tournament list, hung with tapestries showing the arms of the duke, and in front of it began steps of gradations laden with vessels, the lowest of which were the most common, and highest the most costly and delicate.
>
> (Brown and Small 2007: 67–8)

La Marche also goes on to describe the plate and ornament on the table as well as the seating arrangement. At the elevated table of honor sat the bride in the middle, flanked by the duke's mother on one side and the Lady of Argueil on the other, in a manner for all to see and that allowed them to look out over the room.

In addition to the elevated table and cloth of honor, other manifestations of ranking took place. Those seated to the right of the guest were of greater status than those to the left. Katherine McIver notes that such distribution goes back to depictions of the Last Supper with Christ flanked by his disciples (McIver 2015: 125). So, for instance, in the wedding banquet described above in honor of the bride Margaret of York, it was Charles the Bold's mother (Margaret's mother-in-law) who sat to the bride's right. A 1473 banquet given by Cardinal Riaro in Rome, to honor Eleanora, daughter of the King of Naples, she was seated at the middle of the raised table and the Cardinal (host) was to her right (125). The seating in the above scenarios continued an established medieval tradition where the guest of honor and host were visible to the guests who sat facing them on either side of the room. The host on display from this elevated perspective could also supervise table service, as recommended in etiquette and household management books, such as the *Rules* (1240-2) written by Bishop Robert Grosseteste for his recently widowed friend and noblewoman, Countess Margaret of Lincoln (Bumke 1991: 195; Coss 2006: 47). Perhaps because ritual and ceremony were becoming increasingly elaborate, rules and rulebooks from the thirteenth through fifteenth centuries repeatedly note the need for supervision and order (Strong 2002: 102).

Clearly dining throughout this period was more than a means to mere sustenance. Even at its most basic, the table with the head of the family surrounded by others elevated a meal with prayer to a sacred event. At its most grand, dining was an event, with all movements, seating, and object placements orchestrated for an audience, where the event and its participant-diners were on display to each other. Roy Strong describes a most extravagant fifteenth-century banquet given by Duke Philip the Good in 1454 in the great hall of his Lille Castle:

> to witness the event were not only five hundred guests, including members of the ducal family, the aristocracy and representatives of trade and industry, but also onlookers accommodated on five specially constructed platforms known as estrades. It was a display of hierarchy on the grand scale ... the feast lasted until 4 am the next day.
>
> (Strong 2002: 125-6)

In addition to rank, dining displayed finery and wealth. A medieval courtly table for King Ottokar of Bohemia displayed sumptuously made gold and silver plate (Bumke 1991: 192). Dining also featured hygiene as a form of table etiquette. Refined diners could begin their meals with ceremonial hand-washing with servers bringing costly vessels with washing water, and fine cloths for hand-drying (Bumke 1991: 193; Strong 2002: 105). By the end of the fifteenth century in Florence, *sale* in the most modern palazzi were updated with *acquaii* (wall fountains), which included running water (Preyer 2006a: 284–5; b: 38). Though few survive, these substantial immobile furnishings certainly impressed guests and diners.[8] Medieval etiquette books discuss hygiene as a desirable example of table manners. For instance, Fra Bonvincino da Riva's 1290 manual, *Fifty Courtesies for the Table*, encouraged hand-washing, as well as eating slowly and in moderation, and not talking with your mouth full. It also explained how to behave when women, guests, and people greater than oneself were present— in other words, your manners "at board" were on display.[9]

The scale of grand festivities required large spaces and tables, and due to the elaborate nature of these dining events more records of them exist than more mundane meals. However, small and intimate dining around a table could also be elegant. Dining in pairs at cloth covered small tables had become fashionable for courtly couples by the later Middle Ages, even associating this more intimate table gathering with expressions of "courtly love" (Bumke 1991: 188). For such meals around a smaller table, chairs, not benches, were used and these additional pieces of furniture might also connote greater prestige. Peter Thornton included an example of such a refined scene, though not one of courtly love: a 1473 painting by Giovanni Boccati from the *Life of S. Savino* depicts the saint dining in the *anticamera*, a more intimate space, at a small, three-legged, cloth-covered round table with a cloth of honor hanging behind him (Galleria Nazionale delle Marche-Palazzo Ducale, Urbino; Thornton 1991: 215). A 1472 banquet with trestle tables in a chamber, not a hall, merged fashionable intimacy with expressions of power, order, and presentation. This intimate luxury event at Windsor was hosted in the chambers of Queen Elizabeth of Woodville (queen to King Edward IV of England) in honor of Louis de Gruuthuse, a Burgundian courtier who sheltered Edward during the king's exile in Bruges in 1470–1. At the banquet, according to a Bluemantle Pursuivant, one of Edward's officers of arms, Gruuthuse and his son sat at the main table with the king and queen, the Duke and Duchess of Buckingham, and the king's sister, while other guests and courtiers sat at two other tables (Eames 1977: 218; Seward 2007: 1317–22).

Because of a table's versatility, other domestic purposes, such as food preparation, have to be acknowledged along with other kinds of work including intellectual or pious work when tables were used as desks or altars. Trestle tables could be used as desks, as noted in the inventory of goods after Lorenzo de' Medici's death in 1492. On the ground floor of the Palazzo Medici in a room known as the "chamber of the clerks" a trestle table was used to support portable writing desks (Stapleford 2013: 77).[10] Any flat surface was suitable for business, intellectual activities, and even for home worship. But a domestic desk, though ostensibly utilitarian, was prestigious furniture, which potentially had sacral associations, such as to Saint Jerome in his study. To a fortunate guest to the study, then, the desk-owner's status could be seemingly elevated to that of a scholar, collector, or erudite humanist. A 1490 painting of Saint Gregory at a proper desk with an elevated footrest, for example, helped to communicate this Pope's "superior rank" (Giovanni Pietro Birago, "Sforza Hours," British Museum, MS 34294; Thornton 1991: fig. 259). The fusion of sacred and secular regarding domestic tables is hinted at in such depictions of theologian scholars, but the association was very real and tangible to residents who used home tables specifically and exclusively for devotional purposes. This is the case for families who were given altar rites, or official church permission, to have domestic chapels (Mattox 2006: 658–73). For portable domestic altars, all that was required was a flat table-top surface on which the consecrated stone would rest (664). The consecrated or holy stone allowed the table to be transformed into an altar at which sacred rituals could take place. The fifteenth-century Florentine Tornabuoni family had permission for a domestic altar, apparently a portable one, which was a trestle table in an upstairs hall, outfitted with "precious vessels and missals, some with the family arms" (Musacchio 2000: 154; Cooper 2006: 199).

While benches were the most convenient choice for large trestle tables at events with many guests, when such tables were used for other, more singular purposes, such as a desk, other seating forms were more logical, such as stools. In general, chairs were less common for ordinary seating in the Middle Ages as they held social connotations whereby use of them might be determined by rank and precedence (Morley 1999: 75). In other words, if you had a chair in your own house, should someone of higher rank arrive, you would give up your chair to that person. Like a bed, canopies and fabrics further denoted prestige and authority, as would the addition of a footstool (Eames 1977: 202; Morley 1999: 76). Since antiquity, the X-frame chair, folding chair, and faldstool had connoted imperial, royal, or ecclesiastic authority (Eames 1977: 181–4; Morley 1999: 78). To that point, in Italian inventories, the X-chair may be referred to as "alla cardinalesca (cardinal's chair)" (Stapleford 2013: 16). Recalling this tradition, fifteenth-century Italian domestic chairs were likewise prestigious, so esteemed that, like beds, they could be given as diplomatic gifts (Thornton 1991: 191). More commonplace were rustic stools, three- or four-legged seats that could be dressed up with a back, with paint, or with leather as noted in a desk stool for Lorenzo de' Medici (148).

Buffets

Complementary to tables were buffets or *credenze* found in *sale* or halls (and occasionally chambers). Buffets provided storage and were also display furnishings, which ranged from simple to extravagant depending on the status of the family or the significance of the event for which it was in use. Throughout the later Middle Ages, the simplest buffet was an elaboration of the table boards to create a sideboard or cupboard. Auxiliary to tables, buffets were typically against walls; a buffet was a table with an additional tier or platform to aid in service or to display wares, and in some cases used for storage of those wares. However, despite the potentially rudimentary nature of such a structure, its ceremonial display function, like that of a bed or a table, was enhanced and confirmed through its adornment with fabrics and textiles. Indeed, no buffet or *credenza* in this era was complete without these associated items (Eames 1977: 56–8; Thornton 1991: 220). The growing popularity of buffets in the late Middle Ages is demonstrated by their documented use at various ceremonial, domestic functions, such as hosting esteemed guests, weddings, births, and even at funeral gatherings. The purpose of the buffet is best appreciated in the context of the hall or *sala*. Comparable to the role of tables, buffets communicated the family's/host's wealth, power, dignity, and status. Like beds, buffets were subject to social convention so that for those with a higher social rank, it was acceptable to have several tiers or stages on a buffet. In fact, because buffets were covered with cloth, the wooden buffet itself could be very simple and still communicate high status through the number of its tiers (Morley 1999: 78). A noteworthy breach of protocol associated with multitiered buffets occurred in Bruges in 1478 when Mary, the Duchess of Burgundy, used a five-stage buffet when, according to custom, Mary should have only used four shelves (Karaskova 2012: 320). The buffet was in her chambers as part of formal celebrations following the birth of her son Philip. According to Aliénor de Poitiers, the number of shelves on a buffet communicated rank; if a common local woman had a buffet in her chambers, she could have one shelf, a noblewoman two or three, and a princess or duchess such as Mary could have four (320). Five shelves was reserved only for the Queen of France (Eames 1977: 57; Morley 1999: 70).

Unfortunately, but not surprisingly, no stepped or tiered buffet from the Middle Ages has survived, so scholars rely on documentary evidence that recorded them as central fixtures of important family events. Wedding celebrations were a cause to set up a buffet, cover it in fine cloth, and display and arrange plate on it making the furniture and its adornments a dominant visual element in the hall on such occasions. The impending 1429 marriage between Philip the Good and Isabelle of Portugal included festivities in a newly constructed hall in Bruges in which the "buffet of five stages, measuring 70' long and 20' high" allowed the finery on the stages to be ranked, with the most precious objects on the uppermost stages (Eames 1977: 57, n. 140).[11] The description of one of the marriage banquets for Margaret of York and Charles the Bold (1468) by Oliver de la Marche quoted earlier also cited a buffet (in this case, a "lozenge-shaped sideboard") with storage and many shelves. Though storage of finery was possible in some buffets, not all had fixed, lockable doors. Storage was a secondary feature of buffets, one that certainly allowed for appropriate household management, but above all, in feudal aristocratic households the primary role was to promote the status of the family.

From this aristocratic tradition elite mercantile families in republican Florence adopted, adapted, and used their *credenze*. The *credenza* is essentially the Italian version of the buffet: it was typically placed against a wall, often in the *sala*, and comprised a lower-level cabinet and shelves above it. A few recorded *credenze* were described as elaborately carved wood pieces, such as the one owned by Niccolò III, Lord of Ferrara, in 1436 for his private dining room (Thornton 1991: 220). However, most *credenze* up to and through the fifteenth century were typically simple wooden forms with the cabinet (cupboard) below for safekeeping objects and with shelves or stages above for displaying prized objects. Like so many objects and furnishings in the Italian palazzo, the *credenza* was accessorized for receptions. When it was clad in textiles and decorated with plate, maiolica, and crystal, the display heralded the status and dignity of the homeowner, as well as conveying connections to past domestic events and celebrations when the *credenza* was likewise ornamented. James Lindow's discussion of this furniture included examples of how and when it was used by various Florentine families. Specifically, the journal of the wealthy Florentine merchant Giovanni Rucellai described his *credenza* as a sumptuous display vehicle for their silver during the wedding festivities for his son Bernardo in 1466 (Lindow 2007: 139; see also Maso Fineguerra's 1460 drawing that includes a *credenza*). In describing this type of furniture, Lindow integrated it into a larger discussion on the decorum of the "splendid" interior and, accordingly, cited Giovanni Pontano's *De Splendore* (1498), which highlighted the appropriateness of elite families owning, and therefore displaying, various quality objects (Lindow 2007: 138; Welch 2002). Though Welch argued that Pontano's *De Splendore* was not a prescriptive guide, Pontano's writing provides insights into how domestic objects and furnishings were elevated beyond mere utility to promote their role in eliciting "admiration" (Welch 2002: 215).

Whether for daily family use, celebration, or pretensions, there was remarkable consistency among critical furnishings during the entire period discussed here. Great and humble families all had domestic rituals wherein furniture was used, for instance, to display and welcome guests on various occasions. Over generations, particular furnishings became requisite actors around which family dramas and events took place. The durability of family traditions existed together with the longevity of specific objects; as familial customs provided continuity from year to year and between generations, so too did certain furniture, such as chests or *credenze*, thereby making them touchstones to the family's past and foundations to the family's future.

CHAPTER FIVE

The Public Setting

MATTHEW M. REEVE

This chapter considers the most public monuments of medieval furniture in the period 500–1500 from both the great household and the great church. It explores the furnishings of the physical and performance spaces of power and authority of medieval Europe, from the thrones of kings, their tapestries and beds, to the liturgical furnishings of its great cathedrals, their choir stalls, altars, and *cathedrae*. Although we can certainly lament a dearth of evidence—both documentary and material—for the early centuries under consideration here, the years between 1000 and 1500 offer a remarkable range of monuments, only a handful of which can be considered. The later Middle Ages also offer a wealth of evidence derived from literature, written accounts, household manuals, and other sources that substantially buttress the material record. This chapter shall be focused on movable objects. As such, tapestries, tables, thrones, lecterns, beds and chests fall within its domain, while stone choir screens, pavements, and wall paintings do not, unless they relate in a significant way to the uses or meanings of the furniture. To lend some coherence to the evidence, I shall focus in particular upon England, although I shall have occasion to refer to furnishings throughout Europe.

Having raised the issue of definitions, it is useful to consider some of the terms that will be used in this account. The concept of the public setting, for example, poses some problems when applied to the Middle Ages. The idea of public space (and therefore of private space) follows modernist divisions and allegorizations of space that have few straightforward analogies in the medieval world. These divisions are reflected in the canonical texts of modern furniture, such as Penny Sparke's influential *The Modern Interior* (2008), which employs them to divide the book into two halves, but were never employed in this sense in the Middle Ages. While the period certainly witnessed profound social changes that created certain divisions of public and private that might be understood to anticipate the divisions of the eighteenth century (most famously in Norbert Elias's influential account of *The Civilizing Process* [2000]), these must be treated with great care. The bedchamber of Henry III at Westminster Abbey (of which more will be said below) is a useful case in point: although a "private" space of rest with a significant canopied bed that was framed by wall painting, Henry's chamber also appears to have been used to receive guests, conduct aspects of administration, and even to observe the Mass, thereby challenging any modern sense of the functions and meanings of "public" and "private" (or for that matter "sacred" and "secular") space.

Here, as elsewhere in this volume, the terms "furniture" and "setting" also require some qualification. Our sense of furniture, and of furniture history as a discipline, is premised on the modernist appraisal of architecture and the built environment generally. The modern movement that significantly gave birth to the discipline of furniture history sought to separate ornament from architecture: the cornices, moldings, applied ornament such as stucco and so on were replaced by the now familiar unadorned walls and rectilinear glass planes familiar to moderns. The signally important statement of this division is surely Adolf Loos's canonical essay "Ornament and Crime" (1908) that posits an ethical split of architecture (or structure) from ornament, in which ornamentation becomes a criminal perversion of architecture itself (Loos 1997; Canales and Herscher 2005). The modern period saw not only the reduction of architectural ornament from buildings, but, crucially for our purposes, the displacement of this ornamentation and its meanings to the furnishings of the interior, which gained meaning in part through sheer visual contrast with their un- or minimally articulated settings. This revaluing of furnishings surely informs Fernand Léger's view that the "most significant event of our times is the rise in importance of the object" (Payne 2012: 1). This conception of architecture as a sphere of cultural production somehow emancipated from its objects and ornamentation informed the creation of the modern categories of the decorative arts and of furniture history, discourses in which objects and furnishings serve to frame, interpret, and narrate architecture.

I open with this brief excursus on the shaping of the disciplines of furniture history and the history of the interior to remind us of the stark differences between modern and premodern approaches to architectural space and its furnishings, and to public space in particular. This division of architecture and furniture, however much our current language of critique is grounded in it, had little to do with medieval conceptions of furniture and its role in the built environment. In many respects, the public monuments under consideration here—which by their inherent nature are deliberately contrived displays designed to be experienced via or through formal ritual activity—are far closer to the installation art or site-specific art of postmodernity than these modernist paradigms. Consider the Museum of Contemporary Art (MOCA) in Los Angeles' definition of installation art:

> The everyday meaning of installation refers to the hanging of pictures or the arrangement of objects in an exhibition. The less generic, more recent meaning of installation is a site-specific artwork. In this sense, the installation is created especially for a particular gallery space or outdoor site, and it comprises not just a group of discrete art objects to be viewed as individual works but an entire ensemble or environment. Installations provide viewers with the experience of being surrounded by art, as in a mural-decorated public space or an art-enriched cathedral.
>
> (MOCA n.d.)

While I take the inherent differences between pre- and postmodern art practices as read, their congruities have not gone unnoticed in recent scholarship (Nagel 2011). MOCA's definition provides a useful working definition of public art spaces in general that is readily employed for my present purposes. The possibility of works being viewed discretely as singular objects in space and then appraised holistically as an ensemble or environment usefully transfers to the realities of premodern public art.

This is underscored by several features inherent in the making and experience of medieval furniture. The religious and secular settings under discussion here, like installation art in the present, became animated and narrativized through ritual interaction with their viewers/users. Simply put, the monuments only became fully artful when they were experienced and understood in relation to their spaces by their viewers, and in relation to a series of prescribed ritual ceremonies, whether religious or secular. In terms of style there was a fluid stylistic relationship between architecture and furniture. Especially from the thirteenth century onward, furnishings frequently bore the same microarchitectural designs of macroarchitecture, and were often designed by architects as installations within broader environments. While naturally conceived within the existing conventions of their retrospective typologies (i.e., choir stalls had misericords, thrones were often backdated to emphasize their venerability, etc), medieval furnishings frequently bore a common stylistic or ornamental vocabulary with the buildings they graced. There was, in other words, no distinct furniture style in the Middle Ages, or at least not a dominant one. A major reason is that, for much of the period under consideration here, furniture making was a profession that was synonymous with, related to, or conducted alongside carpentry, sculpture, architecture, and painting (e.g., Eames 1997: 230–4). It is clear from extensive documentation that architects were responsible for monumental buildings as much as their furnishings, from chairs in marble to wooden choir stalls, or that makers of marble furniture also worked in the same material as pavers, tomb makers, and so on.

To set this study in context, we might look at two famous visual descriptions of interior spaces: the first is the "plan" of the east end of St Augustine's Abbey in Canterbury drawn by Thomas of Elmham around 1410 (Hyatt 2000; Kaneko 2018) (Figure 5.1); and the second is the January page from the Duc de Berry's *Très Riches Heures* (c. 1411–16), which shows the Duc and his court in the traditional labor of feasting (Plate 15). Thomas of Elmham's drawing appears in his *Speculum Augustinianum*, a chronicle of the history and antiquities of St Augustine's Abbey. In contrast to our modern plotting of architectural space on proportionally accurate plans that indicate the negative and positive spaces of architecture, the criss-crossing of vault patterns, etc., Elmham's plan dissolves the building into an abstract envelope devoid of elevation or scale, much less "structure" or "style." He focuses on what he manifestly took to be the dominant physical and thematic anchor points of the building, namely its furnishings: the choir screen with its two doors or *ostia*—which officially separated lay and sacred space, its altars and reliquaries. These provide a sacred itinerary for the east arm—its performance script—moving the eyes and mind of the viewer from altar to altar within the *locus sanctus* or holy place. Elmham's drawing also functions as a visual inventory or relic list of the abbey's relics, albeit one plotted out in the space of the abbey's eastern arm rather than the textual accounts more common in the Middle Ages (e.g., Howley 2009). In all of these features, Elmham's drawing echoes the approaches employed in medieval texts: while chroniclers were loquacious about the qualities, materials, and significance of liturgical furnishings (and the furnishings of secular buildings for that matter), emphasizing the preciousness of material, the quality of craftsmanship (as in Abbot Suger's use of the Horatian tag *materiam superbat opus* [the workmanship surpassed the materials] in his description of Saint Denis) and their spiritual and political significance, we look in vain for careful stylistic accounts of medieval buildings. Turning to the *Très Riches Heures*, our perspective is lowered and focused into an intimate scene presumably set in one of the Duc de Berry's great halls. The somewhat claustrophobic scene—tightly cropped by the Limbourg Brothers—gives the eye little rest as it darts from character to character and object to object, invariably fixing on the Duc himself, positioned at center right, silhouetted against the woven firescreen and beneath the projecting tester. Despite its stunning verisimilitude, the January page does not present anything like a "portrait" of the interior of a specific hall. Indeed, aside from the ornamentation on the fireplace, the hall could be any hall owned or used by the Duc (it has not been identified securely as an individual place by scholars). Here too, the focus of the image is its objects—it is the colorful bodies of the courtiers, the walls wrapped in a stunning tapestry celebrating

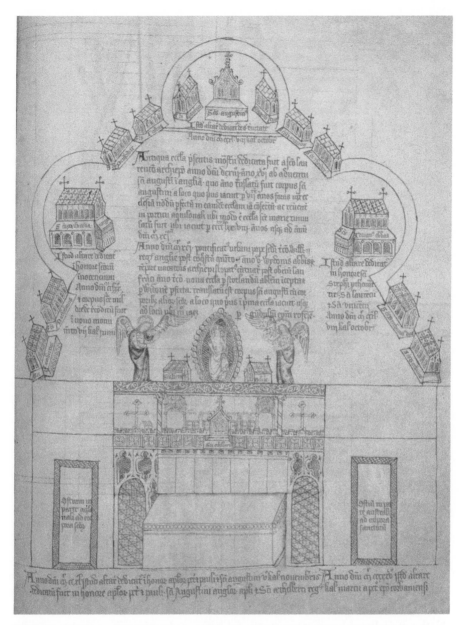

FIGURE 5.1 Plan of St Augustine's Abbey. Cambridge University, Trinity Hall
MS 1, f. 77r. Photograph courtesy of Master and Fellows of Trinity Hall, Cambridge.

the Trojan Wars, and its gleaming furnishings that populate the space. The approach here is thus not dissimilar to the Canterbury drawing: it provides a carefully articulated visual inventory of the furnishings of a great room rather than of the room itself, again providing a close analogy with textual inventories (in this case the famous household inventories of the Duc de Berry). This must in some sense be a response to the tastes and desires of a great collector: it has often been suggested that the oversized *salière du pavillon* (salt cellar in the shape of a ship) pictured was that listed in the Duc's household inventories (Longnon and Cazelles 1989: 173; cf. van Rijen 2000: 166–73). As Michael Camille has argued, the January page is remarkable not only for its display of the interior of a great hall, but also for its complex psychosexual pictorialization of the Duc's acquisitional and sexual attitudes: as he collected objects, so he collected young men, both of which are on display in this idealized image of his court (Camille 2001).

THE GREAT HOUSEHOLD

The vicissitudes of postmedieval history throughout Europe mean that the furnishings of the great church survive in far greater numbers than those of the great household. Fundamental changes in the social structure of Europe meant the disruption of a traditional aristocratic life centered around the great or seigniorial household and a dismantling of its contents. Few great households have continuous inventories of their furnishings stretching from our period through to the present. Much of the furniture that does now exist has been carefully cataloged but unfortunately its dispersal means we can no longer know its original functions or contexts within the household (if indeed it was used in the household at all). As such, to a far greater extent than the great church, the great household requires careful reconstruction of its furnishings and their architectural contexts. But here too some of the furniture under consideration was meant to function differently: throughout our period, the furnishings of the great household were often meant to be collapsible and portable, as the lord traveled throughout his lands with his retinue. High-status furnishings that were likely used in this capacity include monuments such as the Newport Chest, an "altar chest" with painted imagery of the crucifixion under its lid that could also have functioned in a devotional capacity, or even the Wilton Diptych (now in the National Gallery, London), a small, foldable, and eminently portable wooden diptych (53 × 37 centimeters), which features Richard II being presented to the Virgin and Christ Child by the Plantagenet saints John the Baptist, Edward the Confessor, and Edmund (Eames 1977: 111–25, 135; Alexander and Binski 1987: no. 345; Gordon, Monnas, and Elam 1997).

The great hall is deservedly understood as the center of the great household, a feature that it shares with a range of high-status seigneurial buildings, including the town halls of the Low Countries and Italy, episcopal see palaces, and early university colleges. Its status as the nodal point of the great household—in its many manifestations—stretches deeply into the period under consideration here. The well-known descriptions of Heorot in the eighth-century poem *Beowulf* provides a useful starting point:

> Then, as I have heard, the work of constructing a building
> Was proclaimed to many a tribe throughout this middle earth.
> In time—quickly, as such things happen among men—
> It was all ready, the biggest of halls.
> He whose word was law
> Far and wide gave it the name "Heorot."
>
> (lines 74–9)

> The men did not dally.
> They strode inland in a group until they were able to discern the timbered
> hall, splendid and ornamented with gold.
> The building in which that powerful man held court was the foremost of
> halls under heaven
> Its radiance shone over many lands.
>
> (lines 306–11)

> The wall hangings shone,
> Embroidered with gold with many a sight of wonder
> For those that delight to gaze upon them.
>
> (lines 730–2)

The visual prominence and cultural status of the hall as a center of hospitality and governance, its function as a signifier of its lord's authority, and its allegorical significance as a structure that radiated light figuratively illuminating its environment, were topoi that would often be repeated in subsequent descriptions of great halls, whether real or imagined. Its decorations are a focus of the description, particularly its mural decoration. Great halls were richly ornamented with wall paintings, or, in the case of Heorot, hung with hangings that might be permanent or could be folded up and moved from hall to hall as a great lord and his retinue traveled. In either case, visual pleasure or wonder was manifestly a desideratum of mural decorations of the hall interior, from the richly instructional and moralizing imagery of Carolingian Ingelheim, on the Rhine (*c.* 825) drawn from the Old Testament, the New Testament, antique and Frankish history, to the equally historical and moralizing images of the Bayeux Tapestry, quite certainly intended to hang in the episcopal hall of Odo of Bayeux, although its first recorded appearance was in Bayeux Cathedral in the fifteenth century (Davis-Weyer 1986: 84–8; Heslop 2009).

The great hall was the setting of much of what the sociologist Norbert Elias would call *The Civilizing Process*, and it developed a highly sophisticated, quasi-liturgical code of etiquette and conduct. Developed in the schools and transferred to the courtly milieu, the hall, its imagery and furnishings, were governed by an increasingly refined and hierarchical set of social and ethical precepts about bodily comportment. Embodying the ultimately Ciceronian concept that "manners maketh man" later employed by William of Wykeham (1320–1404), clerics penned a new category of conduct literature that informed how the hall, and the household generally, should be used and how the lord should best present his own image of majesty to his followers during the social meal. These conduct manuals sought to transform and remodel aristocratic life along the lines of the cathedral schools into a religious/aristocratic code of living, a Christian habitus now broadly categorized as "chivalry." Significantly, the interior of the great hall changed considerably in the twelfth and thirteenth centuries, adopting many of the architectural features of Gothic religious architecture—notably including tall traceried windows—by which the great hall began to look and feel like the luminous interior of the great church (Reeve 2011) (Figure 5.2). Understanding these codes for the hall, and for its furnishings, usefully underscores the problematic division of sacred and secular in the great household.

While feasting and the communal meal were its main functions, the hall was an inherently multifunctional space, and its furnishings and fittings were generally designed to be moved or removed to allow the hall to function in various administrative and festive capacities. Even before the thirteenth century, great halls were generally divided between a communal feasting space and a separate chamber or "camera" located in the end bay of the hall. These spaces were divided by wooden screens and passage between them (the "screens passage") was accessed via axially-positioned doors on either side of the hall. Thirteenth-century estate literature advises that lords not retreat to their private chambers, but maintain a majestic presence in the great hall to earn "fear and reverence" from their subjects during the social meal. Given their inherently quotidian nature, it is not surprising that these furnishings survive principally in literary and occasionally documentary accounts (for general accounts, see Eames 1977; Boccador 1988; Tracy 1988; Wilson 1991). Our physical evidence for the period up to the fourteenth century derives largely from high-status environments, and from the royal milieu in particular, where documentation exists that substantially buttresses the physical record.

The great hall at the royal palace in Westminster, now known as Westminster Hall, is a case in point. Unlike many halls to which it might be compared, however, it was not designed with feasting as its primary function. From its origin in the eleventh century (the Hall was substantially remodeled by Richard II in the late fourteenth century), the Hall was not intended as a place of regular

FIGURE 5.2 Winchester Hall and Round Table. Photograph by the Author.

feasting (this took place in the Lesser or White Hall in the Palace) but rather as a place of administration and justice (holding the King's Bench, Chancery, and Common Pleas), royal ceremonial (housing the coronation feasts), and even commerce (from the late thirteenth century the hall housed a series of market stalls) (Wilson 1997). While a little is known about the sturdy wooden furniture and screens used in the hall, more is known about the high-status ceremonial furniture used by the king and his court. Located on axis at the center of the south wall of the hall atop the royal dais was the marble throne, commissioned by Henry III in 1245. Although the throne is now lost, its commission is recorded in royal documentation. Featuring a bronze leopard at the foot of each side of the throne (to which two further lions were added in 1267) the throne was raised upon a dais of stone steps to elevate it, creating a visual and thematic focus for the room as a whole. The marble throne at Westminster is quite certainly that rendered in Henry III's great seal of 1259 (Figure 5.3). The iconography of Henry's throne followed the throne of Solomon described in

FIGURE 5.3 Great Seal of Henry III. Durham Cathedral Archives, 1.2.Reg.6a. Photograph reproduced by Kind permission of the Dean and Chapter of Durham Cathedral.

I Kings 10: 18–20 and in 2 Chronicles 9: 17–19 (Collins et al. 2012: 7–11). The design of Henry's throne was not only topical, in that it served to reinforce his status as a wise and judicious judge following hallowed biblical precedent, but it also followed a long-standing royal and imperial tradition of Solomonic allusion in high-status furniture. Most obvious, perhaps, is Charlemagne's marble throne in his palace chapel at Aachen, Germany, which was raised upon six steps in evocation of Solomon's. The tribune screen and baldachin (ceremonial canopy) in the Saint Chapelle in Paris created by Louis IX by 1248 likewise alluded to the Solomonic prototype: transforming the iconography of a seat into the architecture of a monumental screen, it features a central baldachin with flanking steps in microarchitectural tabernacles (Weiss 1995). Solomonic allusions also extended to the other major royal seats of power in England for which we have evidence, namely the Coronation Chair at Westminster Abbey, designed as a seat of power and a reliquary container for the sacred stone of Scone (Binski 2003) (Plate 16).

Returning to Westminster Hall, it is undoubtedly not a coincidence that the other great Purbeck marble throne in England was the archbishop's throne at Canterbury, thus seating the respective secular and religious heads of medieval England. The royal throne was one of at least two marble pieces of furniture used in the hall, including the king's high table that stood below it at the south end. The making of the table is not documented, but the royal accounts mention its existence (as in a 1253 account dictating Peter de Hispania and other painters create a painting behind or above the table [*ultra mensam*]) (Collins et al. 2012: 210). The iconography of the painting is not known, but it remains significant that the painting served as a visual (and doubtlessly thematic) backdrop for the king's table. Fortunately, the discovery of three of the original Purbeck marble trestles for the table has allowed for a reliable reconstruction: current interpretations indicate that the twelve-foot table had marble slabs carried upon six trestles that allowed for five settings—two flanking the king on each side. Here too, it is not coincidental that an analogous marble high table graced the Grand Salle at the Capetian royal palace in Paris, the Palais de la Cité. It was recorded in Jean of Jandun's encomium *Tractatus de laudibus parisius* (1323):

> There is a marble table there, set so that it reflects the light of the western windows in its smooth and highly polished surface while the guests sit facing east. It is so large in fact, that I fear I would not be believed were I to give its measurements without offering some kind of proof.
>
> (Inglis 2003: 68)

Furniture of this sort was manifestly exceptional: emphasizing royal largesse and splendor, and created in a material that signified both nobility and venerability, the two royal tables speak of a politics of emulation in art and architecture that defined court patronage in the period.

Great halls also had a wide range of festive, heraldic, and purely decorative furnishings. Among the most spectacular examples from our period are the so-called Dacre Beasts (*c.* 1520) (Marks and Williamson 2003: no. 156). Four full-sized oak beasts (measuring between 185 to 206 centimeters), they are rare survivors of a tradition of heraldic ornament in the great hall. Each was designed to hold a staff and a flag bearing family heraldry. In this case the Red Bull is the crest of the commissioner, Thomas, Lord Dacre (1467–1525); the Dolphin represents his wife Elizabeth de Greystoke (1471–1516); the Black Gryphon represents the Dacres of Gilsland (Lord Dacre's forebears); and the White Ram is the supporter of the arms of the Multon family (the barony of Gilsland was acquired when Ranulph de Dacre wed Margaret de Multon in 1317). There remains now some dispute about which Dacre hall these were intended to grace: they stood in Naworth Castle in Cumbria until 1999, although they were possibly intended for the great hall at Kirkoswald, another Dacre household, also in Cumbria. In any case, these beasts served to emphasize the antiquity of the Dacre family and its formation through dynastic alliances. Also worthy of discussion here is the Round Table at Winchester, Hampshire (Figure 5.2). Measuring 5.5 meters in diameter, the table is a monumental piece of furniture made from English oak, intended as a recreation of the fabled round table of Arthurian romance. Even before the table's construction, Winchester had established connections to the Arthurian legend via Geoffrey of Monmouth's *Historia Regum Britaniae* (*c.* 1130), which would be developed by Chrétien de Troyes, who made Winchester the capital of King Arthur. The table now hangs on the end wall of the great hall at Winchester Castle, where it was recorded in 1464 in John Hardyng's *Chronicle*, but it was clearly meant to be usable at least occasionally, since it bears holes for twelve removable legs (Biddle 2000). Dendrochronological analysis and carbon dating has confirmed that it was most likely constructed in the late thirteenth century during the reign of Edward I (1272–1307). The painted surface divides the table radially into twenty-six seatings (with King Arthur naturally at the cardinal point), each identified with an inscription (i.e., "S[ir] gauen," "S[ir] galahallt," "S[ir] p[er] cyvale," etc.). A recent study of the table suggests that it may have been created in 1289 in anticipation of the celebration of the engagements of Edward's three children and a great tournament held in Winchester in 1290. In this context, it can be understood as a natural extension of the cult of Arthur during Edward's reign, a manifestation of the overtly chivalric glamour of Edward's so-called Arthurian enthusiasm (Loomis 1953: 114–27). A monumental piece of state furniture, the Round Table was used by various monarchs to different political and dynastic ends: for its patron Edward I, Arthur was a royal ancestor and an established political allusion, because like Arthur, Edward reunited England,

Scotland, and Wales under a single king. The table was transformed from a functional piece of furniture to a symbol of royal dynasty under Edward III when it was first hung up and probably covered by a painted covering in leather or another material. Its present painting dates to the sixteenth century; previous to this time the table must have seemed an austere if awesome relic of ancient British kingship.

The room known as the chamber—briefly alluded to above—likewise served myriad functions, from dining, to administration and retirement from court life (see also Chapter 4 in this volume). The significance of the chamber as a semi-private space within aristocratic life is underscored in a lengthy literary tradition that celebrated it and its furnishings. Consider Boudri of Bourgueil's famous account of Countess Adele of Blois's chamber (*c.* 1107):

> The walls are covered with tapestries, woven according to her design, and all seem alive: on one wall, creation, the fall and fratricide, the flood with fish on mountain tops and lions in the sea; sacred history from Noah through Abraham, Jacob, Joseph, the glory of Moses, and David to Solomon on a second wall; the Greek gods and myths, Phaethon, Ganymede, Cadmus, Pyramis and Thisbe, Hermaphroditus, Orpheus, Troy, and Roman kings on a third; around her bed the conquest of England, William's claims to the throne as Edward's chosen successor, the comet, the Norman council and preparations, the fleet, the battle of Hastings with the feigned flight of the Normans and the real one of the English, and the death of Harold.
>
> On the ceiling, the sky with its constellations, the signs of the zodiac, the stars and planets described in detail. On the floor, a map of the world with its seas, rivers, and mountains, named along with their creatures, and the cities on the land masses of Asia, Europe, and Africa. The bed is decorated with three groups of statues, of Philosophy and the liberal arts, the quadrivium (music, arithmetic, astronomy, geometry) at the head of the bed, the trivium (rhetoric, dialectic, and grammar) at the foot. The third group represents medicine, with Galen and Hippocrates, the humors and physical characteristics, herbs and unguents.[1]

Baudri was clear that the "lovely chamber" he "painted" was as much an imaginative fantasy as anything based upon the realities of Adele's or any other contemporary chamber. The account nevertheless describes a spectacular chamber hung with tapestries apparently designed by its dedicatee recounting Old Testament, Greek and Roman history, and the Norman Conquest of England—most famous being its miniature copy of the Bayeux Tapestry—a bed decorated with sculptures (?) of philosophy and the liberal arts, a painted (?) ceiling of the cosmos, and a floor mosaic formed as a *mappa mundi*. While we cannot consider this to be an accurate account of her chamber, this site-specific environment does speak (in overtly flattering terms) to the intellectual, historical, and ethical tenor of interior decoration within the elite chamber.

It reflects the conception of a bedchamber and its furnishings and imagery inherited from the antique world as a place for thought and reflection, for the bedchamber to function as a "meditational machine" (Carruthers 2000: 171–8, 213–20). As such, Adele's chamber in Baudri's account becomes an imaginative pictorialization of the tastes and historical knowledge of an elite woman *via* its furnishings.

That the chamber and its furnishings were considered in certain elite contexts as a space for pedagogy, instruction, and moral and ethical reflection is suggested in a range of texts. Saint Hugh of Lincoln's hagiography recounts, for example, that he would retire to his chamber after dining in the hall with his guests to entertain them with instructive tales of the famous men of history (Douie and Farmer 1962: 202). It is rare in the high Middle Ages that we have direct documentary evidence for the forms and furnishings of an actual great chamber. The King's or Painted Chamber at Westminster is thus of significance. A room of state forming one side of a cloister with St Stephen's Chapel and the Lesser Hall, and adjoining the Queen's Chamber and Chapel, the Painted Chamber was a significant room of state in the royal palace. Measuring 24.5 × 7.9 meters it was a substantial chamber, with the royal bed at the east end of the north wall. The lion's share of attention on the Painted Chamber has deservedly been paid to its remarkable thirteenth-century wall paintings, their dating and patronage. For the present purposes, it will do to focus on the royal bed. Documentary evidence from the 1240s indicates that Henry III (1216–72) ordered the bed to be made with green posts powdered with gold stars with a canopy or *celour* painted by Master William, from which hung curtains (Binski 1986: 13–15, 35–8). Henry's bed is an early documented example of a bed of state with a projecting tester or canopy that would become common in elite contexts during the fourteenth century. Evidence for beds of this sort, and particularly for rich hangings on or around beds complete with heraldic blazons and other motifs are evident later in the century in the household inventories of Mahaut, Countess of Artois and Burgundy (1268–1329) and can be charted with frequency in later fourteenth- and fifteenth-century manuscript painting (Eames 1977: 74–6). Henry's bed appears to have been carefully coordinated with the imagery in his chamber: its canopy framed hagiographical imagery in mural painting of the coronation of Saint Edward the Confessor, his royal ancestor and the subject of much of his patronage at Westminster. Edward's profound devotion to Saint Edward is well known, and in his own chamber it became the mise-en-scène to his sleeping and waking activities in bed—it too was imagery and furniture to "think with." To either side of the coronation were two soldiers—on both sides of the bed—who perpetually stood guard over the king in evocation of Solomon (Canticles 3:7–8). The splays in the windows were painted with virtues and vices: enjoying a long pedigree in medieval art, these illustrated moral lessons for the king, such as *Debonereté* trampling

Ire, or *Largesce* choking the figure of *Covoitise* with gold coins (Binski 1986; Hyams 1998). This imagery was glossed by the painted inscription above the door stating "He who does not give what he most prizes does not get what he most desires" (*Ke ne dune ke ne tine ne prent ke desire*) (Binski 1986: 35). Positioned in the wall behind Henry's bed at 1.5 meters from the floor was a glazed quatrefoil squint that allowed the king to gaze through the wall into the chapel beyond, presumably to watch the elevation of the host from the comfort of his own bed. Unfortunately we know less than we would like about the actual functions of the Painted Chamber during Henry's reign and thus about the bed itself: it appears to have served as the king's own chamber for private meetings and assemblies, and occasionally as an overflow room for public almsgiving.

THE GREAT CHURCH

Like the furnishings of the Great Household, the furnishings of the Great Church can be usefully examined according to the broad spatial and functional (liturgical) divisions of the building itself. The influential liturgical commentator William Durandus (*c.* 1237–96) frequently evoked a threefold structure for church furnishings: the furnishings of the altar, the furnishings of the choir, and the furnishings of the spaces to the west of the choir screen. As a liturgical commentator, Durandus offered a rich, multifaceted allegory of the church and its spaces and furnishings: the chancel—the "head" of the church—holds the altar (signifying Christ) and thus represents humility; the choir, holding the monks' or canons' choir stalls—"is the harmonious gathering place of the singers, or the multitude gathered for the sacred mysteries"; while "the remaining part extending to the west is seen as the rest of the body" (Thibodeau 2007). Durandus manifestly imposes a sacred and spatial hierarchy on the spaces of the church, moving from east to west. Durandus based his text closely upon the wisdom of earlier commentators, leaving no doubt that these were well-established divisions in the great church. I shall follow them here and focus in particular on the furnishings east of the choir screen.

At the physical and thematic center of the liturgy, the high altar was the focus of the great church. It receives a lengthy subchapter in Durandus's account, which should be required reading for all students of medieval furniture. First, the altar itself: a semipermanent stone or marble table raised on four legs and decorated with Eucharistic symbols (XP or Chi Ro, vines referring to Chapter 15 of Saint John's Gospel, etc.) were a development of the fourth and fifth centuries, such as can be seen on the Minerve altar in Marseille (Musée Borély), which is associated with Saint Rusticus, around 456 (wooden altars were banned at the Council of Epaone in 517). A later example of this type is the stunning altar at Saint-Sernin in Toulouse carved from a monolithic slab of (probably spoliated) marble, consecrated May 16, 1096, by Pope Urban II and signed by the sculptor Gislebertus (although it is raised on a pedestal base) (Lyman 1982) (Plate 17).

Through the course of the Middle Ages, the high altar became a multimedia ensemble comprising frontals, altarpieces, and a host of liturgical furnishings—notably the pyx, paten, chalice, and mass books required for celebration of the Mass. The altarpiece—the wooden, metalwork, or stone image behind the altar—is surely its most significant development. Conceived in wood, stone, and occasionally wall painting and stained glass, the altar image sits somewhat uneasily within the rubrics of furniture employed in this volume. This specific type of monument, nevertheless, demands consideration, particularly when created in unfixed and portable wood. Most famous, perhaps, is Duccio's *Maestà*, the monumental wooden high altarpiece of the Duomo in Siena, Italy, created between 1308 and 1311, which was carried through the streets of Siena and around the Piazza del Campo (the main square) before being interred in the Duomo (Norman 1999: 21–2). Another example is suggested by Henry III's 1237 commission of five painted panels (*tabulae quadratae*) featuring a Majesty of Christ, a Virgin Mary, a Crucifixion with Mary and Saint John, a Coronation and a Transfiguration to be employed in royal processions (Binski 2004: 163). It is hardly possible here to explore fully the development of the altar image (for a recent treatment, see Binski 2010). It will suffice to state that, even if the earliest physical evidence we have dates from the thirteenth century, the altarpiece was a much earlier development. Its origins are obscured by a dearth of physical evidence—caused by regular remaking during the Middle Ages and by subsequent religious reformations in different parts of Europe. While much debate surrounds when and why imagery began to be placed upon the altar, and the extent to which practice was influenced by legislation, it is surely significant that from the beginnings of the organized Catholic rite, images—often in painting or mosaic on the apse above the altar, provided a vital pictorialization of the mysteries of the Eucharist (Thunø 2015). The altarpiece was, in one sense or another, an elaboration of this well-established relationship.

In England, the earliest extant wooden altarpiece is the Westminster Retable, a monument now datable to between 1259 and 1269 (Binski and Massing 2009) (Figure 5.4). Scholars largely agree that the retable was employed as the

FIGURE 5.4 Westminster Retable. Photograph by the Author.

high altarpiece of Westminster Abbey and was thus commissioned by Henry III (1216–72) for whom the altar area served as a kind of family chapel. Made from oak panels, the retable was a substantial piece of liturgical furniture, measuring 333 centimeters wide × 95 centimeters high. Its side panels (now comprising Saint Peter and Saint Paul, respectively) were a late alteration to the original design that substantially lengthened the panel prior to its decoration. Due to its deleterious postmedieval history, the painted surface and the wooden microarchitectural frames and inlays have suffered considerable damage. Still, the general iconography of the panel is known: at the center is Christ, the Virgin, and Saint John beneath canopied microarchitectural niches, the left section containing the miracles of Christ within four interlocking eight-pointed stars, the right section is now lost, and the lateral panel of Peter (left) is extant while Paul (right) is now lost. As Christopher Wilson has pointed out, the applied microarchitectural and inlaid frames of the altarpiece—and particularly the central panel with its fashionably French triple gables—clearly reflect the influence of the west façade of Amiens Cathedral, which most concisely parallels the crocketed gables divided by rising spires (Wilson 2009). Other features of the retable, the *kufesque* or pseudoscript hem of Saint Peter's robe, and particularly the eight-pointed stars inlaid with pointed crosses, manifestly hail from the Islamic or Mediterranean world, even if both features had been employed in European art in the years before and during the construction of the retable (Michael 2009; on pseudoscript in medieval painting, see Nagel 2011). The broad appraisal of taste and style reflect in a very real sense the internationalism of the Plantagenet court during the Henrician period (1216–72).

Thrones provide a second category of furniture within the sanctuary or chancel of the great church. Intended as ceremonial seats of their abbots or bishops, even if they seldom sat in them (especially in the later Middle Ages), thrones served to articulate the very status of a great church—as the *cathedra* or *sede episcopi*—literally the seat of a bishop, thereby functioning as a permanent signifier of the institution's exalted cathedral status. Articulating pedigree and concomitant mythologies of institutional power, thrones share strategies of historical self-fashioning common to medieval institutions generally. Key to this was the appeal to tradition. Thrones engaged in complex practices of rustication and even forgery to enhance their venerability. This could be achieved by the addition of inscriptions that assigned their manufacture to the distant past, by back-dating them stylistically, or by giving them the names of a venerated original throne. The *sella curulis* at Saint-Denis is a case in point. During his celebrated rebuilding of Saint-Denis, Abbot Suger records remaking (*refici*) the ancient chair (which probably only entailed renewing the backrest and arms of the ninth-century Carolingian original) but does not record that the appellation *of Dagobert* (King Dagobert [r. 603–39]) was also his own invention (Weinberger 1964; Gaborit-Chopin 1991). Suger's remaking and backdating of the throne was part of a broader campaign to emphasize the abbey's status as the royal abbey par excellence via its hallowed role as royal necropolis and keeper of the royal regalia. Functioning as the throne upon which the kings of France sat to receive homage from the lords of the kingdom, and appearing on the great seal of Louis VII (ascended the throne in 1137), Saint-Denis's throne of Dagobert was a tangible sign that the abbey in fact sustained and connected *Les Trois Races*: Merovingian, Carolingian, and Capetian (Bedos-Rezak 1986).

As Lawrence Nees has shown, the celebrated group of Italian twelfth-century episcopal thrones at Bari, Monte Sant'Angelo, Casosa di Puglia, Salerno, Saint Clemente (Rome), and elsewhere also participated in this retrospective artistry. Forming two relatively distinct groups, the Apulo-Sicilian monuments with their distinctive pedimental backs appear to descend from the celebrated *cathedra Petri* in the Vatican (connected in the period to Saint Peter himself), while the circular-backed Roman thrones descend from a lost throne in the Vatican associated with Pope Sylvester (r.314–35) and Constantine (d.337). But more than suggesting a formal and iconographic succession from a venerated prototype, these monuments variously employed forged inscriptions to backdate them to a previous period (as in the case of Bari), or even employing ancient spolia. The thrones at Salerno (1120s) and Saint Clemente, for example, each incorporate ancient fabric into their construction: Salerno's lion armrests are third or fourth century, and the backrest at Saint Clemente, bearing the inscription MARTYR that breaks from the borders of the top and bottom, leaves no doubt that it is indeed a repurposed monument, meant to be readily understood as such (Nees 1993, 1996). This tradition extends to Venice, where the eleventh- or twelfth-century throne at San Pietro di Castello (the so-called chair of Saint Peter) incorporates an Islamic funerary stele as its backrest (Carboni 2007: 325, cat. no. 87). Although conceived in metalwork rather than marble, the aforementioned Throne of Dagobert engages in a related form of retrospective artistry by refashioning an ancient seat: indeed, its pedimental back pierced by round oculi clearly reflect the Saint Peter's model.

While such Italian monuments survive to a far greater extent than their northern European relatives, an important exception is the so-called throne of Saint Augustine—the archiepiscopal throne of England at Canterbury Cathedral. Saint Augustine's chair was positioned within a truly site-specific context: located atop the stairs leading to the upper church and cult center, the throne was a visible sign of Canterbury's archiepiscopal authority from both the stalls in the choir and the upper church (Figure 5.5). In the upper church, it was set on an axis with the shrine of Thomas Becket (from 1220) and with the head reliquary in the "Corona" chapel, forming a line of episcopal monuments connecting the current bishop with his saintly predecessor. Carved from three pieces of gray-green Purbeck marble, the chair can be dated with precision by the monastery's treasurer's accounts, which record payments over three years for a

FIGURE 5.5 "Throne of St. Augustine" at Canterbury Cathedral. Photograph courtesy of Wikimedia Creative Commons.

sede archiepiscopi. As argued elsewhere, the monastery's patronage of the chair was a symbolic response to an acrimonious dispute between two archbishops who planned to build a new college at Hackington to the north of Canterbury, which would have taken much of the prestige away from Canterbury and largely removed its archbishop. Paid for by the monks, the chair served as both a "gift" to the archbishop for abandoning his plans for a new church and also a solid assertion of their rights to hold the archiepiscopal seat (Reeve 2003).

Typical of the traditions of making thrones discussed so far, the archbishop of Canterbury's throne has a pronounced retrospective character. Although comparanda are hardly abundant, its paneled elevations manifestly hark back to early prototypes, including the sixth-century ivory throne of Maximian of Ravenna. The somewhat anachronistic tau cross termination is difficult to parallel in other monuments, but it is possible that the two partial circles are meant to be an echo of the oculi on the *cathedra Petri*. Given these features it is tempting to suggest that the archiepiscopal throne (the *cathedra Augustini*) was a remaking of the earlier throne from the Romanesque church. In any case, it is significant that the chair fit into a broader institutional aesthetic for the cathedral that reflected its particular relationship to Saint Peter's (with whom it shared a dedication to the Savior "Christ Church") and to the authority of Rome. Gervase of Canterbury, the famous monastic chronicler, usefully epitomizes this relationship: "As Rome is to France and England, and to the Universal Church, so is Canterbury to the church in England" (Gervase of Canterbury 1879: 1:79; Sayers 2000). This idea was reflected in a continual policy of Romanization in the arts of Canterbury from the Anglo-Saxon period to the present. The chronicler Eadmer, for example, was clear that the Anglo-Saxon church was built in the Roman fashion, including a *confessio* modeled after Saint Peter's; this tradition was continued in the early Gothic choir (1174–1220), the marble columns of which reflected Roman prototypes such as Santa Costanza.

The fourteenth century witnessed profound changes in the design and integration of church furnishings, and episcopal thrones in particular. Conceived as parts of wider campaigns to rebuild and refurnish the eastern arms of Exeter, Hereford, Wells, and Durham cathedrals, new thrones were manufactured in wood or stone (Tracy and Budge 2015). These were not thrones in the sense of singular seats of authority, but monumental microarchitectural canopies that held or were integrated with episcopal seats. Employing the technology of microarchitecture developed in architectural draughting, in stained glass canopywork, and realized in monuments such as the Eleanor Crosses, these monuments reflect a new type of episcopal monument. They also reflect the breaking of the *synthronon* arrangement that characterized the Christian church from late antiquity through the thirteenth century, in which the bishop was centrally placed (or his throne was) typically in or near the eastern apse, with his flock of religious seated in flanking choir stalls or other seating (as at Canterbury and elsewhere). Instead, these new monuments were typically placed just east of the choir stalls and on the south side.

Moving westward, Durandus's second division was the choir, which held the stalls of the monks or canons. In England, as in France, there is less evidence than we would like for choir stalls before the thirteenth century. In England, the earliest complete set of choir stalls are those designed for the new cathedral at Salisbury (built from 1220) (Tracy 1987). A reference in the Close Rolls for 1236 records a gift from Henry III to the cathedral from the royal forest of Chippenham. Happily the 106 stalls at Salisbury are in situ. Larger stalls were provided for the elevated positions of the Dean and Precentor on the west side, and the Chancellor and Precentor on the east. Stacked in three tiers of seating, the stalls are perhaps most notable for their extraordinarily restrained character. Although some seats bear their original misericords, the upper canopywork is nineteenth century in date. The stalls were originally backed by the choir enclosure wall, which, as Sarah Brown has suggested, may well have been painted (Brown 1999). Although the Salisbury stalls now seem minimal and even corporate in their regularity and lack of ornamentation (a description that has been applied to the cathedral in general), an understanding of the stalls must engage with the broader allegorical understanding of the cathedral spaces in general. As argued elsewhere, Salisbury's eastern arm was divided into clearly articulated spaces, each ornamented with paintings located upon the vaults directly above. The choir vaults featured a symmetrical arrangement of twenty-four Old Testament worthies, each unfurling a scroll with a prophecy inscribed upon it anticipating the coming of Christ. The Old Testament imagery intersected in many ways with the activities that took place in the choir enclosure directly below, providing a kind of thematic and allegorical gloss on contemporary clerical endeavor. The crucial nexus between the canon's stalls and the Old Testament prophets was a well-established typological conceit, in which the contemporary religious were the successors to the prophets, since as the prophets of the Old Testament anticipated Christ's first coming, so too did contemporary religious await Christ's Second. This allegorical relationship of wall painting to liturgy, furniture, and space was exploited throughout the eastern arm: the eastern crossing held the high altar and on the vaults directly above was an image of Christ in Majesty. As such, as we move from west to east we move through Salvation History itself, from Old Testament prophecy in the choir to fulfillment with Christ at the high altar (Reeve 2008).

Surveys of church furniture such as this can often overlook the fact that throughout the period under consideration here, liturgical spaces, and choir spaces in particular, were not static installations but were frequently decorated or redecorated (*ornatur* or *paratur*) for significant feast days during the liturgical year. Altars were covered with special cloths, choir spaces were hung with tapestries, sacred images and objects were veiled and unveiled for particular liturgical ceremonies, and even the clergy were adorned with particular liturgical vestments. In their cyclic variability, tapestries and textiles—such as the Lenten Veil—were fundamental to the theatricality of the religious rite. For Durandus, these tapestries that decorated the church were allegorized as the virtues that adorn the Christian body, a conceit that ran through much medieval writing on the issue. As Laura Weigert (2004) has shown, choir tapestries were central to late medieval clerical identity and religious devotion. The 1402 choir tapestry at Tournai Cathedral (now in Belgium), hung on the stone wall above the choir stalls and wrapped around the stalls and the west wall of the choir (rood screen), and it represented the lives of the founding bishops Piat (d.286) and Eleutherius (d.532). But more than being simple hagiographies, the saints' lives were carefully intermeshed with that of the city of Tournai itself, representing its early history to the eyes and minds of the cathedral canons. But the tapestry also potentially provided a saintly allegory of clerical endeavor, as the canons gazed across the choir to witness the mise-en-scène of Tournai saints hung directly above their clerical successors in the choir below (Weigert 2004).

It has only been possible in this brief chapter to allude to the potential richness of furniture in the great church and household in the later Middle Ages. In doing so, the interconnectedness of medieval furnishings with the art and architecture of the church and court in general has been emphasized, in part because they are connected at the level of style and manufacture. More profoundly, these premodern connections indicate a broader, ontological relationship of furnishings to their architectural settings that is akin in some respects to postmodern installation art. Like installation art, medieval public furnishings were made meaningful and narrativized through sacred and secular ritual, serving both as their performance script. Pursuing "furniture history" in the Middle Ages demands nothing less than a reexamination of its fundamental premises as a modernist discourse and a reengagement with the modes of producing and using art in the Middle Ages.

CHAPTER SIX

Exhibition and Display

LEAH R. CLARK AND CAROLINE CAMPBELL

The modern relationship between function and display makes it hard to comprehend the concept—so key to the medieval and Renaissance periods—that part of an item of furniture's function existed in its ability (or potential) to perform. Today the word functional is used to describe objects or actions, which do no more than they need to do. A chair that serves its function, for example, enables someone to sit on it and nothing more. During the period under discussion here furniture was of course purposeful, but that purpose might be multifaceted, and more strongly related to display and show than is often the case in the early twenty-first century. In the medieval period, this was partly because the ownership of furniture or movable objects, including beds, chairs, tables, and chests, was restricted very largely to the church and the nobility. The very possession of furniture in the secular sphere, to a surprisingly late date, was reserved to the relative elite, the higher middling and upper orders of society. Very little movable furniture was made, except for noblemen, royalty, and senior clerics. Even in 1418, the Medici family of Florence possessed only six chairs in their principal residence in the Tuscan city (Goldthwaite 1993: 225–9). They were not yet the city's rulers, but they were already renowned throughout Europe for their extraordinary wealth. These six precious seats—objects of desire and status far more than of necessity—were only the beginning of the great expansion in disposable wealth and of conspicuous consumption that played such a part in the development of European furniture. The exhibition and presentation of furniture both to members of the family and household, and to specially invited guests, became central to these objects adequately performing their function.

The rise of movable furniture as a vehicle for display and exhibition in social situations beyond the worlds of the highest-ranking clerics and secular courts is closely related to the culture around luxury, magnificence, and consumption. The fifteenth century witnessed a building boom in large urban family palaces, which influenced and was influenced by theories regarding magnificence and righteous living. The display of a family's wealth and power was thus expressed through their material surroundings, including furniture. These theories are often linked to Italian humanism, but furniture was certainly a social marker in other countries. Indeed, the Burgundian court, for example, was renowned for the display of lavish textiles and gold and silver displayed on *dressoirs*, which certainly impressed and influenced Italian visitors (Belozerskaya 2002). Members of the English royalty and nobility possessed a similar range of opulent movable goods. For instance, the inventories made for the Countess of Suffolk (Geoffrey Chaucer's granddaughter) at Ewelme in Oxfordshire in 1466 record the great chamber with its ceremonial bed, as well as tapestries, hangings, other beds, heirlooms, and even children's clothes (Goodall 2001: 281–5). Across Europe, changes to the layout of rooms and consequently their functions also affected the use, variety, and purpose of furniture. Since homes and palaces were built both for the family who lived there and for visitors, their layout, decoration, and furniture could serve family members and guests alike. As a result these spaces and the possessions that adorned them had a more public function than domestic spaces today and could play a performative role in social rituals (Preyer 1998). Rather than being merely background adornments or practical objects, items of furniture were active performers in conveying the owner's wealth, status, and even knowledge.

This chapter is particularly attentive to the social roles that furniture played in exhibition and display from domestic contexts and courtly entertaining spaces to shops and even ecclesiastical settings. That is, chests, beds, daybeds, dressers, cabinets, cradles, and *credenze* (roughly translated as sideboards or buffets) are examined as social agents within and outside the home. Most of these items were movable, serving varied functions in different locations, and were often integral to displaying or conveying symbolic meaning at particular events. This chapter begins with an examination of cultural approaches to furniture and its changing display functions in the medieval period and the Renaissance, drawing upon primary sources that discuss furniture as well as the layout and function of rooms. It then turns to specific examples of types of display in differing contexts. These vary from the cabinets and rooms built to exhibit worldly goods to cradles, seats, or beds designed to display the body. Categories of types of furniture—chests, beds, cradles, cabinets, and *credenze*—are examined as fluid; many pieces of furniture could serve multiple purposes, as objects of display, as functional pieces, as symbolic actors, or as a combination of all three.

PLATE 1 Jan Van Eyck, *The Arnolfini Portrait*, 1434. London, National Gallery. Photo: VCG Wilson/Corbis/Fine Art/Getty Images.

PLATE 2 Jean de Wavrin, Dukes of York, Gloucester, and Ireland dining with Richard II, in the *Anciennes et Nouvelles Chronique d'Angleterre*, after 1471, before 1483. British Library, Royal MS 14 E IV, f. 265v. Photo © The British Library, Royal 14 E. IV, f.265v 61607 / add_ms_18850_f015v Add. 18850, f.15.

PLATE 3 Daphni Monastery Church, *Birth of the Virgin*, late eleventh century. Dumbarton Oaks. Photo: Irina Andreescu, North Adriatic Project fieldwork records and papers, circa 1974–1990, Dumbarton Oaks, Trustees for Harvard University, Washington, D.C.

PLATE 4 Crib of the Infant Jesus, fifteenth century. Photo: Gift of Ruth Blumka, in memory of Leopold Blumka, 1974, Metropolitan Museum of Art, NY.

PLATE 5 The Carpenter with his Auger. Relief in rue de Bayeux, Caen. Photograph: Roi.dagobert, CC BY-SA 3.0/Wikimedia Commons.

PLATE 6 Master of the Bedford Hours, "The Construction of Noah's Ark," *Bedford Hours* (1410–30). British Library, Add. MS 18850, f. 15v. Photograph courtesy of the British Library Board.

PLATE 7 Giovanni da Verona, Intarsia with master of perspective instruments, from choir stalls, 1502, Abbey, Monte Oliveto Maggiore, Italy. Photograph courtesy of Scala/Art Resource, NY.

PLATE 8 A Romanesque bed, stained glass, early thirteenth century, Trinity Chapel, Canterbury Cathedral. Photograph by the Author.

PLATE 9 A boarded chest with decorative ironwork from Rydaholm, Sweden, oak, 1246–70. Photograph courtesy of the Swedish History Museum, Stockholm.

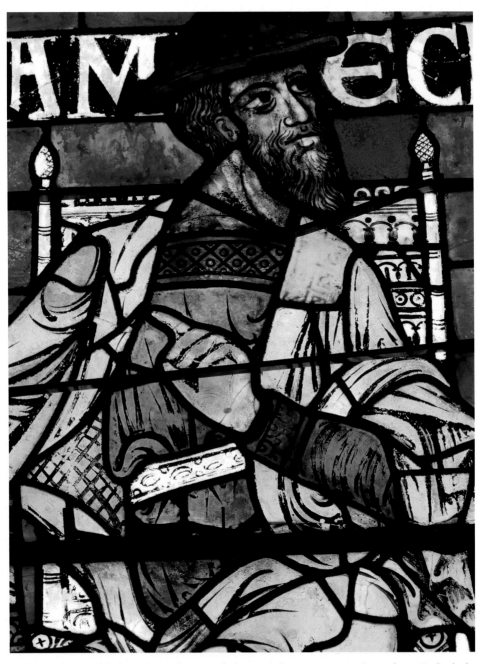

PLATE 10 A turned chair, Lamech, stained glass, southwest transept, Canterbury Cathedral, 1178. Photograph by the Author.

PLATE 11 A turned chair, Vallstenna, Gotland, oak, 1250–1350. Photograph courtesy of the Swedish History Museum, Stockholm.

PLATE 12 Christine de Pizan Presents a Manuscript to Isabeau of Bavaria in her Bedroom. Manuscript illumination attributed to Master of the Cité des Dames from the *Book of the Queen* by Christine de Pizan (c. 1410–c. 1414). British Library, Harley MS 4431 [f. 3]. Photograph courtesy of Wikimedia Creative Commons.

PLATE 13 Hieronymus Bosch, *Death and the Miser, c.* 1485–90. National Gallery of Art, Washington, DC (1952.5.33). Oil on panel. Photograph courtesy of National Gallery of Art, Washington, DC.

PLATE 14 How the Noble King Alexander was Poisoned. Manuscript illumination by Jean Vauquelin in *Histoire du Grand Alexandre* (1460). Musée des Beaux-Arts de la Ville de Paris. Photograph courtesy of Bridgeman Images.

PLATE 15 January, *Très Riches Heures*. MS 65 Musée Condé, Chantilly. Photograph courtesy of Wikipedia Commons.

PLATE 16 Coronation Chair, Westminster Abbey. Photograph by the Author.

PLATE 17 Saint-Sernin altar table. Photograph by the Author.

PLATE 18 Petrus Christus, *A Goldsmith in his Shop*, 1449. Robert Lehman Collection, 1975. Photograph courtesy of Metropolitan Museum of Art, 1975.1.110.

PLATE 19 Biagio d'Antonio, Jacopo del Sellaio, and Zanobi di Domenico, the Morelli-Nerli chests. Photograph © The Courtauld Gallery, Samuel Courtauld Trust: Lee Bequest.

PLATE 20 King Solomon giving audience from his *lettuccio*. From the Malermi Bible (printed in Venice by Giunta, 1490). Photograph courtesy of Metropolitan Museum of Art, Harris Brisbane Dick Fund, 1933 (33.66).

PLATE 22 Hans Hammer, Pulpit, Strasbourg Cathedral, 1484–5. Photograph courtesy of Wikimedia Creative Commons.

PLATE 23 Adam Kraft, Sacrament House (Dais), St. Lorenz, Nuremberg, 1493–6. Photograph courtesy of Wikimedia Creative Commons.

PLATE 24 Anton Pilgram, Pulpit, St. Stephen's, Vienna, *c.* 1505. Photograph by the Author.

FIGURE 25 Anton Pilgram, Organ Tribune, Church of St. Stephen, Vienna, 1513.
Photograph by the Author.

PLATE 26 "Ezra writing" in the *Codex Amiatinus*. Laurentian Library, MS Amiatino 1, f. 5r. Photograph courtesy of DeAgostini/Getty Images.

PLATE 27 Antonello da Messina, *St. Jerome in His Study*, 1474–5. Photograph courtesy of the National Gallery, London.

PLATE 28 "Gregory dictating his epistles" in the *Registrum Gregorii*. Trier Stadtbibliothek MS 171/1626. Photograph courtesy of Archiv Gerstenberg/ullstein bild.

PLATE 29 King Arthur's Round Table. Photograph courtesy of Bibliothèque nationale de France, fr. 116, f. 610v.

PLATE 30 Villard de Honnecourt, Choir stalls. Photograph courtesy of Bibliothèque nationale de France, fr. 19093, f. 27v.

PLATE 31 The First State Bed of Henry VII and Elizabeth of York, *c.* 1486. The Langley Collection. Photograph reproduced by permission of Ian Coulson, the Langley Collection.

PLATE 32 Detail from the *Pricke of Conscience* window, All Saints North Street, York, *c.* 1420. Photograph courtesy of Wikimedia Creative Commons.

CONCEPTS OF DISPLAY

The concept of display was central to medieval society and culture both in religious and secular spheres. In the religious context, the performance of the Mass was a key part of Christian devotion. Churches were constructed as settings for the most important of Christian objects, such as altarpieces that acted as the central focus and backdrop of the Mass, or reliquaries that housed holy objects and became sites of pilgrimage. Perhaps the most striking is the church of Sainte Chapelle in Paris, commissioned by King Louis XI of France to house what he believed was Christ's Crown of Thorns, purchased for the jaw-dropping sum of 135,000 livres (half the annual expenditure of France) in 1239 in Constantinople. In the early medieval period, the overwhelming majority of furniture was made in an ecclesiastic context, for divine glory, and this expenditure and earthly splendor were fundamentally related to the devotional purpose of furniture. Most church furnishing was performative, from the bishop's throne to the stalls for clerics to the altars and their accoutrements. Central to this display was the adornment of altars and of sacred shrines. This was a continual and additive process. For instance, at the heart of Canterbury Cathedral, rebuilt following the fire of 1174, was one of the great sites of medieval pilgrimage: the tomb of Saint Thomas à Becket, the Archbishop murdered in his cathedral church four years earlier. Becket's tomb continued as a site for pilgrimage, and for further enrichment, throughout the Middle Ages. Around 1500, an Italian visitor stated that "the magnificence of the tomb of St Thomas the Martyr ... is that which surpasses all belief" (Sneyd 1847: 83–4). Some decades later, the humanist Erasmus (1466–1536), recounting a visit to Canterbury that took place before 1519, describes:

> A coffin of wood (covered) a coffin of gold which, being drawn up by ropes and pullies, an invaluable treasure was discovered. Gold was the meanest thing to be seen there. All shone and glittered with the rarest and most precious jewels of an extraordinary bigness ... When this sight was shown, the prior with a white wand touched every jewel one by one, telling the name, the value, and the donor of it.
>
> (Erasmus 1849: 55–6)

When, less than twenty years later, Canterbury Cathedral was stripped of its most valuable possessions by King Henry VIII's commissioners, much of the twenty-six cartloads of silver and gold that were removed from Canterbury must have been plundered from this shrine (Campbell 1987: 162). This example—and there are many, although not perhaps so opulent, from all over medieval Europe—serves to remind us that ecclesiastical furniture and furnishings was of exceptionally high monetary, as well as devotional, value.

The earliest recorded medieval furniture has been found in churches, such as the seventh-century peace stools still surviving in the English churches of Hexham Abbey and Beverley Minster (Blair 2005: 223). Ecclesiastical furnishings did honor primarily to God, but also to their patrons. They could also on occasion serve a wider social purpose, as in the case of the benches and choir stalls recorded in the Florentine Benedictine convent of San Pier Maggiore. These items of furniture, installed in the fourteenth century, and recorded in inventories prior to their removal in the early sixteenth century, were commissioned by elite laymen living in the neighborhood surrounding the church. They were not employed solely for devotional purposes, as it seems that they were the site for local community gatherings of these male citizens.[1]

The expansion of a middle class, largely due to trade and mercantile growth between the late fourteenth and middle of the seventeenth centuries, ensured that furniture moved from the almost exclusive possession of the lay and clerical elite into the hands of the middling sort. It seems that most members of the middle ranks of European society from the later fifteenth century onward possessed items of furniture. And, although the documentary record is much richer and more informative about the possessions of royalty, noblemen, and the richest of merchants—and most surviving items of furniture were made for those at the top of the social scale—it is also evident from inventories, court records, and other sources that furniture was also owned, and certainly used, by many of those far below them in the social hierarchy. The extent of furnishings and the layout of rooms in a dwelling varied largely depending on the economic level and the needs of the occupants, but throughout the fifteenth and sixteenth centuries, there was an increase in the types of furniture to serve specific needs, used across a widening social spectrum (Ariès and Duby 1988: 172–84). Furniture varied according to status: peasants and the urban poor slept on straw mats, while the urban middle classes and aristocrats were likely to own different varieties of beds, from simple beds used solely for sleeping in to "day beds" and even grand ceremonial structures in which they might receive family members or specifically invited guests.

Well into the sixteenth century, the regular travel of monarchs, senior clerics, and noblemen between a series of residences meant that their most valuable possessions were generally of a size and flexibility that they could be packed up and transported without the danger of extensive damage. The fact that private devotional paintings—which could also be classified as quasi-liturgical furniture—were often hinged until the sixteenth century so that the central, most significant elements could be protected from chance damage is also significant (Dunkerton et al. 1991: 68). Triptychs or diptychs, assemblies of three or two sacred stories, usually painted on wood, or carved in ivory, were distinctly portable. While small-scale folding paintings, such as the "(i)cone" or panel painting commissioned by Queen Sancia of Naples in 1331, seem to have been the preserve of the clergy and the most elevated levels of the laity, the large quantity of surviving diptychs and single panels of Christian devotional subjects in ivory suggest that these had a much wider clientele (Gordon 2011: 379, n. 33). Indeed, the Parisian workshops that dominated the market and fashion for ivory diptychs were operating a mass-production market by the fourteenth century, producing objects of greatly varying quality.

The interior spaces of the home were often transformed through the use of furniture and accompanying textiles, and were thus fluid and transitional entities, becoming sites of display at important points in one's life, while also acting as the backdrop against which day-to-day household life took place— from birthing children to daily meals. The growth of urban centers in the later fourteenth and fifteenth centuries meant a burgeoning market for household furnishings, which both gave rise to and was influenced by a new attitude to the home and the objects that filled it, resulting in a culture of display (Goldthwaite 1987, 1993: 153–75; Musacchio 2008: 52–4). Novel textiles, glass, and metalwork coming into Europe from the Silk Road as well as new tastes for antique and *all'antica* objects, meant that homes were becoming increasingly places where movable wealth could be put on display. Such new habits were remarked upon by preachers of the time who condemned the "luxuries" no longer only found in the "palaces of the great, but in the houses of common citizens" including the "size and softness of the beds" painted and gilded with "precious coverlets" (Musacchio 2008: 58). In discussing money, the fifteenth-century Florentine apothecary and humanist Matteo Palmieri (1406–75) singled out "magnificent dwellings" and the "luxury of living splendidly" as things that were sought not because they were useful in themselves but for comfort and dignity and because they could enhance and ennoble life (Rubin 2007: 38). Palmieri's own life, as recorded in his writings and from documents, shows that he lived out such ideals in his purchasing of domestic furnishings (Sliwka 2015: ch. 1).

This accumulation of new furnishings was largely related to a shift that took place within the organization of the home and the changing functions of rooms. In the early medieval house, there was typically one main room equipped with a fire, which could serve as living room, dining room, bedroom, and even kitchen. In wealthier households this room, usually referred to as a hall, would still serve as the main space for most activities, from eating and entertaining guests and even work, but the owners might have their own quarters for sleeping often on another storey, with servants using the hall as a place to sleep (or they were given their own quarters depending on the size of the house) (Mercer 1969: 18– 21; Ariès and Duby 1988: 60–1). For example, the house of the Lord of Ardres in northern France had, in 1129, cellars and granaries on the ground floor, while the first floor was made up of a hall where meetings were held and meals were eaten, flanked by small rooms for the servants, with the "great chamber" reserved for the lord and his lady, with an adjoining room used as a dormitory for the children and servants. Few medieval halls survive, however, to flesh out the documentary record. One of the best preserved is Penshurst Place in Kent, built by the successful London merchant Sir John de Pulteney as his country residence, in the years after 1341, when he received his license to crenellate (to fortify his property). The central hearth, which lit and heated the room, survives in the center of the floor. The screen, which separates the offices from the main body of the hall, is of sixteenth-century manufacture, but it probably replicates an original, earlier structure. Yet even in this grand house we have no evidence of the furnishings—probably because they were far less valuable than the carved wood and stone that made up the structural elements of the hall.

Peasants' homes were far simpler, usually consisting of only one room where a range of activities would take place throughout the day. It has been argued, however, particularly in the case of England, that differences between urban middling households and rural peasants' houses in the medieval period were not simply a case of more rooms and more furniture, but rather were linked to different value systems (Kowaleski and Goldberg 2008). For example, studies of English inventories from the late medieval period have revealed that choice of investment in types of goods varied depending on social status and thus reveals different priorities, whereby peasant households in the countryside placed emphasis on kitchen tools, for instance, whereas bourgeois homes in urban centers spent more money on a wide range of material culture dedicated to display, from furnishings such as beds to more elaborate dining ware such as silver spoons (the ability to own a variety of cutlery was a sign of wealth) (Goldberg 2008: 124–44). The makeup of the household, that is the people who lived there, also varied depending on profession and social class. In middle-class houses where merchants and artisans lived, a new style of domestic living emerged in the fourteenth century, which combined working and trading with domestic life. This type of household thus comprised parents, children, apprentices, and servants, as well as day-laborers who might not actually live there. This in turn required new spatial differentiations within the home that also gave rise to, and influenced, new conceptions of privacy. The one-room house of the poor became ideologically different from the multiroom house, where working, eating, and sleeping could take place, if chosen, in different rooms (Riddy 2008: 17).

By the fourteenth century, a marked shift is clearly evident in elite homes. Eating began to take place in the more private chamber, which also served as the main bedroom, while the hall was reserved for larger gatherings. In England, this is reflected in the emergence of withdrawing rooms, such as the "privé parlour" appearing in inventories in London from the 1370s, while the relocation of storerooms—from the cellar connected to the lord's chamber to a room off the main hall—reveal increasingly elaborate and hierarchical rituals around dining that worked to display the lord's generosity and largesse to guests (Kowaleski and Goldberg 2008: 5). In Dijon the 1412 inventory of Jean Suivard demonstrates his chamber served as a place to sleep, eat, cook, and receive visitors, rather than the *salle* or hall (Wilson 2016). At the top end of the scale, by the early fourteenth century the chamber at Westminster Palace had achieved a prominence it had not had before, as the king now began to use the chamber as a place to dine, as a refuge from the more public hall (Vale 2001: 60).

Increasingly, the structure of the elite home was becoming even more complex, resulting in new approaches to living, where activities took place in more distinct places, and an increasing need for different types of furniture to fulfill specific functions, which also reflected new approaches to dining. For instance, the Florentine Jacopo di Rosso's inventory from 1390 reveals that his house had a grand entryway, a wine cellar, two halls (one recorded as "grand"), two bedrooms off each hall, a kitchen, and servants' quarters (Ariès and Duby 1988: 2, 174). Thomas Mocking, a fishmonger in London who died in 1373, had a house with eight rooms, including two chambers, a hall with a fireplace, a storeroom, a parlor, a servant's room, another room with two tables, and a kitchen (Riddy 2008: 24). In the fishmonger's case furniture was designed to be adaptable for the changing function of the rooms depending on the time of day: a trestle table and a folding bed allowed for flexibility. Inventories of elite households from Dijon demonstrate that by the early fifteenth century, living quarters had become more elaborate and the furnishings could vary depending on who was using the spaces (Wilson 2015: 335–59). Jean Aubert, who worked for the Burgundian dukes, for example, had a house in Dijon that spread over three floors with the basement comprising a stable and a cellar. The first floor was subdivided into eight rooms, which served a variety of functions, from eating and sleeping to accounting. The top floor had three rooms, comprised of two chambers, one of which had its own *garde robe* (a more private room used to store valuables). These numerous rooms resulted in numerous and varied furnishings: the rooms on the lower floors were less richly decorated than those on the top floor, which reflects their uses: simpler beds and chests were reserved for Aubert's staff, while the galleries were decorated with tapestries and elaborate chests as a way to display the wealth of the family to those who visited. The chamber attached to the *garde robe* contained a large bed with elaborate tapestry hangings and ornaments, a stool, a chest, a donor portrait, chests of oak and walnut, and a bench. The *garde robe* contained numerous chests as well as a small bed. In the other chamber, there was a bed, a couch with bedcover, a bench with backing, a chest, a small table and two stools, and a variety of books (342). The furnishings were thus much more elaborate on the top floor, the spaces that were specifically used by the family, underlining in some ways a paradox: as rooms became more "private" their furnishings became more elaborate to display the wealth of the family to those who were fortunate enough to be invited into these spaces.

By the early fifteenth century in cities such as Florence, the building of large family *palazzi* or palaces gave rise to an unprecedented number of rooms, such as the Da Uzzano brothers' palace that contained thirty rooms across three floors (Ariès and Duby 1988: 2, 174). This expansion of rooms and thus of display furniture was connected to an essential component of building, buying, or furnishing the Renaissance house—the concept of magnificence. In the Italian courts, magnificence was a virtue not only becoming of but also expected of a ruler, while in the republics wealthy merchant-banking families such as the Medici (or indeed the less wealthy Matteo Palmieri), used the term to justify outward displays of wealth as contributing to the glory of their city and to the common good (Fraser Jenkins 1970: 162–70; Shepherd 2007: 47–70). The Italian humanists, drawing on classical sources but reinterpreting them for Renaissance society, developed the concept of magnificence further by introducing the notion of splendor, which divided forms of spending and display into public and private. The Neapolitan humanist Giovanni Pontano (1426–1503) described this distinction in the late fifteenth century. He remarked that magnificence is related to "grandeur and concerns buildings, spectacle and gifts, while splendour is primarily concerned with the ornament of the household, the care of the person and with furnishings" (Welch 2002: 214). Pontano dedicated a whole treatise to *On Splendor* (1498), looking closely at a new range of objects that had hitherto been ignored by those writing about magnificence, from knives and goblets to furniture.

By doing so, Pontano praised a virtue (splendor) that was more obtainable for the middling sorts of society than magnificence, thus providing varying ways to display wealth according to one's status. Indeed, display is an underlining theme of Pontano's whole treatise and it provides us with a rich account of the attention given to furniture and the other furnishings of the home. As Pontano points out these could range from the more utilitarian to the ornamental, writing that: "seals, paintings, tapestries, divans, ivory seats, cloth woven with gems, cases and caskets variously painted in the Arabic manner, little vases of crystal and other things of this type with which the house is adorned ... bring prestige to the owner of the house, when they are seen by the many who frequent his house" (Pontano 1999; translated in Welch 2002: 215). Pontano thus underlines the more "public" roles such "private" furnishings could perform. As was often the case in the fifteenth and sixteenth centuries, Pontano discusses furnishings and furniture together, which demonstrates how these societies did not always see a distinction between the ornaments of the home and pieces of furniture.

Display and the reception of visitors were crucial components in the choice, look, types, and decoration of household furnishings, which could convey symbolic messages to those who visited, used, and experienced the furniture in a home. The tailoring of furniture with coats of arms or portraits further personalized these pieces. But furniture, like furnishings in general, were often movable objects and therefore multipurpose. Elite furniture was an integral part of display, whether it was a piece designated specifically for the display of goods that reflected the owner's material wealth, such as a *credenza* (sideboard/ buffet), or one meant for the display of a particular body (an heir or a person of standing), such as a state cradle or a *lettuccio* (daybed). For Mimi Hellman, furniture is a social actor, which when used sets up a mutual relationship between itself and the body that uses it, resulting in a "joint performance" by both the person and the thing. For example, the particular nature of a daybed could further the sociability of the object, as one gave audience from it or received visitors, thus as Hellman argues, furniture "shape[s] the form and content of social exchange" rather than merely acting as a backdrop (Hellman 1999: 416). Although Hellman writes primarily about eighteenth-century France, her model also has utility for the study of medieval and Renaissance furniture, which was also used for sociability and display.

Special occasions called for the display and performative roles of these objects to come to the fore, but many of the same items had a function in everyday life. It was this social interaction between inanimate objects and subjects that brought these articles of furniture to life, endowing both the user and the thing itself with higher status and importance. A chair is just a chair, until placed at the head of a table—the user gains status and recognition by its placement while the chair takes on new meaning as being occupied by a person of standing. Similarly, a bed might just be a bed that one sleeps in, until it is used in ritual and becomes the site of festivity, for instance when a mother lies in it to receive friends, family, and business associates at the birth of her child. At this point it takes on new meaning and becomes a site of display, functioning as a mediator and a source of assembly, association, and conversation (Appadurai 1986; Campbell, Miller, and Carroll Consavari 2013; Campbell 2014).[2] This social performance alludes to the ways that one piece of furniture could often serve different functions and underscores how approaching furniture in terms of typologies often sidesteps the multifaceted ways in which furniture was used, adapted, and transformed.

PRIMARY SOURCES AND DISPLAY

A closer look at contemporary accounts of the use of furniture reveals its performative nature. For example, there is a group of primary sources detailing the suites of furniture provided for the Neapolitan princess Eleanora d'Aragona on her visit to Rome in 1473. In these documents, some objects are singled out as being special or noteworthy as individual items while others are listed as part of a larger ensemble. This example is useful in understanding the variety of furniture—from *credenze* to beds—that were ornamented with textiles, pillows, and other decorations, in a number of separate yet interconnecting spaces.

In June 1473 Eleonora, the daughter of King Ferrante of Naples, was hosted in Rome for several days by Pope Sixtus IV and his nephews (the cardinals Pietro Riario and Giuliano della Rovere), as part of her bridal procession from Naples to the court of her new husband Ercole d'Este in Ferarra. Numerous festivities and banquets were arranged for Eleonora's retinue and the Ferrarese contingent accompanying her who were all lavishly housed by the pope. In the two letters and a diary recording the event, attention is given to describing the furniture, which adorned both the temporary structure and the permanent palace. A temporary wooden building erected in the piazza flanking the Roman Church of Santi Apostoli connected the palaces of the Riario and della Rovere families, and was the site of banquets and festivities, while Eleonora's accommodation amounted to over fourteen rooms in the nearby Riario palace.[2] These documents are scrupulous in their detail, revealing the importance attached to the display of furniture and the social function of the decorative arts. On the Monday, as a Ferrarese courtier tells us, a feast was served in one of the large rooms temporarily erected outside in the piazza, which displayed

> an enormous credenza with twelve shelves full of, even overloaded with, great vessels of silver and gold with so many precious stones that it was miraculous to look at; but what was even more stupendous was that even with so many dishes served and so many varieties of those … there was always enough silver and nothing was ever moved from the credenza.
>
> (Licht 1996: 20)

As discussed below, the *credenza* was a piece of furniture dedicated to display and the number of stages or shelves was indicative of one's status, as were the things displayed upon it. Pope Sixtus IV not only wanted to reflect his own power and status, but also that of Eleonora d'Aragona and, by extension, that of her father and her husband, the King of Naples and the Duke of Ferrara, respectively—both of whom were imbricated in political ties with the pope.

The suite of apartments was also key in displaying the host's (in this case Pietro Riario's and by proxy the pope's) as well as Eleonora d'Aragona and her family's wealth and power. Eleonora's accommodation was arranged on the *piano nobile* of Riario's palazzo and the accounts provide us with a detailed description of the layout of the rooms and their contents, including furniture and textiles. As exemplified by these accounts, contemporaries often focused on describing the textiles that decorated pieces of furniture rather than the furniture itself, and did not often make a distinction between the two. For example, one bedroom off the chapel contained a bed, which one visitor described as having:

a mattress of blue Venetian silk, two covers of white damask, and another cover of crimson cut-velvet that covered the whole bed clear down to the ground. Above there was a canopy and curtains of white damask with golden fringe, a blue headboard, four cushions of gold and four of violet velvet, then two others of violet velvet and two of green velvet ... Also in this room, folded above the chest, was a cover of violet velvet lined with green velvet.

(quoted in Licht 1996: 15–16)

In addition, there were two chairs covered in green velvet, that were repeatedly singled out as individual items worth describing, estimated by those who viewed them to be worth 600 ducats each, an enormous sum for the time (Bryant 2012: 365). In a letter, Eleonora d'Aragona noted that all the rooms were covered with tapestries on the walls and carpets on the floor. She also made sure to note that on the evening before they departed, Cardinal Riario sent one of his servants with the keys to the chests in the rooms, and showed the guests all of their contents, which revealed curtains and long robes in fine materials. The viewing of these textiles apparently lasted close to six hours, which caused Eleonora to claim that by the end they were so bored they "begged those servants not to show [them] any more" even though the "silk brocades were really perfect and very worthy" (Licht 1996: 20). Such a description demonstrates how furniture—chests in this case—were used to house precious furnishings such as textiles and became part of the display process. Opening the lid would reveal hidden treasures within, underlining not only a bodily engagement with the piece of furniture as the lid was lifted, but a performative act within social rituals of display as well as secrecy.

Descriptions of furniture, their contents, and the decoration of rooms—from *credenze* to beds to chairs to chests to textiles—demonstrate the ways early modern viewers paid close attention to their material surroundings. On such occasions, display was paramount and furniture did not play a background role, but indeed a central one in displaying magnificence and denoting status. This was not only apparent for those present but became a crucial element in the reports that would be sent to family, rulers, friends, and allies, which could either ruin or bolster reputations. For example, ambassadors' reports and letters from guests who visited a palace provide us with crucial information on what visitors were supposed to pick up on and often describe both the display of furniture and the display of objects on (and in) furniture. *Ricordanze* (diaries) and account books indicate how much these pieces and their decorations cost (either new or second hand), and also often provide us with the motive behind these purchases, such as pride, honor, and status, which were then materially translated into the furnishings purchased and used.

FUNCTIONS AND TYPES OF DISPLAY

Extremely lavish displays of textiles and *credenze* such as those described in Rome were usually restricted to special events—coronations, marriages, and births, for instance—and were generally limited to the upper echelons of society, although less lavish displays were also increasingly becoming common among the middling sort. In Renaissance Italy, the time of greatest financial outlay in terms of furnishing one's home was at marriage when a groom would furnish his apartment with important pieces of furniture—the most luxurious suites comprised a bed, a *lettuccio*, and marriage chests to welcome his new wife, although this custom was not restricted to Italy (French and German prints and poems suggest this also took place in other countries) (Lydecker 1987: 112–24; Musacchio 2008: 51; Campbell 2009). The wedding feast itself would require the use of particular types of furniture from tables and chairs (or stools) to a *credenza* to display the wealth of the family. The life cycle also called for different uses and displays of furniture—from the nuptial bed where the marriage would be consummated to the use of the same bed (or an additional daybed) for a new mother to lie in and receive visitors when celebrating the birth of an heir, who would often be displayed in a cradle. Furniture could serve differing forms of display—from the display of bodies to the display of things.

Displaying worldly goods

New trade routes, voyages of exploration, and diplomatic negotiations throughout the fifteenth and sixteenth centuries meant that European interiors soon had a proliferation of objects that required new types of furniture to accommodate them. The furniture and the spaces used to exhibit such objects was also linked to new ways of approaching the material world. Marvellous objects that represented the miraculous works of God, from relics of saints and precious stones to elephant tusks, ostrich eggs, and unicorn horns, were commonly housed in church treasuries in the medieval period. In the Renaissance, due to increased trade, these items also made their way into patrician and aristocratic homes, becoming part of a secular collecting culture (Shelton 1994; North 2010). This relocation of precious and rare things from the church to the home was not simply a change of setting, but a reflection of shifting attitudes to the world of goods and the world at large.

The increased complexity of interior spaces also gave rise to new functions for rooms, such as the emergence of the study. In Europe, collectors built dedicated spaces in their homes to display a variety of objects. In Italy, this room or study was usually referred to as a *studiolo* and emerged in the fifteenth century, while in German-speaking countries such a room became popular in the sixteenth century and was called a *Kunstkammer* (chamber of art) or

Wunderkammer (chamber of wonders) (Kauffmann 1994; Thornton 1997). In the sixteenth and seventeenth centuries, these spaces were also called cabinets of curiosities—a reference to the furniture that displayed "curiosities" as well as the inquisitive impetus behind collecting (Impey and Macgregor 1997).

European collecting spaces and the furniture that filled them took many forms. Aristocratic families who ruled courts acquired goods to reflect their magnificence and power, as well as to demonstrate taste and knowledge, dedicating whole rooms to collecting where the walls were decorated with complex painting programs and cabinets filled with precious objects. Increasingly, collecting became a pastime that merchants, humanists, and others increasingly undertook, where goods were collected and displayed to show sophistication, worldly knowledge, and a successful business. In homes of the middling sorts, a closet or a small room could serve as a study and a collecting space, similar to a monastic cell. But many middle-class homes simply housed their collectibles in one part of the bedchamber or throughout their home, placed on shelves, above doorframes and in cabinets.

The types of furniture built to showcase collections are often described in inventories. Small collectibles such as gems, coins, and plaquettes were displayed in a wide range of forms—some dangling on strings and attached to shelves, while others were kept in caskets, boxes, and bags, which in turn were then placed in chests, desks, and cabinets. Indeed, furniture was sometimes used to hide objects rather than display them, which added to the allure of the objects and the process of viewership and handling when they were finally taken out of their compartments and exhibited for the viewer. A Ferrarese collector described his cabinet (referring here to a piece of furniture rather than a room) in the sixteenth century as "very beautiful, made of walnut, with many secret compartments and little drawers, some of which are made in cypress wood" (Thornton 1997: 70). The 1494 inventory of the Este in Ferrara listed 437 coins (or medals?) of various sizes displayed on "nineteen wooden panels" (Archivio di Stato di Modena, Guardaroba 117 55R; Syson 2002a: 241). The 1559 inventory of the Este possessions in the *camerini*, the rooms that Duke Alfonso d'Este famously renovated in Ferrara, indicate that Titian's *Christ with the Coin* located in the *camerino adorato* served as the cover to the coins and medals cabinet, indicating how paintings might be integral to the furniture and serve an iconographic purpose (Nygren 2016: 455). Throughout the other rooms, furniture was used as a means to display the collections such as the wood table on which various silver and gold vases "for drinking water" were placed, in addition to the inkwell, wooden boxes with portraits on them, and four metal portraits of the King and Queen of Poland that were also placed on the table (Marchesi 2012). From the middle of the sixteenth century, cabinets had become rather complex pieces of furniture, and their drawings were circulated amongst the elite. Gerolamo Garimberto, the archaeological adviser to Cesare

Gonzaga, describes in detail the design of a cabinet from 1564, which was "very beautiful and rich in fine stones and accompanied by those [alabaster] columns ... which ... have turned out to be very lovely and beautiful .... Put together with the ornament of many ancient figurines, the cabinet has proved a great success" (Thornton 1997: 70).

Dedicated built-in cabinets within a *studiolo* could be extremely elaborate, such as the intarsia cabinets in the *studioli* of the Montefeltro at Urbino and Gubbio from the end of the fifteenth century (Figure 6.1). Here, the intricate intarsia (inlaid wood) decorations, a craft first developed in church interiors, depict the types of objects held within the cabinets—from musical to scientific instruments. These representations are indeed extremely complex, operating as cerebral games, while also playing on the viewer's perception of space (Kirkbride 2008). While some of these were indeed doors that could be opened, the walls are largely trompe l'oeil—doors that pretend to be open and benches that appear functional, but are entirely fictitious. The intarsia here could be said to *perform* furniture, making the viewer aware of the functions of furniture in such spaces.

FIGURE 6.1 Giuliano da Maiano with Benedetto da Maiano, Studiolo from the Ducal Palace at Gubbio, *c.* 1478–82, wood. Photo: Rogers Fund, 1939, Metropolitan Museum of Art.

Representations of saints in their studies often depict an ideal *studiolo*, a quiet place for contemplation and devotion, well furnished with a desk, shelves, and cabinets that house books, writing utensils, and collectibles. A woodcut by Albrecht Dürer for example (Figure 6.2), shows Saint Jerome in a study, possibly located in a bedroom, where shelves display candlesticks, glass vessels, and books, while the desk provides a place to read and write as well as additional storage where scissors and writing implements are attached. In front of the desk is a chest with a pillow on it, serving the dual function of seating as well as storage. The walls are also used to display paternoster beads, an hourglass, letters, and brushes.

Goods of course were also displayed in shops, spaces that served as semi-public rooms, sometimes on the ground floor of a residence. A painting by Petrus Christus (Plate 18) of a goldsmith in his shop displays many similar objects that might be found in a study, arranged on shelves to showcase the merchandise to the viewer. Vases on the top shelf are similar to those that would be found on *credenze*. Indeed, it has been suggested that this painting is a portrait of Willem van Vleuten, a Bruges goldsmith who worked for Philip the Good, Duke of Burgundy who was known for his lavish services. On the shelf below are a range of goods from the natural world (coral and a nut set into a mount) as well as jewelry and a reliquary. The presence of a curtain suggests it could be drawn to protect the goods. The counter provides a means to distinguish between the outside world and the interior of the shop, while also serving as a place to weigh wares. This threshold is further underlined by the mirror, which reflects the outside world of the public square.

One particularly instructive example of the public and sociable dimension of mercantile spaces is the apothecary shop or pharmacy, which in the sixteenth century became a comfortable place to gather, converse, and even exchange news (De Vivo 2007). These shops might even be seen as the precursors to the coffeehouses or salons of the eighteenth century, whereby individuals did not just purchase objects from a counter but, indeed, lingered, discussed, and even gambled and played chess, suggesting there was furniture in place to do so (De Vivo 2007: 508–9). Indeed, benches and stools in descriptions of pharmacies suggest they encouraged lingering, although such furniture could also serve the activities associated with the apothecary, such as seats and writing desks, which were used by doctors who saw their patients in the shop. In barbers' shops, where activities associated with medicine could take place, such as blood-letting alongside the cutting of hair, rooms were lavishly furnished and decorated with pictures and antiquities, suggesting it was a comfortable, even homely space, and would have reflected the successful business of the owner.

In the sixteenth and seventeenth centuries, apothecaries also served as cabinets of curiosities, furnished with shelves to display rare specimens and objects, from "unicorn horns" (narwhal tusks) to stuffed crocodiles, operating as

FIGURE 6.2 Albrecht Dürer, *Saint Jerome in his Study*, 1514, woodcut. Photo:
Fletcher Fund, 1919, Metropolitan Museum of Art.

a proto-museum, where cases were specifically tailored for this sort of display. In the fifteenth century, textual and visual evidence suggests that shelves in apothecary shops were specifically built to display the colorful *albarelli*, which housed spices, while built-in counters facilitated the weighing of ingredients and attendance to customers. In contrast, the furniture of itinerant apothecaries and other street sellers appear in numerous literary references as promoting a chaotic form of mobility, where individuals might stand up on their bench and shout to, or even grab, passersby. The bench, however, was a piece of furniture that authorities hoped could also control chaos, such as the decree from 1507 in Venice, which stated that bread sellers were not to "shout and thrust bread at clients, they must stand with composure behind their *bancone*" (Welch 2008: 132). In some instances, furniture could be made from the merchandise itself, such as a grocer who used parmesan cheese rounds as seats for some customers who wanted to play cards. Such furniture—temporary or sedentary—which encouraged customers to linger might have also served as a form of display for the merchant. By flaunting their clientele, it could indicate to potential customers that it was a successful business where clients were happy to return and linger.

Furniture such as chests, which were used to store and transport goods, became movable display pieces in themselves and are recorded in all types of spaces—from bedrooms to studies to ecclesiastical settings. The chest is a broad term with which to describe a wide variety of individual types of object. They could be immensely simple, or highly decorated, such as with delicate intarsia work, pastiglia (objects decorated with lead-based paste), carving (whether metal, wood, or ivory), or painting (Paolini 2006: 120–1). Chests were commissioned by secular or ecclesiastical magnates, for cathedrals and for churches; for colleges and other collective bodies, and by more modest individuals; for instance an Anglo-French manuscript of the mid-thirteenth century shows a chest in use as a merchant's trading counter (Tracy 1987: 119, 278, cat. 204). A late medieval inventory at Château Cornillon in Burgundy records a total of seventy-four chests in forty-two chambers or offices (Eames 1977: 108, n. 280). Chests often marked the change in status associated with the removal of women from their father's care to their new, marital family (even if they were not commissioned by the bride's family). A nun, leaving her father to be the "bride of Christ" would also be furnished with a chest, decorated appropriately for her particular circumstances. Those women entering a secular marriage might use bundles or baskets to move their possessions, but on entering their husband's houses, chests would be provided to store these (and other) items (Rubin 2007: 362–4, with a summary of the preceding literature).

Chests were decorated according to wealth or status, and depending on the fashions and customs of each region or nation of Europe. In England and France, for instance, chests were most usually made of oak, and carved, the decoration following pattern books or prints, or even architectural tracery

(Tracy 1988: 172–9; Neuschel 1998: 595–622; Thirion 1998: 76). In Italy, there was a greater variety of decoration. Chests could be carved, but they were also (particularly during the fifteenth century) decorated with painted elements. In Italian, these highly worked and fine-quality chests were known as *forzieri*—regardless of their decoration. This word, which has sometimes been translated into English as "great chests," refers to the fact that they were supplied with a lock, often placed in the center of the front panel of the chest (Paolini 2006: 120). Although painted chests were a rarity in France, Germany, and the British Isles, their production flourished in much of Italy from the late fourteenth to the early sixteenth centuries. Chests decorated with fine painting are documented all over the peninsula, but few have survived (either in totality, or simply their painted sections) outside Tuscany, Venice, and the Veneto (Baskins 2008; Campbell 2009; Rutherglen 2012).

The mixed function of chests was closely connected to their location. Inventories of the fifteenth and sixteenth centuries show that chests could be found in most household rooms, but painted chests were intended for spaces which had designated public and private purposes (Lindow 2007: 119–52). In fifteenth- and early sixteenth-century Florence we know that pairs of painted chests were often destined for the *camera*, or chamber, a room which was often the focus of substantial redecoration by a male patrician around the time of his first marriage, a moment when he was often emancipated from his father's control. From surviving inventories, it is clear that these pairs of objects (such as that in Plate 19) were among the most costly movable items commissioned at this moment in a young man's life (Lydecker 1987; Preyer 2006b: 40–1).

The subjects narrated on the fronts and sides of these chests were drawn from a repertoire of storytelling, which drew both on popular and oral as well as intellectual and written culture (Bayer 2008: 230–8; Campbell 2009: 31–47). The central Italian artist and historian Giorgio Vasari, writing in the late 1560s, and the first person to accord any intellectual status or merit to painted chests, commented in the "Life of Dello Delli" (who he describes as a specialist in painted furniture) that "for the most part they told tales from Ovid and other stories" (Vasari [1568] 1966–87: 3:38). The range was in fact somewhat greater, encompassing Greek and Roman mythology, ancient and modern history (Lucretia's suicide [see Figure 6.3], was particularly popular), the Old Testament, and more contemporary poetry, including the works of Dante, Petrarch, and Boccaccio. The thread linking those subjects, which were deemed acceptable for inclusion on chests, was that they could, in some sense or other, be linked to marriage (Bayer 2008: 230–8, 303–6; Campbell 2009: 1–19). These pictures, like the chests they adorned, were also intended to be noticed and commented on. There is some evidence to suggest that they were utilized, on occasion, to instruct their users—children, as well as adults—in ways of thinking and behavior which were appropriate to their familial status, gender and their role within the household (Campbell 2009: 45, 73; Baskins 2008). And one of their most important performative functions was to cast honor upon the families who were participating in the marriage alliances that occasioned their production. Chests were often decorated with heraldry, and *imprese* (intellectual symbols and visual conceits associated with a particular individual) (Paolini 2006: 120). Indeed, the way in which these chests could stand as physical memories of a particular alliance probably explains the reluctance of many Italian families to sell or dispose of painted chests, even after they had long ceased to be items of furniture in general use (Campbell 2009: 41).

Displaying the Body

Furniture that was used specifically to serve the body, such as beds, also became symbolic objects as they functioned within rituals. Beds varied in their decoration, but monumental beds and daybeds were a sign of prestige and were often an imposing presence in a room, and like chests were often adorned with family arms, painted decoration, or intarsia, which could convey symbolic meaning (Figure 6.4) (Ariés and Duby 1988: 106–14). Types of beds of course varied depending on social status. Owning a bed in itself was seen as a sign of particular standing, as large portions of society in the medieval and Renaissance periods simply slept on straw mats. A variety of types of beds could thus be found in the same household—simple beds on the ground floor for servants and household staff, while more elaborate beds with coverings and tapestries could be found in the upper rooms, as is evidenced from some of the inventories already mentioned.

In royal circles, there was a distinction between display (state) furniture and furniture that was meant to be functionally used. In England by the Tudor period, the three pieces of state furniture comprised the bed, the seat of authority, and the buffet, all of which were singled out especially in household regulations as items not to be touched by anyone except the king (Thurley 1993: 234). Beds of state were not always meant to be slept in, but simply to be displayed or used during ceremony. State beds across Europe, like other luxury pieces of furniture such as thrones, cradles, chairs, and daybeds, were often marked by a large canopy indicating privilege, prestige, and status. These canopies were sometimes designed by court painters, such as the one designed by Cosmé Tura of Ferrara for Duke Ercole d'Este, and they could also feature in sumptuary legislation, underlining their ability to convey signs of wealth and display status (Thornton 1991: 129, 133; Morley 1999: 77). One of the earliest records of an English state bed dates to the 1240s made for Henry III for his bedchamber at Westminster Palace, where he would give audience and hold meetings with council. Above the bed was a large wall painting from the 1260s, which depicted the coronation of the king's predecessor, Edward the Confessor, providing a clear symbolic message and a powerful visual connection between

FIGURE 6.3 Biagio d'Antonio, *The Death of Lucretia*. Photo: Galleria Giorgio Franchetti alla Ca' d'Oro, Veneto Museum complex, on grant from the Ministry of Cultural Heritage and Activities and Tourism.

the two rulers (Eames 1977: 75; Vale 2001: 64). By the time of Henry VIII, state beds had become so elaborate that they were merely used for the ritual of going to bed and rising in the morning, and the King would sleep in smaller, more comfortable beds elsewhere (Thurley 1993: 235–6). In 1380, when King Charles of France was dying, he was transported from his everyday bed into his state bed in his private bedchamber, where he could die with respect and honor (if less comfort) (Thornton 1991: 41).

Beds and *lettucci* could also be used to receive visitors when ill, as attested by a print from Savonarola's *The Art of Dying Well* (Figure 6.4), which shows a sick man reclining on his bed while visitors come to attend to him (Thornton 1991: 148). There was not always a clear distinction between beds and furniture for sitting, especially during the day, when beds were often used to receive visitors as chairs of state by elites. The large chests around beds also often provided seating for visitors. Throughout the centuries it was not uncommon for the pope to receive guests in his bedchamber, sometimes receiving them while he was in bed, such as in 1238 when a Franciscan from Germany, Jordon of Ciano, visited the pope or in 1526 when Isabella d'Este was given audience by the pope in his bedchamber (Mercer 1969: 63; Thornton 1991: 294).

Lettucci had multiple functions, as they could be used to lie or sit down as a daybed. Visual imagery suggests that when used by royalty, they could serve as a piece of furniture from which to give audience, displaying the authority of the ruling family. For example, a print from the late fifteenth century (Plate 20) depicts King Solomon giving audience from his *lettuccio* decorated with lavish textiles, using it as a quasi-throne (Mercer 1969: 74; Trionfi Honorati 1981: 40; Thornton 1991: 148). *Lettucci* were certainly gifts worthy for a king, as the Florentine merchant-banker Filippo Strozzi commissioned a *lettuccio* depicting a view of Naples from Benedetto da Maiano in 1473 to

li tucti appartengono ad te che se sano:ma debbi penfare che
ad ogni hora tu puoi infermarti & morire:perche quefto pen
fiero della morte e regola molto utile nella uita fpirituale.
Hor fa quefto bafti , quanto alla prima cartha del libro che io
ti ho decto che tu tifaccia dipingere. Vegnamo hora alla fe,
conda cartha.

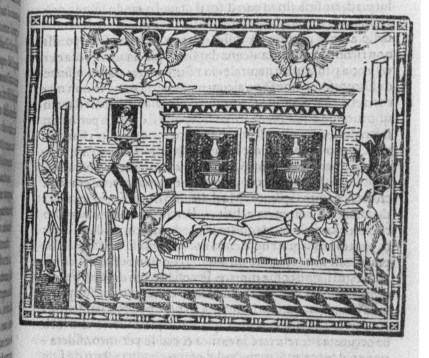

 La feconda cartha che io tidiffi gia altra uolta e quefta ch
tu tifacci dipingere uno huomo cominciato ad infirmarii con

FIGURE 6.4 Woodcut from Girolamo Savonarola's *Predica dell'arte del ben morire*
(Florence, 1496). Photograph courtesy of Metropolitan Museum of Art, Harris
Brisbane Dick Fund, 1925 (25.30.95).

give to King Ferrante d'Aragona of Naples, where it was highly admired and sparked a taste for *lettucci* in that city (Borsook 1970: 14; del Treppo 1994: 488–9; Clark 2009: 146–69). The following year, Filippo sent some additions to the *lettuccio*, including textiles, noting that these "adornments" will make the "beautiful *lettuccio* … even more beautiful" demonstrating how important the accoutrements were for furniture (del Treppo 1994: 489; Santoro 2000: 45). Beds, too, were conceived as prestigious gifts: John de Vere, thirteenth Earl of Oxford was given one as part of his fee for acting as Lord Great Chamberlain at Henry VII's coronation, while Henry VIII received a "rich bed" in 1529 from Francis I of France (Stratford 1993: 85; Thurley 1993: 234).

The throne-like quality of the *lettuccio* played upon the historic significance of the seat of honor, seen as a place of privilege on which the sovereign, judge, or bishop sat (Eames 1977: 181). Such symbolic seats usually had a religious significance alluding to the throne of Solomon, and in the medieval period frequently appeared in church space to mark earthly and heavenly authority. Some examples of these seats still exist such as the well-known Throne of Maximian in Ravenna from the middle of the sixth century; the tenth-century throne in the palace chapel at Aachen; or the later thirteenth-century archbishop's throne in Canterbury Cathedral (Reeve 2003: 131–42). It is these sorts of wooden boarded seats with high backs that also appear in medieval manuscript illumination, occupied by religious figures from Mary to the Evangelists, underlining their symbolic function.

The social nature and display function of beds and *lettucci* in the Renaissance are highlighted when one considers the reception of visitors coming to see a new mother in bed as commonly seen in depictions of biblical births, where furniture was used not only to display the mother and baby, but also the material culture of the family—from *deschi da parto* (painted birth trays) to maiolica bowls. As bedchambers were not intended only for sleeping but could be the focal point of special events such as marriages, births, funerals, and more casual receptions, the furniture and the decorations in those spaces were meant to be viewed by more than just the individuals who might sleep there (Preyer 1998: 357–74).

Cradles too were important markers of status and were integral to rituals associated with different stages of life for both the aristocracy and the middle classes. Cradles for show were used in houses of the elite in republics, as more than one cradle can be found in inventories in Venice, often one in a nurse's or servant's room, while more lavishly decorated ones could be found in the greater *camera* (Fortini Brown 2004: 77, 81, 96). Cradles belonging to royal babies were elaborately decorated, intended to impress and dazzle, and to reflect the status of the heir as well as the family. These were almost always intended only for display and ceremonial purposes, while more practical cradles, usually lower to the ground, were actually used for nursing and tending to the child. In 1403, Margaret of Flanders, Duchess of Burgundy purchased two cradles, "1 of state and the other for rocking and feeding the said infant." The accounts for the state cradle record fine textiles including crimson and ermine, as well as the cost of burnished gold for the painting of the coat of arms as decoration (Eames 1977: 97). An English manuscript dating from the fifteenth century, *The Christening of a Prince or Princess*, stresses the need for two cradles; the "cradell of Estate" was distinguished as larger and more richly decorated (Mercer 1969: 81).

Cradles were central to rituals around births and baptisms, often accompanied by feasting and other festivities in royal courts, and they could often be lavish gifts of state in themselves. Duke Borso d'Este of Ferrara paid his court painter to decorate a cradle with stars, a Madonna and Child, Saint Francis, an Annunciation, and Saint George along with foliage and the arms of Borso, which he gifted to his sister Isotta who was married and living in Croatia (Thornton 1991: 97). Such a gift would reflect the status of both giver and receiver, as well as the child. In 1493 Eleonora d'Aragona wrote home from Milan to her husband, Duke Ercole d'Este, in Ferrara about the cradle they had given to the son of their daughter Beatrice d'Este and Ludovico Sforza, commenting that all the ambassadors and gentlemen had come to admire it, while it was displayed in the *camera del thesoro* (Archivio di Stato di Modena, C&S 131–2, 1683 x-34). Such an item was not only meant to display the child, but also to reflect the magnificence of his grandparents and his parents. Ludovico Sforza estimated the gift at 8,000 to 10,000 ducats, an incredible sum, but this was surely an exaggeration. The cradle itself likely cost below 400 ducats, but the cloth furnishings and accoutrements would have cost more than 3,500 ducats, so lavish were they that they were later displayed on tables set up in the treasury (Tuohy 1996: 233). This was not the only state cradle the baby used, as another one of Milanese manufacture was also displayed nearby in a *camera del putino*, which was completely gilded with four columns and a large canopy (*spavero*) with gold cords and blue silk. It stood next to a great bed decorated with Sforza devices and a canopied *lettuccio*, from either of which the mother, Beatrice d'Este, likely received visitors. The Milanese cradle was described by a Ferrarese lady-in-waiting to Eleonora d'Aragona as "bellissima" but she made sure to note that the Ferrarese cradle was also on display and was "worthy of an emperor"—both were presumably state cradles, which reflected their respective courts (Thornton 1991: 253; Welch 1995: 226–7, 319, n. 84). Birthing rituals also gave the family the opportunity to show off their material wealth, either through the display and use of the furniture in their home, or for the higher echelons of society, through the display of treasury items and the practice of guided tours of the palace to visiting dignitaries.

Displaying honor and wealth

Credenze in Italy (buffets in England and *dressoirs* in France) were a particular piece of furniture that emerged to coincide with the increasing emphasis on display, especially in dining rituals. *Credenze* were made specifically to display precious vessels, some of which were only collected to testify to their owner's wealth rather than to be used in dining. It was significant events that would require that the treasures of the household to be removed from lock and key and to be put on display to reflect the status and honor of the family. It is striking that few of these valuable objects have survived, perhaps due as much to their fragility as well as their material value if melted down, we have many accounts and descriptions of the less costly items of furniture on which they were displayed. *Dressoirs* appear regularly in manuscript illumination depicting activities associated with the Burgundian court, which highlights their symbolic function and the status they hoped to convey (Plate 21). Like beds and thrones, they were often accompanied by lavish canopies made out of expensive textiles.

The close relationship between the display of the heir and the display of wealth is evident in the fact that the treasury also served as the "antechamber to the illustrious birthing chamber" during the 1493 Sforza birth festivities in Milan, where a *credenza* of silver vases was shown off to visitors (Welch 1995: 223–5). Ludovico Sforza presumably wanted to take advantage of showing off his wealth, his heir, and his wife to ambassadors and fellow princes, but such an arrangement was fairly common in Sforza and Visconti castles where the women's quarters were traditionally placed next to the treasury. This arrangement would have served both a symbolic and practical function, as a lady-in-waiting at the birth ceremony commented that "each room had its own doormen and its own seneschal and its own guards for each bed," underlining the need to safeguard the duchess's chastity and the duke's wealth (225–7). Similarly, at the court of Burgundy in 1457, the room in which the duchess gave birth to Mary of Burgundy also contained a *dressoir* with tiers "fully charged with rock crystal vessels set in gold and studded with gems, and there were vessels of pure gold ... all the most precious vessels of duke Philip the Good were there, ... which were never put on display except for such occasions" (Helfenstein 2013: 432–6). In middle-class Renaissance homes it was also common to store treasures in the bedchamber, as Alberti instructed "where they are safe from fire and other natural disaster, and where I can frequently, whether for my pleasure or to check them over, shut myself up alone or with whomever I choose while giving no cause for undue curiosity to those outside" (Alberti 1956: 207–20; Musacchio 2008: 105–6).

Credenze were also used by the merchant classes, especially in Florence, where numerous *cassoni* and *spalliere* (painted backboards or wainscoting) depicting marriage feasts show the *credenza* on central display, alluding to the ways the *credenza* and the objects on it were part of the staging of identity within the theatrical performance of social life and its rituals, and it is not surprising that the number of stages and the vessels displayed figured in sumptuary legislation. One or two stages were fairly common amongst the wealthy, but special occasions called for more, such as in 1476 when the Florentines wanted to impress the sons of the King of Naples and the *credenza* was set with nine stages full of silver and gold vases. A similar display at Ferrara impressed Ludovico Sforza so much that he asked Duke Ercole d'Este in 1483 for drawings of his spectacular service (Thornton 1991: 207–9; Syson and Thornton 2001: 65–8; Syson 2002b: 45). In England, a variety of buffets were reported in different rooms from the king's bedchamber to the great hall—some were functional while others were dedicated to display in ceremonial. On occasions of state, Henry VIII had twelve stages while Cardinal Wolsey in 1527 was reported at Hampton Court to have half that number, which reflected Wolsey's high status while at the same time not daring to rival the king's (Thurley 1993: 242). Marital *credenza* also appear in wedding scenes, such as a well-known *spalliera* by Botticelli, which depicts the final wedding feast in Boccaccio's tale of Nastagio degli Onesti, providing a moral tale around conspicuous consumption (Olsen 1992).

In the courts, visits from foreign dignitaries could also be an excuse to show off a ruler's wealth. A typical tour of an elite palace would involve a visit to the treasury, *studiolo*, or chamber where precious stones, gems, vases, and jewels would be displayed on tables or cabinets (Thornton 1997; Clark 2013: 171–84). But *credenze,* treasuries, or specific rooms dedicated to collecting such as *studioli* were not the only places where collectibles were displayed; rather, tables, shelves, beds, *lettucci,* and chests were also used to exhibit or store collections. Inventories and images attest to the display of works of art and other objects on the ledges of *lettucci,* or attached on the wall above them, while some even had hat pegs to hang things on (see Figure 6.3). Other items for display were incorporated into the structure of the room itself, such as on ledges above doors, constructed cornices running along the wall, or built-in shelves (as in Dürer's woodcut, Figure 6.2) (Smith 1975: 31–40; Braham 1979: 754–63, 65; Thornton 1991: 150–1; Ajmar-Wollheim and Dennis 2006b: 272; Warren 2006: 302). Among the many *lettucci* in the Medici inventory of 1492 one incorporated cupboards and "caskets" or small chests (*chasette*), which contained arms, armor, cuirasses, daggers, and damascened candlesticks. The same inventory describes a cupboard with seven shelves set into paneling that held a variety of ceramic dishes, including porcelain vases, all of which were evaluated at a considerable sum, suggesting these were precious objects both worthy of display and protection (Kemp 1997: 141). In the *camera d'oro* in the Da Lezze house in sixteenth-century Venice there were two *scrigenti* or cabinets filled with the family's treasures including jewelry, silver cutlery, and other wares, while the room also contained a harpsichord, five chairs, a walnut stool for doing needlework, a walnut *cassone* (which contained dresses), and a bed on wheels, suggesting this space was likely used for multiple purposes (Fortini Brown 2004: 77). Caskets or small storage containers could also be purpose-built and valued items of furniture in their own right. The humanist Angelo

Poliziano, Secretary to Lorenzo de' Medici, noted that his master's gems had been put in armoires opened for viewing when Cardinal Raffaele Riario visited, underlining the flexibility and use of furniture (Fusco and Corti 2006: 194–5).

CONCLUSION: EXHIBITION AND DISPLAY

This chapter has outlined how the display function of furniture was closely linked to its performative nature in the medieval period and during the Renaissance. Many items of furniture—from chests to daybeds and cradles to *credenze*—had multifaceted functions, which were malleable and altered according to context. The interior rooms of the home were likewise not static, but often changed depending on what rituals or activities were taking place in those spaces. Furthermore, some items of furniture, such as chests, were movable, and thus were used as portable storage items, stationary objects of display, as well as mnemonic and symbolic devices, marking a marriage and often reinstating gender expectations. Sometimes these objects were subjected to immense structural changes, being altered so that they conformed with new fashions, or even in some cases completely changing form. For instance, a Florentine sale of household furniture in 1549 records two chests that were put together to make a *lettuccio*. Yet even in such radically altered states such objects retained considerable value: the *lettuccio* of this 1549 sale had an estimated price of twenty-eight lire, but it sold for forty (Matchette 2006: 711).

The adaptability and flexibility of Renaissance furniture may explain its durability over the centuries; although the predominance of family symbols and coats of arms on the external surfaces of many of these items must also have been an important factor. Only in recent years, thanks to the development of technical art history, has there been any appreciation of the extent to which most surviving pieces of what purports to be fifteenth- and sixteenth-century furniture were radically reshaped, remade out of existing fragments, or even made from scratch in the late nineteenth and early twentieth centuries. Chests, which survived in larger numbers than any other category of furniture, have been subject to particularly heavy reconstruction. Many apparently fifteenth-century painted chests were remade in the nineteenth century, out of pieces of damaged yet more historically true objects (Callmann 1999: 338–48). A considerable number were reconstructed, in a small number of Florentine workshops, on the basis of one of the woodcuts made to illustrate Savonarola's *The Art of Dying Well* (Figure 6.4). This shows a chest, displayed as a sideboard, to which an ornately carved *spalliera* has been attached. On the basis of this contemporary print, and one apparently intact pair of chests with their *spalliera* panels (now in the Courtauld Gallery, London; Plate 19) it was believed that *cassoni* were always made in conjunction with these backboards. Curiously, the Morelli-Nerli chests and *spalliere* do always seem to have belonged to the same decorative ensemble. They were commissioned in 1472 to mark the marriage of the Florentine patrician Lorenzo Morelli to Vaggia Nerli, and they are recorded as such, although—significantly—with "una spalliera" running above them, in inventories of the Morelli family long into the sixteenth century (Campbell 2009: 73–4). However, in the late nineteenth century, and probably in Florence, the backboards were screwed onto the chests. This made it impossible for the chests to fulfill their original dual purpose as storage chests as well as objects of show and display, as they could no longer be opened without causing damage to the *spalliera* panels (Barraclough 2009: 78–9). This simple but important piece of evidence shows that these items of furniture were no longer configured as they would have been in the late fifteenth century. The alteration to their structure, however, made them better able to perform their new function, as massive and impressive pieces of Renaissance Florentine furniture, destined for a private or public museum.

The Morelli-Nerli chests are therefore, in their way, a palimpsest of how issues of display and show have continued to impact Renaissance furniture. Since the late 1940s these objects have been a constant feature of the permanent collection of a leading university art gallery and their prominent public presentation has arguably contributed to the revival of academic interest in Renaissance furniture (Campbell 2009: 69). In their altered state they not only bear witness to the display purpose of much Renaissance furniture, but they show how exhibition and display—in a very different context—remain a constant of these objects' identity, more than five centuries after they were made in late fifteenth-century Italy.

CHAPTER SEVEN

Furniture and Architecture

ETHAN MATT KAVALER

Philip Johnson's AT&T Building in New York, whose postmodern pediment was famously mocked as a reference to a "Chippendale highboy," highlights the contemporary assumption that architecture and furniture should have little if anything in common ("AT&T Building" 1987; Glynn 2001). This belief is largely the legacy of modernism with its polemical dismissal of ornament as a sensual or structuring element. Historians and critics today tend to endorse this assessment, despite the fact that many modernist architects such as Mies van der Rohe, Gerrit Rietveld, and Arne Jacobsen designed paradigmatic articles of furniture. Their famous chairs, however, are often considered discrete and quasi-ludic projects, removed from their more serious buildings.

The relationship between furniture and architecture was much more complex in the late Middle Ages and early modern period, their boundaries porous. Many genres of ecclesiastical furniture in particular adopted the larger forms and ornamental elements of chapels, churches, and cathedrals. Not all church furniture displayed architectural features, of course. The pulpit in Aachen Cathedral (the Ambon of Henry II) of around the year 1020 is gilded and bejeweled like an oversized piece of precious metalwork. Its costly materials signify rather than its form. Nor was architectural emulation the invention of the Gothic period. The Romanesque choir bench from the church of Sant Climent de Taüll in Catalonia is a set of three stalls sheltered by as many round arches, while the side mimics the façade of a Romanesque cathedral (Museu Nacional d'Art de Catalunya, Barcelona, accession no. MNAC 15898).

Yet the concordance between "architecture proper" and church furniture reached an unparalleled level of exchange during the late Gothic age, especially in central Europe. It is necessary to remember that the Gothic mode (pointed arches, geometric tracery, ribbed vaults, etc.) continued to be practiced in northern Europe and Spain well into the sixteenth century, at a time when we usually think of classical or Renaissance forms having already superseded these earlier creations. In fact, from about 1450 until 1540 Gothic design was revitalized across the continent, revealing new structural and ornamental forms—new ways of building, shaping space, and articulating surfaces—that had not been seen before in "classic" Gothic architecture (Kavaler 2012). The Gothic was, in fact, a cutting-edge design mode in northern Europe until the second third of the sixteenth century, attracting the most prestigious artists and patrons and effectively competing with the newly voguish antique manner, which has come to characterize for us the "Renaissance" period.

We should not worry too much about the precise definition of "furniture" in the period between 500 and 1500, this concern with categories of objects being much more relevant today than in the medieval period. There is also disparity between different languages. The English word "'furniture," for example, can signify a "means of equipment" necessary for a certain use, "decoration," or a "receptacle" or "container"—all of which relate in different degrees to our present-day notion of furniture (*Compact Oxford English Dictionary* 1971: 2:615–16). The French *meubles* and the German *Möbel*, on the other hand, derive from the Latin *mobilis* and imply movability—much as in the inclusion of these objects in Dutch inventories under the category "movable goods" (*roerende goederen*). With the exception of lecterns and a few other pieces of limited scale, church furnishing during the period covered here is generally not movable, though it is equipment necessary for the performance of the liturgy and can well be seen as an ornament to the building.

Nor should we take for granted the definition of architecture during this period. As Tara Bissett has emphasized, "architecture" was more an idea figured across texts and different visual media—a shifting *topos* in the imagination—than it was a distinct set of buildings or physical constructions (Bissett 2017). Medieval romances and devotional treatises introduced earthly and celestial—tangible and intangible—palaces as spaces for action and as visions of divine and secular power (Bucher 1976). Furthermore, the most innovative and fashionable architectural conventions were realized not only in churches, town halls, and palaces, but also in portals, pulpits, sacrament houses, gold reliquaries, carved altarpieces, paintings, and engravings. Thus, much furniture was not only *like* architecture, it *was* architecture—to the extent that it substantially helped define this protean and floating concept.

Whereas our modern notion of "architect" is fairly stable, the late medieval and early modern counterpart was more ambiguous. Architects themselves were a varied lot and came from many different traditions (Klein 2009: 13–17; Hurx 2012: 14–65). There were the designers of buildings as well as the *Baumeistern* or Masters of the Works, who often rose through the masons' guild. Architectural projects, however, might be drafted by other craftsmen as well. Sculptors generally needed to provide architectural frames for their carved figures. Consequently, they had to be well versed in current architectural conventions. The Flemish theorist Pieter Coecke van Aelst, for instance, specifically dedicated his classical architectural treatise of 1539, *The Design of the Orders* (*Die Inventie der Colommen*) to "painters, sculptors, masons, etc. and all who take pleasure in ancient buldings" (Coecke van Aelst 1539).

It was not unusual for sculptors to receive architectural commissions. The most prominent sixteenth-century Italian examples were Michelangelo and Giambologna (Cole 2011: 158–254). Their Netherlandish equivalents were Jacques Dubroeucq, who built several châteaux for Mary of Hungary and her court, and Cornelis Floris, the principal designer of the Antwerp town hall (Van Damme 1996: 115–20; De Jonge 2005: 95–112). Painters might also qualify. The northern "architects" sent to Italy around 1400 to work on the Cathedral of Milan included Jacques Coene, one of the most eminent Flemish painters then working in Paris (Welch 1995: 104–8).

The classification of professions was not cut and dried. Disputes over who could construct furniture were frequently resolved in court. A legal case concerning the choir stalls in the church of Saint Gertrude in Leuven, Belgium, is instructive (Glover 2017). In 1544 the Leuven masons' guild brought charges against Mathys de Wayere, the maker of the stalls. Mathys was registered as a joiner (*schrijnmaker*) and should have been restricted to fashioning the structural elements of the stalls, or so the masons contested. Yet he and his team had also carved the figural parts: the statuettes and biblical reliefs. Of course, prestigious choir stalls generally held statuettes of saints and narrative carvings; this was hardly a unique commission. Mathys succeeded in convincing the authorities that the images on his stalls enjoyed a different status from independent sculpture, that they qualified as "ornament" (*cyrate* or *sieraad*), which joiners were permitted to include in their work.

In fact, ecclesiastical furniture has for some time been considered a species of "micro-architecture," a concept that has drawn increasing attention since François Bucher's seminal article of 1976. His essay, "Micro-architecture as the 'Idea' of Gothic Theory and Style," introduced certain notions that will be refined in the present chapter. For Bucher, microarchitecture could be anything from miniature gold reliquaries to expansive Spanish retables that clothed cathedral apses. Bucher regarded microarchitecture, in its scalelessness, small size, and accessibility to optimal materials, best able to represent the ideals of Gothic design, which could be only imperfectly realized in monumental buildings (Bucher 1976).

There have been two traditions in the study and development of this concept. Medievalists have tended to follow Bucher's lead. They use the term "microarchitecture" and apply it to a wide variety of artifacts from embossed depictions of Gothic edifices on wax seals, coins, and medals, to sculptural representations of churches held by statues of saints, to pulpits, sacrament houses, and other works of church furniture. Clearly, our references here to microarchitecture are limited to this final category. The term has enjoyed increased popularity in the last decade and has served as the subject for conferences in Nuremberg ("Mikroarchitektur im Mittelalter" 2005) and Paris ("Microarchitecture et figures du bati" 2014).

The second tradition has always had more to do with Italian Renaissance art. Works of limited size in this mode have been labeled with the German word *Kleinarchitektur*. Jacob Burckhardt was the first to isolate these creations in his study of Italian Renaissance architecture. He dedicated a large part of his book to what he called "decoration"; the subsection titled "Decoration in Stone" treated such works of *Kleinarchitektur* as pulpits, tombs, and mantelpieces (Burckhardt 1987: 193–218). Recently, Alina Payne and others have followed Burckhardt's lead, discussing reduced architectural objects in terms of *Kleinarchitektur* and the German art historical discourse (Payne 2010: 365–86).

References linking microarchitecture to monumental architecture in these works serve several functions. Most directly, they relate furniture to the encompassing edifice, suggesting that it was an integral part of a whole, sharing the same cultural genetic code. The adoption by furniture of particular features, such as tower-like projections, for example, could suggest—as they do with cathedrals—a fortress-like protective capacity. The display of tracery could signify the role of geometry as the essential language of design in Gothic architecture and might further convey the Platonic associations with geometry as the instrument of creation, uncorrupted by materialization in the world and approximating the ideal language of divine thought. In addition, late Gothic furniture could serve as an experimental ground for developments in Gothic architecture in general—its materials and reduced scale permitting innovations in design that were not yet possible in heavy stone or in the size of large buildings.

Church furniture could serve as an exalted stage for the liturgy or sermons of the church. Sacrament houses or tabernacles for keeping the consecrated host, for instance, which became ever larger and more prominently placed throughout the fifteenth century, publicly celebrated the Eucharist. Many of these towering receptacles offered a dais for the priest, who would stand in full view of the congregation as he retrieved the Host from a compartment in the structure and transported it to the altar, where he would celebrate the Mass. Consuming the wine and wafer was still unusual for European laity in the fifteenth and sixteenth centuries; the mere sighting of the Host frequently sufficed. Sacrament houses provided a dramatic and conspicuous container and platform for the sacred materials of the Eucharist.

Well-crafted pulpits could similarly accentuate the importance of the preacher delivering his sermon. In Protestant churches the pulpit was, perhaps, the primary item of furniture; certain Lutheran chapels included the pulpit within the permanent architecture of the edifice (Hitchcock 1981: 125–7). In 1484–5, Hans Hammer built for Strasbourg Cathedral a highly elaborate pulpit (Plate 22) specifically commissioned to celebrate the eminent local theologian, Johann Geiler von Kaisersberg (Entz 1992: 7–10; Fuchs 1992; Schock-Werner 2012). Hammer was the Master of the Works of Strasbourg Cathedral, but since the building was largely completed by his tenure, he had relatively little to do on this edifice, one of the most prominent in the German lands. He did design a project for a north tower, which was never built, but his principle constructions were for other churches in the city and in other towns in Alsace.

Hammer, like so many Strasbourg architects, was enormously sophisticated and widely traveled. He had crossed southern Germany on his way to Hungary, where he had seen projects initiated by the king, Matthias Corvinus. And he may have visited Italy. His most recognized works, though, were items of church furniture such as the pulpit of 1495 for the Alsatian town of Saverne. His principal works of this genre, however, were for Strasbourg Cathedral: the lost Sacrament House of 1483, the organ buffet and *positif* of 1489, and his highly esteemed pulpit. The stair to Hammer's Strasbourg pulpit was itself a splendid invention, with a complex and undulating openwork tracery pattern serving as the balustrade. The basket or *Korb* rises from a "foundation" of intersecting arches holding additional filler tracery that screens its substantial supports. The ornate baldachins along the top of the basket sheltered statuettes carved by such prominent Strasbourg sculptors as Veit Wagner and Nikolaus Hagenauer (Kavaler 2012: 167–9).

Like Hans Hammer, many celebrated architects of the late medieval and early modern period designed church furniture. Because of its possibilities for innovative design and the relatively free reign they offered architects, works of furniture might stand as signature pieces in an artist's oeuvre. Unlike churches themselves, furniture could be completed within a limited period of time and according to its original design. A church could easily take more than a century to complete, and its plan might be altered by later architects. A work of furniture could, thus, allow both artist and patron to enjoy the fruits of their collaboration.

Partly for these reasons, works of church furniture became the signature pieces of several architects. The German sculptor and architect Adam Kraft reserved his most distinctive sign of identity for the imaginative and elaborate sacrament house of 1493–6 (Plate 23) that he built for St. Lorenz Church in Nuremberg (Bauer and Stolz 1974: 8–12; Kavaler 2012: 172–3). The dais is supported by life-size kneeling figures. Instead of the expected apostles or patriarchs, however, these supporting men are clearly craftsmen. The figure at the front is a self-portrait of Kraft himself, with recognizable facial features, who is holding a chisel and mallet, the tools of his trade. In Vienna, Anton

Pilgram, the Master of the Works of the Church of St. Stephen (now cathedral) likewise included his self-portrait on the pulpit, peering out of a small window in the base and holding his architect's compass (Plate 24 and Figure 7.1). Pilgram later added a self-portrait at the base of his Organ Tribune in the same church (Plate 25), a magnificent gallery that adapts cutting-edge techniques of vaulting to its new venue (Kavaler 2012: 173–9). In the Low Countries, the sculptors Jan Borman II, Jan Borman III, and Jean Mone all signed exemplary carved altarpieces with their extensive architectural frames (Saintenoy 1931: 37; D'Hainaut-Zvweny 2005: 170–1, 193). In Ulm, the famous sculptor Jörg Syrlin the Elder, who carved the famous choir stalls and High Altarpiece in Ulm Minster, chose to inscribe his lettered signature on a sacristy cabinet now in the Ulm Museum (Gropp 1999; Roller and Roth 2002).

These "signatures" on furniture partook of a general revolution in signs of authorship across the arts. Albrecht Dürer's famous painted self-portraits are, perhaps, the best-known examples, but they were hardly alone. Conventional architects had for centuries played with different types of signatures. The labyrinth inscribed in the pavement of the Gothic Cathedral of Amiens was a sign of both the architect's ingenuity and identity (Klein 1998: 63). A more direct sign of authorship is found in the triforium of the choir of St. Vitus in Prague: a series of portrait busts that represent Emperor Charles IV, his family, and archbishops—but also includes portraits of the architects Matthieu d'Arras and Peter Parler (de la Riestra 1998: 211). Tomb slabs in churches likewise testified to the author of the edifice. On St. Martin's Church in Landshut, an epitaph with a portrait bust of the builder Hans von Burghausen rests on the façade (Kurman and Kurmann-Schwarz 2010: 44–60). In the Austrian town of Feistritz an der Drau, furthermore, the remarkable architect Bartlmâ Firtaler painted his signature above the gallery on the inner west wall (Brucher 1990: 282–4).

The relationship between furniture—or microarchitecture—and monumental architecture depended partly on the geometric nature of Gothic design (Bork 2011). Because most architectural elements were drafted in terms of geometrical figures and their permutations and transpositions, Gothic design enjoyed an essential scalelessness. The geometric plan and elevation for the openwork spire of a miniature gold reliquary could be easily adapted to a stone sacrament house rising ten meters or to a church spire of significantly greater height. It is indicative of this lack of fixed scale that a Gothic drawing in the collection of the Akademie der bildenden Künste in Vienna, now thought to represent the ground plan of a baptismal font, was previously considered the plan of the spire of the church of Maria am Gestade in that city (Bucher 1976: 74–5; Böker 2005: 133).

Among the most impressive works of late medieval church furniture is a 1467 ciborium, the skeletal and tower-like celebratory case that covers the baptismal font (Figure 7.3), in the Church of Saint Severus in Erfurt (Thuringia). The sinuous lines of tracery that weave the skeletal enclosure about the font suggest

FIGURE 7.1 Anton Pilgram, Pulpit (Self-portrait), St. Stephen's, Vienna, *c.* 1505.
Photograph by the Author.

FIGURE 7.2 Anton Pilgram, Pulpit (basket), St. Stephen's, Vienna, *c.* 1505. Photograph by the Author.

FIGURE 7.3 Ciborium and Baptismal Font, Saint Severus, Erfurt, 1467. Photograph courtesy of Open Source.

the transformation of advanced two-dimensional window tracery patterns into a palpable three-dimensional object. Small statuettes of saints are supported by the structure, but the visual impact is overwhelmingly due to the abstract, curving, and intersecting bars of tracery that break out of their plane. The ciborium seems to be a stone index—the trace—of its process of design: the original lines drafted on paper or vellum with the aid of a compass and straightedge. Achim Timmermann (2007) has suggested that the author of this work emerged from the architectural lodge of the Cathedral of Strasburg, perhaps the premier institution for architectural innovation in the German-speaking lands at this time. It was in these progressive workshops on the Upper Rhine that the architect Johann Dotzinger, Master of the Works at Basel Minster, for example, developed his skills. In the cloister at Basel, his vault in the bay nearest the south portal employs looping, floral-like tracery, while the top of the portal's arch is filled with complex open tracery. Significantly, Dotzinger also designed church furniture, such as the great sacrament house of 1435–8 for the Minster, which is no longer extant (Kavaler 2012: 6–7; Schock-Werner n.d.).

Another paradigmatic piece of ecclesiastical furniture is the pulpit to the Church of St. Stephen in Vienna mentioned above (Plate 24 and Figure 7.2). Every part is a manifesto of sixteenth-century Gothic design. The basket or *Korb*, which holds the preacher (Figure 7.2), is veiled in successive sheets of astonishingly delicate tracery that clothe the structure and thereby hide its necessarily heavy supportive elements. These openwork pointed arches emerge as fully three-dimensional, concave projections channeled with moldings and intricate tracery motifs within their contours. Similar, smaller, more complex arches act as baldachins for the four busts of the church fathers that occupy niches around the basket. These smaller tracery figures establish an almost musical counterpoint with their larger cousins beneath the portrait sculptures.

This intricate complex tracery that dresses the forms and conceals the substantial foundation is closely related to the façades of the well-known flamboyant churches of the turn of the sixteenth century. When we regard one of the most famous examples, that Church of Saint Trinité at Vendôme north of the Loire and designed by Jean Texier de Beauce around 1500, we note a closely related dependence on elaborate pointed arches filled with openwork tracery figures that spread unbroken from the tympana atop all three portals, to the spandrels above, and through the openwork galleries, finally intersecting with the large arched window that takes the place of the more common rose (Figure 7.4) (Hamon 2008: 522, n. 106).

Perhaps even more unexpected is the relationship between the transparent tracery of the pulpit and the development of vaults in central Europe with flying ribs—ribs suspended in open space without any webbing. This, too, was an invention of the early sixteenth century. A good example is the vaulting of the Holy Cross Chapel in the Willibrordi Church at Wesel in the Lower Rhine,

FIGURE 7.4 Jean Texier de Beauce, Saint Trinité, Vendôme, *c.* 1500. Photograph by the Author.

completed before 1518 by Johann Langenberg (Figure 7.5). The webbing of the chapel is painted white and supported by intersecting looping ribs that inscribe a tracery figure at the crown of the vault. Yet hanging in mid-air beneath this construction is a second network of curvilinear ribs that enframe their own tracery motifs (Nussbaum 2000: 197–9).

Relations between furniture and vaulting were more extensive than the chapel at Wesel might suggest. The crossing springers (ribs emerging from the pier) that we find in so many late Gothic churches, for instance, seem to find their origin in these smaller ecclesiastical objects. Hans von Burghausen's music oratory in the Church of St. Lawrence of about 1430 in Landshut is supported by an abrogated vault that displays these crisscrossing ribs, and the underside to the stair of Pilgram's pulpit in Vienna is decorated with "broken ribs" that

FIGURE 7.5 Johann Langenberg, vault, Wesel, Willibrordi Church, Holy Cross Chapel, *c.* 1518. Photograph by the Author.

were then being introduced into large halls by architects such as Benedikt Ried in Prague (Nussbaum 2000: 202–3; Kavaler 2012: 176–9, 236–9).

Near the Vienna pulpit in St. Stephen's, against the north wall, is the organ tribune that also bears Pilgram's self-portrait (Plate 25). Seen from beneath, the ribbed support of the tribune appears as an abrogated model of the looping, curvilinear vaults introduced into central European architecture about 1500 (Kavaler 2012: 172–6). Classic examples are found in the Church of St. Anne in Annaburg, Saxony, and Most, Czech Republic, both of which devolve from the radical designs of Benedikt Reid at Prague (Nussbaum 2000: 207–11). There are, however, many examples scattered throughout the Austrian provinces such as the parish church of Weistrach in Upper Austria (Figure 7.6). Double-curved ribs (curved in plan and elevation) spring from the piers and intersect each

FIGURE 7.6 Vault, Parish Church, Weistrach. Photograph by the Author.

other as they extend their winding rings to the crown of the vaults (Brucher 1990: 197–8).

The Vienna organ tribune also emphasized the scalelessness and geometrical basis of the Gothic that allowed furniture to exploit and even innovate techniques of Gothic design. As François Bucher demonstrates, the tribune, shown upside down, strongly resembles drawings for the bases of chalices and other small receptacles of precious metal (Bucher 1976: 82). Metalwork and engraving have been seen as links between architecture and various other media. The engraved tracery lines on chalices, reliquaries, and monstrances— and their delicate skeletal towers—were generally more elaborate than their counterparts in stone and could serve as models for less refined emulation on a monumental scale.

Further, the skills used in engraving on metal surfaces were those necessary to produce engraved prints. A great many intaglio prints of architectural subjects were made by a variety of artists in the late medieval and early modern period. These works broadly disseminated cutting-edge architectural designs, quite often as church furniture. Established masons such as Wenzel von Ölmutz in central Europe, Hans Böbblinger in southern Germany, and Alart Duhamel in the Low Countries produced such prints. But painters like Albrecht Dürer, the Master ES, Dirk Vellert, Hans Burgkmair, and Hans Holbein the Younger also contributed to the genre. Around 1470, von Ölmutz produced an engraving of an elegant sacrament house that was closely followed some thirty years later by the Augsburg architect Stephan Weyrer, when the latter created the sacrament house for the church of St. George in Nördlingen (Timmermann 2009: 141–2).

Duhamel, a colleague of Hieronymus Bosch's in the Brabantine town of 's-Hertogenbosch, issued prints of a stone baldachin and an intricate monstrance. These spire-like forms were among the most fungible designs of the Gothic, as we have seen. Duhamel was at the time in charge of the collegiate church of St. John in 's-Hertogenbosch, and his expertise was also requested for numerous projects elsewhere. At St. John's he authored the north portal with its graceful, intersecting, and openwork balustrade of inverted arches. He also planned the remarkable baldachin atop the (now nineteenth-century) statue of a saint on the northeast pier of the crossing (Figure 7.7). This surprising piece of microarchitecture or church furniture appears to be caught in the moment

FIGURE 7.7 Alart Duhamel, "Collapsing Baldachin," St. John's, 's-Hertogenbosch, c. 1500. Photograph by the Author.

of collapse. Its lower uprights are tilted at an angle and seem to be shifting under the weight of the upper elements, destabilizing the object. Such a creation was a game, a *jeu*, for laypeople and professionals who understood the basic principles of Gothic design and were presumably amused by this contravention of expectations. But the 's-Hertogenbosch baldachin was also an up-to-date experiment in the deconstruction of the Gothic system, of its statics and its ideational bases that allowed it intimate impressions of physical and spiritual stability. It belongs to the same movement as Benedikt Ried's broken ribs on the vaults to the Rider Stair at the Royal Castle in Prague of about 1500 (Figure 7.8), to which Anton Pilgram playfully referred in the vaulting to his pulpit in Vienna (Kavaler 2012: 232–40). It also relates to Freiberg's so-called Tulip Pulpit, which appears to be pulling apart and is visually secured by the life-size figure of a man bracing the stair on his back (Körner 1990: 68–9).

Material was a central issue. Wood furniture might come even closer to the imagined ideal of transparency and intersection than stone—even stone furniture—could achieve. The tall spire-like baldachins of choir stalls frequently exceeded the limits of church spires and sacrament houses. The spindly canopies of the choir stalls in Chester Cathedral of *c.* 1370, are far more delicate, airy, and open than the famous skeletal spire of the Minster at Freiburg im Breisgau. The Bishop's throne in Exeter Cathedral, moreover, also from the fourteenth century, develops interlocking geometrical figures into a magnificent and fully three-dimensional baldachin, with "nodding" arches that break away from the plane (Binski 2014: 134–8). It is not only far less substantial than contemporary church building, it also better demonstrates the paradigm of Gothic design as a spatial assemblage of geometrical elements.

The epitome of this development—of the ideals achievable in wood Gothic—may be the oak choir stalls (1508–22) in Amiens Cathedral (Tracy and Harrison 2004; Lemé-Hébuterne 2007). The canopy above the seat for the King of France is an extremely complex and airy tower, an extreme elaboration of what we have been surveying in this chapter. Yet even more impressive are the ends of the stalls that draw their form from both church façades and carved altarpieces (Figure 7.9). Intricately detailed, paradoxically skeletal buttresses rise along the sides of the stall ends, which culminate at the top in an encompassing ogee arch that simulates a gable. Between the faux-buttresses is an extraordinarily delicate array of intersecting arches, miniature canopies, and pendants (with tiny bosses). The arches that decorate the buttresses and the drop tracery inside them are extraordinarily fine. They resemble threads and recall the pen lines that mark the original drafting of their geometrical course. The lace-like appearance of the stall ends, executed in hard oak, testifies to the highest level of virtuoso craftsmanship among wood carvers and, consequently, furniture makers.

FIGURE 7.8 Benedikt Ried, Rider Stair, vault, Hradchin, Prague, *c.* 1500. Photograph by the Author.

Three narrative carvings from the Life of the Virgin and Infancy of Christ have been set within this architectural frame, just as we would find in one of the carved altarpieces from the Low Countries or northern France. There are, however, distinct differences between the genres. At Amiens, the figural reliefs are not at the same height, as they would be in an altarpiece. They are situated, instead, at different levels. They, thus, resemble the reliefs and statues that are occasionally inserted in church façades, especially in the northern provinces of Picardy and Flanders. They depart visibly, however, from even these models through the exceedingly diaphanous and fragile nature of their encompassing support.

In suggesting the incorporeal linearity of Gothic design, the Amiens stall ends might call to mind the Platonic, metaphysical connotations of this mode of architecture. Geometry, a language of pure mathematical relations uncorrupted by materialization in the real world, could stand as a semblance of the purity of divine thought. "Every mathematical name is less improperly said of God than is a concrete name," wrote Alan of Lille, the twelfth-century theologian and philosopher who enjoyed particular popularity at the end of the Middle Ages (Jolivet 1980: 83–99; Butterworth 1991: 89–90; Hudry 1995: 7–80). Nicolas of Cusa was one of several authorities who followed earlier authors such as Boethius in stating that God had created the world through the use of geometry along with arithmetic and music (Cusanus 1954: 1:46, 2:118–19). The image of God as geometer, fashioning the world with the aid of a compass, was still current in the fifteenth century (Friedman 1974: 419–39).

The narrative scenes representing human figures and props like altar tables and sheds could be understood as the imperfect materialization of the divine idea as matter. Nicolas of Cusa was one of many who supported this concept when he asserted that "Thus materialized, no form is true, but rather only an image of the truth of true form, since the truth of form is separated from all material" (Cusanus 1967: 3:231). These ideas easily migrated from high theological texts to popular works such as the *Pilgrimage of Human Life*, a fourteenth-century devotional work that enjoyed a vogue in the fifteenth and sixteenth centuries and was published in both French and Spanish editions around 1500 (Deguileville 1992).

Such lattices of tracery might also serve other functions. The "pure" geometrical armature that encases the biblical scenes could represent God's plan with respect to time as well as space. The three different narrative moments are all experienced by mortals on earth as distinct and sequential. But the observer of the choir stall end can see all three events simultaneously. The ability to see the entirety of divine history in a single moment is the privilege of God; the Amiens ends offer an image that approximates this divine perception of time. It makes visible the notion of the "eternal present" through which God sees in an instant all events that have passed and all that will come to pass. Boethius and

FIGURE 7.9 Choir Stall (End), Amiens Cathedral, *c.* 1515. Photograph by the Author.

Saint Augustine famously discussed this mystical faculty; the relevant passages in Boethius's *Consolation of Philosophy* received numerous commentaries at the end of the fifteenth century (Boethius 1978: 5:77–80; Augustine 1982: § 13; Lloyd 1999: 56–9; Kavaler 2017).

This property was more commonly suggested by another genre of church furnishing, the carved wood altarpieces of the Netherlands. These retables were immensely popular, both in the Low Countries themselves and in nearly every European land to which they were exported in great numbers. The Altarpiece of the Life of the Virgin, made in Antwerp in 1518–22 and shipped to the wealthy Baltic city of Lübeck, is a fine example (Figure 7.10) (Borchgrave d'Altena 1958: 95; Hasse 1983: 146–8). Such works and their local imitations were desired acquisitions of prominent churches from Scandinavia, to England, to northern Italy (Jacobs 1998: 149–208; Woods 2007: 106–42). Although nearly a third of these altarpieces have been stripped of their original polychromy, they were nearly all originally painted and gilded, their extensive and elaborate baldachins reflecting the vagaries of daylight and candlelight on their brilliant gold surfaces. The gilding, thus, distanced the altarpieces from

FIGURE 7.10 Antwerp Artists, Altarpiece of the Life of the Virgin, Marienkirche, Lübeck, 1518–22. Photograph by the Author.

the encompassing chapel or church in which they were located and set them in an ideal realm, recalling, perhaps, the golden city of the heavenly Jerusalem as described in the Book of Revelations (Jacobs 1998: 132–44). The framing of the biblical scenes might that much more easily be accepted as a physical and metaphysical register of God's plan, both spatial and temporal.

Finally, church furniture could also introduce a new architectural mode. This was particularly true with the voguish antique manner of the early sixteenth century. Before monumental buildings were constructed in this Italianate fashion in France, the Low Countries, or Germany, its architectural features were already present in a number of microarchitectural genres from tombs and epitaphs to altarpieces. In France, the Renaissance candelabra pilasters on the architectural frame to the Holy Sepulchre at Solesmes are dated 1494—before any "Renaissance" château or church was built (Zerner 2003: 351–4). The same could be said for the Tomb of Francois II of Brittany at Nantes, planned in 1499, or the frame of the altarpiece for Georges d'Amboise's chapel at Gaillon (Blunt 1973: 40–2). In the Netherlands, Jean Mone's Italianate tombs, mantelpieces, and altarpieces of the 1520s likewise preceded any secular or religious building on a large scale (Lipińska 2015: 57–67). And in Germany, epitaphs such as that of Anton Kress of around 1513 by Peter Vischer in Nuremberg's church of St. Lorenz preceded the dedication of even that incunabulum of German Renaissance architecture, the Fugger Chapel, which was completed in 1519 (Smith 1994: 129–31).

Church furniture of the period around 1500 maintained a close relation with architecture. To an extent, it *was* architecture, since it frequently embodied decorative and structural aspects less fully apparent in monumental building. Thus, it greatly contributed to the notion of architecture, a flexible concept defined across numerous media. The architectural features of this furniture— pulpits, jubés (rood-screens), sacrament houses, baldachins (for statues of saints), choir stalls, baptismal fonts, and many other such objects—were concentrated and used specific expositions of principles of architectural design that could never have the same focus in full-size churches and monasteries with their multifarious parts and functions.

The adoption of architectural forms helped relate furniture to the containing edifice—implying that it partook of the service and symbolism of the larger structure. Such furniture was integrated with daily performances. Sacrament houses offered a dramatic stage for the Eucharist, baptismal fonts for the sacrament of baptism, choir stalls for the recital of the offices, and pulpits for sermons.

This furniture—or microarchitecture, as it has been called—could demonstrate advanced techniques in architectural design—closely related to innovations in contemporary development of church façades and even vaults. Furniture might even initiate a new architectural mode—the "Renaissance" antique manner, which often appeared in microarchitecture before it was manifested in palaces, town halls, or churches. This development was especially prevalent in the late Gothic period. The geometrical basis of Gothic design allowed for a certain scalelessness in conception, which heightened the relationship of furniture to monumental building. All architectural objects were drafted with a compass and straightedge—they were conceived as disembodied lines and might be realized in almost any size. For this reason, Gothic furniture could also carry Platonic associations with geometry as a pure language of divine thought, removed from the imperfections of material existence.

Because furniture might be constructed within a limited period of time—from a matter of months to a few years—while churches could takes decades if not centuries to complete, these modestly scaled works could better stand as signature pieces of leading architects. Architects in important cities such as Vienna and Nuremberg might include a sculptural self-portrait in these creations.

Church furniture was a principal genre of the arts in the late medieval and early modern period. Although dismissed in much of the modernist twentieth century as part of the minor "decorative arts," attention is now being redirected to these creations as instrumental to many of the issues that now concern cultural historians.

CHAPTER EIGHT

Visual Representations

Setting the Stage—The Structural Roles of Furniture in Medieval Art and Illustration

DIANE J. REILLY AND ELIZABETH MOORE HUNT

A comparison between the scriptorium of the Old Testament scribe Ezra depicted in the eighth-century Anglo-Saxon *Codex Amiatinus* (Plate 26), and the study carrel staged for the biblical translator and commentator Saint Jerome painted by Antonello da Messina around 1475 (Plate 27), reveals how furniture can provide the art historian with the most basic visual tools of formal analysis. The orthogonal lines allow the viewer to measure objectively the artist's success in rendering space. The physical structure of furniture within medieval representations functions only in part to suggest spatial setting, however, for its structural role more importantly helps to convey the iconographic content of the image. Both Ezra's and Jerome's scriptoria contain custom-shelved furniture to support the books that they used for translation and elevated platforms to suggest their divine appointments. In providing the structural armature of the image's spatial setting, furniture could be used to expand, amplify, or assign meaning to their sitters from within.

Most of the roles ascribed to furniture stem from the types of people using it—the author writing at his desk, rulers seated on thrones, or mothers and elders attended from bedsides. The compositions for such scenes were fairly standardized, but the choice and elaboration of furniture forms allowed the artist to stage more complex nuances for the events depicted. As Penelope Eames emphasizes in her 1977 catalog of medieval furniture, ceremonial pieces and accessories such as daises, footboards, and textile canopies were assigned according to the social hierarchy, or "precedence," of figures within an image, so shifts in the usage or appearance of furniture forms can suggest something in particular about the status of an individual (1977: xix). For example, a mortise-and-tenon footstool grounds the labor of the scribe Ezra in the opening folio to the *Codex Amiatinus*, but a floating, marquetry platform is used to elevate Christ's feet over the cosmos in the *Maiestas Domini* image opening the New Testament later in the same codex. This chapter describes how artists manipulated such nuances in depicting three of the most common furnished settings—the desk, the throne, and the bedside—to set the stage for the reading of a particular manuscript and to offer ways for the viewer to connect to the scene.

Particularly in early manuscript illumination from before 1200, a scene is typically rendered with minimal furniture, limited often to a single rudimentary but symbolically meaningful piece. Before the late fourteenth century, manuscript painters were typically no more interested in depicting a realistic environment surrounding the figures that populated their narratives than they were in creating portrait likenesses. Blank, diapered, or tooled gold backgrounds often formed the backdrops for narrative scenes, while figural groupings were sometimes framed with assemblages of disproportionately small architectural motifs meant to symbolize "church," "city," or "heavenly Jerusalem." Among early medieval European manuscripts only biblical texts and saintly *vitae* were regularly illustrated with narrative images that called for furnishings. Items of furniture were props added to the events that were unfolding on the page; depictions of the Nativity like the one in the *St. Lambrecht Gospelbook* (Graz Universitätsbibliothek cod. 185, f. 13v) could incorporate a bed and throne, although the details of the Gospel account make it unlikely that Mary and Joseph would have serendipitously encountered such furnishings in their humble Bethlehem lodgings (Nicka 2010: 18–19). Thus artists deployed the repertoire of furniture forms they inherited from late antique art, such as bejeweled thrones and linen-draped beds, not to create realistic settings but rather to encode the temporal and spiritual condition of the figures and objects depicted. Simplified and rearranged, the vocabulary of shapes and animal heads found on the surviving depictions of luxury furnishings (such as bench thrones or the folding chairs known as faldstools) could transmit the iconography of secular and ecclesiastical governance. Like the pseudo-architectural frameworks surrounding a scene, the items of furniture found within it could also be composites of other furniture types designed to link themes and events symbolically. To impart theological significance to an image, artists depicted utilitarian furniture such as beds, tables, and lecterns by combining the component parts of furniture with ceremonial functions, for instance, thrones and altars. Genres of furniture, whether explicitly liturgical in function or superficially more prosaic, were thus freighted with symbolic weight.

As book illumination expanded with new types of texts such as illustrated histories and romances, which were made for the increasingly literate aristocracy during the thirteenth century, so too did the pool of scenes placing interior furnishing into narrative roles. By the fifteenth century, furniture ensembles were being used to create a class-specific setting that was not limited to the liturgical or the historical, and that also promoted a consciously contemporary point of view. Complex arrays of furniture were now frequently inspired by contemporary furniture fashion. Just as fabrics and tapestries enhanced the layers of depth in an image, the carved decorations on furniture embedded the setting with meaningful designations. In searching for the "hidden symbolism" of early Netherlandish paintings, Erwin Panofsky suggested that the decorative elements of the furniture were manipulated as "disguised" or "transfigured" symbols of theological significance (1934: 126), although any symbolism was likely recognized by their original viewers. When decorated pieces, composite forms, and ceremonial accessories appear in manuscript illuminations, the context of the manuscript itself can suggest ways to interpret the message that the artist wished to transmit to her or his intended viewers. In essence, artists used furniture in a supporting role to frame their subjects for particular manuscript contexts and viewers. By the later Middle Ages, the depiction of furniture for its own sake remained rare, but its role to engage the contemporary surroundings of its viewer gained center stage.

SEATING CAPACITY

At the eleventh-century Benedictine abbey of Saint-Omer, the scriptorium's monks illuminated a singular moment in the life of their patron saint (Figure 8.1). Omer (d. *c.* 670) sits opposite the Merovingian King Dagobert (*c.* 603–39), and is invested with his insignia of office as the bishop of the diocese of Thérouanne. The artist juxtaposed the two in a composition adapted from the venerable formula for a *disputatio*, a formal method of debate (Svoboda 1983: 129–30), and delineated the marks of secular and ecclesiastical governance carefully: the king wears a crown and cope and carries a foliate staff while the bishop wears a chasuble and receives a crozier, the curved staff symbolizing his role as shepherd of his flock. Although the two have matching footstools, an insignium of office derived from Roman custom (Wanscher 1980: 154–6), their seats are differentiated: the king sits in a zoomorphic faldstool, the medieval incarnation of the Roman *sella castrensis*, or portable folding camp throne (138, 191–4), while the bishop perches on a substantial masonry bench throne similar to that occupied by the bishop who received Omer and his father into holy orders on folio 6r.

Although in the later Middle Ages the zoomorphic faldstool became a symbol of episcopal administration, in the early Middle Ages the folding

FIGURE 8.1 Life of Saint Omer. Saint-Omer Bibliothèque municipale
MS 698, fol. 7v. Photo: Photo12/UIG/Getty Images.

stool embellished with animal heads and feet was associated with holders of both sacred and secular offices (Wanscher 1980: 191–2). This is reasonable considering that, as with Bishop Omer and King Dagobert, both secular and ecclesiastical duties as well as the origins of both types of power were understood to overlap. In the Saint-Vaast Bible, discussed below, biblical rulers occupy both animal faldstools and masonry bench thrones while leaders holding purely religious office never sit in faldstools. In other manuscripts the type of throne depicted served to signal the sitter's sphere of office, although which office was symbolized could shift according to the whim of the artist.

In the course of the eleventh century bishops and secular rulers were pitted against one another by the Investiture Controversy, a struggle over what rights lay leaders had to select bishops and install them in office. The manuscripts made by monks in the region mirror this debate by either inserting or removing ritual furnishings. In a manuscript of the *Life of Saint Amand* from the second half of the eleventh century (Valenciennes Bibliothèque municipale MS 502, f. 11r), a giant enthroned king holding an orb presides over the consecration of the bowing Saint Amand (*c*. 584–*c*. 676), whose head is partially obscured by an oddly placed pillar. In contrast, in two versions of the consecration found in a copy of the same *vita* made a century later (Valenciennes BM MS 500), the standing saint takes center stage while a smaller, standing king has been compositionally marginalized (65v) or eliminated altogether (57r) as fellow clerics acclaim Amand bishop, signaling the waning power of the lay elite to control religious office (Abou-el-Haj 1997: 173–4).

Relative placement of furniture could also telegraph power relationships. At Saint-Omer, the artist of the *vita* chose to depict a lay investiture even though none was described in the accompanying text (Svoboda 1983: 128), and signaled the distinction between secular and ecclesiastical governance by seating the king on the manuscript's only depiction of a faldstool. Although Barbara Abou-el-Haj claims that the Saint-Omer investiture "is represented as a transfer between equals, saint and king enthroned side by side, vested, frontal, both grasping his crozier" (1997: 38), the king's faldstool appears to hover in the air, raising the king slightly higher than his prelate, while the faldstool's clawed right leg also overlaps the substantial masonry throne of the bishop, signaling the king's hegemony (Svoboda 1983: 129).

Sometimes an assemblage of furniture parts was designed to convey overlaps between sacred and secular authority. In the late tenth-century *Registrum Gregorii*, a collection of the epistles of the sixth-century saint Gregory the Great commissioned by Archbishop Egbert of Trier (*c*. 950–93), the occupants assigned to each type of throne have been reversed and a puzzling hybrid created. In one miniature, an Ottonian emperor receives tribute from the personifications of four subject nations (Chantilly Musée Condé MS 14b, detached leaf). Grasping a staff and orb, he sits on a massive masonry bench throne, his feet resting on a footstool that hovers in the air before it. The bench itself floats in front of a tile-roofed ciborium. Peeking out from underneath a green drapery that cascades over what must be the bench throne's backrest are two roaring beast heads of the same type usually found on a faldstool's seat. This combination resembles no surviving throne of the era.

In what was once a pendant image to that of the enthroned emperor (Plate 28), Gregory receives divine inspiration from a dove of the Holy Spirit while his scribe spies through a hole he has poked in the intervening drapery with his stylus. Gregory sits on a cushioned and draped zoomorphic faldstool while the scribe perches sideways on a cushioned masonry bench throne. As in the emperor image, space in this miniature is rendered ambiguously. An architectural canopy performs several functions: it forms a backdrop for Gregory's faldstool and lectern, supports the drapery through which the scribe peeks, allows a votive crown, symbolizing Gregory's divinely inspired wisdom, to hover over his head and signals his location in an ecclesiastical structure.

The fathers of the early Church frequently dictated their works to scribes who recorded them temporarily with a stylus on wax tablets (Williams 2006: 201–3). As this author portrait was intended to preface Gregory's *registrum*, or register of papal letters, one might expect the saint to be represented with a certain amount of ceremony, but his scribe's seat and ghostly floating footstool seem grand for one of such a humble occupation. Biblical and patristic authors were almost always portrayed in manuscripts as working while seated—on faldstools, monumental benches, or high-backed thrones—and writing in bound books that rested on lecterns, despite the fact that ancient and medieval scribes worked almost exclusively on their laps or on lap desks while seated on stools, as we see in the *Codex Amiatinus*'s portrait of Ezra (Plate 26), and wrote on loose sheets of parchment. Grander furniture served to elevate the author, the act of writing, and the contents of their text.

The origin of the enthroned author formula can be found in ancient depictions of authors and philosophers. It would have been inappropriate to portray these elevated individuals as wielding a tool as prosaic as a pen. The late Roman Sidamara sarcophagus, now in the Istanbul Archeological Museum at the Topkapi Palace, contains the seeds of the *Registrum Gregorii*'s author portrait: a bearded man, likely a stand-in for the aristocratic owner of the tomb, wears a draped himation (outer garment); sits in profile on a cushioned magistrate's seat, or *sella curulis*, rendered with curved animal legs; and reads from a scroll that he grasps in his left hand (Elderkin 1939: 101–15). He and his seat rest on a masonry platform and are flanked by spiral-fluted columns crowned by an elaborately carved entablature and pediment, complete with akroteria (architectural ornaments), possibly meant to recall an ancient library, like that of Celsus in Ephesus. Seated in front of a backdrop evoking aristocratic pursuits, the figure epitomizes the scholar-intellectual, a virtuous and well-educated man of leisure.

Medieval Evangelist portraits simply adapted this preexisting type, the seated or enthroned author, by adding tools that were the stock-in-trade of the medieval author-monk. For example, in the Carolingian *Ebbo Gospelbook*'s portrait of Luke (Épernay Bibliothèque municipale MS 1, ff. 90v and 135v), the writing Evangelist sits in profile on a *sella curulis* that has been truncated to a single, swelling animal leg attached to a roaring head. John sits instead on a masonry throne. In the *Coronation Gospels* (Vienna Schatzkammer Inv. XIII 18, f. 15r) Matthew sits in profile on a cushioned, straight-legged *sella castrensis*, a folding camp seat related to both the faldstool and the curved-legged *sella curulis*. Each Evangelist grasps a codex and wields a quill and inkhorn, and is accompanied by a book on a lectern.

In the *Registrum Gregorii*, the artist has divided such props between Pope Gregory and his scribe. Unlike in the *Life of Saint Omer*, the *Registrum*'s artist did not discriminate between royal and episcopal offices when he furnished his scenes. The emperor received a throne that combined the masonry and faldstool forms. Both emperor and pope are framed by classicizing architectural canopies often associated with sites of sacramental liturgy. This iconographic slippage between the secular and ecclesiastical realms is typical of Ottonian art: both emperors and popes were consecrated to their offices, the emperor taking on a form of sacral kingship, the pope the role of Christ's high priest on earth (Mayr-Harting 1999: 60–8). The visual symbolism of sacred and secular power moved easily between the two.

The portrait of the Old Testament scribe Ezra in the eighth-century, Anglo-Saxon *Codex Amiatinus* (Plate 26) seems at first glance more realistic. In this grand pandect, or single volume Bible, Ezra sits on a low, cushioned stool, his feet raised on a footstool, and writes in a codex resting on his lap, the tools of a scribe scattered around him on the floor. As Paul Meyvaert explains, the convention of littering the surroundings of an artisan with his tools derives from Roman tomb images showing humble craftsmen such as gravediggers (1996: 870–1). Ancient authors could also be accompanied by piles of scrolls or a *capsa* (scroll chest), well into the early Middle Ages as in the late fifth-century Roman Vergil (Vatican Library Vat. Lat. 3867; Wright 2001: 16). This image of Ezra is innovative, however, in combining both the tools of the scribe's trade and the assembled scholarly collection that would have been the domain of the author or theologian.

Ezra was renowned for having transcribed the Old Testament from memory after its destruction during the Babylonian Captivity in the sixth century BCE. Wearing the *tallith* (mantle worn by Jews at prayer) and jeweled breastplate of a priest, Ezra sits before a book press, or *armarium*, the open doors of which reveal nine bound volumes lying on their sides labeled as parts of the Old and New Testaments (Meyvaert 1996: 876). This cabinet exemplifies the common means of storing books from ancient times until the advent of the well-stocked, chained libraries of the later Middle Ages in which books stood on edge. Books were locked by the *armarius* (monastery librarian) into the *armarium* closest to the location where they were used, whether it was the church, cloister or chapter house. More than in any of the other illuminations we have seen, this ensemble of furniture suggests the kind of realistic, three-dimensional milieu that would have been familiar to the eighth-century viewer.

While this miniature depicts a scribe at work in his miraculous task of revivifying the Old Testament, some scholars have argued that its model depicted a different but related scene: the sixth-century Christian author Cassiodorus seated before his prized possession, a multivolume Bible (Marsden 1995: 14–15). Cassiodorus's *Codex Grandior*, a Bible that contrasted six different versions of the text in parallel columns, was made at Cassiodorus's Calabrian villa-monastery of Vivarium. It was likely brought to the Anglo-Saxon monastery of Wearmouth-Jarrow by Abbot Ceolfrith a century after it was made (Marsden 1995: 4). Whether or not the Wearmouth-Jarrow artist copied the earlier Italian miniature, he created several anachronisms: the Old Testament scribe Ezra is seated before a collection of codices that includes parts of the Bible that had not yet been written; the *amarium* holding the volumes is covered with Christian symbolism, such as peacocks and crosses; and Ezra is shown writing in a bound codex rather than the scroll that was the customary vehicle for text transmission in the pre-Christian world. In fact, in all but his priestly insignia Ezra is depicted as a monastic scribe sitting before his abbey's *armarium*, endeavoring to preserve scripture, much as the monks of Wearmouth-Jarrow intended by copying their three giant Vulgate pandects (DeGregorio 2011: 123–5).

In the Gothic period commercial scriptoria expanded the production of large-scale illuminated Bibles to include fully illustrated versions, a luxury afforded by few, such as the King of France, Louis IX (1214–70). One type, called the "Moralized Bible," contains verbal and visual commentaries that relate biblical stories to contemporary events. Dating between 1227 and 1234, the dedication page in one copy acknowledged the grandeur of the undertaking by elevating the roles of both the author and the scribe below the enthroned rulers, Louis IX and his mother and regent, Blanche of Castile (Pierpont Morgan Library MS M. 240, f. 8) (Figure 8.2). The artist assembled the four figures in a grid of microarchitecture (for a discussion of this term, see Chapter 7 in this volume) against a glowing gold background and assigned each a seat that denoted relationship and status. Below the royal pair a tonsured Dominican cleric sits in a turned-rod chair at a lectern supported by a column and dictates from his open codex to a capped, lay scribe, one of many trained in Paris's burgeoning manuscript market, seated on a bench and writing on a folio spread on a lectern pierced with two arches. The royals' thrones are similarly

FIGURE 8.2 Queen Blanche of Castile and King Louis IX, in the Moralized Bible
(Paris, 1226–34). Photograph courtesy of the Pierpont Morgan Library and Museum,
New York. MS M. 240, f. 8r.

differentiated, with the queen seated on a masonry throne flanked by curved, foliated arms, perhaps echoing the regal appearance of the faldstool, and the king seated on a hexagonal chair composed of turned rods with knobs and an arcaded balustrade. Just as the clerical author dictates the scribe's written text, the queen regent directly above him instructs her son, for which the Moralized Bible was likely created to assist her. The authority of each figure, however, is counterbalanced by the positions and forms of the seats supporting them: the scribe's stone slab echoes the form of the queen's bench, underlining her adjunct role to the authority of the king, whose elaborate turned-rod chair mirrors that of the clerical author demonstrating his exegetical authority.

An interest in viewing biblical stories through a contemporary thirteenth-century pictorial lens is evident in another commission for Louis IX, the so-called Crusader Bible (c. 1244–54; Pierpont Morgan Library MS M. 638), which illustrates over 346 episodes from Genesis to Samuel. Its contemporary settings and props have provided modern historians with a plethora of images illustrating medieval military garb, weapons, wares, mores, and manners. With over seventy-five seats and thrones required in the illustrations, only three types were employed: a faldstool, a masonry bench, and a high-backed, arcaded chair, or "palace" throne. As the illuminators of the Crusader Bible deliberately deployed structural elements to stage these scenes, the choice of one seat over another may have been suggested purely by narrative needs, as is shown by the lower backed chairs that catch the collapses of Eli and Nabal, whose stories appear in the books of Samuel (ff. 21r and 33v). The masonry bench is commonly used for any rank, but the faldstool and the palace throne seem to be required for certain settings that underline the military and jurisdictional roles of the kings, who served as models of kingship for Louis IX and his descendants.

Most thrones in the Crusader Bible include a footstool for their sitters, while a curtain hung above, ringed on a rod and slung upward, is added to scenes with Isaac and Jacob (ff. 4r, 5r, 6r, and 7r), framing the Judaic patriarchs with a conventional accessory of honor. The faldstool—depicted in this manuscript with claw feet and armrests ending in lion-head terminals—appears in fourteen scenes as the throne for the biblical kings, Saul and David, and is not used at all for the Egyptian pharaoh. Its utilization for both coronations in this manuscript may have been inspired by the gilt bronze "throne of Dagobert," a *sella curulis* housed in the Abbey of Saint-Denis at the time and used for the coronations of the French kings (Bedos Rezak 1986: 98; Noel and Weiss 2002: 16). The manuscript's faldstools provide seating during military campaigns and for certain judicial or advisory decisions, such as when demons whisper at Saul's ear or when David dispenses justice for crimes against him. Saul's faldstools are gilded, save for one, while David's are colored white. This distinction may be attributed to the hands of the artists, as the master of the team of six illuminators was responsible for Saul's illustrations (Noel and Weiss 2002: 144). Yet the painted lead-white used to color the faldstool may subtly evoke the ivory material of the throne of Solomon, David's successor, in contrast to Saul's depravity. Another difference in the settings of these two kings is that whereas Saul often sits in isolation with his spear or scepter held aloft, David cradles his scepter and his advisors surround his seat.

Of the Crusader Bible's seventy-five seats, nearly half (thirty-six) are composed of a high back, four posts with cone knobs, and arcades supporting the boarded seat (Figure 8.3). Usually painted white, although those by the master artist are polychrome, this "palace" throne type is used alike for the Egyptian pharaoh, the Israelite kings, and the Judaic patriarchs. In one of the Crusader Bible's last scenes, King David stands before an elaborately arcaded palace throne at the gate of Mahanaim as he greets his people following Absalom's rebellion (f. 43r). The text of 2 Samuel (19:8) does not specify a throne yet emphasizes that David sits at the gate ("sedit in porta" and "rex sederet in porta"). David's upright stance exposes the palace throne in full, perhaps reminding the viewer that his kingship persists through exile and rebellions. Unlike the ceremonial faldstools of Saul and David, the palace throne harkens to the seats of the pharaoh and patriarchs to reify the terrestrial place of the king. Its pictorial centrality in the microarchitectural setting foreshadows the throne's role in

FIGURE 8.3 The Crusader Picture Bible (Paris, c. 1240–50). Photograph courtesy of the Pierpont Morgan Library and Museum, New York. MS M. 638, f. 43r.

establishing Solomon's kingdom, to which the Capetian kings of France aligned their aspirations.

The Crusader Bible's limited captions have led scholars to suggest that the volume's meaning was to be transmitted through oral exposition, especially for members of the royal household who were preparing to embark on Crusade (Noel and Weiss 2002: 98, 108). The scenes including palace thrones contributed to the emphasis on the established stability of the home front. For example, Ruth, the great-grandmother of David, noted for her loving-kindness, is the only female figure who is accorded a high-backed palace throne, versus a bench or bed as in other depictions of women. The story of Ruth's continuation of her mother-in-law's genealogical line, in the absence of her husband or sons, may have helped to reassert the sense of stability during Louis IX's minority or his Crusades (Sand 2008: 554). Similarly, in the Parisian *History of Outremer*, an image of the coronation of the Frankish Queen Melisende of Jerusalem (1105–61) with her husband, Fulk of Anjou, following her father's death, deliberately depicts the pair as equals together on the same masonry bench throne colored with marbleized green and gold (British Library MS Yates Thompson 12, f. 82v). Jaroslav Folda observes that here, unlike in other ceremonies typically shown with royalty standing, the coronation scene contains certain realistic details that address dynastic inheritance when the king is deployed, an issue important to an audience keenly attuned to the current theory of kingship that necessitated a female regent's authority (Folda 1993: 103–4).

In twenty-three scenes from the Crusader Bible other minor characters as well as kings sit on masonry benches, which was the most common type of seat in medieval representations. This is reflected in one of the few pattern books to survive the Middle Ages, the early thirteenth-century sketchbook of Villard de Honnecourt (Bibliothèque nationale de France [hereafter "BnF"] MS fr. 19093), which contains drawings of architectural structures, figurative subjects, and some furniture pieces. Among the 250 drawings in Villard's "portfolio," most of the seated figures are provided with plain stone benches, sometimes with molded lips or bases. Only two contain additional articulation: a blind arcade decorates a bench beneath a noble couple and freestanding colonettes support the figure of a blessing Christ (ff. 14r and 16v; Barnes 2009: 218). Faldstools and palace thrones of the type enhanced in the illuminated manuscripts are absent among Villard's sketches. Villard endeavored, however, to record an ancient monumental throne in a folio-scale drawing of the "Sepulchre of a Saracen" (f. 6r; Barnes 2009: 53–4). The throne surrounds a semi-nude figure with a multilevel, architectural structure, but the construction betrays a lack of familiarity with a classical vocabulary, including pilasters supporting columns and a pediment at the base. The sculptural dimension of the source, which has been suggested to be a tomb that Villard saw en route to Hungary, has been reduced to a complex pattern of dipping, arcing lines and flattened plinths barely supporting the sitter and framing his subject as "Other."

By contrast, the realistic throne depicted in one of the earliest portraits of a contemporary ruler, that of Richard II at Westminster Abbey (*c.* 1395), is a palace throne with microarchitectural details that mimic the appearance of Saint Edward's Coronation Chair, constructed to house Scotland's "Stone of Scone" in 1296, and kept at Westminster Abbey. The Perpendicular-style finials, crockets, arcaded back, and pierced armrests also echo those of kings and bishops on contemporary wax seals, the very means by which they exercised their terrestrial authority (Alexander and Binski 1987: 230, 493–4). Set against a gilded tin-relief background, the throne's architectural cavity situates the ruler frontally to create a "perpetual presence" within the choir where the portrait was originally placed (134, 517–18). The throne would have resonated visually with the wood-carved furniture within the choir, and such high-backed chairs have surviving counterparts preserved in ecclesiastical collections (Eames 1977: plate 69). The microarchitectural designs created for thrones in these large-scale and "from life" examples visualize the terrestrial power of the king as centered in a palatial armature.

The capacity of seats to carry meaningful variations in manuscript illumination allowed for the nuances of decoration and accessories to shift rather fluidly according to the subject being depicted and the manuscript's intended viewers. The compositions of the enthroned ruler and the writing author were often repeated formulae in the dedication of a manuscript. The familiar lexicon of furniture forms allowed artists to conflate and juxtapose signs of status to explore the relational roles of their subjects, such as female regents and scribes in relation to their kings and bishops.

BEDSIDE MANNERS

Although an equally static composition, the figure in repose on a bed was more often used to illustrate a narrative or text. Therefore the artists' manipulation of the bed's form and accessories created a platform to stage certain events. Proportionally speaking, more seats than beds survive in physical form from the period under discussion here. In manuscript illuminations, the physical forms of these beds are difficult to assess as they are often subsumed in linens and cushions, which reveal very little in terms of the bed's structure. Artists use these textile elements, however, to add layers to an image's setting. Beds fashioned from less mundane components are less common and therefore warrant particular attention to the artist's intended associations. The relative embellishment of a bed, then, provides reposed, bed-ridden subjects with a vehicle to expand the narrative structure and potential of a scene.

Two miniatures painted almost a hundred years apart and in scriptoria separated by more than 6,500 kilometers illustrate the narrative role played by the bed. The Psalter of Queen Melisende was illuminated for the reigning queen of Jerusalem as a gift from her once-estranged husband Fulk, Count of Anjou and Main, probably in the mid-1130s (Folda 2012: 437). A product of the scriptorium attached to the Church of the Holy Sepulchre in Jerusalem, the manuscript fused Byzantine and Western iconography, style, and textual content. This combination probably pleased the multicultural Melisende, daughter of a French noble and an Armenian princess, but was also appropriate to a scriptorium that was situated within a former territory of the Byzantine patriarchate then governed by French-dominated conquerors and that housed artists trained in both traditions (Folda 2012: 452–7).

The Psalter begins with an elaborate prefatory cycle of miniatures aligned with the *Dodekaorton*, the cycle of feasts celebrated in the Orthodox tradition. Near the end of the series one finds the *Koimesis*, or Dormition of the Virgin (f. 12r) (Figure 8.4), the "falling asleep" that preceded the assumption of her soul through the intervention of her son, Jesus. Jerusalem was home to an unusually complex celebration of the feast of the Dormition, August 15, including a stational liturgy, or procession between churches, in imitation of the actions of the Apostles, who were said to have escorted Mary's body to its grave at Jehosephat next to the Garden of Gethsemane after her death (Shoemaker 2002: 38, 105, and 132–40). Western communities such as the Augustinians who served the Church of the Holy Sepulchre celebrated the Feast of the Assumption on the same day, but also marked the procession from the Virgin's house to her tomb on the vigil before the feast, as recorded in the calendar of a liturgical book made in the Holy Sepulchre scriptorium for Jerusalem's Knights Templars (Dondi 2004: 166–76).

In the Dormition image in Melisende's psalter, before a burnished gold backdrop and flanked by stacks of brightly colored architectural elements, the Virgin lies on a red pallet that mimics the one on which she lay after giving birth in the manuscript's Nativity miniature (f. 2r). Both western European and Byzantine artists commonly depicted individuals sleeping or reclining on such pallets, which could rest either on the ground or on a bedstead, as in the ninth-century Carolingian Utrecht Psalter (Utrecht Universiteitsbibliotheek MS Bibl. Rhenotraiectinae I Nr 32, p. 14), or the tenth-century Byzantine Paris Psalter (BnF MS Gr. 139, f. 446v). In Melisende's psalter, the pallet balances atop a slab-like platform of marine blue, framed in gold and embellished with red, trellised flourishes enclosing gold spades. Before this stands a gilded and bejeweled footstool. One of the bowing and mourning apostles censes the structure in accordance with Byzantine funerary ritual (Velkovska 2001: 27).

Jaroslav Folda surmised that the artist of the psalter's prefatory cycle, Basil, may have traveled from western Europe or been born to Western parents, but had then been trained in the Byzantine artistic tradition (Folda 2012: 452), and

FIGURE 8.4 Psalter of Queen Melisende, f. 12r, "Dormition of the Virgin." British Library MS Egerton 1139, fol. 12r. Photograph courtesy of British Library Image Services.

the style and iconography of the cycle as a whole aptly display the hybridity that resulted. The iconography of the Dormition originated in the Byzantine world, however, and the Psalter's image hews to Byzantine norms in its overall composition, the appearance of the pallet and footstool, and a censing apostle. In Byzantine examples the Virgin's pallet lies on either a bedframe or bier, most often shown with spindle or spooled legs, spade feet, and draped in gathered folds of luxuriously embroidered and edged fabrics. Although other Western artists copied this part of the Dormition formula almost exactly (Mayr-Harting 1999: 139–52), the Holy Sepulchre artist transformed it into a solid, block-like platform enhanced with a tapestry pattern resembling an altar cloth.

It is difficult for the modern observer to tell whether this bed was intended to represent an actual piece of furniture, or was designed with specific symbolism in mind. In an almost contemporary image at the Panagia Phorbiotissa church in Àsinou on nearby Cyprus the Virgin's red pallet lies on a similar, slab-like rectangle, but framed with turned legs, and her head is propped up by an integrated headboard (Weyl Carr and Nicolaïdès 2012: 80–1). Perhaps the artist of Melisende's psalter Dormition was inspired by a depiction such as this but simply misunderstood his source image and removed the bedframe's legs. Alternatively, he may have intended to represent a contemporary bench bed. By the twelfth century many Byzantine households employed stone benches integral to the dwelling's structure rather than portable wooden frame beds. Portable beds were assembled to host honored guests, the sick, the dying, and those in childbirth (Oikonomides 1990: 209–10).

If instead the artist wanted to invest the bed with symbolism, it is possible that he merged the Virgin's bed with the sarcophagus venerated as the tomb of Mary in her burial church at Gethsemane. Recently renovated by Melisende's family (Folda 2012: 435), the same church served in 1126 as the burial place for Melisende's mother, Queen Morphia, and later for Melisende herself. It was also the destination of the holy procession on the eve of the Feast of the Assumption. Miniatures in two Byzantine manuscripts of the homilies on Mary by the twelfth-century monk Jacobus Kokkinobaphos (BnF MS Gr. 1208, f. 109v, and Vatican Library Gr. 1162, f. 80v), almost exactly contemporary with Melisende's psalter, depict the same type of platform with the same ornamentation in an image that interprets Mary's betrothal in Christological terms. In this case, the "bed" is the Couch of Solomon, drawn from Song of Songs 3:7–8, which according to Jacobus and his source, the fourth-century bishop Gregory of Nyssa, prefigured the mother of God and the souls of Christians awaiting mystical union with Christ. In Jacobus's sermon, and in the sermon manuscript's image, however, it is not Mary who lies in the bed, but Christ/God (Linardou 2011: 142–4). Perhaps in Melisende's psalter, the Virgin and the bed symbolically become one and the same, a subtle transference not unknown in Western settings, where beds themselves could become contact relics and be venerated in place of the saintly beings who once occupied them (Wade 2007: 140; Schulenberg 2014: 165–7).

Hundreds of kilometers away, a northern French monk referenced Solomon's couch in a much more explicit manner by creating hybrid forms. In the Saint-Vaast Bible (Figure 8.5), illuminated in the Benedictine abbey of Saint-Vaast in the early eleventh century, an artist painted stacked images of Kings David and Solomon reclining in distinctively royal beds while they address members of their court as the frontispiece to 3 Kings, which describes the end of the reign of David, and that of his son and successor, Solomon. In the upper register of the image, David, swaddled tightly in green, lies before a plain, purple backdrop on a lavishly draped bedstead supported by prominent orange, spiral-decorated legs with clawed animal feet. Solomon's matching bed, below, sports white, spiral-decorated legs with green feet and is set against an unpainted parchment background. Each king has a pillow beneath his head, a detail unusual in this period.

In this case the bedsteads signal two disparate conditions typically associated with beds: infirmity and sleep. Helpful inscriptions identify the scenes. Above, as described at the very beginning of 3 Kings, David's courtiers, seeking to warm their aged, frail king, present him with the young maiden Abishag, interpreted in biblical commentaries as Wisdom. Solomon stands at the foot of the bed grasping a scepter while being admonished to walk in the ways of the Lord. Below, Solomon, having performed a massive fiery sacrifice of a thousand offerings as described in the third chapter of 3 Kings, experiences a dream vision in which God rewards him with wisdom (Reilly 2006: 197–200). The artist has asserted the regal status and divinely inspired wisdom of the supine rulers by dangling votive crowns above them and grafting onto the bed the type of animal legs more typically found on a faldstool.

Unexplained by the Bible's text are the six tunic-clad men, one holding a sword, who stand at the foot of Solomon's bed. They may hint at an inspiration for some of the image's more unusual details. Once again, the description of Solomon's bed from the Song of Songs 3:7–10 provides the key:

Behold: threescore valiant ones of the most valiant of Israel, surrounded the bed [*lectulum*] of Solomon, all holding swords, and most expert in war, every man's sword upon his thigh, because of fears in the night. King Solomon hath made him a litter [*ferculum*] of the wood of Lebanon; the pillars thereof he made of silver, the seat [*reclinatorium*] of gold, the going up [*ascensum*] of purple; the midst he covered with charity for the daughters of Jerusalem.

In the Carolingian era, Archbishop Hincmar of Reims crafted a *carmen figuratum*, or poem with its words arranged to form an image, and an accompanying *explanatio* interpreting this passage (Ernst 2012: 235–93). The way in which Hincmar arranged the words into an image is no longer known, however the words themselves suggest possible furniture types. Along with the

FIGURE 8.5 Saint-Vaast Bible, Arras 559, f. 144, "David and Solomon in Beds."
Photograph by Diane Reilly. Reproduced courtesy of Médiathèque d'Arras.

Church Fathers Jerome, Ambrose, and Bede, Hincmar considered both the *ferculus* and the *lectulus* to be the same thing, and he and his contemporaries interpreted Solomon's bed as a metaphor for the Church and the presence of Solomon, a type of Christ, in it as representing Christ's union with the Church. Textual scholars reconstruct the poem's visual layout more literally as either a bed or a throne, perhaps the empty *hetoimasia*, the throne prepared for Christ's Second Coming that in this case includes pillars, a space on which to recline and a cushion. The eleventh-century Saint-Vaast monk who illuminated 3 Kings, living in the archdiocese of Reims and no doubt familiar with the works of Hincmar and his fellow commentators, may have intended to allude to this allegorical understanding of Solomon's bed by inserting the sword-bearing "valiant ones" of the Song of Songs passage, the cushion or pillow suggested by Hincmar's *carmen*, and creating a bed-throne hybrid by adding the zoomorphic faldstool's prominent animal feet.

The reclination of kings is one type of biblical illustration requiring furniture that was easily transferred and adapted to the relatively new genre of illustrated romances in the thirteenth century (Cooper 2005: 26). In Arthurian literature, significant pieces of furniture, such as Solomon's Bed, the Round Table, or the Perilous Seat, which was a vacant seat at the Round Table for the most virtuous knight, play fairly active narrative roles. The pseudo-religious content of two Holy Grail stories, the *Estoire del Graal* and the *Queste del Graal*, provides a comparative example for the challenging illustration of Solomon's bed, which conveys the Grail upon a "marvelous boat." The story describes how the bed was made from three grafts of red, green, and white that originated from the Tree of Life. In the most extensively illuminated cycle (British Library, Add. MS 10292, f. 31r), the three grafts appear as tapers on either side of a multicolored cushion with a sword and a crown resting upon it, yet their support of what the narrator describes as a "curious canopy" over the bed is not depicted (Cooper 2005: 36; Stones and Kennedy 2009: 156). In another extensively illuminated cycle at Yale University (Beinecke Library MS 229 [hereafter "Yale Arthur"] f. 257v) the bed appears without colored spindles or a canopy but is enhanced instead with six gold knobs on posts and a balustrade railing cropped by the boat's edge (Hahn 2007: 81). Based on her research on the illustrated tradition, Alison Stones suggests that the omission of symbolic details may be attributed less to the artist's ignorance of the text than to the preference for seeing the same ordinary objects that befuddle the questing knights (1996: 214).

In romance illustration, the adventures of wandering knights necessitated both the repetitive forms and the occasional embellishment of furnishings to highlight significant points of arrival and departure throughout the meandering narrative. Within the sequence of numerous illustrations in a deluxe prose or verse romance, depictions of furniture could function structurally to establish a framework in which to stage parallel events, allowing the artist to stitch thematic threads across similar scenes. In her essay on the roles of beds in the Yale Arthur, Stacey Hahn notes how, in Arthurian romance, beds were strategically placed at points where a narrative shift from one tale to another occurs. For instance, Queen Guenevere's lovesickness for Lancelot is shown in two successive miniatures (Yale Arthur, ff. 25r and 27v). She appears in her bed beneath a vair-fur cover hemmed with red fringe and leaning upon a diapered pillow, details distinguishing this bed from the sixteen others illustrated in this manuscript (Hahn 2007: 70). From within the lower curve of a historiated initial, her body leans and turns toward the outer margin of the page where a gilt-clad knight rides his warhorse toward the fore-edge. Although the text conveys that Guenevere swoons (Stones 1996: n. 8), the placement of the bed in the scene visually initiates a new section of tales that follows Lancelot's adventure and his return to the queen, alone in her bed two folios later (f. 27v).

As Hahn argues, the narrative needs of the bed changed over the course of the decline of Camelot, and in the Yale Arthur bedroom scenes were allotted smaller spaces and minimal linens. In the *Queste* the bed becomes "associated with *luxuria* and the creature comforts that lead men astray," as evidenced by the times that knights refuse beds in the *Queste* as a form of "physical abnegation" (Hahn 2007: 76). By contrast, the Yale Arthur's pendant volume in Paris—BnF MS fr. 95 containing the *Estoire del Graal* and *Estoire de Merlin* (hereafter the Paris *Estoire*)—features a more elaborately decorated bed in two scenes that feature clandestine intercourse. An intricate latticework of roundels and quatrefoils forms the railings, and six posts with gilded knobs surround the frame and flank an opening to the cushion. In the first miniature, a demon beds with a maiden to engender Merlin (BnF fr. 95, f. 113v) (Figure 8.6); in the second, Uterpendragon (King Uther of post-Roman Britain) beds with Arthur's mother, Igerne (Lady Igraine, the wife of Uther's enemy Gorlois) (f. 149v). Serving as framing devices, the ornate beds visually sequester the rapes and parallel the character flaws of the king and his counselor that are explored later through the narrative.

Creating a frame within a frame, a draped curtain parted over a bed often functioned to reveal the subject rather than conceal it. For example, in the Crusader Bible, parted drapes appear over four birth scenes (ff. 7v, 19r, 19v, and 42v), David's tryst with Bathsheba (f. 41v), the pharaoh's dream (f. 5v), and the death of Jacob (f. 7r). A disheveled drape, rather than a neatly parted one, sets a moralizing tone over Amnon's rape of his half-sister, Tamar (2 Samuel 13) (BnF Nouv. Acq. Lat. 2294, f. 1r). The illustration of a celour, or a hanging canopy over the bed, appears more developed by the middle of the fourteenth century. The celour extends from the top of the tester, or

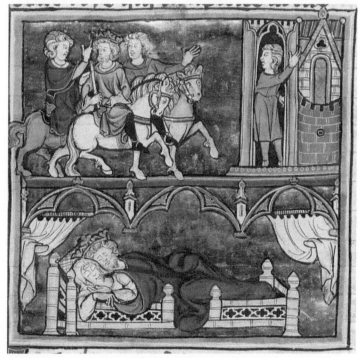

FIGURE 8.6 *L'Estoire de Merlin*. Photograph courtesy of Bibliothèque nationale de France, fr. 95, f. 113v and fol. 149v.

headboard, and is held aloft with cords over the length of the bed cushion; often, one corner of the hanging drapery is tied into a "curtain sack," which appears as a teardrop shape of cloth revealing the bed inside (Eames 1977: 74; Koslow 1986: 9). The use of celour canopies may have begun earlier, according to the inventories and receipts belonging to itinerant courtly households, for example, those of Mahaut, Countess of Artois (1268–1329), which include mentions of textiles for bedding (Dehaisnes 1886: 207–20). Depictions of hung beds multiplied alongside heightened representations of spatial depth that accommodated more ensembles including chairs, prie-dieus, or lavabos, which ultimately enhanced the impression that a scene took place in the contemporary period.

A scene with a bed sets the stage for one of the most popular illustrated poems of the Middle Ages, the *Roman de la Rose*, begun by Guillaume de Lorris around 1230 and continued forty years later by Jean de Meun. Contrary to the typical author portraits containing a lectern and seat that open the first page of historical texts, the opening miniatures of late thirteenth- and fourteenth-century *Rose* manuscripts show the author or narrator asleep in a cushioned bed with a rose-budded vine springing from its side. By the fifteenth century, the celour-hung beds became a feature of the *Rose* openings that could visually articulate the liminal state of the narrator as he rises in his dream, changes his clothes, and exits to a garden. Just as curtains often encouraged looking into the picture (and the ensuing text) in earlier manuscript illustrations, the three dimensions of the hung celour invite the *Rose*'s viewer to enter the textual landscape, or virtual reality, of the dream sequence that starts the poem. The expansion of the sequence in several scenes also provides a narrative role for furnishing to convey actions in the text where furniture is not explicitly described (Figure 8.7). The expanded ensemble includes a bedside chair or couch for changing clothes, a freestanding lavabo with which to wash, and an outdoor element, either a window, a tapestry, or an adjoining garden scene.

In the *Rose* illustrations the author's role as writer is conflated with his narrative position as dreamer, lover, and visionary (Guillaume de Lorris and Jean de Meun [1971] 1995: 8–9). The action that takes place through the furniture's framework in the initial stanzas encourages the reader to accompany the author-narrator into the text, and thus into the dream allegory. The framework provided by the hung-celour bed functions in these cases as a kind of tactile aureola for the transcendent threshold entered by the narrator, signified by both the changing of clothing and the outdoor excursion as specified in the opening stanzas. While the clothed bed surrounds the narrator, or the lover, Amans, additional furniture belonging to an author—a chair for changing or a desk for writing—establishes the

FIGURE 8.7 *Roman de la Rose*. Photograph courtesy of Bibliothèque nationale de France, fr. 1665, f. 1r.

written authority of the ensuing allegorical truths. Eight opening miniatures include a rounded seat next to the bed, and Amans dresses in the chair in two fourteenth-century miniatures (Paris Arsenal MS 5209, f. 1r, and Oxford Bodleian Library MS Selden Supra 57, f. 1r). By the fifteenth century such a "tub-shaped" seat, or *pozzetto*, was frequently used for images of authors, masters, and members of the educated elite (see Plate 27). Together the hung bed and changing chair structure the traditional site of the author portrait as progenitor of the textual body. The ensemble was a novel mash-up for the author portrait, creating a liminal threshold between reality and allegory, waking and dreaming, that advanced the narrative's progress.

The ensemble of a bed and chair on the opening page of the *Roman de la Rose* manuscripts anticipates the illustration of the "chambre de parement," or "reception room," which was a public area staged with furniture for receiving visitors. During the fifteenth century, reception rooms appear more frequently in dedication portraits and Annunciation scenes. The "state beds" became structures upon which to display kermes-dyed and gilt-damask textiles, eventually blazoned with heraldry. Often in the frontispieces of Valois-Burgundian manuscripts a recipient is presented with a codex and is simultaneously framed by the display of wealth in textiles and heraldry on the hung celour, tester, and bedspread. Rather than serving as private domestic chambers, such *chambres des parements* include the recipient's entourage and stage the exchange of official business, particularly in historical *Chronicles* commissioned during the fifteenth century. As Edwin Hall emphasizes, contemporaries viewed the celour-hung bed's role in the "furniture of estate" as a staged formal ensemble for display rather than as a site of consummation or procreation (1994: 113; Ridderbos 2005: 65). For example, an account of the birth of Margaret of Austria's mother referred to a kind of "bed where no one sleeps," and next to it a high-backed chair akin to the "great chairs of earlier times" (Hall 1994: 83–7, 157, n. 72). Viewed within the hands of the manuscript's intended reader, frontispieces containing such displays of heraldry, textiles, and furniture certainly reflect the patron's aspirations for the formal appearance of the estate. When such a traditional subject is framed three-dimensionally with a celour-hung bed, the interior domestic space invites the viewer's entry.

In later miniatures, an ensemble of furniture that combined a hung bed with a chair, bench, chest, prie-dieu, desk, or *armarium* could extend the sense of spatial reality and further support the symbolic weight of literacy, piety, and status desired by the book's owner. Similar *chambres des parements* became a favorite choice to frame the subject of the Annunciation in panel painting and in manuscript illumination (Harbison 2005: 380). According to Craig Harbison, Rogier van der Weyden's earliest placement of a bed at the Annunciation in 1440 reflected the desire to set historical events within a contemporary reality. A contract dating to 1447 specified an interior setting like that of the "seigneurs et bourgeois" (379). Although one scholar has argued that the hanging curtain-sack's resemblance to a womb in anatomical drawings made it a "disguised symbol" for the Incarnation, the sack's unequivocal presence in ducal reception rooms and both birth and death scenes casts doubt on the theory that gestational symbolism was desired (Koslow 1986: 32). Rather, as with the *Rose* miniatures, the celour-hung bed facilitated the visual articulation of transitional space, structuring the coming and going of the subjects within a scene of such transitive importance as the advent of the New Testament.

The particular details applied to the basic cushioned bed in manuscript illumination highlight that the bed's roles were not merely to support their subjects. Quite literally this driving role can be seen with the beds on litters and boats that function as moving bedframes to transit time and space in the illustrated Arthur romances (Hahn 2007: 80). Whether through the inclusion of fine textiles and cushions, the articulation of the bedframe itself or its pairing with other furnishings, enhancements to the standard bed bolstered its use as a structural device to frame the status or role of a subject in a spatially significant setting.

FURNITURE IN THE ROUND: REAL OR IMAGINED?

Grounded in a lexicon of furniture forms that could be grafted and interchanged, the furniture in manuscript illumination was often manipulated to convey the status and the stories of their subjects. During the fourteenth and fifteenth centuries, illuminated miniatures increasingly contained furniture pieces that were literally rounded in form, calling particular attention to their spatial occupation. One type of tester or dossier—a wood-planked backboard with a vaulted "half-celour" or hooked arch—appears next to the bed in two *Roman de la Rose* author portraits (University of Chicago, Regenstein Library, MS 1380, f. 1r, and Oxford University, Bodleian Library, MS Douce 195, f. 1r) (Figure 8.8). In one of the miniatures, the author's space is separated from the narrator's; the author sits on the hooked-vaulted chair and writes at a polygonal lectern while Amans sleeps in a draped bed next to an empty rounded chair. Hooked-vault testers also appear as headboards on beds in an opening miniature of a *Rose* that was illustrated by the prolific Parisian illuminators, Richard and Jeanne Montbaston (BnF fr. 25526, f. 1r), as well as for other illustrations, such as a wife tricking her husband in a *Rose* miniature (Douce MS 332, f. 153v) and Louis IX's scourging by his confessor in the *Grande Chroniques de France de Charles V* (BnF fr. 2813, f. 265) (Hedeman 1991: 124). Surviving angular constructions for tall headboards, such as a "baldachinbett" in the Bayerisches Nationalmuseum in Munich, may provide parallels to the headboards or backboards of this type, but there are no surviving counterparts to the wood-planked hooked arch (Eames 1977: 91).

Despite a dearth of models in reality, the depiction of rounded-form furniture may have been encouraged by the spatial possibilities of interior settings. The depiction of fictional pieces of furniture, such as Solomon's Bed or the Perilous Seat, in the Arthurian romances relied on the lexicon of available forms. Despite its eponymous shape, the most famous of the fictional furnishings, King Arthur's Round Table, had been depicted in manuscripts as any other table set out for a feast or the Last Supper: a mobile rectangular board covered with white cloth and supported by trestles. Not until the later fourteenth century does the Round Table appear as circular in shape (Plate 29). In one manuscript the knights are seated on a continuous bank of low benches with low backs and armrests (BnF fr. 343, f. 3r); in a much later manuscript the benches are carved with quatrefoil oak leaves, which are carved on the end-grain to expose tree-rings, and inscribed with gilded letters (BnF fr. 116, f. 610v); and in a third the backs are high, like choir stalls (BnF fr. 120, f. 524v). In these examples, the table is annular, or ring-shaped, in response to the narrative's visualization of the Grail floating aloft in the center of the company. Common to other tables

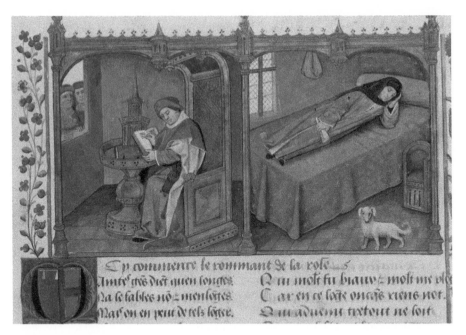

FIGURE 8.8 *Roman de la Rose*. Photo: The Bodleian Libraries, The University of Oxford.

and altars, however, the Round Table's construction is concealed beneath a veil of white linen.

The appearance of furniture forms in manuscript illumination provides little information as to the actual construction or appearance of furniture forms in reality. The few "pattern books" that survive from the Middle Ages were not used as patterns for actual furniture but rather to model their representation in other media (Scheller 1995: 6). For example, on two folios in his portfolio, Villard de Honnecourt extended the details of furnishing that he recorded, presumably, on site to demonstrate three examples of carved choir stalls (ff. 27v and 29r). On folio 27v, Villard drew the profile section of a choir stall accompanied by a blown-up detail of a "poppet," or carved fretwork that ends the row of stalls (Barnes 2009: 179) (Plate 30). The profile seat features a column leg with a capital at the front, a tapered peg leg in the back, a single folded acanthus-leaf armrest, and a dot to mark the hinge of the misericord, which Villard used for the point of his compass. The end-screen is composed of a twinned arcade topped by a carved acanthus scroll resembling a letter "E," from which leaves sprout on the ends and spray from the center Plate. On folio 29r, the decorative foliage multiplies with berries and oak leaves covering the vinescroll "E," also atop a twinned arcade with added trefoil tracery. The foliage and construction of the stall on folio 27v resemble that of surviving thirteenth-century choir stalls, such as those at Notre-Dame Cathedral in Lausanne, Switzerland, while the ornament on folio 29r's poppet may have been enlarged as a model for furniture yet to be carved, possibly for the choir in Cambrai, France (Barnes 2009: 186).

Villard's drawings are ostensibly two-dimensional, but he expressed interest in conveying the three-dimensionality of form in his written instructions for a lectern. He describes arranging carved "serpents" and triangular slabs around a central rod that supports an eagle atop and refers to his drawing "to see for yourself in what manner the lectern is made." Not included in his written description are three authors seated at lectern-armed desks and twisting in various poses around the platform on which the Gospel book would rest. Their placement would enhance the authority of the written word opposed to the bestial decoration at the base. By the end of the fifteenth century, artists frequently depicted polygonal and two-sided lecterns on pedestals from which an author read and copied multiple texts. A freestanding *intarsia* lectern among the choir furniture of the Church of Santa Maria in Organo, Verona, represents an example of the two-sided lectern form. Others show a rounded platform with a centered tower, as in the *Roman de la Rose* at the Bodleian Library (MS Douce 195, f. 1r) (Figure 8.8).

As patterns, Villard's drawings of choir furniture lack the occupation of figures or a setting for illustration. Conversely, the painted wood panel of *St. Jerome in His Study* by Antonello da Messina amplifies the spatial realism of the traditional author portrait. Jerome's bookshelf-lined enclosure with a lectern desk, a low chest or *capsa*, and a rounded chair, or *pozzetto*, often associated with authors, all encased beneath a spacious vaulted interior, exemplifies the physical expansion of furniture in the later Middle Ages (Plate 27). According to Dora Thornton, structures for study carrels such as these existed in the fifteenth century, but as fixed architectural additions, they were not mentioned in inventories. However, a descriptive entry in the inventory of Lorenzo di Pierfrancesco de' Medici, for the residence at Fiesole, echoes Antonello's fabrication: "a large writing desk ... with boards and a backrest, and with a cupboard with a cornice made of walnut, and compartments decorated with inlay. Underneath the desk, where one puts one's feet, is a wooden platform raised up from the ground" (Thornton 1997: 54, n. 5). Such written descriptions of furniture corroborate the realistic appearance of furniture in fifteenth-century paintings for which models are no longer extant. Meanwhile, the studio props of hutches, cabinets, and chests that reappear in the "bourgeois settings" of panel paintings and illuminations are more easily comparable to the numerous surviving examples preserved in ecclesiastical collections.

The strong visual contrast between an eleventh-century miniature such as the author portrait of Gregory, with its monochrome backdrop and restricted repertoire of furniture types, and the fifteenth-century *Roman de la Rose*'s naturalistic recession into depth and panoply of luxuriously draped elite furnishings, disguises the fact that in both cases the artists have positioned these pieces as devices to reinforce messages of status or narrative subtexts. Rather than simply providing a passive setting for the action or props on which characters are arrayed, furniture played a powerful role in manipulating the stage on which the visual actors in a painting performed. Whether used as framing elements, supports or as characters in and of themselves (as with the Round Table), furnishings fleshed out the language of the image. Those who seek to mine medieval illuminations for clues to a chronology of furniture style or type must be mindful that artists self-consciously incorporated anachronistic, imaginative, and hybrid forms to create meanings more understandable to their original audience than to modern viewers schooled in realism and trained to believe that depictions of furniture placed in a seemingly realistic environment should be trusted as reflections of the real.

CHAPTER NINE

Verbal Representations

Making "an Honest Bede"—Encountering God in Bed in Late Medieval England

HOLLIE L.S. MORGAN

Medieval verbal representations of furniture are few and far between. While everyday objects and surroundings consistently affected the ways in which people thought, acted, and produced literature and art, the ubiquitous objects themselves were rarely the focus of any written production.[1] Instead, most of the information to be gleaned from written sources on furniture and the roles it had to play in medieval society is to be found in the sidelines: the incidental details and the patterns and slippages, which become visible when the corpus is viewed as a whole.

The two pieces of furniture most prevalent across the genres are those that often formed part of marriage vows: the bed and the board (or, as we would think of it now, the table). In the Salisbury marriage vows, the woman promises "to be bonour and buxom[2] in bed and at board"[3] and in the York marriage vows, both the man and the woman use the phrase "to have and to hold, at bed and at board" (Maskell 1846: clv; Henderson 1875: 27; Staley 1911: IX, 156; McCarthy 2004; Morgan 2017: 80).[4] The "bed and board," as a pairing, is something that we might only encounter these days in reference to holiday lettings or rooms for rent; in the later Middle Ages, the bed and board were considered to be at the very center of marriage and, by extension, the household. The bed and board represented the two areas of the house in which a husband and wife were expected to share. Such can be seen in the bargain made between the late medieval mystic Margery Kempe (*c.* 1373–1438) and her husband John, when Margery wishes to take a vow of chastity in 1413, after many years of marriage and the birth of at least fourteen children.[5] In *The Book of Margery Kempe*, written in the late 1430s, the couple are described discussing the terms of a chaste marriage. While John releases Margery from any sexual debt, he makes three requests:

> My first desire is that we shall lie still together in our bed as we have done before; the second is that you shall pay my debts before you go to Jerusalem; and the third is that you shall eat and drink with me on the Friday as you were wont to do.[6]
>
> (Staley 1996: lines 545–8)

As Lynn Staley argues, John Kempe sees the essential parts of marriage to be "the creature comfort of sharing a bed and a weekly meal" (Staley 1996: 62). John is willing to forgo sex and does not expect Margery to be present at every meal, and so marriage to him really does come down to the shared use of two items of furniture: the bed and the table. Sharing a bed and board was so much a part of what was understood to be marriage that judicial separation was known as "divorce *a mensa et thoro*": divorce from bed and board (Butler 2002: 2; 2013). Such a phrase was not only confined to pragmatic texts: in Thomas Malory's *Le Morte Darthur* written in the late fifteenth century, King Meliodas' wife attempts to poison the young Tristram, after which "King Meliodas would never have ado with her as at bed and at board" (2008: 172–3). Beds and boards, metonymically representing the two main sections of the house in the architecture of the late medieval English imagination—the chamber and the hall—occur throughout late medieval written culture as a backdrop upon which real and fictional lives were played out. Together, they represented marriage and the effective running of a household. Separately, they had wider and more nuanced cultural meanings, which affected and were affected by the ways in which people interacted with them (cf. Morgan 2017).

IN BED WITH JESUS

A rare example of a text in which a piece of furniture is the focus rather than something that exists in the background is the mnemonic allegory of conscience, *Bonum lectum*, which survives in seven extant fifteenth- and sixteenth-century manuscripts, but as Ian Doyle argues, probably existed in some form from an earlier date, as the variations between the texts of the extant manuscripts suggests a wider and longer circulation than is now apparent (1995: 186–90).[7] It instructs the addressee to "take heed and learn how you shall make a good and honest bed, pleasing unto God and worshipful unto your soul" (186–7).

What follows is a step-by-step account of the construction of the bed, with each component of the bed assigned an attribute, virtue, or devotional activity required to make the "chamber of your soul" a suitable resting place for Christ (187). As *Bonum lectum* is arguably the most detailed late medieval English verbal representation of a single piece of furniture, this chapter will discuss the text as a representation of a bed, before moving on to the broader context of the bed verbally represented as a place in which to encounter God.

Bonum lectum is one of the most useful sources of evidence for the construction of physical beds in late medieval England, given the paucity of archaeological evidence (see Figure 9.1). As it mentions both men and women as possible readers and has a wide readership in mind, which, as Doyle points out, was "without limitation of status, clerical, religious or lay" (1995: 180), the material bed it describes is probably not exceptional, except in the fact that it is imaginary. For the allegory to work, it requires a level of understanding from its readers. It is wholly a bed and wholly not a bed at the same time, but the shared knowledge required to use and understand this text suggests that the aspect that we could consider to be wholly a bed is representative of the typical bed for its readership. This is not to say that every bed was the same in late medieval England (which is certainly not the case), nor that each component of the "honest bed" found in the text would be found in one's own bed in some form or another, but that it would be recognizably a bed to its audience. The instructions encompass the whole process of putting a bed together, beginning with the reader being entreated to gather straw and use a "shake fork" (a fork used to shake hay) "of kindness" to remove "the dust of sin and foul thoughts" (186). The reader is then guided through the process of placing a canvas over the straw, adding a mattress, two blankets, a "nether-sheet" and "over-sheet," a

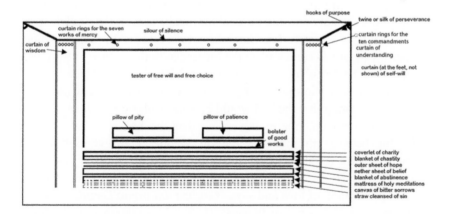

FIGURE 9.1 A representation of the bed in the *Bonum Lectum*, "chamber of the soul." Photograph by the Author.

coverlet, two pillows, and a bolster. The text then moves on to discuss the bed frame: the boards holding the straw in place, the tester, three curtains, canopy, cords, and hooks, and how the entire bed is set up in the chamber. Wills and probate inventories, while invaluable sources of data on the materials, colors, patterns, and monetary value of bedding, are by their nature lacking in detail when it comes to how a bed is actually constructed. *Bonum lectum* allows us to understand the order in which the components are layered and the method of keeping the tester and canopy up, in an era before four-poster beds. According to the text, the canopy is held in place by cords nailed to the wall. Some of the components of the bed and their corresponding attributes are delightfully mnemonic: the virtue ascribed to the coverlet is "charity," for "charity covers a multitude of sins," while one must be careful that none of the "ten [curtain] rings of the ten commandments … be broken, for if they are broken the enemy the fiend may look over into the bed of Jesus" (187–8). The mnemonic nature of this text invites readers to apply the allegory to their own beds.

As well as being an invaluable source for our understanding of how medieval beds were put together, it also demonstrates a strong connection between beds and faith in the late medieval cultural imagination by encouraging its audience to treat the act of making the bed as devotional. Given the level of detail in which the construction of the bed is described, from the pillows right down to the nails and cords supporting the canopy, it is very unlikely that anyone would rebuild their bed repeatedly and systematically as a prayerful activity. However, the wide circulation of this text and its mnemonic qualities point toward the text's use as extraordinarily suitable bedtime reading. One can easily imagine that the audience, once having read *Bonum lectum*, would then lie in bed recalling the divine attributes associated with the components of her or his own bed. The text—starting from the bottom (the straw) and working through the layers of the bed up to the top (the canopy) then spreading out to the walls, door, and window of the chamber—would be ideal for meditation, and the bed the perfect space in which to meditate (cf. Carruthers 1998: 116–70). Where would be more perfect a place to contemplate the intricacies of the creator of the universe than upon the "mattress" of "holy meditations" (Doyle 1995: 186)?

Bonum lectum, while noteworthy in its attention to detail, is not entirely unusual in suggesting that the bed would be a particularly appropriate object— and site—for devotion, nor in suggesting that the bed is an allegory for a relationship between the believer and the Divine. The text itself hearkens back to an earlier tradition of considering the bed to be a suitable space in which to encounter God: the allegorical bed "is the bed that our lord Jesus speaks of in his book of love and says, '*Canticorum primo Lectulus noster iam floridus est*': our bed is full of flowers" (189).[8] This reference to the Song of Songs (1:15), the Old Testament celebration of sexual love, "behold thou art fair, my beloved, and comely. Our bed is flourishing," illustrates that *Bonum lectum* is the product of a long tradition of thought and reflects theological reasoning of the time. As argued by Daniel Frank, the "frank eroticism" of the Song of Songs required allegorization so that Christians could be reconciled to its place in the canon (2010: 51). Medieval commentaries on the Song of Songs placed great emphasis on its allegorical nature, and such commentaries sparked a renewed appreciation of allegory throughout the Middle Ages. As E. Ann Matter discusses, medieval commentaries of the Song of Songs "tell a story of the triumph of the allegorical" (Matter 1990: 10) and pre-Reformation commentaries of the text had much more appreciation of allegory than those post-Reformation (3–16). The bed in the Song of Songs is treated in medieval commentaries such as the *Glossa Ordinaria*[9] and those by Gregory the Great (590–604) and William of Saint Thierry (1085–1148) as a metaphor for the relationship between the two speakers and between the believer and God, as well as a physical space in which the soul seeks the bridegroom Christ (Hart 1970: 77, 82; Dove 2004: 194; Gregory the Great 2012: 116). It is usually translated into a female voice, which commentaries often take as a representation of the believer, the Church as the bride of Christ, or the Virgin Mary (Matter 1990: 151–77). Interestingly, *Bonum lectum* takes the opposite approach, attributing the Bible verse to Christ, so that the "honest bed" is "the bed that our lord Jesus speaks of" (Doyle 1995: 198). This attribution has the effect of making the bed appear sanctioned and requested by God, as if God were waiting for the believer in the bed, rather than the other way around. In this reappropriation of Solomon's text, *Bonum lectum* illustrates that in the late medieval English cultural imagination the bed, like the church or private chapel, was where one should expect to find God and, indeed, where God lay waiting for his believers.

A pattern across several devotional texts and commentaries indicates that the bed was considered across centuries a suitable place in which to meditate on one's relationship with God. Hugh of Saint-Victor's twelfth-century *De Archa Noe*, an interpretative spiritual essay on Noah's Ark as a vessel for spiritual wisdom, refers to God "in the soul as the bridegroom in the wedding-chamber" and refers to those who love God as "His house, to the intent that He who made you may also dwell in you" (Squire 1962: 49–50). In the thirteenth century, nuns' visions in Helfta, Saxony "include images of God's grace as a bed with pillows" (Oliva 2008: 145), while Ida of Neville refers to the "spiritual dormitory" (Hamburger 1997: 145; Voaden 1997: 74). The fifteenth-century Middle English adaptation of *The Doctrine of the Hert*, a text written for a religious female readership, which pairs the gifts of the spirit with actions of the heart, uses the metaphor of "the house of your heart" with a bed by which "you shall understand peace and rest of conscience" (Whitehead, Renevey, and Mouron 2010: 8–9). This symbolism recalls Gregory the Great's seventh-century portrayal of the Church as a house, which has "an entrance," a "staircase of hope," "banquet halls" of "charity," and "the bedchamber of the king":

lest anyone exalt himself and fall into pride when he comes to know the secrets of God, when he scrutinizes God's hidden commandments, when he is raised up to the lofty heights of contemplation, it is said that he enters "the bedchamber of the king". In other words, the more a soul is brought to the knowledge of his secrets, the greater the reverence that should be shown.

(Matter 1990: 96; Gregory the Great 2012: 128–9)

Gregory's use of the "bedchamber of the king" is interesting because it equates the chamber with a certain level of intimacy and knowledge, arguing that the Church has reached the spiritual level of "bedchamber" (after the entrance, staircase, and banquet hall) due to being "already filled with and rooted in the mysteries of God," reaching "the lofty secrets and even penetrat[ing] them" (Gregory the Great 2012: 128). It also implies that the most appropriate space for "reverence" is the "bedchamber" (129). As chambers became more frequent in the later Middle Ages, their owners may well have recalled such teaching.[10] The idea of the chamber as an intimate space and one that is close to God is an interesting one, as unlike our modern ideas of bedrooms as private and cut off from the rest of the house, chambers would have been relatively busy. Probate inventories show that chambers often contained tools, merchandise, cooking utensils, and other items and the number of beds in the room was not necessarily limited to one. Despite the reality of many people's chambers, the idea persisted that the chamber, and the bed within it, were at a higher spiritual level in relation to other spaces in the house.

Richard Rolle, a mystic writing in the fourteenth century, specifically locates prayer in bed. In his commentary on the Psalter, of which over twenty extant copies remain (Allen 1988: 66), he equates "my bedding" to "the nether region of my soul" in reference to Psalm 6 and suggests, in reference to Psalm 62, that meditation on God in bed is necessary because "for he that does not think on him in rest, in his work he holds not his thought in him" (Rolle 1884: 23, 219). Adding a new layer to the relationship between physicality and allegory, Rolle interprets Matthew 6:6, "enter into your chamber, and having shut the door, pray to your Father," metaphorically rather than literally: "'Enter, he says, your bed,' that is, call your heart home, 'and then lock your door,' that is, hold your wits inside yourself, so that none come out" (Horstmann 1896: 142). This reading recalls texts such as *The Doctrine of the Hert* and implies that the bed and chamber are obvious symbols for the heart in relationship with God.

The mixed life followed by both Rolle and Margery Kempe means that their ideas are only representative of a small yet growing minority, and yet their texts reached out to a number of people. The proliferation of Rolle's manuscripts indicates that his ideas were well respected (Hanna 2010), so it is probable that some of his instructions were followed by some of his audience. Similarly, while *The Book of Margery Kempe* exists in only one manuscript, it had at least four early readers, probably at Mount Grace Priory, Yorkshire, so it was deemed worthy of study within a religious institution (Brown Meech 1940: xxxv–xlv; Staley 1996). Both writers assume that praying in bed is normal. However, Kempe takes the idea of prayer in bed a step further than Rolle. In *The Book of Margery Kempe* there are several occasions where Margery encounters God in bed. It is clear that the bed is not the only space in which God is physically present to Margery: God reportedly tells Margery that "when you go to church, I go with you; when you sit at your meal, I sit with you; when you go to your bed, I go with you; and when you go out of town, I go with you" (Staley 1996: lines 704–6). However, it is apparent throughout the *Book* that Kempe understands the bed to be a particularly appropriate space in which to spend time with God. For instance, after the birth of her first child, Margery "went out of her mind" (line 149) for over six months (perhaps a case of postpartum depression). She attributes her recovery to a bedside visit from Jesus:

> as she lay alone and her keepers were from her, our merciful Lord Christ Jesus, ever to be trusted, worshipped be his name, never forsaking his servant in time of need, appeared to his creature, which had forsaken him, in the likeness of a man, most seemly, most beauteous, and most amiable that ever might be seen with human eye, clad in a mantle of purple silk, sitting upon her bed's side, looking upon her with so blessed a cheer that she was strengthened in all her spirits, [and] said to her these words: "Daughter, why have you forsaken me, when I never forsook you?"
>
> (lines 167–73)

Margery had been restrained in bed due to her sickness, so if a vision of Jesus were to appear at any time, it would have had to have been in her chamber. However, the link between the bed and heavenly visitations does not stop there. The description of Christ "sitting upon her bed's side" emphasizes the bed as the locus of this visitation. Later in the narrative, as she "lay in her bed with her husband" (line 241), she hears heavenly music. Elsewhere in her *Book*, perhaps more famously, Margery literally marries God, as "the Father took her by the hand in her soul" (lines 2027–8) before the other two members of the Trinity, Mary, the saints, apostles, holy virgins, and angels and declared, "I take you, Margery, for my wedded wife" (lines 2030–1). He then discusses the physical consummation of that marriage in bed:

> For it is the convention that the wife be homely with her husband ... they must lie together and rest together in joy and peace. Right so must it be between you and me .... Therefore I must be homely with you and lie in your bed with you. Daughter, you desire greatly to see me, and you may boldly, when you are in your bed, take me to you as your wedded husband, as your

dearest darling …. And therefore you may boldly take me in the arms of your soul and kiss my mouth, my head and my feet as sweetly as you will.

(lines 2097–108)

There is some debate as to whether *The Book of Margery Kempe* should be taken as an autobiographical account, so it is unclear whether this is an accurate portrayal of the vision of a medieval mystic or a construction by one or more independent authors. Regardless of the authorship, intention, or accuracy of this report, what is important to this discussion is that the author (whoever that may be) describes "the Father of Heaven" giving instructions specifically for "when you are in your bed" and suggests that a tangible presence of God can be (and must be) present within the bed. While the fact that Margery is repelled by many of her contemporaries within the text implies that her experiences are not necessarily the norm, the placement of God within the bed is concurrent with contemporary writings and reminiscent of the flourishing bed in the Song of Songs. Margery has taken a vow of chastity, rejecting the physicality of a relationship with her husband in favor of one with God. As such, it makes sense that Christ fills the space in bed, which a husband would otherwise occupy. Like the author of *Bonum lectum*, Kempe puts forward the abstract idea of meditating on God, by using physical characteristics associated with the physical bed. The *Bonum lectum* author uses the physical construction of the bed; Margery Kempe uses its recognized role as a space for sex (Morgan 2017: 139–70). One could argue that the late medieval bed is seen to be a space in which a different sort of prayer is performed: where physical actions are just as holy and effective as recited Paternosters.

HEAVENLY BEDFELLOWS

The idea of the bed as a meeting place for God and the believer is not only articulated through explicitly religious writings. There are a significant number of examples in Middle English romance in which encounters with God, heavenly voices, and angelic apparitions often occur within the chamber, which shows that the idea of the bed as a meeting place for God was widespread and not exclusive to those in religious positions, as Middle English romances were consumed by a mostly secular audience. Just as in *Bonum lectum*, in romance texts God often appears to seek people out in bed: characters encountering God or God's works in bed do not usually initiate prayer. For example, in *Le Chevelere Assigne*, probably composed in the late fourteenth century, "an angel came to the hermit and asked if he slept" (Gibbs 1868: line 193). The role of a hermit is to remove himself from the world so that he is in constant communication with God, and yet the divine message still arrives while he is in bed, which suggests that the bed is a locus particularly suited to communing with the supernatural. Similarly, in the late thirteenth-century *Havelok the Dane*, a romance generally considered to be part of the Matter of England and one which purports to explain the origins of the Lincolnshire town of Grimsby, the only instance in which a "voice" of an angel is heard is when Havelok, the rightful heir to the throne of Denmark, and Goldeboru, the daughter of the deceased king of England, are in bed together (Sands 1986: line 1265). The angelic voice explains to Goldeboru that she has married a mistreated prince, not the peasant she thought he was, and that they must devise a plan to reconquer their respective kingdoms. In addition, the "noble cross" (line 1264), a birthmark that emits light and marks Havelok as a king anointed by God, is only witnessed in the chamber, first by Goldeboru and then by soldiers peering into his "bower" (line 2094). Further divine encounters in bed occur in *The Siege of Milan*, written in the second half of the fourteenth century: Sir Alantyne prays to God both inside and outside of his chamber, but he only hears "by him on a wall / An angel" when he is in "bed" (Lupak 1990: lines 85–91).

Some encounters with heavenly beings occur in romance through the medium of a dream. In *The Siege of Milan*, on "the same night" (Lupak 1990: line 109) in which Alantyne hears an angel, Charlemagne lies "in his bed" (line 110) and has a dream in which an angel comes to him with a message from God. The angel gives him a sword, saying it is a gift from God:

> When Charles wakened from his dream,
> He saw a brightness of a beam
> Up unto heavenward glide.
> But when he rose, the sword he found
> That the angel gave him in his hand
> Upon his bed's side.
>
> (lines 133–8)

Not only does this text suggest that it was considered appropriate to communicate with holy beings in bed, but a physical manifestation of God's favor upon Charlemagne is delivered through the medium of sleep and the bed. In a similar way, in the early fourteenth-century romance *The King of Tars*, the female protagonist has a dream in which she is almost ravaged by hounds twice, but is saved "through Jesus Christ's passion" (Chabot Perryman 1932: line 443). One of the dogs is then transformed into a knight "in white clothes" (line 451), who calls her "my sweet wight" (line 452) and reminds her that "your lord that suffered passion / Shall help you at your need" (lines 455–6). Upon waking up, "on her bed she sat all naked" (line 457) to pray to Jesus.

The bed is also used in late medieval literature as a site for miracles. In the late thirteenth-century *Amis and Amiloun*, the chamber is an important locus of divine activity. Toward the end of the romance Amiloun, who has become leprous as a punishment after sacrificing his honor to help his friend and sworn brother Amis, is cast out by his wife and eventually arrives at Amis's house, where it is assumed he will die. Shortly afterward, "an angel came from heaven bright / And stood before [Amis's] bed," before visiting the bed-ridden Amiloun in his dreams, explaining that Amis must sacrifice his children if he wishes to save Amiloun (Foster 2007: lines 2200–22). Carrying out the angel's instructions, Amis "alone himself, without anyone else, / Into the chamber he began to go, / There where his children were" (lines 2281–3), anointing Amiloun "in bed" with the children's blood and covering him with rich bedclothes (lines 2343–6). God restores Amiloun and resurrects the children, both miracles taking place in bed. After Amis slays his children, "he laid them in their bed again" (l. 2311), then leaves the chamber, locks the door and hides the keys, even though he intends to blame his children's death on a burglar (lines 2314–20). While this deception would be more believable if the door remained unlocked, the writer highlights the fact that the chamber is locked and the key hidden from human eyes. This fact is important, as it emphasizes that the resurrection of the children occurs inside a locked chamber, as Jesus was resurrected in a sealed tomb (John 20).

One reason why many divine encounters in romances occur in bed is that messages from God and visions are more credible if given through the medium of a dream, avoiding any accusations that the author is putting words in God's mouth. However, it is clear that there is more to the bed in relation to encounters with the divine in late medieval literature than simply being the place in which a character falls asleep. Dreams do not account for the resurrection of Amis and Belisaunt's children within a locked chamber, nor for occasions where romance characters specifically decide to pray in bed. For instance, in *Sir Eglamour of Artois*, written around 1350, Eglamour wishes to marry the earl's daughter and prays in bed for the marriage:

> To his bed he went,
> That richly was wrought.
> Both his hands he cast up soon,
> To Jesus Christ he made his boon,
> To the Lord that us bought.

(Hudson 1996: lines 98–102)

There is a tradition of heartsick romance characters taking to their beds but unlike many lovelorn characters, Eglamour does not throw himself on the bed to soliloquize on his sorrow. Instead, he deliberately chooses to pray in bed. Similarly, the fifteenth-century romance *Sir Gowther* emphasizes the importance of the chamber as a space for domestic piety. Originally a wild, evil child spawned from a demon, Sir Gowther eventually repents and carries out his penance in an emperor's castle, where he is treated like a fool, remaining mute and only eating food that has been given first to the dogs. His use of a chamber as a space in which to pray can be seen to be an important step toward salvation, as it is far removed from the orchard in which he was conceived and the physical and spiritual wilderness in which he committed his many sins. Upon hearing the news that the emperor's daughter is at risk from heathen invaders, "Sir Gowther went to a chamber smart / And prayed to God in his heart" (Laskaya and Salisbury 1995: lines 403–4). The adverb "smart" (meaning "straight away") emphasizes his conscious change of location: he did not pray straight away, but first went to the chamber. The chamber as the site for prayer is emphasized when the answer to his prayer arrives in the form of a horse and armor "at his chamber door" (line 411), and when it disappears from within the "chamber" (line 439) after he has used it. After his prayers are answered a second time, Gowther chooses to lie in bed while the rest of the court celebrates "in the hall" (line 529), so that he can think about how he can achieve salvation: "he had no thought but of his sin, / And how he might his soul win / To the bliss that God can buy him" (lines 538–40). As the chamber and hall are often used as binary opposites within the romance genre, the emphasis on Gowther "in his chamber" (line 532) and not "in the hall" (line 529) marks it out as a space specifically chosen by Gowther for prayer and contemplation. Because of the three occasions in which Sir Gowther literally puts on "the armor of God" (Ephesians 6:10–17) in his chamber, and the sincerity with which he strives for repentance in the chamber, he is absolved of all his sins. The repeated reference to his "chamber" and lying down suggests that the chamber and the bed within it played an integral part in his salvation, while his active role in seeking out the chamber in which to pray suggests that Gowther—and by extension the author and audience—understood it to be a space for prayer.

AS I LAY ME DOWN TO SLEEP …

So far this chapter has explored how the bed was considered to be a particularly suitable space in which to communicate with God. It will now discuss the ways in which that might be done. While, on the one hand, the bed was used for prayer and expressions of piety because devotional texts and popular literature modeled such behavior, on the other hand, it was done out of a sense of anxiety. The night was understood to be full of dangers. Rumors of ghosts, demons, and satanic influences abounded, propagated by Christian teachings on the contrast between light and darkness as the difference between good (Christ as the light of the world) and evil (all who are against him) (Youngs and Harris 2003: 136–8). Sleep had its own terrors, as a sleeper relinquishes control of her or his mental faculties. Such a problem was understood to allow the devil to get a foothold, as is seen in *Bonum lectum*: if the curtains of "reason" and "your own will sag down, then the enemy the fiend may look over into the bed of Jesus"

(Doyle 1995: 187). Practically, night was when people were most at risk of crime or house fires, and when they were least equipped to protect themselves. Sleepers' increased vulnerability did not go unnoticed. For instance, the late fifteenth-century semi-hagiographical romance *Le Bone Florence of Rome* illustrates how easily one might be killed or deceived in bed. Both Florence and her bedfellow Beatrice are attacked in the middle of the night, on separate occasions. While Florence manages to hit her attacker in the mouth with a handy stone (Falvo Heffernan 1976: lines 1605–13), Beatrice dies in her sleep with Florence sleeping peacefully beside her (line 1655). As a result, Florence is blamed for the murder of her bedfellow. In other texts, such as the fourteenth-century romance *Octavian* or *Le Chevelere Assigne* discussed above, new mothers, exhausted after childbirth, fall asleep and wake to find that mischief has been done to them. Such anxieties were not only played out in romance. For example, in the York divorce case of *Nesfeld v. Nesfeld* (1396), Margery Nesfeld is reported to have told her husband that "she could kill him in bed at night if she wanted" (Goldberg 1995: 142; Pederson 2000: 134). Because of the vulnerability associated with sleep, prayers upon sleeping and waking were intended to protect against spiritual and physical harm. Rolle recounts the advice given to Saint Edmund by his apparition:

> This is my Lord's name that you see thus written. I want you to have it in mind and imprint it into your soul; and cross your breast with this name before you go to sleep: it shall protect you from attack from the fiend that night, and from sudden death; and all that you might encounter at night.
>
> (Horstmann 1896: 152)

The two main horrors of the night, "the fiend" and "sudden death," are kept at bay through keeping the name of Jesus in mind and performing an act of devotion, in this case by crossing oneself. Elsewhere, Rolle instructs his audience to "whenever you wake, lift your heart to God with some holy thought, and rise and pray to your lord that he grant release of pains to the dead, and grace to the living and life without end" (Horstmann 1896: 152). In *The Book of Margery Kempe*, Margery is described praying in bed: "lying in her bed the next night following, she heard with her bodily ears a loud voice calling 'Margery'. With that voice she awoke, greatly afraid and, lying still in silence, she made her prayers" (Staley 1996: lines 3090–2). Margery's conversations with God parallel an episode in the fourteenth-century hagiographical text *The Life of Christina of Markyate*, which describes how when the twelfth-century Christina—or Theodora as she was called before she changed her name—was a small child, "she used to talk to [God] at night and on her bed as if he were a man whom she could see" (Talbot, Fanous, and Leyser 2008: 4). The young Theodora was "teased" for talking to God in bed "in a high, piping voice," and so "changed her ways" (4). This information, combined with Margery's recollection that she prayed "in silence" despite the fact that God spoke aloud (Staley 1996: line 1092), might suggest that it was normal practice to pray silently when in bed.

There is very little concrete evidence of specific prayers said morning and night in the chamber, due to the fact that if they were said morning and night, they were likely to be either memorized formulae such as the Paternoster or a spontaneous prayer for God to grant a specific boon or afford protection, such as we find mirrored in romance. Evidence of more tangible aids to salvation is found in descriptions of beds and chambers in wills. For instance, John Baret, who made his will in Bury St. Edmunds in 1463, certainly understood both the bed and chamber as spaces to remember God and the Virgin Mary, as can be seen in his instruction to his executors:

> I give and bequeath to Dame Margaret Spurdaunce, of Norwich, my crucifix, which is in my white chamber; and the canopy of cloth above, with the valance of scripture about the image, must not be removed nor had away; and I will that there be made at my expense such another crucifix, to be set up in the white chamber where the other crucifix was.
>
> (Tymms 1850: 36)

As Diana Webb comments, this action is "as if to say that *a* crucifix was an indispensable feature of this chamber" (2005: 42–3; original emphasis). It indicates that the crucifix itself was not of utmost importance, but that the white chamber was understood to be a space which contained a crucifix, and would have been lacking without. One could argue that such bedding required a crucifix to be placed nearby, or just that it was obvious that there should be a crucifix near the bed. In Caxton's *Golden Legend*, for instance, we are told that "there was a Christian man who had rented a house for a year and he had set the image of the crucifix by his bed to which he made daily his prayers and said his devotion" (Richardson 1884–5: 166). Crucifixes and religious imagery were often found close to or part of the design of the bed. John Baret so much associated religious iconography with the bed that he took a bed containing a Marian image on his travels: he bequeathed to his boy, John Aleyn, "a tester with two small blue-striped curtains, with an image of Our Lady in gold leaf, that I used to truss with me ... and the canopy belonging to it" (Tymms 1850: 34). John Baret was not alone in his penchant for beds decorated with religious iconography. In a York will of 1526 William Nelson left his son "a covering of a bed with imagery" (Raine and Clay 1869b: 200). Cecily Lepington's York will of 1526 includes her "best over-see bed called the Baptist," which presumably refers to an image of John the Baptist on the bed (2224). In Lincoln, a "bed called the maiden's bed" is left by William Gibbins to his son in 1535

(Clark 1914: 191–2). Given that the bed is not left to a "maiden," and in conjunction with the bequest of his soul "to Our Lady Saint Mary" and the bequest of three shillings four pence "to our lady light in the chancel," it can be assumed to be a bed representing the Virgin Mary. Lillechurch Priory in Higham, Kent, owned several bed hangings of saints and a red coverlet with an image of Christ (Cussans 1870–1: 268), while the prioress had a chamber hanging containing a prayer to the Virgin Mary (Scott 1913: 404–7). The bedding in St. Mary's Priory in Langley, Warwickshire, included one coverlet of crosses and roses and one of Mary as Queen of Heaven (Walcott 1868: 121–2).

Diverging slightly from verbal representations of beds, the recently discovered frame of the fifteenth-century State Bed of Henry VII and Elizabeth of York (Plate 31), thought to have been presented to Henry VII and Elizabeth of York for their marriage ceremony in 1486, contains richly layered religious imagery and has implications for the ways in which God could have been understood as belonging at the center of the royal marriage by being firmly associated with the bed (Morgan 2017: 68–9, 97–9). While it is an actual bed rather than a verbal representation, it is so deeply entrenched in text that it deserves a place in this chapter. The triptych arrangement on the tester portrays Adam and Eve as agents of the Fall of Man (Figure 9.2). This scene, with its resonances of both creation and temptation, reminds its audience that the bed is a site of procreation and temptation. At the same time, the figures of Adam and Eve, who arguably also represent Henry and Elizabeth, are shown to be transmuted through the cross of Christ's sacrifice into Jesus and the Virgin Mary, as figures of redemption. They are pictured holding an apple and rejecting the serpent's fruit, as they flank the Tree of Life, promised in Revelation 22:2, which grows several different types of fruit, which could represent the Fruits of the Spirit (Galatians 5:22). The two figures are encircled in a scroll that presumably contained scripture, now replaced by later script.[11] The visual representation of the creation story is reminiscent of royal genealogies, in which the family line is traced back to Adam and Eve, such as London, British Library, Harley Rolls C. 9 (Anglo 1961). In addition to the bed carvings of Adam and Eve, the representations of Christ and symbols of fertility, the bed frame has carvings of seven stars referencing the message of healing and conciliation between peoples in Isaiah 30:26 as well as the stars in Christ's right hands in the book of Revelation 1:16. The occupiers of this bed, whether they were the royal couple or not, would be visually situated in the middle of the story of the world, from Creation to the Apocalypse, so that they were literally lying at the center of God's plan.

Returning to texts, then, the Household Ordinances of Henry VII show that Henry's bed (whether this one or another, as his beds became progressively larger) was treated with a great degree of reverence, and that the making of his

FIGURE 9.2 Detail from tester of the First State Bed of Henry VII and Elizabeth of York, *c.* 1486. The Langley Collection. Photograph reproduced by permission of Ian Coulson, the Langley Collection.

bed every day was a ritual in itself. Every night, after several yeomen put the bed together, an "esquire for the body" sprinkled it with holy water, "then shall the esquires and the ushers, and all others that were at the making of the bed, go into an antechamber, where they would be met with bread, ale and wine; and so to drink altogether" (Anonymous 1790: 122). The practice of sprinkling holy water on the bed was normally reserved for marital beds of newlyweds, or to heal the sick (Woolgar 1999: 4; Egan 2007: 74; Wolfthal 2010: 3). Sprinkling the king's bed every night sanctified the space, while suggesting that the bed is also a marriage bed, so that each night became a consummation of the marriage between king and state. The ritual act of eating and drinking following the making of the king's bed added to the sense of ceremony. The rituals attached to its preparation combined with the rich religious imagery on the bed all point toward the bed as a sacred space for the king and his subjects. Given that the bed was culturally understood to be a meeting point between God and the believer, the king's bed is arguably the most important object in his possession: the space where he receives divine instruction and guidance.

TAKING THE BED OUT OF THE CHAMBER

The cognitive link between beds, chambers, and God in the late medieval English collective mindset is obvious, from evidence of religious imagery within the chamber to the late medieval understanding that God could literally communicate with a believer in bed. However, evidence of this cultural connection does not stop at the chamber door. Written evidence of the practice of displaying bedding in churches for bedding's own sake, as found in Holy Trinity Church, Kingston-upon-Hull, shows that the beds themselves were considered to have some religious meaning. The parishioners of Holy Trinity bequeathed bedding to the church so that they were used in remembrance of the donors on specific days and also displayed more generally on St. George's day. Thomas Wood's will of 1490 contains detailed instructions for the church's use of his bedding:

> To the Trinity church one of my best beds of Arras work, upon this condition: that after my decease the same bed shall yearly cover my grave at my *Dirige* and *Masse*, carried out in the said Trinity church with note for evermore; and also that I wish that the same bed be hung yearly in the said church at the feast of Saint George the Martyr among other worshipful beds; and, when these beds are taken down and delivered, then I wish that the same bed be redelivered into the vestry, and there to remain with my cope of gold.
>
> (Raine and Clay 1869a: 60)

The term "bedde" in Middle English could be used to refer to the whole bed structure or to part of the soft furnishing, which could be the stuffed mattress or featherbed or the coverlet (Morgan 2017: 22–38). In this case, as he wishes it to be "hung" (Raine and Clay 1869a: 60), "bed" probably refers to the coverlet. The repetition of "beds" throughout Wood's bequest suggests that the articles of bedding he mentions were still considered to be beds, rather than altar cloths or sepulcher hangings, which were often made out of bedding bequeathed to churches. One may wonder, then, what it is about them that marked them out as "beds" rather than other hangings. The difference between beds and wall hangings is, of course, their function, and as Wood wishes for his bed to "yearly cover [his] grave," one might say that it is still performing one of its functions as a cover for a reclined body, if in a somewhat macabre fashion. One of its other functions, as a space set aside for devotions, is hinted at in the phrase "other worshipful beds." "Worshipful" is synonymous with "honorable" or "worthy" and does not necessarily carry with it the suggestion of a god or idol. It does, however, suggest that the beds themselves were valued as objects of worship. Kate Heard argues that the inclusion of personal symbols or insignia on vestments bequeathed to the church encouraged remembrance of the donor and inspired frequent prayer for their soul (2011: 164). As the church was instructed to use the bedding on remembrance days associated with the donors, the church would have been required to have a record of which bed belonged to which donor, so it is possible that something similar is happening here. Considering these beds within the literary context in which texts such as *Bonum lectum* a soul's relationship with God, we can read each of these beds as a representation of its owner's soul. As Jenny Kermode points out, Wood's intention to store his earthly bedding until resurrection "raises interesting theological questions" (1998: 140). While it is not clear from his will whether Wood expected to make use of his bed upon or after Judgment Day, it might suggest that beds were understood to play a part in the Apocalypse, as is implied by the *Pricke of Conscience* window in All Saints North Street, York (Plate 32), in which even during the Apocalypse, people die in beds and have the last rites performed.

If the bed was a physical symbol of one's soul, Wood's "worshipful bed" might be kept safe for God's inspection (Raine and Clay 1869a: 60). It is clear that, for the merchant community of Holy Trinity Church, Hull, beds played an important part in the church's calendar, as they were hung up every year on the Feast of St. George the Martyr. As such, parishioners, not yet deceased, witnessing these church practices, would have understood their late acquaintances' beds in terms of their religious meaning. This understanding, in turn, would have affected the way in which they regarded their own beds.

One final piece of written evidence shows that, like Wood's "worshipful bed," beds that were still used to cover the living had another function as decoration and played a part in the collective worship of God. As recorded in the York *House Books* of 1544, during the feast of Corpus Christi:

> it is further agreed ... that for the honor of God and worship of this city ... on the morning after Corpus Christi day every householder that dwells in the highway on which the said procession proceeds shall hang before their doors and forefronts beds and coverings of beds of the best they can get ... for the honor of God and worship of this city and this [practice] be firmly kept hereafter upon pain of every man that if he does to the contrary of this agreement, he shall forfeit and pay to the Common Chamber of this City three shillings four pence.
>
> (Johnston and Rogerson 1979: 283)

The threat of a fine for those who did not comply suggests that the public display of bedding was not instigated by the owners of the beds themselves, and therefore was not only a competitive demonstration of personal wealth, although it is probable that a display of the city's collective wealth was one of the factors in the decision. The repeated rhetoric of "the honor of God and worship of this city" implies that beds lining the streets will, somehow, honor God. Like

Wood's will, it is specifically beds and bed coverings that are mentioned, rather than any other type of hanging or decorative cloth, indicating that beds had a certain meaning, in the cultural imagination, which made them appropriate and necessary decorations for the event. Lining the Corpus Christi procession route with bedding effectively kept the body of Christ and everyone taking part in the event between bedclothes, placing God and his worshippers in bed together. The practice also mirrored the plays themselves: just as the mystery plays sought to bring out the secrets and wonders of the Gospels, which were otherwise hidden in Latin texts and read only by authorized priests, it allowed the citizens of York to identify with the humanity of Christ, the most intimate spaces and objects associated with the citizens' sense of self are turned inside-out, so that the beds are unhidden before the Corpus Christi.

CONCLUSION

This chapter has shown that there was a very clear link between the domestic and the divine in the late medieval collective psyche. The bed was widely understood to be the site of communication between the believer and Christ, as can be seen through the wide dissemination of devotional works and biblical commentaries expounding this view. However, the idea of the bed and the "chamber of your soul" as the locus for divine encounter was not merely theoretical (Doyle 1995: 186). The devotional images upon the beds, the bequest of bedding for specific religious use, and the repeated insistence that one must serve God immediately upon waking up all point toward an inherent understanding that the bed was a sacred space. With this idea in mind, Margery Kempe and her nocturnal encounters with Jesus may not have been as transgressive as they now appear to a modern reader.

Let us return, briefly, to *Bonum lectum*. Toward the end of the text the addressee is instructed to use a "hammer" to nail together the four boards keeping the straw together around the base of the bed and to drive the hooks supporting the canopy into the four walls of the chamber (Doyle 1995: 188). The shaft of the hammer is made from "the cross that our lord Jesus died upon," while its head is made "of the hard nails of iron that nailed the hands and the feet of our lord Jesus Christ to the cross" (189). According to *Bonum lectum*, without the crucifixion, there would not be the tools required to make the bed. Without the "honest bed," there would be no space "which our lord Jesus Christ will have liking to rest in" (186); without God's sacrifice, there would be no bed to begin with. Christianity, *Bonum lectum* suggests, means being able to share a bed with God.

NOTES

Chapter 1

1   Sogdiana, around the area of Samarkand in Central Asia, was the homeland of an ancient Iranian people.

Chapter 2

1   More generally, the history of technology in the period under consideration, see Singer et al. (1956, 1962), Long (1985, 2005). On the level reached in antiquity in the wood processing industry, see Baker (1966).

2   See the medieval architecture contribution of Carlo Tosco in Crivello (2006: 14–35, esp. 18–21, with further bibliographical references).

3   For an introduction to the history of medieval furniture, see the pioneering contributions of John Hunt and Douglas Ash in Hayward (1965: 20–4), Symonds (1962), Eames (1977), and Tracy (1988).

4   Clear documentation of the type of furniture in a medieval house is offered by inventories compiled at the time of the owner's death. Among these, some of the most detailed are the inventories of the palace of Francesco Datini in Prato, see Paolini (2012). On medieval construction techniques for portable furniture, see Dieh (1997).

5   About the art of connections and joints, see Hoadley (1980: 180–8), Drury (1988: 20–1, 34–5), and Borghini and Massafra (2002: 305–8).

6   See the contributions of the medieval sculpture of Saverio Lomartire and Guido Gentile in Crivello (2006: 223–71, esp. 252–4, with further bibliographical references).

7   See the contribution of Elisabetta Ingrid Basile in Maltese (1990: 315–99, esp. 328–30).

8   About the tools of woodworker, see Haines et al. (1948), R.H.G. Thomson in Singer et al. (1962: 395–402), Goodman (1964), Welsh (1966), and Walker (1980). Some precious old tools used in wood processing are stored in Nessi collection of Lugano, see Carter (2004). On the vocabulary related to the various tools and for

their historical description, see Simona Rinaldi in Borghini and Massafra (2002: 289–304), and Paolini and Faldi (2005 ad vocem).

9   See the contribution of Bertrand Gille in Singer (1962: 653–5), Symonds (1962: 252–4), Drury (1988: 22–3), Bernabo and Mocali (1998), and Simona Rinaldi in Borghini and Massafra (2002: 296).

10 See, for example, the various and detailed woodcuts in the known volume of Jost Amman and Hans Sachs of 1568. See Amman (1973: 95 [The Carpenter], 96 [The joiner], 97 [The wagonwright], 98 [The cooper], 99 [The turner]).

11 An overview of the guilds of the woodworkers in Italy is provided by contributions from Daniela Cuomo in Galetti (1985: 13–26, with further bibliographical references).

12 On chests made between the Middle Ages and the Renaissance there is an extensive bibliography, in particular relating to the chests that have painted imagery. Among the most recent publications, in relation to the topic, see Paolini (2002, 2004c: 81–5, for further bibliographical references; 2006: 120–1), Campbell (2009), Paolini, Parenti, and Sebregondi (2010: 51–67), and Randolph (2014: 139–67).

13 Ferretti (1982), an essay considered to be a fundamental contribution on the subject.

14 For a more extensive discussion on the inlay techniques see Edi Baccheschi in Maltese (1973: 383–7), Raggio and Wilmering (1999: 2:3–59 [Materials and Tools of the Intarsia Cutters], 61–81 [Intarsia Techniques in Renaissance Italy]), Paolini (2006), and Fedeli (2013).

Chapter 3

1   Henry VIII's inventory shows clearly how textiles were used to decorate furniture (Starkey and Ward 1988).

2   These are based on Chinnery (1979: 69–74, 104–24), but his term "clamp-fronted" is not precise since the front, back, and side boards are all clamped by joints that hold the wide tenons in long mortises in the stiles (uprights). In practice, chests may combine pure types. Chinnery's typology treats as secondary features such as lid shape, the presence of legs and plinths, which are given more importance by Eames (1977: 108–80).

3   The Brasenose College, Oxford, chest of c. 1510 is one of the earliest framed and paneled chests in England. It has a single panel front but when two additional locks were added in 1517 they were fixed to a new internal panel, suggesting some diffidence about the construction method.

4   At the basilica of Valère a plan of twenty-two probable chest locations has been drawn up based on a document of 1364 (Charles and Veuillet 2012: 1:55–60).

5   Compare this with the 1.75 × 0.80 × 0.65 meters size of the later iron-bound, clamped Westphalian chests (Baumeier 2012).

6   Thanks to Karl Heinrich von Stülpnagel for this information (personal communication, 2013).

Chapter 4

1   For example, in a Genoese artisan's house, often only a bed and chests were found in the bedroom, and with no other furniture, the only seating were the bed and chests (serving as benches), therefore, on most days the *camera* in an artisan's home

was better suited to family interactions rather than to "accommodating external visitors" (Cavallo 2006: 74).

2   A novel bed treatment in the space-restrictive environment of Venice is worthy of note. Though here, too, the typical freestanding bed was common, but "the built-in alcove bed was a characteristically Venetian accoutrement" (Fortini Brown 2006: 61). It maximizes space within the room by having this furniture a part of the architecture. Just like freestanding beds, curtains accompanied the beds and when not in use they were "tucked" into the bed, hiding it. Furthermore, the Venetian casa might have a separate, small bedroom above this unobtrusive bed alcove called a *sopraletto* ("above the bed") for children and childcare, which was accessible by a small staircase in the wall on either side of the alcove bed (61).

3   Or, the fabric barrier might suggest a temporary function to the room, such as a birthing room. See Musacchio (1999: 46).

4   Musacchio notes a lavish Venetian confinement room from a 1466 document of a merchant's home; Florence was not known for the same extravagance, but such rooms were often still very luxurious. See Musacchio (1999: 43–6). Sometimes the confinement bed was a daybed (*lettuccio*). This room was typically separate from the husband's or couple's bedroom chamber, allowing female guests to visit without disrupting the husband.

5   Examples of such visits are recorded in Gaspare Nadi's diary (Nadi 1969: 174, 282–3; in Cavallo 2006: 73, n. 50).

6   The 1448 inventory is for Antonio di Marsilio Vecchietti; the 1495 inventory is for Gismondo della Stufa, also from Florence.

7   The *portego* also served as a receiving hall and like a *sala*, tended to keep its terrazzo floors free of furniture.

8   The Duke of Urbino (Federico da Montefeltro [1422–82]) was famous for ceremony and display and his preoccupation with ritual hand-washing. See Jennifer Webb (2013) and Maria Grazia Pernis and Laurie Schneider Adams (2003).

9   Fra Bovincino da Riva's 1290 poem, *The Fifty Courtesies for the Table*. See *Italian Courtesy Books* translated by William Michael Rossetti (da Riva 1869: 17–31).

10 See also Dora Thornton (1997).

11 John the Fearless had a buffet in chambers where he also greeted guests; canopies could also be attached to buffets. At funerals, the buffet would be covered with cloth, but not laden with finery. See Eames (1977: 56, n. 138 and 61).

Chapter 5

1   I have necessarily followed the abbreviation of the text at https://epistolae.ctl. columbia.edu/letter/94.html. For a full account of the text in Latin and English, see Otter (2001).

Chapter 6

1   The San Pier Maggiore inventories will shortly be published by Joanne Allen, in her forthcoming book on the transformation of Florentine churches in the sixteenth century. We are grateful to her for sharing this material, delivered at a meeting of the National Gallery Research Seminar devoted to San Pier Maggiore, 6 November 2015.

2   There are three authors that record the event: Eleonora d'Aragona in a letter to her former tutor and councilor to the king of Naples, Diomede Carafa (the Count of Maddaloni); Teofilo Calcagnini a Ferrarese courtier writing to Duke Ercole d'Este;

and Bernardino Corio. All three share similar reports, noting the lavishness of the banquet and the suites of rooms, although details such as the number of stages on the *credenza* vary according to each account. For discussions, transcriptions, and translations of these documents, see Licht (1996: apps. I, II), Bryant (2012: 365, doc. 5), and Corvisieri (1878: 475–96; 1887: 629–87).

Chapter 9

1   See, for example, Appadurai (1986), Sarti (2002: 199–23), Smith (2003), and Daston (2008).
2   "Bonour and buxom" does not really survive translation. Essentially, it is a promise to be good natured and generous of heart.
3   All spellings are modernized.
4   McCarthy (2004) conflates the various marriage vows, suggesting that only the women use the phrase "at bed and board" in York. This is not the case.
5   Much scholarship has been done on the authorship of Margery Kempe, whether the protagonist can be seen to be an accurate representation of the real Margery Kempe, whether the events in the narrative took place, and whether it was actually dictated by a woman of that name. For the purposes of clarity, I use "Kempe" to refer to the author(s) and "Margery" to refer to the protagonist. For a discussion on the authorship of Margery Kempe, see, for example, Hirsch (1975), Atkinson (1983), Mueller (1986), Staley Johnson (1991), Beckwith (1992), Lawton (1992), and Glenn (1992).
6   All translations are my own.
7   According to Doyle (1995: 179–86), the text survives in seven manuscripts: Cambridge, St. John's College, MS G. 8, ff. 49v–52r; Oxford, Bodleian Library, MSS Douce 302, ff. 32v–33v, Laud Misc. 19, ff. 22v–30v, Laud Misc. 99, ff. 123r–124r, Eng. Theol. C. 57, ff. 131v–32v; Oxford, Jesus College, MS 39, pp. 560–2; and Oxford, University College, MS 123, ff. 74v–75v. U, S, D, and M are separate versions and do not derive from any others. J, E, and L have significant variations but sometimes agree with D, "pointing to a common parent nearer the original" (p. 186). There are some linguistic links between U and S, S and D, D and M.
8   The Latin text between the chevrons is interlinear.
9   The *Glossa Ordinaria* (literally "ordinary gloss") is a twelfth-century collection of biblical glosses drawn from patristic and medieval authors, which was disseminated across hundreds of manuscripts. See Smith (2009).
10 For more on the increased frequency of chambers in houses, see Faulkner (1958), Blair (1993), and Quiney (1999: 42).
11 Paint analysis revealed evidence of secondary graining, where the current lettering, which reads "The sting of death is sinne: The strength of sinne is the law," is incised. Jonathan Foyle suggests that the original lettering was raised and was planed off, though it could also have been painted on.

BIBLIOGRAPHY

Primary Sources

Archivio di Stato di Modena, Caso e Stato (C&S) 131-2, 1683 x-34.
Archivio di Stato di Modena, Guardaroba 117 55R.
Cambridge, St. John's College, MS G. 8.
London, British Library, Additional MS 61823.
Oxford, University College, MS 123.
Oxford, Bodleian Library, Douce MS 302.
Oxford, Bodleian Library, Eng. Theol. MS C. 57.
Oxford, Bodleian Library, Laud Misc. MS 19.
Oxford, Bodleian Library, Laud Misc. MS 99.
Oxford, Jesus College, MS 39.

Secondary Sources

Abou-el-Haj, Barbara (1997), *The Medieval Cult of Saints: Formations and Transformations*, Cambridge: Cambridge University Press.
Aguilo, Maria Paz (1987), *El mueble classico espanol*, Madrid: Catedra.
Aguilo, Alonso and Maria Paz (1993), *El mueble en Espana: siglos XVI–XVII*, Madrid: CSIC/Ediciones Antiqvaria.
Ajmar-Wollheim, Marta and Flora Dennis (2006a), "Introduction," in Marta Ajmar-Wollheim and Flora Dennis (eds.), *At Home in Renaissance Italy*, 10–31, London: Victoria & Albert Museum Publication.
Ajmar-Wollheim, Marta and Flora Dennis, eds. (2006b), *At Home in Renaissance Italy*, London: Victoria & Albert Museum Publication.
Alberti, Leon Battista (1956), *On Painting*, trans. John R. Spencer, New Haven, CT: Yale University Press.
Alberti, Leon Battista (1969), *Della Familia*, trans. Neu Watkins, Columbia, South Carolina: University of South Carolina.
Alexander, Jonathan and Paul Binski, eds. (1987), *Age of Chivalry: Art in Plantagenet England 1200–1400*, London: Royal Academy.

Allen, Rosamund, ed. (1988), *Richard Rolle: The English Works*, Mahwah, NJ: Paulist Press.

Amman, Jost (1973), *The Book of Trades (Standebuch)*, New York: Dover.

Anderson, J.C. (1991), "The Illustrated Sermons of James the Monk: Their Dates, Order, and Place in the History of Byzantine Art," *Viator*, 22: 69–120.

Angar, Mabi (2015), "Furniture and Imperial Ceremony in the Great Palace: Revisiting the *Pentapyrgion*," in Michale Featherstone, Jean-Michel Spieser, Gülry Tanman, and Ulrike Wulf-Rheidt (eds.), *The Emperor's House: Palaces from Augustus to the Age of Absolutism*, 181–200, Boston: de Gruyter.

Anglo, Sydeny (1961), "The *British History* in Early Tudor Propaganda, With an Appendix of Manuscript Pedigrees of the Kings of England, Henry VI to Henry VIII," *Bulletin of the John Rylands Library Manchester* 44 (1): 17–48.

Anonymous, ed. (1790), *A Collection of Ordinances and Regulations for the Government of the Royal Household, Made in Divers Reigns, from King Edward III. to King William and Queen Mary*, London: Society of Antiquities.

Appadurai, Arjun (1986), "Introduction: Commodities and the Politics of Value," in Arjun Appadurai (ed.), *The Social Life of Things: Commodities in Cultural Perspective*, 3–63, Cambridge: Cambridge University Press.

Ariès, Philippe and Georges Duby (1988), *A History of Private Life. Revelations of the Medieval World*, trans. Arthur Goldhammer, vol. 2, Cambridge, MA: The Belknap Press of Harvard University Press.

"AT&T Building" (1987), *New York*, June 15: 85. Available online: https://books.google.ca/books?id=ruMCAAAAMBAJ&pg=PA35&lpg=PA35&dq=at%26t+building+chippendale&source=bl&ots=TwT_LNM8nx&sig=J-YxJCUY_npJYgkyzgLHFsenJ5U&hl=en&sa=X&ei=39qfVajuGsGuyATun6qgCg&ved=0CDoQ6AEwBzgK#v=onepage&q=at%26t%20building%20chippendale&f=false (accessed July 10, 2015).

Atkinson, Clarissa W. (1983), *Mystic and Pilgrim: The Book and the World of Margery Kempe*, Ithaca, NY: Cornell University Press.

Augustine, Saint (1982), *Confessions*, trans. R.S. Pine-Coffin, Harmondsworth, UK: Penguin.

Bagatin, Pier Luigi (1987), *L'arte dei Canozi Lendinaresi*, Triestre: Lint.

Bagatin, Pier Luigi (2000), *Preghiere di legno: tarsie e intagli di Fra Giovanni da Verona*, Florence: Centro Ed. Toscano.

Bagatin, Pier Luigi (2004), *Le pitture lignee di Lorenzo e Cristoforo da Lendinara*, Treviso: Antilla.

Baker, Hollis S. (1966), *Furniture in the Ancient World: origins and evolution 3100–475 B.C.*, London: The Connoisseur.

Barnes, Carl F. (2009), *The Portfolio of Villard de Honnecourt (Paris, Bibliothèque Nationale de France, MS Fr 19093): A New Critical Edition and Color Facsimile*, New York: Ashgate.

Barnet, Peter and Nancy Y. Wu (2012), *The Cloisters: Medieval Art and Architecture*, 75th Anniversary edn., New York: The Metropolitan Museum of Art.

Baron, J.H. (1990), "The Hospital of Santa Maria della Scala, Siena, 1090–1990," *British Medical Journal*, 301: 1449–551.

Barraclough, Graeme (2009), "Technical Notes," in Caroline Campbell (ed.), *Love and Marriage in Renaissance Florence: The Courtauld Wedding Chest*, 78–9, London: The Courtauld Gallery.

Bartlett, Robert, ed. (2001), *Medieval Panorama*, London: Thames and Hudson.

Barton, Richard (2009), "Aristocratic Culture: Kinship, Chivalry, and Courtly
    Culture," in Carol Lansing and Edward D. English (eds.), *A Companion to the
    Medieval World*, 500–24, Chichester, UK: Blackwell Publishing.
Baskins, Cristelle (2008), *The Triumph of Marriage: Painted Cassoni of the Renaissance*,
    Boston: Gutenberg Periscope Publishing.
Bauer, Herbert and Georg Stolz (1974), *Engelsgruß und Sakramenthaus in St. Lorenz
    zu Nürnberg*, Königstein in Taunus: Langewiesche.
Baumeier, Stefan (2012), *Beschlagene Kisten: Die altesten Truhen Westfalens*, Essen:
    Klartext.
Bayer, Andrea, ed. (2008), *Art and Love in Renaissance Italy*, New York: Metropolitan
    Museum of Art.
Bebb, Richard (2007), *Welsh Furniture 1250–1950*, 2 vols., Kidwelly, UK: Saer
    Books.
Beckwith, Sarah (1992), "Problems of Authority in Late-Medieval English Mysticism:
    Language, Agency, and Authority in *The Book of Margery Kempe*," *Exemplaria*, 4:
    172–99.
Bedos Rezak, Brigitte (1986), "Suger and the Symbolism of Royal Power: The Seal
    of Louis VII," in Paula Lieber Gerson (ed.), *Abbot Suger and Saint Denis: A
    Symposium*, 95–103, New York: Harry N. Abrams.
Bellavitis, Anna and Isabelle Chabot (2006), "People and Property in Florence
    and Venice," in Marta Ajmar-Wollheim and Flora Dennis (eds.), *At Home in
    Renaissance Italy*, 76–85, London: Victoria & Albert Museum.
Belozerskaya, Marina (2002), *Rethinking the Renaissance: Burgundian Arts Across
    Europe*, Cambridge: Cambridge University Press.
Bernabò, Massimo and Carlotta Mocali (1998), *Spasso di principi e ingegno di artigiani.
    Disegni di strumenti e ricette di un maestro artigiano del Seicento*, Florence:
    Polistampa.
Biddle, Martin (2000), *King Arthur's Round Table: An Archaeological Investigation*,
    Woodbridge, UK: Boydell.
Binski, Paul (1986), *The Painted Chamber at Westminster*, London: Society of
    Antiquaries Occasional Paper IX.
Binski, Paul (2003), "'A Sign of Victory': The Coronation Chair, Its Manufacture,
    Setting and Symbolism," in Richard Welander, David J. Breeze, and Thomas Owen
    Clancy (eds.), *Stone of Destiny: Artefact and Icon*, 207–20, Edinburgh: Society of
    Antiquaries of Scotland Monograph 22.
Binski, Paul (2004), *Becket's Crown: Art and Imagination in Gothic England 1170–
    1300*, New Haven, CT: Yale University Press.
Binski, Paul (2010), "Statues, Retables, and Ciboria: The English Gothic Altarpiece in
    Context, Before 1350," in Justin E.A. Kroesen and Victor M. Schmidt (eds.), *The
    Altar and Its Environment 1150–1400*, 31–46, Turnhout: Brepols.
Binski, Paul (2014), *Gothic Wonder: Art, Artifice and the Decorated Style 1290–1350*,
    New Haven, CT: Yale University Press.
Binski, Paul and Ann Massing, eds. (2009), *The Westminster Retable: History,
    Technique, Conservation*, Cambridge: The Hamilton Kerr Institute and University
    of Cambridge.
Bissett, Tara (2017), "Architecture as Idea in the French Renaissance," Ph.D. thesis,
    University of Toronto.
Black, Anthony (1984), *Guilds and Civil Society in European Political thought from
    the Twelfth Century to the Present*, London: Methuen.

Blair, John (2005), *The Church in Anglo-Saxon Society*, Oxford: Oxford University Press.

Blair, W. John (1993), "Hall and Chamber: English Domestic Planning 1000–1250," in Gwyn Merion-Jones and Micahel Jones (eds.), *Manorial Domestic Planning in England and France*, 1–21, London: Society of Antiquaries.

Blanc, Monique (1999), *Le mobilier francais: Moyen age—Renaissance*, Paris: Massin.

Bloom, Jonathan M., Ahmed Toufiq, Stefano Carboni, Jack Soultanian, Antoine M. Wilmering, Mark D. Minor, Andrew Zawacki, and El Mostafa Hbibi (1998), *The Minbar from the Kutubiyya Mosque*, New York: The Metropolitan Museum of Art.

Blunt, Anthony (1973), *Art and Architecture in France 1500–1700*, Harmondsworth, UK: Penguin.

Boccador, Jacqueline (1988), *Le mobilier francais du moyen age à la renaissance*, Saint-Just-en-Chaussée: Editions d'art Monelle Hayot.

Boethius (1978), *The Consolation of Philosophy*, trans. S.J. Tester, Cambridge, MA: Harvard University Press.

Böker, Johann Josef (2005), *Architektur der Gotik/Gothic Architecture: Bestandskatalog der weltgrößten Sammlung an gotischen Baurissen der Akademie der bildenden Künste Wien*, Salzburg: Verlag Anton Pustet.

Bonde, Niels, Ian Tyers, and Thomas Wazny (1997), "Where Does the Timber Come From? Dendrochronological Evidence of the Timber Trade in North Europe," in Anthony Sinclair, Elizabeth Slater, and John Gowlett (eds.), *Archaeological Sciences 1995*, 201–4, Oxford: Oxbow Books.

Borchgrave, d'Altena, Joseph De (1958), *Notes pour server a l'Étude des retables anversois*, extract from the *Bulletin des Musées Royaux d'Art et d'Histoire 1957–1958*, 1–168, Antwerp: Imprimeries Générales Lloyd Anversois.

Borghini, Gabriele and Maria Grazia Massafra, eds. (2002), *Legni da ebanisteria*, Rome: De Luca.

Bork, Robert (2011), *The Geometry of Creation: Architectural Drawing and the Dynamics of Gothic Design*, Farnham, UK: Ashgate.

Borsook, Eve (1970), "Documenti relativi alle Capelle di Lecceto e delle Selve di Filippo Strozzi," *Antichità Viva*, 9 (3): 3–20.

Braham, Allan (1979), "The Bed of Pierfrancesco Borgherini," *The Burlington Magazine*, 121 (921): 754–63, 765.

Breckenridge, James D. (1980–1), "Christ on the Lyre-Backed Throne," *Dumbarton Oaks Papers*, 34/35: 247–60.

Brett, Gerard (1954), "The Automata in the Byzantine 'Throne of Solomon'," *Speculum*, 29 (3): 477–87.

Bridge, Martin C. and Daniel W.H. Miles (2011), "A Review of the Information Gained from Dendrochronologically Dated Chests in England," *Regional Furniture*, 25: 25–55.

Brotton, Jeremy (2002), *The Renaissance Bazaar: from the Silk Road to Michelangelo*, Oxford: Oxford University Press.

Brown, Andrew and Graeme Small (2007), *Court and Civic Society in the Burgundian Low Countries, c. 1420–1530*, Manchester, UK: Manchester University Press.

Brown, Michelle P. (2003), *Painted Labyrinth: The World of the Lindisfarne Gospels*, London: British Library.

Brown, Sarah (1999), *Sumptuous and Richly Adorn'd: The Decoration of Salisbury Cathedral*, London: The Stationery Office.

Brown Meech, Sanford, ed. (1940), *The Book of Margery Kempe*, New York: Oxford University Press.

Brubaker, Leslie (2004), "The Elephant and the Ark: Cultural and Material Interchange across the Mediterranean in the Eighth and Ninth Centuries," *Dumbarton Oaks Papers*, 58: 175–95.

Brucher, Günter (1990), *Gotische Baukunst in Österreich*, Salzburg: Residenz Verlag.

Bryant, Diana (2012), "Affection and Loyalty in an Italian Dynastic Marriage," Ph.D. dissertation, University of Sydney.

Bucher, François (1976), "Micro-Architecture as the 'Idea' of Gothic Theory and Style," *Gesta*, 15: 71–89.

Bumke, Joachim (1991), *Courtly Culture: Literature and Society in the High Middle Ages*, trans. Thomas Dunlap, Los Angeles: University of California Press.

Burckhardt, Jacob (1987), *The Architecture of the Italian Renaissance*, trans. Peter Murray, Harmondsworth, UK: Penguin.

Butler, Sara M. (2002), "Lies, Damned Lies, and the Life of Saint Lucy: Three Cases of Judicial Separation from the Late-medieval Court of York," in Philippe Romanski and Aïssatou Sy-Wonyu (eds.), *Trompe(-)l'œil: Imitation and Falsification*, 1–16, Rouen: Publications de l'Université de Rouen.

Butler, Sara M. (2013), *Divorce in Medieval England: From One to Two Persons in Law*, New York: Routledge.

Butterworth, Edward. J. (1991), "Form and Significance of the Sphere in Nicholas of Cusa's *De ludo globi*," in Gerald Christianson and Thomas Mizbicki (eds.), *Nicholas of Cusa: In Search of God and Wisdom, Essays in Honor of Morimichi Watanabe by the American Cusanus Society*, 89–100, Leiden: Brill.

Callmann, Ellen (1999), "William Blundell Spence and the Transformation of Renaissance *cassoni*," *Burlington Magazine*, 141 (June): 338–48.

Camille, Michael (2001), "'For Our Devotion and Pleasure: The Sexual Objects of Jean, Duc de Berry," *Art History*, 24 (2): 169–94.

Campbell, Caroline, ed. (2009), *Love and Marriage in Renaissance Florence: The Courtauld Wedding Chest*, London: The Courtauld Gallery.

Campbell, Erin (2014), "*Listening* to Objects: An Ecological Approach to the Decorative Arts," *Journal of Art Historiography*, 11 (December): 1–23.

Campbell, Erin J., Stephanie R. Miller, and Elizabeth Carroll Consavari (2013), *The Early Modern Italian Domestic Interior, 1400–1700: Objects, Spaces, Domesticities*, Burlington, VT: Ashgate.

Campbell, Lorne (1998), *The Fifteenth Century Netherlandish Schools*, National Gallery Catalogues, London: National Gallery Publications.

Campbell, Marian (1987), "Metalwork in England, c. 1200–1400," in Jonathan Alexander and Paul Binski (eds.), *The Age of Chivalry. Art in Plantagenet England*, 162–8, London: Royal Academy of Arts in association with Wiedenfeld and Nicolson.

Canales, Jimena and Andrew Herscher (2005), "Criminal Skins: Tattoos and Modern Architecture in the Work of Adolf Loos," *Architectural History*, 48: 235–56.

Carboni, Stefano (2007), *Venice and the Islamic World 828–1797*, New Haven, CT: Yale University Press.

Carruthers, Mary (2000), *The Craft of Thought: Meditation, Rhetoric, and the Making of Images, 400–1200*, Cambridge: Cambridge University Press.

Carter, Claudine (2004), *Antichi strumenti e utensili dalla collezione Nessi*, Milan: 5 Continents Editions.

Cavallo, Sandra (2006), "The Artisan's *casa,*" in Marta Ajmar-Wollheim and Flora Dennis (eds.), *At Home in Renaissance Italy,* 66–75, London: Victoria & Albert Museum.

Cecchi, Alessandro (1998), "L'Arte dei Legnaiuoli in Firenze: gli esordi," in *Arti Fiorentine. La grande storia dell'artigianato,* vol. 1, *Il Medioevo,* 187–213, Florence: Giunti.

Cescinsky, Herbert (1931), *The Gentle Art of Faking Furniture,* London: Chapman and Hall.

Cescinsky, Herbert (1934), "'Post-dissolution gothic' in English Furniture," *Apollo,* 20 (116): 73–9.

Cescinsky, Herbert and Ernest R. Gribble (1922), *Early English Furniture and Woodwork,* 2 vols., London: Waverley.

Chabot Perryman, Judith, ed. (1932), *The King of Tars: A Critical Edition,* Heidelberg: Carl Winter's Universitätsbuchhandlung.

Charles, Claudette and Corinne Veuillet (2012), *Coffres et coffrets du Moyen Age,* 2 vols., Sion: Musées cantonaux du Valais.

Chatelain, Jacques (2006), *Mobilier traditionnel des Alpes Occidentales,* Grenoble: Libris.

Cheng, B. (2010), "The Space Between: Locating 'Culture' in Artistic Exchange," in "Theorizing Cross-Cultural Interaction among the Ancient and Early Medieval Mediterranean, Near East and Asia," special issue, *Ars Orientalis,* 38: 81–120.

Chinnery, Victor, (1979), *Oak Furniture: The British Tradition, A History of Furniture in the British Isles and New England,* Woodbridge, UK: Baron Publishing.

Christie's (1999), *Oak, Country Furniture and Works of Art,* Sale, Christie's South Kensigton, November 3.

Christie's (2015), *Collecting in the English Tradition: Property of the Metropolitan Museum,* Sale, Christie's New York, October 27.

Clark, Andrew, ed. (1914), *Lincoln Diocese Documents, 1450–1554,* Ann Arbor: University of Michigan Press.

Clark, Leah R. (2009), "Value and Symbolic Practices: Objects, Exchanges, and Associations in the Italian Courts (1450–1500)," Ph.D. dissertation, Department of Art History and Communication Studies, McGill University.

Clark, Leah R. (2013), "Collecting, Exchange, and Sociability in the Renaissance Studiolo," *Journal of the History of Collections,* 25 (2): 171–84. https://doi.org/10.1093/jhc/fhs022.

Classen, Constance (2012), *Deepest Sense: A Cultural History of Touch,* Urbana: University of Illinois Press.

Coecke van Aelst, Pieter (1539), *Die inventie der colommen met haren coronementen ende maten. Wt Vitruvio ende andere diversche Auctoren optcorste vergadert, voer Scilders, beeltsniders, steenhouders, &c. En[de] allen die ghenuechte hebben in edificien der Antiquen,* Antwerp: Pieter Coecke van Aelst.

Cole, Michael (2011), *Ambitious Form: Giambologna, Ammanati, and Danti in Florence,* Princeton, NJ: Princeton University Press.

Collins, Mark, Phillip Emery, Christopher Phillpotts, Mark Samuel, and Christopher Thomas (2012), "The King's High Table at the Palace of Westminster," *Antiquaries Journal,* 92: 197–243.

Conseil General de la Haute-Marne (CGHM) (2003), *D'un coffre a l'autre,* Chateau du Grand Jardin exhibition catalog, Joinville, Chaumont: CGHM.

The Compact Oxford English Dictionary (1971), Oxford: Oxford University Press.

Cooper, Donal (2006), "Devotion," in Marta Ajmar-Wollheim and Flora Dennis (eds.), *At Home in Renaissance Italy*, 190–203, London: Victoria & Albert Museum.

Cooper, Lisa H. (2005), "Bed, Boat, and Beyond: Fictional Furnishing in *La Queste del Saint Graal*," *Arthuriana*, 15 (3): 26–50.

Corvisieri, Costantino (1878), "Il trionfo romano di Eleonora d'Aragona nel giugno del 1473," *Archivio della società Romana di Storia*, 1: 475–96.

Corvisieri, Costantino (1887), "Il trionfo romano di Eleonora d'Aragona nel giugno del 1473," *Archivio della società Romana di Storia*, 10: 629–87.

Coss, Peter (2006), "An Age of Deference," in Rosemary Horrox and W. Mark Ormrod (eds.), *A Social History of England, 1200–1500*, 31–73, Cambridge: Cambridge University Press.

Crivello, Fabrizio, ed. (2006), *Arti e tecniche del Medioevo*, Turin: Einaudi.

Crum, Roger (2001), "Controlling Women or Women Controlled: Suggestions for Gender Roles and Visual Culture in the Italian Renaissance Palace," in Sheryl E. Reiss and David G. Wilkins (eds.), *Beyond Isabella: Secular Women Patrons of Art in Renaissance Italy*, 37–50, Kirksville, MO: Truman State University Press.

Crum, Roger J. and John Paoletti (2008), "'... Full of People Every Sort': The Domestic Interior," in Roger Crum and John Paoletti (eds.), *Renaissance Florence, A Social History*, 273–94, Cambridge: Cambridge University Press.

Cusanus, Nicholas (1954), *Of Learned Ignorance*, trans. Germain Heron, New Haven, CT: Yale University Press.

Cusanus, Nicholas (1967), *De ludo globi*, in Nikolaus von Kues, *Philosophisch-theologische Schriften*, ed. Leo Gabriel, trans. Dietlind and Wilhelm Dupré, Vienna: Herder.

Cussans, John E. (1870–1), *A History of Hertfordshire*, vol. 2, *Hitchin, Hertford, and Broadwater*, London: Chatto and Windus.

da Riva, Fra Bovincino (1869), "The Fifty Courtesies for the Table," *Italian Courtesy Books*, trans. William Michael Rossetti: 17–31, London: Published for the Early English Text Society.

Daston, Lorraine (2008), *Things That Talk: Object Lessons from Art and Science*, New York: Zone Books.

Davis-Weyer, Caecillia (1986), *Early Medieval Art Sources and Documents 300–1150*, Toronto: University of Toronto Press.

DeGregorio, Scott (2011), "The Figures of Ezra in the Writings of Bede and the Codex Amiatinus," in Elizabeth Mullins and Diarmuid Scully (eds.), *Listen, O Isles, unto Me: Studies in Medieval Word and Image in Honour of Jennifer O'Reilly*, 115–25, Cork: Cork University Press.

Deguileville, Guillaume de (1992), *The Pilgrimage of Human Life (Le Pèlerinage de la vie humaine)*, trans. Eugene Clasby, Garland Library of Medieval Literature, Series B, vol. 76, New York: Garland.

Dehaisnes, Chrétien César Auguste (1886), *Documents et extraits divers concernant l'histoire de l'art dans las Flandre, l'Artois & le Hainaut avant le xve siècle*, Lille.

De Jonge, Krista (2005), "Le langage architectural de Jacques Du Broeucq," in Krista De Jonge, Marcel Capouillez, Michel De Reymaeker, and Roland Van Caenegem (eds.), *Jacques Du Broeucq de Mons (1505–1584): Maître artiste de l'empereur Charles Quint*, 95–112, Mons: Ville de Mons.

De la Riestra, Pablo (1998), "Gothic Architecture of the 'German Lands,'" in Rolf Toman (ed.), *Gothic: Architecture, Sculpture, Painting*, 190–235, Cologne: Könemann.

del Treppo, Mario (1994), "Le avventure storiografiche della Tavola Strozzi," in
  Paolo Marcy and Angelo Massafra (eds.), *Fra storia e storiografia. Scritti in onore di
  Pasquale Villani*, 483–515, Bologna: Società editrice il Mulino.
de Lorris, Guillaume and Jean de Meun ([1971] 1995), *The Romance of the Rose*,
  trans. Charles Dahlberg, 3rd edn., Princeton, NJ: Princeton University Press.
DePrano, Maria (2013), "*Chi vuol esser lieto, sia:* Objects of Entertainment in the
  Tornabuoni Palace in Florence," in Erin Campbell, Stephanie R. Miller, and
  Elizabeth Carroll Consavari (eds.), *The Early Modern Italian Domestic Interior,
  1400–1700: Objects, Spaces and Domesticities*, 127–42, Farnham, UK: Ashgate
  Publishing.
De Vivo, Filippo (2007), "Pharmacies as Centres of Communication in Early Modern
  Venice," *Renaissance Studies*, 21: 505–21.
D'Hainaut-Zvweny, Brigitte, ed. (2005), *Miroirs du sacré. Les Retables sculptés à
  Bruxelles xve–xvie siècles. Production, Formes et Usages*, Brussels: CFC-Éditions.
Didier, R. (1990), "Sculptures, style et faux," in Hartmut Kruhm and Christian
  Theuerkauff (eds.), *Festschrift fur Peter Bloch zum 11. Juli 1990*, 190–235, Munich:
  Verlag Philipp von Zabern.
Dieh, Daniel (1997), *Constructing Medieval Furniture: Plans and Instructions with
  Historical Notes*, Mechanicsburg, PA: Stackpole Books.
Dondi, C. (2004), *The Liturgy of the Canons Regular of the Holy Sepulchre of
  Jerusalem*, Turnhout: Brepols.
Dorin, Rowan W. (2008), "The Mystery of the Marble Man and His Hat: A
  Reconsideration of the Bari Episcopal Throne," *Florilegium*, 25: 29–52.
Douie, Decimia L. and David H. Farmer, eds. and trans. (1962), *Magna Vita Sancti
  Hugonis*, London: Clarendon Press.
Dove, Mary, ed. and trans. (2004), *The* Glossa Ordinaria *on the Song of Songs*,
  Kalamazoo, MI: Medieval Institute Publications.
Doyle, A.I. (1995), "'Lectulus Noster Floridus': An Allegory of the Penitent Soul," in
  R. Newhauser and J. A. Alford (eds.), *Literature and Religion in the Later Middle
  Ages: Philological Studies in Honour of Siegfried Wenzel*, 179–90, Binghamton, NY:
  Medieval and Renaissance Texts and Studies.
Drury, Elisabeth, ed. (1988), *Segreti di bottega: storia e tecniche delle arti decorative*,
  Novara: Istituto Geografico De Agostini.
Duby, Georges (1988), "The Aristocratic Households of Feudal France, Communal
  Living, Kinship," in Philippe Ariès and Georges Duby (eds.), *A History of Private
  Life: Revelations of the Medieval World*, 35–155, Cambridge, MA: The Belknap
  Press of Harvard University Press.
Dunkerton, Jill, Susan Foister, Dillian Gordon, and Nicholas Penny (1991), *Giotto to
  Dürer*. Early Renaissance Painting in the National Gallery, London: The National
  Gallery.
Durand, Jannic, ed. (1992), *Byzance: L'art byzantin dans les collections publiques
  françaises*, Paris: Editions de la Reunion des musees nationaux.
Eames, Penelope (1971), "Documentary Evidence Concerning the Character and Use
  of Domestic Furnishings in England in the Fourteenth and Fifteenth Centuries,"
  Furniture History, 7: 41–60.
Eames, Penelope (1973), "Inventories as Sources of Evidence for Domestic Furnishings
  in the Fourteenth and Fifteenth Centuries, " *Furniture History*, 9: 33–40.
Eames, Penelope (1974), "An Iron Chest at Guildhall of about 1427," *Furniture
  History*, 10: 1–4.

Eames, Penelope (1976), "Review," *Furniture History*, 12: 101–4.

Eames, Penelope (1977), "Furniture in England, France and the Netherlands from the Twelfth to the Fifteenth Century," *Furniture History*, 13: 1–303.

Eames, Penelope (1997), "The Making of a Hung Celour," *Furniture History*, 33: 35–42.

Egan, Geoff (2007), "Material Culture of Care of the Sick: Some Excavated Evidence from English Medieval Hospitals and Other Sites," in Barbara S. Bowers (ed.), *The Medieval Hospital and Medical Practice*, 65–76, Aldershot, UK: Ashgate.

Elderkin, G.W. (1939), "The Sarcophagus of Sidamara," *Hesperia*, 8: 101–15.

Elet, Yvonne (2002), "Seats of Power: The Outdoor Benches of Early Modern Florence," *Journal of the Society of Architectural Historians*, 61 (4): 444–69.

Elias, Norbert (2000), *The Civilizing Process: Sociogenetic and Psychogenetic Investigations*, Revised edn., Oxford: Wiley Blackwell.

Elston, Ashley (2012), "Pain, Plague, and Power in Niccolò Semitecolo's Reliquary Cupboard for Padua Cathedral," *Gesta*, 51 (2): 111–27.

Entz, Géza (1992), "Le séjour en Hongrie de Hans Hammer, future maître d'oeuvre de la cathédrale de Strasbourg," *Bulletin de la Cathédrale de Strasbourg*, 20: 7–10.

Erasmus, Desiderius (1849), *Pilgrimages to Saint Mary of Walsingham and Saint Thomas of Canterbury*, trans. J.G. Nicholls, London: John Bowyer.

Ernst, Ulrich, ed. (2012), *Visuelle Poesie I: Von der Antike bis zum Barock*, Berlin: De Gruyter.

Evans, Helen C., ed. (2004), *Byzantium: Faith and Power (1261–1557)*, New Haven, CT: Metropolitan Museum of Art, New York.

Falvo Heffernan, Carol, ed. (1976), *Le Bone Florence of Rome*, New York: Manchester University Press.

Faulkner, P.A. (1958), "Domestic Planning from the 12th to 14th Centuries," *Archaeological Journal*, 115: 150–83.

Fearn, Kate (1997), "Medieval and Later Woodwork from the Choir in Ely Cathedral," *Journal of the British Archaeological Association*, 150 (1): 59–75.

Fedeli, Francesca (2013), *Marquetry and Inlaid Woodwork: The Origin and Secrets of "Tinted Woods and Mosaics,"* Florence: Edifir.

Ferrandis Torres, José (1940), "Muebles hispanoárabes de taracea," *Al-Andalus*, 5: 459–65.

Ferrão, Bernardo (1990), *Mobiliáro Portugues*, 4 vols., Oporto: Lello and Irmao.

Ferretti, Massimo (1982), "I maestri della prospettiva," in Giulio Bollati and Paolo Fossati (eds.), *Storia dell'arte italiana*, part 3, vol. 5, *Forme e modelli*, 459–585, Turin: Einaudi.

Fligny, Laurence (1990), *Le mobilier en Picardie 1200–1700*, Amiens: Picard.

Flood, Finbarr B. (2001), "A Group of Reused Byzantine Tables as Evidence for Seljuq Architectural Patronage in Damascus," *Iran*, 39: 145–54.

Folda, Jaroslav (1993), "Images of Queen Melisende in Manuscripts of William of Tyre's *History of Outremer*: 1250–1300," *Gesta*, 32 (2): 97–112.

Folda, Jaroslav (2012), "Melisende of Jerusalem: Queen and Patron of Art and Architecture in the Crusader Kingdom," in Therese Martin (ed.), *Reassessing the Roles of Women as "Makers" of Medieval Art and Architecture*, 429–77, Leiden: Brill.

Forman, Benno (1971), "Continental Furniture Craftsmen in London: 1511–1625," *Furniture History*, 7: 94–120.

Forsyth, William H. (1989), "Popular Imagery in a Fifteenth-Century Burgundian Crèche," *Metropolitan Museum Journal*, 24: 117–26.

Fortini Brown, Patricia (2004), *Private Lives in Renaissance Venice: Art, Architecture, and the Family*, New Haven, CT: Yale University Press.

Fortini Brown, Patricia (2006), "The Venetian *casa*," in Marta Ajmar-Wollheim and Flora Dennis (eds.), *At Home in Renaissance Italy*, 50–65, London: Victoria & Albert Museum.

Foster, Edward E., ed. (2007), *Amis and Amiloun*, in *Amis and Amiloun, Robert of Cisyle, and Sir Amadace*, 2nd edn., Kalamazoo, MI: Medieval Institute Publications.

Frank, Daniel (2010), "Karaite Commentaries on the Song of Songs from Tenth-Century Jerusalem," in Jane Dammen McAuliffe, Barry D. Walfish, and Joseph W. Goering (eds.), *With Reverence for the Word: Medieval Scriptural Exegesis in Judaism, Christianity, and Islam*, 51–69, Oxford: Oxford University Press.

Friedman, John Block (1974), "The Architect's Compass in Creation Miniatures of the Later Middle Ages," *Traditio*, 30: 419–39.

Fuchs, François Joseph (1992), "Introduction au 'Musterbuch' de Hans Hammer," *Bulletin de la Cathédrale de Strasbourg*, 20: 11–67.

Fusco, Laurie and Gino Corti (2006), *Lorenzo de' Medici: Collector and Antiquarian*, Cambridge: Cambridge University Press.

Gaborit-Chopin, Danielle (1991), "Trône de Dagobert," in Danielle Gaborit-Chopin (ed.), *Le Trésor de Saint-Denis*, 63–8, Paris: Réunion des musées nationaux.

Galetti, P. (1985), *Civiltà del legno. Mobili dalle collezioni di palazzo Bianco e del museo degli Ospedali di S. Martino*, Genoa: Sagep.

Geddes, Jane (1999), *Medieval Decorative Ironwork in England*, London: Society of Antiquaries of London.

Gervase of Canterbury (1879), *Opera historica*, 2 vols., London: Longman and Co.

Gibbs, Henry H., ed. (1863), *The Romance of the Cheuelere Assigne*, London: Oxford University Press for EETS.

Gibbs, Henry H., ed. (1868), *The Romance of the Cheuelere Assigne*, London: Pub. for the Early English Text Society, by N. Trübner & Co.

Girouard, Mark, (1978), *Life in the English Country House: A Social and Architectural History*, London: Yale University Press.

Glenn, Cheryl (1992), "Author, Audience, and Autobiography: Rhetorical Technique in the Book of Margery Kempe," *College English*, 54 (5): 540–53.

Gloag, John (1972), *Guide to Furniture Styles: English and French, 1450–1850*, London: Adam and Charles Black.

Glover, Angela (2017), "What Constitutes Sculpture? The Guild Dispute of 1544 over the St. Gertrude Choirstalls in Leuven," in Ethan Matt Kavaler and Anne-Laure Van Bruaene (eds.), *Netherlandish Sixteenth-Century Culture*, 99–112, Turnhout: Brepols.

Glynn, Simon (2001), "AT&T Building." Available online: http://www.galinsky.com/buildings/att/ (accessed July 9, 2015).

Goitein, Shelomo Dov (1967–93), *A Mediterranean Society: The Jewish Communities of the Arab World as Portrayed in the Documents of the Cairo Geniza*, vol. 4, 99–112, Berkeley: University of California Press.

Goitein, Shelomo Dov (1977), "Three Trousseaux of Jewish Brides from the Fatimid Period," *AJS Review*, 2: 77–110.

Goldberg, Jeremy (2008), "The Fashioning of Bourgeois Domesticity in Later Medieval England: A Material Culture Perspective," in Maryanne Kowaleski and Jeremy

Goldberg (eds.), *Medieval Domesticity: Home, Housing and Household in Medieval England*, 124–44, Cambridge: Cambridge University Press.

Goldberg, Peter J.P. (1995), *Women in England, c. 1275–1525*, Manchester, UK: Manchester University Press.

Goldthwaite, Richard A. (1987), "The Empire of Things: Consumer Demand in Renaissance Italy," in F.W. Kent and Patricia Simons (eds.), *Patronage, Art, and Society in Renaissance Italy*, 153–75, Oxford: Oxford University Press.

Goldthwaite, Richard A. (1993), *Wealth and the Demand for Art in Italy, 1300–1500*, Baltimore: Johns Hopkins University Press.

Golombek, Lisa (1988), "The Draped Universe of Islam," in P.P. Soucek (ed.), *Content and Context of Visual Arts in the Islamic World: Papers from a Colloquium in Memory of Richard Ettinghausen, Institute of Fine Arts, New York University, 2–4 April 1980*, 25–38, University Park: Pennsylvania State University Press.

Goodall, John (2001), *God's House at Ewelme: Life, Devotion and Architecture in a Fifteenth-Century Almshouse*, Aldershot, UK: Ashgate.

Goodman, William L. (1964), *The History of Woodworking Tools*, London: Bell.

Gordon, Dillian (2011), *National Gallery Catalogues: The Italian Paintings before 1400*, London: National Gallery Company.

Gordon, Dillian, Lisa Monnas, and Caroline Elam (1997), *The Regal Image of Richard II and the Wilton Diptych*, London: Harvey Miller.

Grabar, André (1954), "La Sedia de San Marco à Venise," *Cahiers Archéologiques*, 7: 19–34.

Gregory the Great (2012), *Gregory the Great on the Song of Songs*, trans. Mark DelCogliano, Collegeville: Liturgical Press.

Gropp, David (1999), *Das Ulmer Chorgestühl und Jörg Syrlin der Ältere: Untersuchungen zu Architektur und Bildwerk*, Berlin: Deutscher Verlag für Kunstwissenschaft.

Hahn, Stacey (2007), "The Enigmatic Contours of the Bed in Yale 229," in Elizabeth M. Willingham (ed.), *Essays on the "Lancelot" of Yale 229*, 69–88, Turnhout: Brepols.

Haines, Margaret (1983), *La Sacrestia delle Messe del Duomo di Firenze*, Florence: Giunti.

Haines, Ray E., John V. Adam, Raymond Van Tassel, and Robert L. Thompson (1948), *Carpentry and Woodworking: A Handbook of Tools, Materials, Methods and Directions*, New York: D. Van Nostrand.

Hall, Edwin (1994), *The Arnolfini Betrothal: Medieval Marriage and the Enigma of Van Eyck's Double Portrait*, Berkeley: University of California Press.

Hamburger, Jeffrey (1997), *Nuns as Artists: The Visual Cultural of a Medieval Convent*, Berkeley: University of California Press.

Hamling, Tara and Catherine T. Richardson (2016), *A Day at Home in Early Modern England: The Materiality of Domestic Life, 1500–1700*, New Haven, CT: Yale University Press.

Hamon, Étienne (2008), *Un chanter flamboyant et son rayonnement. Gisors et les églises du Vexin français*, Besançon: Presses Universitaire de Franch-Comté.

Hand, John Oliver (2004), *National Gallery of Art: Master Paintings from the Collection*, Washington, DC: National Gallery of Art.

Haneca, K. (2010), *Twee gotische koffers uit Kortrijk*, Brussels: Vlaams Instituut voor het Onroerend eregoed.

Hanna, Ralph (2010), *The English Manuscripts of Richard Rolle: A Descriptive Catalogue*, Exeter, UK: University of Exeter Press.

Harbison, Craig (2005), "Iconography and Iconology," in Bernhard Ridderbos, Anne Van Buren, and Henk Van Veen (eds.), *Early Netherlandish Paintings: Rediscovery, Reception, and Research*, 378–406, Los Angeles: J. Paul Getty Museum.

Hart, Columbus, trans. (1970), William of Saint Thierry, *Exposition on the Song of Songs*, Kalamazoo, MI: Cistercian Publications.

Hasenfratz, Robert, ed. (2000), *Ancrene Wisse*, Kalamazoo, MI: Medieval Institute Publications.

Hasse, Max (1983), *Die Marienkirche zu Lübeck*, Munich: Deutscher Kunstverlag.

Hayward, Helena, ed. (1965), *World Furniture: An Illustrated History from Earliest Time*, London: Paul Hamlyn.

Heard, Kate (2011), "Such Stuff as Dreams Are Made On: Textiles and the Medieval Chantry," *Journal of the British Archaeological Association*, 164: 157–68.

Hedemann, Anne D. (1991), *The Royal Image: Illustrations of the Grandes Chroniques de France, 1274–1422*, Berkeley: University of California Press.

Helfenstein, Eva (2013), "Lorenzo de' Medici's Magnificent Cups: Precious Vessels as Status Symbols in Fifteenth-Century Europe," *I Tatti Studies in the Italian Renaissance*, 16 (1/2): 415–44.

Hellman, Mimi (1999), "Furniture, Sociability, and the Work of Leisure in Eighteenth-Century France," *Eighteenth-Century Studies*, 32 (4): 415–45.

Henderson, William George, ed. (1875), *Manuale et Processionale ad Usum Insignis Ecclesiae Eboracensis*, London: Published for the Society by Andrews & Co.

Heng, Geraldine (2003), *Empire of Magic: Romance and the Politics of Cultural Fantasy*, New York: Columbia University Press.

Heslop, T.A. (2009), "Regarding the Spectators of the Bayeux Tapestry: Bishop Odo and His Circle," *Art History*, 32 (2): 223–49.

Hirsch, John C. (1975), "Author and Scribe in the *Book of Margery Kempe*," *Medium Ævum*, 44: 145–50.

Hitchcock, Henry-Russel (1981), *German Renaissance Architecture*, Princeton, NJ: Princeton University Press.

Hoadley, R. Bruce (1980), *Understanding Wood: A Craftsman's Guide to Wood Technology*, Newtown, CT: Taunton Press.

Hoffman, Eva R. (2001), "Pathways of Portability: Islamic and Christian Interchange from the Tenth to the Twelfth Century," *Art History*, 24 (1): 17–50.

Hohler, Erla B. (1999), *Norwegian Stave Church Sculpture*, 2 vols., Oslo: Scandinavian University Press.

Hollis, Edward (2004), "The House of Life and the Memory Palace: Some Thoughts on the Historiography of Interiors," *Interiors*, 1 (1): 105–17.

Horstmann, Carl, ed. (1896), *English Prose Works of Richard Rolle: A Selection*, London: Sonnenschein.

Howley, Martin (2009), "Relics at Glastonbury Abbey in the Thirteenth Century: The Relic List in Cambridge, Trinity College R.5.33, fols. 104r–105v," *Mediaeval Studies*, 71: 197–234.

Hudry, Françoise (1995), "Introduction," in *Alain de Lille, Règles de théologie suivi de Sermon sur la sphère intelligible*, 7–80, Paris: Cerf.

Hudson, Harriet, ed. (1996), *Sir Eglamour of Artois*, in *Four Middle English Romances: Sir Isumbras, Octavian, Sir Eglamour of Artois, Sir Tryamour*, 121–58, Kalamazoo, MI: Medieval Institute Publications.

Hurx, Merlijn (2012), *Architect en aannemer: De opkomst van de bouwmarkt in de Nederlanden 1350–1530*, Nijmegen: Vantilt.

Hyams, Paul (1998), "What Did Henry III of England Think in Bed and in French about Kingship and Anger?," in Barbara H. Rosenwein (ed.), *Anger's Past: The Social Uses of and Emotion in the Middle Ages*, 92–126, Ithaca, NY: Cornell University Press.

Hyatt, Alfred (2000), "The Cartographic Imagination of Thomas of Elmham," *Speculum*, 75 (4): 859–86.

Impey, Oliver and Arthur Macgregor (1997), *The Origins of Museums: The Cabinet of Curiosities in Sixteenth and Seventeenth-Century Europe*, New York: Ursus Press.

Inglis, Erik (2003), "Gothic Architecture and a Scholastic: Jean de Jandun's "Tractatus de laudibus Parisius (1323)," *Gesta*, 42 (1): 63–88.

Jacobs, Lynne F. (1998), *Early Netherlandish Carved Altarpieces, 1380–1550: Medieval Tastes and Mass Marketing*, Cambridge: Cambridge University Press.

Janneau, Guilliaume (1973), *Meubles Bretons*, Paris: Hachette.

Jenkins, A.D. Fraser (1970), "Cosimo de' Medici's Patronage of Architecture and the Theory of Magnificence," *Journal of the Warburg and Courtauld Institutes*, 33: 162–70.

Johnston, A.F. and M. Rogerson, eds. (1979), *Records of Early English Drama: York*, Toronto: University of Toronto Press.

Jolivet, Jean (1980), "Remarques sur les Regulae Theologicae d'Alain de Lille," in H. Roussel and François Suard (eds.), *Alain de Lille, Gautier de Châtillon, Jakemart Giélée et leur temps*, 83–99, Villeneuve-d'Ascq: Presses universitaires de Lille.

Jones, David (1990), "A Sixteenth-Century Oak Cupboard the University of St. Andrews," *Regional Furniture*, 4: 71–80.

Kaneko, Beth (2018), "From the Space of the World to the Space of the Local: Two Maps of Thomas Elmham," in Meg Boulton, Jane Hawkes, and Heidi Stoner (eds.), *Place and Space in the Medieval World*, 74–86, New York: Routledge.

Karaskova, Olga (2012), "'ung dressoir de cinq degrez': Mary of Burgundy and the Construction of the Image of Female Ruler," in Juliana Dresvina and Nicholas Sparks (eds.), *Authority and Gender in Medieval and Renaissance Chronicles*, 318–43, Newcastle upon Tyne, UK: Cambridge Scholars Publishing.

Kauffmann, C.M. (1973), *Catalogue of Foreign Paintings*, vol. 1, *Before 1800*, London: Victoria & Albert Museum.

Kauffmann, Thomas DaCosta (1994), "From Treasury to Museum: The Collections of the Austrian Habsburgs," in John Elsner and Roger Cardinal (eds.), *The Cultures of Collecting*, 137–54, London: Reaktion Books.

Kavaler, Ethan Matt (2012), *Renaissance Gothic: Architecture and the Arts in Northern Europe 1470–1540*, New Haven, CT: Yale University Press.

Kavaler, Ethan Matt (2017), "Mapping Time: The Netherlandish Carved Altarpiece in the Sixteenth Century," in Ethan Matt Kavaler and Anne-Laure Van Bruaene (eds.), *Netherlandish Sixteenth Century Culture*, 31–64, Turnhout: Brepols.

Kemp, Martin (1997), *Behind the Picture: Art and Evidence in the Italian Renaissance*, New Haven, CT: Yale University Press.

Kent, F.W. (1987), "Politics and Society in Fifteenth-Century Florence," *I Tatti Studies*, 2: 41–70.

Kermode, Jenny (1998), *Medieval Merchants: York, Beverley and Hull in the Later Middle Ages*, Cambridge: Cambridge University Press.

Kirkbride, Robert (2008), *Architecture and Memory: The Renaissance Studioli of Federico de Montefeltro*, New York: Columbia University Press. Available online: http://www.gutenberg-e.org/kirkbride/index.html (accessed May 15, 2021).

Kisluk-Grosheide, Danielle O., Wolfram Koeppe, and William Rieder (2006), *European Furniture in the Metropolitan Museum of Art: Highlights of the Collection*, New York: The Metropolitan Museum of Art.

Klapisch-Zuber, Christiane (1985), *Women, Family, and Ritual in Renaissance Italy*, trans. Lydia G. Cochrane, Chicago: University of Chicago Press.

Klein, Bruno (1998), "The Beginnings of Gothic Architecture in France and its Neighbors," in Rolf Toman (ed.), *Gothic: Architecture, Sculpture, Painting*, 28–115, Cologne: Könemann.

Klein, Bruno (2009), "Einleitung: Werkmeister oder Architekten? Ein Problem kunsthistorischer Paradigmen," in Stefan Bürger and Bruno Klein (eds.), *Werkmeister der Spätgotik. Position und Rolle der Architekten im Bauwesen des 14. Bis 16. Jahrhunderts*, 13–17, Darmstadt: WGB.

Koeppe, Wolfram, Clare Le Corbeiller, William Rieder, Charles Truman, Suzanne G. Valenstein, Claire Vincent, and contributors (2012), *The Robert Lehman Collection*, vol. 15, *European and Asian Decorative Arts*, New York: The Metropolitan Museum of Art in association with Princeton University Press.

Körner, Hans, (1990), "Die 'gestörte Form' in der Architektur es späten Mittelalters," in Christoph Andreas, Maraike Bückling and Roland Dorn (eds.), *Festschrift für Hartmut Biermann*, 65–80, Weinheim: Dorn.

Koslow, Susan (1986), "The Curtain-Sack: A Newly Discovered Incarnation Motif in Rogier van der Weyden's 'Columba Annunciation,'" *Artibus et Historiae*, 7 (13): 9–33.

Koukoules, Phaedo (1948–57), *Byzantinon bios kai politismos*, 6 vols., Athens.

Kovalovszki, Julia (1981), *Meubles Gothiques et Renaissance*, Budapest: Corvina.

Kowaleski, Maryanne and P.J.P. Goldberg, eds. (2008), *Medieval Domesticity: Home, Housing and Household in Medieval England*, Cambridge: Cambridge University Press.

Kreisel, Heinrich and Georg Himmelheber (1981), *Die Kunst des deutschen Moebels Vol. 1 Von den Anfangen bis zum Hochbarock*, Munich: C.H. Beck.

Kurman, Peter and Brigitte Kurmann-Schwarz (2010), "Memoria and Porträt. Zum Epitaphdes Hans von Burghausen an der Martinskirche zu Landshut," in Stefan Bürger and Bruno Klein (eds.), *Werkmeister der Spätgotik. Personen, Amt und Image*, 44–60, Darmstadt: WGB.

Landucci, Luca (1927), *A Florentine Diary from 1450 to 1516, Continued by an Anonymous Writer till 1542*, trans. A. De Roben Jervis, London: J.M. Dent and Sons.

Lane, Barbara (1989), "'Requiem aeternam don eis': The Beaune 'Last Judgment' and the Mass of the Dead," *Simiolus: Netherlands Quarterly for the History of Art*, 19 (3): 166–80.

Laskaya, Anne and Eve Salisbury, eds. (1995), *Sir Gowther*, in *The Middle English Breton Lays*, 263–307, Kalamazoo, MI: Medieval Institute Publications.

Lawton, David (1992), "Voice, Authority and Blasphemy in 'The Book of Margery Kempe,'" in Sandra J. McEntire (ed.), *Margery Kempe: A Book of Essays*, 93–115, London: Garland Publishing.

Lemé-Hébuterne, Kristiane (2007), *Les stalles de Notre Dame de la cathédrale Notre-Dame d'Amiens: histoire, iconographie*, Paris: Picard.

Lewer, H.W. and James C. Wall (1913), *The Church Chests of Essex*, London: Talbot.

LeZotte, Annette (2004), "Signature Spaces and Signature Objects in Early Netherlandish Painings of Domestic Interiors," Ph.D. dissertation, University of Texas Austin.

Licht, Meg (1996), "Elysium: a Prelude to Renaissance Theater," *Renaissance Quarterly*, 49 (1): 1–29.

Linardou, Kallirroe (2011), "Depicting the Salvation: Typological Images of Mary in the Kokkinobaphos Manuscripts," in L. Brubaker and M. Cunningham (eds.), *The Cult of the Mother of God in Byzantium: Texts and Images*, 133–49, Farnham, UK: Ashgate.

Lindow, James R. (2005), "For Use and Display Selected Furnishings and Domestic Goods in Fifteenth-Century Florentine Interiors," *Renaissance Studies*, 19 (5): 634–46.

Lindow, James R. (2007), *The Renaissance Palace in Florence: Magnificence and Splendour in Fifteenth-Century Italy*, Aldershot, UK: Ashgate.

Linghor, Michael (2008), "The Palace and Villas as Spaces of Patrician Self-Definition," in Roger Crum and John Paoletti (eds.), *Renaissance Florence, A Social History*, 240–72, Cambridge: Cambridge University Press.

Lipińska, Aleksandra (2015), *Moving Sculptures: Southern Netherlandish Alabasters from the 16th to 17th Centuries in Central and Northern Europe*, Leiden: Brill.

Little, Donald P. (1984), "The Ḥaram Documents as Sources for the Arts and Architecture of the Mamluk Period," *Muqarnas*, 2: 61–72.

Lloyd, Geneviève (1999), "Augustine and the 'Problem' of Time," in Gareth B. Matthews (ed.), *The Augustinian Tradition*, 39–60, Berkeley: University of California Press.

Long, Pamela O. (2005), *Technology and Society in the Medieval Centuries: Byzantium, Islam and the West, 500–1300*, Washington, DC: American Historical Association.

Long, Pamela O., ed. (1985), *Science and Technology in Medieval Society*, Annals of the New York Academy of Science, vol. 441, New York: New York Academy of Science.

Longnon, Jean and Raymond Cazelles (1989), *The Tres Riches Heures of Jean, Duke de Berry*, New York: George Braziller.

Loomis, Roger Sherman (1953), "Edward I, Arthurian Enthusiast," *Speculum*, 28: 114–27.

Loos, Adolf (1997), *Ornament and Crime: Selected Essays*, Riverside, CA: Ariadne Press.

Lucas, Adam Robert (2005), "Industrial Milling in the Ancient and Medieval Worlds: A Survey of the Evidence for an Industrial Revolution in Medieval Europe," *Technology and Culture*, 46 (1): 1–30.

Lucie-Smith, Edward (1979), *Furniture: A Concise History*, London: Thames and Hudson.

Lupack, Alan, ed. (1990), *The Siege of Milan*, in *Three Middle English Charlemagne Romances*, 105–60, Kalamazoo, MI: Medieval Institute Publications.

Lydecker, Kent (1987), "The Domestic Setting of the Arts in Renaissance Florence," Ph.D. dissertation, Johns Hopkins University, Baltimore.

Lyman, Thomas (1982), "La Table d'autel de Bernard Gelduin et son ambiance originelle," *Cahiers de St Michel de Cuxa*, 13: 53–73.

Macquoid, Percy (1925), *The Age of Oak*, London: The Medici Society.

Macquoid, Percy and Ralph Edwards, eds. (1954), *Dictionary of English Furniture*, 2nd edn., 3 vols., Woodbridge, UK: Antique Collectors' Club.

Maierbacher-Legl, Gerdi (2012), *Der Henndorfer Truhenfund: Dokumentation und Datierung von 127 gefassten siebenbürgischen Truhen des 15. bis 18. Jahrhunderts*, Munich: Siegl.

Malory, Thomas (2008), *Le Morte Darthur: The Winchester Manuscript*, ed. Helen Cooper, Oxford: Oxford University Press.

Maltese, Corrado, ed. (1973), *Le tecniche artistiche*, Milan: Mursia.

Maltese, Corrado, ed. (1990), *I supporti nelle arti pittoriche. Storia, tecnica, restauro*, Milan: Mursia.

Marchesi, Andrea (2012), "Robe che si trovano nello studio overo camerino di marmo, et nel adorato di sua Excellentia': Presence e assenze di oggetti d'arte nell'inventario Antonelli del 1559," in Charles Hope (ed.), *Il regno e l'arte: i camerini di Alfonso I d'Este, terzo duca di Ferrara*, 203–34, Florence: L.S. Olschki.

Marks, Richard and Paul Williamson, eds. (2003), *Gothic: Art for England 1400–1547*, London: Victoria & Albert Museum.

Marsden, Richard (1995), "Job in his Place: The Ezra Miniature in the Codex Amiatinus," *Scriptorium*, 49: 3–15.

Maskell, William, ed. (1846), *The Ancient Liturgy of the Church of England According to the Uses of Sarum Bangor York & Hereford and the Modern Roman Liturgy Arranged in Parallel Columns*, 2nd edn., London: W. Pickering.

Matchette, Ann (2006), "To Have and Have Not: The Disposal of Household Furnishings in Florence," *Renaissance Studies*, 20 (5): 701–16.

Matter, E. Ann (1990), *The Voice of My Beloved: The Song of Songs in Western Medieval Christianity*, Philadelphia: University of Pennsylvania Press.

Mattox, Philip (2006), "Domestic Sacral Space in the Florentine Renaissance Palace," *Renaissance Studies*, 20 (5): 658–73.

Mayr-Harting, Henry (1999), *Ottonian Book Illumination: An Historical Study*, 2nd revised edn., London: Harvey Miller.

McCarthy, Conor, ed. (2004), *Love, Sex and Marriage in the Middle Ages: A Sourcebook*, London: Routledge.

McIver, Katherine A. (2013), "Let's Eat," in Erin Campbell, Stephanie R. Miller, and Elizabeth Carroll Consavari (eds.), *The Early Modern Italian Domestic Interior, 1400–1700: Objects, Spaces and Domesticities*, 159–74, Farnham, UK: Ashgate.

McIver, Katherine A. (2015), *Cooking and Eating in Renaissance Italy: From Kitchen to Table*, Lanham, MD: Rowman & Littlefield Studies.

Medieval & Renaissance Material Culture (n.d.), "Home." Available online: www.larsdatter.com (accessed April 22, 2021).

Meiggs, Russell (1982), *Trees and Timber in the Ancient Mediterranean World*, Oxford: Clarendon Press.

Mercer, Eric (1962), *English Art 1553–1625*, Oxford: Clarendon Press.

Mercer, Eric (1969), *Furniture 700–1700*, London: Weidenfeld and Nicholson.

Meyvaert, Paul (1996), "Bede, Cassiodorus, and the Codex Amiatinus," *Speculum*, 71: 827–83.

Michael, Michael A. (2009), "Re-orienting the Westminster Retable: Islam, Byzantium and the West," in Paul Binski and Ann Massing (eds.), *The Westminster Retable: History, Technique, Conservation*, 97–108, Cambridge: The Hamilton Kerr Institute and University of Cambridge.

"Microarchitecture et figures du bati. L'échelle à l'épreuve de la matière" (2014), Paris, Institut national d'histoire de l'art, December 8–10.

"Mikroarchitektur im Mittelalter" (2005), Nuremberg, Germanisches Natinalmuseum, October 26–29.

Miller, Stephanie R. (2013), "Parenting in the Palazzo: Images and Artifacts of Children in the Italian Renaissance Home," in Erin Campbell, Stephanie R. Miller, and Elizabeth Carroll Consavari (eds.), *The Early Modern Italian Domestic Interior, 1400–1700: Objects, Spaces and Domesticities*, 67–88, Farnham, UK: Ashgate.

Morgan, Hollie L.S. (2017), *Beds and Chambers in Late Medieval England: Readings, Representations and Realities*, Woodbridge, UK: York Medieval Press in association with Boydell.

Morley, John (1999), *The History of Furniture: Twenty-Five Centuries of Style and Design in the Western Tradition*, Boston: Little, Brown and Company.

Mueller, Janel M. (1986), "Autobiography of a New 'Creatur': Female Spirituality, Self-hood, and Authorship in *The Book of Margery Kempe*," in Mary Beth Rose (ed.), *Woman in the Middle Ages and the Renaissance: Literary and Historical Perspectives*, 155–72, Syracuse, NY: Syracuse University Press.

Musacchio, Jacqueline Marie (1999), *The Art and Ritual of Childbirth in Renaissance Italy*, London: Yale University Press.

Musacchio, Jacqueline Marie (2000), "The Madonna and Child, a Host of Saints, and Domestic Devotion in Renaissance Florence," in Gabriele Neher and Rupert Shepherd (eds.), *Revaluing Renaissance Art*, 147–64, Farnham, UK: Ashgate.

Musacchio, Jacqueline Marie (2008), *Art, Marriage, and Family in the Florentine Renaissance Palace*, New Haven, CT: Yale University Press.

Museum of Contemporary Art (MOCA) (n.d.), "Installation." Available online: http://moca.org/pc/viewArtTerm.php?id=18 (accessed April 11, 2016).

Nagel, Alexander (2011), "Twenty-Five Notes on Pseudoscript in Italian Art," *RES: Journal of Anthropology and Aesthetics*, 59 (60): 229–48.

Nees, Lawrence (1993), "Audiences and Reception of the *Cathedra Petri*," *Gazette des Beaux Arts*, 122: 57–72.

Nees, Lawrence (1996), "Forging Monumental Memories in the Early Twelfth Century," in Wessel Reinink and Jeoren Stumpel (eds.), *Memory and Oblivion: Proceedings of the XXIXth Internation Congress of the History of Art held in Amsterdam*, 773–82, Dordrecht: Kluwer Academic Publishers.

Neuschel, Kristen B. (1998), "Noble Households in the Sixteenth Century: Material Settings and Human Communities," *French Historical Studies*, 15 (4): 595–622.

Nicka, Isabella (2010), "Möbel als Analysekategorie," *Medium Aevum Quotidianum*, 60: 17–35.

Noel, William and Daniel Weiss, eds. (2002), *The Book of Kings: Art, War, and the Morgan Library's Medieval Picture Bible*, London: Third Millennium.

Norman, Diana (1999), *Siena and the Virgin: Art and Politics in a Late Medieval City State*, New Haven, CT: Yale University Press.

North, Michael (2010), "Introduction—Artistic and Cultural Exchanges between Europe and Asia, 1400–1900: Rethinking Markets, Workshops and Collections," in Michael North (ed.), *Artistic and Cultural Exchanges between Europe and Asia, 1400–1900*, 1–8, Farnham, UK: Ashgate.

Northedge, Alastair (2005), *The Historical Topography of Samarra*, Samarra Studies 1, London: British School of Archaeology in Iraq and Fondation Max van Berchem.

Nussbaum, Norbert (2000), *German Gothic Church Architecture*, trans. Scott Kleager, New Haven, CT: Yale University Press.

Nygren, Christopher J. (2016), "Titian's *Christ with the Coin:* Recovering the Spiritual Currency of Numismatics in Renaissance Ferrara," *Renaissance Quarterly*, 69: 449–88.

O'Connell, Monique and Eric Dursteler (2016), *The Mediterranean World: From the Fall of Rome to the Rise of Napoleon*, Baltimore: Johns Hopkins University Press.

Oikonomides, Nicolas (1990), "The Contents of the Byzantine House from the Eleventh to the Fifteenth Century," *Dumbarton Oaks Papers*, 44: 205–14.

Oledzka, Eva (2016), *Medieval and Renaissance Interiors*, London: British Library.

Oliva, Marilyn (2008), "Nuns at Home: The Domesticity of Sacred Space," in Maryanne Kowaleski and P.J.P. Goldberg (eds.), *Medieval Domesticity: Home, Housing and Household in Medieval England*, 145–61, Cambridge: Cambridge University Press.

Olsen, Christina (1992), "Gross Expenditure: Botticelli's Nastagio Degli Onesti Panels," *Art History*, 15 (2): 136–70.

Oosterwijk, Sophie (2006), "'Mouz ich tanzen und kan nit gan?': Death and the Infant in the Dance Macabre," *Word and Image*, 22 (2): 146–64.

Otter, Monika (2001), "Baudri of Borgueil, 'To Countess Adela'," *Journal of Medieval Latin*, 11: 60–141.

Panofsky, Erwin (1934), "Jan Van Eyck's Arnolfini Portrait," *The Burlington Magazine*, 64: 117–27.

Paolini, Claudio (2002), *Il mobile del Rinascimento: la collezione Herbert Percy Horne*, Florence: Edizioni della Meridiana.

Paolini, Claudio (2004a), "L'arredo ligneo ecclesiastico nel territorio pistoiese: tipologie, trasformazioni e restauri tra XV e XIX secolo," in Chiara d'Afflitto and Maria Cristina Masdea (eds.), *Arte Sacra nei Musei della Provincia di Pistoia*, 135–54, Florence: Edifir.

Paolini, Claudio (2004b), *I luoghi del cibo. Cucine, tinelli e sale da banchetto nella casa fiorentina tra Xv e XVII secolo*, Florence: Polistampa.

Paolini, Claudio (2004c), *I luoghi dell'intimità. La camera da letto nella casa fiorentina del Rinascimento*, Florence: Polistampa.

Paolini, Claudio (2006), *Il pavimento del Battistero di Firenze: con una nota sul commesso di pietra e di legname*, Florence: Polistampa.

Paolini, Claudio (2012), "Mobili, 'masserizie e chose' negli inventari delle case di Francesco Datini," in *Palazzo Datini a Prato: Una casa fatta per durare mille anni*, vol. 1, 231–43, Florence: Polistampa.

Paolini, Claudio and Manfredi Faldi (2005), *Glossario delle tecniche artistiche e del restauro*, Florence: Edizioni Palazzo Spinelli.

Paolini, Claudio, Daniela Parenti, and Ludovica Sebregondi (2010), *Virtù d'amore: pittura nuziale nel Quattrocento fiorentino*, Florence: Giunti.

Parani, Maria G. (2003), *Reconstructing the Reality of Images: Byzantine Material Culture and Religious Iconography (11th–15th Centuries)*, Leiden: Brill.

Payne, Alina (2010), "Materiality, Crafting, and Scale in Renaissance Architecture," *Oxford Art Journal*, 32: 365–86.

Payne, Alina (2012), *From Ornament to Object: Genealogies of Architectural Modernism*, New Haven, CT: Yale University Press.

Pedersen, Frederick (2000), *Marriage Disputes in Medieval England*, London: Hambledon Press.

Pernis, Maria Grazia and Laurie Schneider Adams (2003), *Federico da Montefeltro and Sigismondo Malatesta*, New York: Peter Lang.

Pickvance, Christopher G. (2007), "Medieval Tracery-Carved Clamp-Fronted Chests: The 'Kentish Gothic' Chests of Rainham, Faversham and Canterbury in Comparative Perspective," *Regional Furniture*, 21: 67–94.

Pickvance, Christopher G. (2012), "Domed Medieval Chests in Kent: A Contribution to a National and International Study," *Regional Furniture*, 26: 105–47.

Pickvance, Chrostopher G. (2014), "The Tracery-Carved, Clamp-Fronted, Medieval Chest at St Mary Magdalen Church, Oxford in Comparative North-West European Perspective," *Antiquaries Journal*, 94: 153–71.

Pickvance, Christopher G. (2015), "The Slow Arrival of Renaissance Influence on English Furniture: A Study of the 1519 Silkstede, Shanklin and the 1539 Garstang, Cirencester Chests," *Regional Furniture*, 29: 101–30.

Pickvance, Christopher G. (2017), "Kentish Gothic' or Imported? Understanding a Group of Tracery-Carved Medieval Chests in Kent and Norfolk," *Archaeologia Cantiana*, 138: 105–28.

Pontano, Giovanni (1999), *I libri delle virtù sociali*, ed. Francesco Tateo, Rome: Bulzoni Editore.

Pousset, Didier (2004), *Analyse xylologique et etablissement du profil dendrochronologique du coffre Cl. 21545 conserve au Musee National du Moyen Age, Hotel de Cluny, Paris (75)*. Available online: http://www.dendro.fr/mobilier.html (accessed May 15, 2021).

Preyer, Brenda (1998), "Planning for Visitors at Florentine palaces," *Renaissance Studies*, 12 (3): 357–74.

Preyer, Brenda (2006a), "The Acquaio (Wall Fountain) and Fireplace in Florence," in Marta Ajmar-Wollheim and Flora Dennis (eds.), *At Home in Renaissance Italy*, 284–7, London: Victoria & Albert Museum.

Preyer, Brenda (2006b), "The Florentine *Casa*," in Marta Ajmar-Wollheim and Flora Dennis (eds.), *At Home in Renaissance Italy*, 34–49, London: Victoria & Albert Museum.

Qaddumi, G., trans. and ed. (1996), *Book of Gifts and Rarities: Kitāb al-Hadāya wa al-Tuhaf*, Harvard Middle Eastern Monographs 29, Cambridge, MA: Harvard University Press.

Quiney, Anthony (1999), "Hall or Chamber? That is the Question: The Use of Rooms in Post-Conquest Houses," *Architectural History*, 42: 24–46.

Raggio, Olga and Antoine M. Wilmering (1999), *The Gubbio Studiolo and its Conservation*, 2 vols., New York: The Metropolitan Museum of Art.

Raine, James and John Williams Clay, eds. (1869a), *Testamenta Eboracensia: A Selection of Wills from the Registry at York*, vol. 4, London: Surtees Society.

Raine, James and John Williams Clay, eds. (1869b), *Testamenta Eboracensia: A Selection of Wills from the Registry at York*, vol. 5, London: Surtees Society.

Ramirez, Janina (2009), "Sub culmine gazas: The Iconography of the Armarium on the Ezra Page of the Codex Amiatinus," *Gesta*, 48 (1): 1–18.

Randolph, Adrian W.B. (2014), *Touching Objects: Intimate Experiences of Italian Fifteenth-century Art*, New Haven, CT: Yale University Press.

Reeve, Matthew M. (2003), "A Seat of Authority: The Archbishop's Throne at Canterbury Cathedral," *Gesta*, 42 (2): 131–42.

Reeve, Matthew M. (2008), *Thirteenth Century Wall Painting of Salisbury Cathedral: Art, Liturgy, and Reform*, Woodbridge, UK: Boydell Press.

Reeve, Matthew M. (2011), "Gothic Architecture and the Civilizing Process: The Great Hall in Thirteenth Century England," in Robert Bork, William W. Clark, and Abby McGhee (eds.), *New Approaches to Medieval Architecture*, 93–112, Farnham, UK: Routledge.

Reilly, Diane (2006), *The Art of Reform in Eleventh-Century Flanders: Gerard of Cambrai, Richard of Saint-Vanne and the Saint-Vaast Bible*, Leiden: Brill.

Riall, Nicholas (2012), "A Tudor Cupboard at Cotehele and Associated Carpentry Work in the Welsh Marches," *Regional Furniture*, 26: 23–72.

Richardson, Octavia, ed. (1884–5), *The Right Plesaunt And Goodly Historie of the Foure Sonnes of Aymon. Englisht from the French by William Caxton, and Printed by Him about 1489*, London: Published for the Early English Text Society by Trübner.

Ridderbos, Bernhard (2005), "Objects and Questions," in Bernhard Ridderbos, Anne Van Buren, and Henk Van Veen (eds.), *Early Netherlandish Paintings: Rediscovery, Reception, and Research*, 4–173, Los Angeles: J. Paul Getty Museum.

Riddy, Felicity (2008), "'Burgeis' Domesticity in Late-Medieval England," in Maryanne Kowaleski and P.J.P. Goldberg (eds.), *Medieval Domesticity: Home, Housing and Household in Medieval England*, 14–36, Cambridge: Cambridge University Press.

Robinson, James (2008), *Masterpieces of Medieval Art*, London: British Museum.

Rodwell, Warwick (2013), *The Coronation Chair and Stone of Scone*, Oxford: Oxbow Books.

Roe, Fred (1902), *Ancient Coffers and Cupboards*, London: Methuen.

Roe, Fred (1905), *Old Oak Furniture*, London: Methuen.

Roe, Fred (1920), *History of Oak Furniture*, London: The Connoisseur.

Rolle, Richard (1884), *The Psalter, or Psalms of David and Certain Canticles*, trans. Henry Ramsden Bramley, Oxford: Clarendon Press.

Roller, Stefan and Michael Roth (2002), *Michel Erhart und Jörg Syrlin d.Ä.: Spätgotik in Ulm*, Stuttgart: Theiss.

Romby, Giuseppina Carla (1976), *Descrizioni e rappresentazioni della città di Firenze nel XV secolo con la trascrizione inedita dei manoscritti di Benedetto Dei e un indice ragionato dei manoscritti utili per la storia della città*, Florence: Libreria editrice fiorentina.

Rubin, Patricia Lee (2007), *Images and Identity in Fifteenth-Century Florence*, New Haven, CT: Yale University Press.

Rutherglen, Susannah (2012), "Ornamental Paintings of the Venetian Renaissance," Ph.D. thesis, Princeton University.

Ryder, R.D. (1975), "Three-Legged Turned Chairs," *The Connoisseur*, 190 (766): 242–7.

Ryder, R.D. (1976), "Four-Legged Turned Chairs," *The Connoisseur*, 191 (767): 44–9.

Sadān, Yusūf (1976), *Le mobilier au Proche-Orient medieval*, Leiden: E.J. Brill.

Saintenoy, Paul (1931), *Jehan Money: Le Statuaire Jan Mone, Maître Artiste de Charles-Quint*, Brussels: Maurice Lamertin.

Sand, Alexa (2008), "Inseminating Ruth in the Morgan Picture Bible," in Albrecht Classen (ed.), *Sexuality in the Middle Ages and Early Modern Times: New Approaches to a Fundamental Cultural-Historical and Literary-Anthropological Theme*, 535–64, Berlin: Walter de Gruyter.

Sands, Donald B., ed. (1986), *Havelok the Dane*, in *Middle English Verse Romances*, 66–140, Exeter: University of Exeter.

Santoro, F. Sricchia (2000), "Tra Napoli e Firenze: Diomede Carafa, gli Strozzi e un celebra 'lettuccio'," *Prospettiva*, 100: 41–54.

Sarti, Raffaella (2002), *Europe at Home: Family and Material Culture, 1500–1800*, trans. Allan Cameron, New Haven, CT: Yale University Press.

Sauer, Michelle M. (2014), "Architecture of Desire: Mediating the Female Gaze in the Medieval English Anchord," in Joanna de Groot and Sue Morgan (eds.), *Sex, Gender, and the Sacred: Reconfiguring Religion in Gender History*, 150–69, Chichester, UK: Wiley Blackwell.

Sayers, Jane (2000), "Peter's Throne and Augustine's Chair: Rome and Canterbury from Baldwin (1184–90) to Robert Winchesley (1297–1313)," *Journal of Ecclesiastical History*, 2: 249–66.

Schapiro, M. (1952), "The Joseph Scenes on the Maximianus Throne in Ravenna," *Gazette des Beaux-Arts*, 40: 27–38.

Scheller, Robert W. (1995), *Exemplum: Model Book Drawings and the Practice of Artistic Transmission in the Middle Ages (ca. 900–ca. 1470)*, Amsterdam: Amsterdam University Press.

Schmitz, Hermann (1956), *The Encyclopaedia of Furniture*, London: Zwemmer.

Schock-Werner, Barbara (2012), "Hans Hammer," *Grove Art Online*. https://doi.org/10.1093/gao/9781884446054.article.T036421.

Schock-Werner, Barbara (n.d.), "Johann Dotzinger," *Grove Art Online*. https://doi.org/10.1093/gao/9781884446054.013.9002294293.

Schulenberg, Jane (2014), "Female Religious as Collectors of Relics: Finding Sacrality and Power in the Ordinary," in Michael Frassetto, John Hosler, and Matthew Gabriele (eds.), *Where Heaven and Earth Meet: Essays on Medieval Europe in Honor of Daniel F. Callahan*, 152–77, Leiden: Brill.

Scott, Robert Forsyth (1913), *Notes from the Records of St John's College*, Cambridge: Cambridge University Press.

Scranton, Robert L. (1957), *Mediaeval Architecture in the Central Area of Corinth*, Princeton, NJ: American School of Classical Studies at Athens.

Seward, Desmond (2007), *A Brief History of the War of the Roses: The Bloody Rivalry for the Throne of England*, London: Robinson.

Shelton, Anthony Alan (1994), "Cabinets of Transgression: Renaissance Collections and the Incorporation of the New World," in John Elsner and Roger Cardinal (eds.), *The Cultures of Collecting*, 177–203, London: Reaktion Books.

Shepherd, Rupert (2007), "Republic Anxiety and Courtly Confidence: The Politics of Magnificence and Fifteenth-Century Italian Architecture," in Michelle O'Malley and Evelyn S. Welch (eds.), *The Material Renaissance*, 47–70, Manchester, UK: Manchester University Press.

Sherlock, David (2008), *Suffolk Church Chests*, Ipswich, UK: Suffolk Institute of Archaeology and History.

Shoemaker, Stephen J. (2002), *Ancient Traditions of the Virgin Mary's Dormition and Assumption*, Oxford: Oxford University Press.

Singer, Charles, Eric John Holmyard, Alfred Rupert Hall, and Trevor I. Williams, eds. (1956), *A History of Technology*, vol. 2, *The Mediterranean Civilization and the Middle Ages: c. 700 B.C. to c. A.D. 1500*, Oxford: Clarendon Press.

Singer, Charles, Eric John Holmyard, Alfred Rupert Hall, and Trevor I. Williams (1962), *Storia della tecnologia*, vol. 2, *Le civiltà Mediterranee e il Medioevo*, Turin: Boringhieri 1962.

Sleep, J. (2004), "Chests, Coffers and Trunks in East Anglia, 1650–1730: A Step towards Definition," *Regional Furniture*, 18: 62–7.

Sliwka, Jennifer (2015), *Visions of Paradise. Botticini's Palmieri Altarpiece*, London: The National Gallery Company.

Smith, D. Vance (2003), *Arts of Possession: The Middle English Household Imaginary*, Minneapolis: University of Minnesota Press.

Smith, Lesley (2009), *The Glossa Ordinaria: The Making of a Medieval Bible Commentary*, Leiden: Brill.

Smith, Jeffrey Chipps (1994), *German Sculpture of the Later Renaissance c. 1520–1580: Art in an Age of Uncertainty*, Princeton, NJ: Princeton University Press.

Smith, Webster (1975), "On the Original Location of the Primavera," *The Art Bulletin*, 57 (1): 31–40.

Sneyd, Charlotte Augusta, ed. (1847), *A Relation … of the Island of England about the year 1500*, vol. 37, London: Camden Society.

Snyder, James, John Silver, and Henry Luttikhuizen (2005), *Northern Renaissance Art*, Upper Saddle River, NJ: Prentice Hall.

Sparke, Penny (2008), *The Modern Interior*, Chicago: University of Chicago Press.

Sparkes, Ivan (1980), *An Illustrated History of English Domestic Furniture (1100–1837)*, Bourne End, UK: Spurbooks.

Squire, Aelred, ed. and trans. (1962), *Hugh of Saint Victor: Selected Writings*, London: Harper and Row.

Staley, Lynn, ed. (1996), *The Book of Margery Kempe*, Kalamazoo, MI: Medieval Institute Publications.

Staley, V., ed. (1911), *The Library of Liturgiology and Ecclesiology for English Readers*, vol. 9, *The Sarum Missal in English*, London: De La More Press.

Staley Johnson, Lynn (1991), "The Trope of the Scribe and the Question of Literary Authority in the Works of Julian of Norwich and Margery Kempe," *Speculum*, 66 (4): 820–38.

Stapleford, Richard (2013), *Lorenzo de' Medici at Home: The Inventory of the Palazzo Medici in 1492*, University Park: Pennsylvania State University Press.

Starkey, David and Philip Ward, eds. (1988), *The Inventory of King Henry VIII: The Transcript*, London: Harvey Miller.

Steane, John M. (2001), *The Archaeology of Power*, Stroud, UK: Tempus.

Stones, Alison (1996), "The Illustrations of BN, fr. 95 and Yale 229: Prolegomena to a Comparative Analysis," in Keith Busby (ed.), *Word and Image in Arthurian Romance*, 203–60, New York: Garland.

Stones, Alison and Elspeth Kennedy (2009), "Signs and Symbols in the *Estoire del saint Graal* and the *Queste del saint Graal*," *Proceedings of the 2006 Harlaxton Symposium*, 18: 150–67.

Stratford, Jenny (1993), *The Bedford Inventories. The Worldly Goods of John, Duke of Bedford, Regent of France (1389–1435)*, London: The Society of Antiquaries of London.

Stratford, Jenny (2012), *Richard II and the English Royal Treasure*, Woodbridge, UK: Boydell Press.

Strocchia, Sharon T. (1989), "Death Rites and the Ritual Family in Renaissance Florence," in Marcel Tetel, Ronald Witt, and Rona Goffen (eds.), *Life and Death in Fifteenth-Century Florence*, 120–45, Durham, NC: Duke University Press.

Strocchia, Sharon T. (1992), *Death and Ritual in Renaissance Florence*, Baltimore: Johns Hopkins University Press.

Strong, Roy (2002), *Feast: A Grand History of Eating*, London: Random House.

Svoboda, Rosemary A. (1983), "The Illustrations of the Life of Saint Omer," 2 vols., Ph.D. thesis, University of Minnesota.

Symonds, R.W. (1962), "Il mobilio nell'epoca postromana," in Charles Singer, T.I. Williams, A.R. Hall, and E.J. Holmyard (eds.), *Storia della tecnologia*, vol. 2/1, *Le civiltà Mediterranee e il Medioevo*, 243–61, Turin: Boringhieri.

Syson, Luke (2002a), "Holes and Loops. The Display and Collection of Medals in Renaissance Italy," *Journal of Design History*, 15: 229–44.

Syson, Luke (2002b), "'Tura and the "Minor Arts': The School of Ferrara," in Stephen Campbell and Alan Chong (eds.), *Cosmè Tura: Painting and Design in Renaissance Ferrara*, 31–70, Boston: Isabella Stewart Gardner Museum and Electa.

Syson, Luke (2006a), "Fifteenth-Century Interiors in the Netherlands," in Jeremy Aynsley and Charlotte Grant (eds.), *Imagined Interiors: Representing the Domestic Interior Since the Renaissance*, 46–7, London: Victoria & Albert Museum.

Syson, Luke (2006b), "Representing Domestic Interiors," in Marta Ajmar-Wollheim and Flora Dennis (eds.), *At Home in Renaissance Italy*, 86–101, London: Victoria & Albert Museum.

Syson, Luke and Dora Thornton (2001), *Objects of Virtue: Art in Renaissance Italy*, Los Angeles: J. Paul Getty Museum Publications.

Talbot, C.H., Samuel Fanous, and Henrietta Leyser, eds. (2008), *The Life of Christina of Markyate*, Oxford: Oxford University Press.

Taylor, Valerie (2005), "Banquet Plate and Renaissance Culture: A Day in the Life," *Renaissance Studies*, 19 (5): 621–33.

Thibodeau, Timothy M. (2007), *The Rationale Divinorum of William Durand of Mende*, New York: Columbia University Press.

Thirion, Jacques (1998), *Le mobilier du Moyen-Âge et de la Renaissance en France*, Dijon: Faton.

Thirion, Jacques, Thierry Crépin-Leblond, and Anne Dion (2002) *Parures d'Or et de Pourpre: le mobilier à la cour des Valois, exhibition*: Chateau de Blois; Paris: Somogy.

Thomas, Natalie (2008), "Did Women Have a Space," in Roger Crum and John Paoletti (eds.), *Renaissance Florence: A Social History*, 311–30, Cambridge: Cambridge University Press.

Thornton, Dora (1997), *The Scholar in His Study: Ownership and Experience in Renaissance Italy*, New Haven, CT: Yale University Press.

Thornton, Peter (1990), "The Restello: What Was It?," *Furniture History*, 26: 174–82.

Thornton, Peter (1991), *The Italian Renaissance Interior 1400–1600*, New York: Harry Abrams.

Thun, Terje and Elling Alsvik (2009), "Dendrochronological Dating of Four Chests: A Surprising Result," *Dendrochronologia*, 27: 71–4.

Thunø, Erik (2015), *The Apse Mosaic in Early Medieval Rome: Time, Network, Repetition*, Cambridge: Cambridge University Press.

Thurley, Simon (1993), *The Royal Palaces of Tudor England. Architecture and Court Life*, London: Yale University Press for the Paul Mellon Centre for Studies in British Art.

Timmermann, Achim (2007), "A Promise of Paradise: Microarchitecture, Baptism and the Font coborium of St. Severus in Erfurt," *Biuletyn Historii Sztuki*, 69: 177–88.

Timmermann, Achim (2009), *Real Presence: Sacrament Houses and the Body of Christ c. 1270–1600*, Turnhout: Brepols.

Tracy, Charles (1987), *English Gothic Choir Stalls 1200–1400*, Woodbridge, UK: Boydell and Brewer.

Tracy, Charles (1988), *English Medieval Furniture and Woodwork*, London: Victoria & Albert Museum.

Tracy, Charles (2001), *Continental Church Furniture in England: A Traffic in Piety*, Woodbridge, UK: Antique Colllectors' Club.

Tracy, Charles (2014), *Britain's Medieval Episcopal Thrones*, Oxford: Oxbow Books.

Tracy, Charles and Andrew Budge (2015), *Britain's Medieval Episcopal Thrones: History, Archaeology and Conservation*, Oxford: Oxbow Books.

Tracy, Charles and Hugh Harrison (2004), *The Choir-Stalls of Amiens Cathedral*, Reading, UK: Spire Books.

Trionfi Honorati, Maddalena (1980), "Mobili," in Paola Barocchi (ed.), *Palazzo Vecchio: committenza e collezionismo medicei*, 205–14, Florence: Edizioni Medicee.

Trionfi Honorati, Maddalena (1981), "A proposito del 'lettuccio'," *Antichità Vivax*, 20 (3): 39–48.

Tuohy, Thomas (1996), *Herculean Ferrara: Ercole d'Este, 1471–1505, and the Invention of a Ducal Capital*, Cambridge: Cambridge University Press.

Tymms, Samuel, ed. (1850), *Wills and Inventories from the Registers of the Commissary of Bury St. Edmund's and the Archdeacon of Sudbury*, London: Camden Society.

Vale, Malcolm (2001), *The Princely Court: Medieval Courts and Culture in North-West Europe 1270–1380*, Oxford: Oxford University Press.

Van Damme, Jan (1996), "De architectuur," in Antoinette Huysmans, Jan van Damme, Carl van de velde, and Christine van Mulders (eds.), *Cornelis Floirs 1514–1575: beeldhouwer, architect ontwerper*, 115–20, Brussels: Gemeentekrediet.

van Rijen, Jean Pierre (2000), "Precious Metalwork in God Leaf. Everyday Lustre at the Court of Jean de Berry, as Depicted by the Limbourg Brothers," in Rob Dückers and Pieter Roelofs (eds.), *The Limbourg Brothers: Nijmegen Masters at the French Court*, 165–78, Nijmegen: Ludion.

Vasari, Giorgio ([1568] 1966–87), "Vita di Dello Delli," in *Le vite de' più eccellenti pittori, scultori ed architettori nelle redazioni del 1550 e 1568*, ed. Paola Barocchi and Rosanna Bettarini, 6 vols., Florence: Sansoni Editore.

Vasari, Giorgio (1906), *Le vite de' più eccellenti pittori scultori ed architettori*, ed. Paola Barocchi and Rosanna Bettarini, edizione a cura di Gaetano Milanesi, 9 vols., Florence: Sansoni Editore.

Velkovska, Elena (2001), "Funeral Rites According to Byzantine Liturgical Sources," *Dumbarton Oaks Papers*, 55: 21–51.

Voaden, Rosalynn (1997), "All Girls Together: Community, Gender and Vision at Helfta," in Diane Watt (ed.), *Medieval Women and Their Communities*, 72–91, Toronto: University of Toronto Press.

Von Falke, Otto (1924), *Deutsche Mobel des Mittelalters und der Renaissance*, Stuttgart: Julius Hoffman.

Von Stülpnagel, Karl Heinrich (2000), *Die Gothische Truhen der Lüneberger Heidekloster*, Cloppenburg: Museumsdorf Cloppenburg.

Wade, Susan (2007), "Miraculous Seeing and Monastic Identity: Miracles of the Visual from the Monasteries of Lobbes and Nivelles," Ph.D. thesis, New York University.

Walcott, MacKenzie E.C. (1868), "Inventories of St Mary's Hospital, Dover, St Martin New-Work, Dover, and the Benedictine Priory of S. S. Mary and Sexburga in the Island of Sheppy for Nuns," *Archaeologia Cantiana*, 7: 272–306.

Walker, Philip (1980), *Woodworking Tools*, Aylesbury, UK: Shire Publications.

Wanscher, Ole (1980), *Sella Curulis, the Folding Stool: An Ancient Symbol of Dignity*, Copenhagen: Rosenkilde and Bagger.

Warren, Jeremy (2006), "Bronzes," in Marta Ajmar-Wollheim and Flora Dennis (eds.), *At Home in Renaissance Italy*, 20, London: Victoria & Albert Museum.

Webb, Diana (2005), "Domestic Space and Devotion in the Middle Ages," in Anthony Spicer and Sarah Hamilton (eds.), *Defining the Holy: Sacred Space in Medieval and Early Modern Europe*, 27–48, Aldershot, UK: Ashgate.

Webb, Jennifer (2013), "All That is Seen: Ritual and Splendour at the Montefeltro Court in Urbino," in Erin Campbell, Stephanie R. Miller, and Elizabeth Carroll Consavari (eds.), *The Early Modern Italian Domestic Interior, 1400–1700: Objects, Spaces and Domesticities*, 191–204, Farnham,UK: Ashgate.

Weigert, Laura (2004), *Weaving Sacred Stories: French Tapestries and the Performance of Clerical Identity*, New York: Cornell Press.

Weinberger, Martin (1964), "The Chair of Dagobert," in Lucy Freeman Sandler (ed.), *Essays in Memory of Karl Lehmann*, 375–82, New York: Institute of Fine Arts.

Weiss, Daneil (1995), "Architectural Symbolism and the Decoration of the Ste.-Chapelle," *Art Bulletin*, 77 (2): 308–20.

Weitzmann, Kurt (1966), "Various Aspects of Byzantine Influence on the Latin Countries from the Sixth to the Twelfth Century," *Dumbarton Oaks Papers*, 20: 1–24.

Welch, Evelyn S. (1995), *Art and Authority in Renaissance Milan*, New Haven, CT: Yale University Press.

Welch, Evelyn (2002), "Public Magnificence and Private Display: Giovanni Pontano's *De Splendore* (1498) and the Domestic Arts," *Journal of Design History*, 15 (4): 211–21.

Welch, Evelyn S. (2008), "Space and Spectacle in the Renaissance Pharmacy," *Medicina e Storia*, 15: 127–58.

Wells-Cole, Anthony (1997), *Art and Decoration in Elizabethan and Jacobean England: The Influence of Continental Prints 1558–1625*, New Haven, CT: Yale University Press.

Welsh, Peter C. (1966), *Woodworking Tools 1600–1900*, Washington, DC: Smithsonian Institution.

Weyl-Carr, Annemarie and Andreas Nicolaïdès (2012), *Àsinou Across Time: Studies in the Architecture and Murals of the Panagia Phorbiotissa, Cyprus*, Washington, DC: Dumbarton Oaks.

Whelan, Fiona (2017), *The Making of Manners in Twelfth-Century England: The Book of the Civilized Man*, London: Routledge.

Whitaker, Muriel (1999), "The Chaucer Chest and the 'Pardoner's Tale': Didacticism in Narrative," *The Chaucer Review*, 34: 174–89.

Whitehead, Christiana, Denis Renevey, and Anne Mouron, eds. (2010), *The Doctrine of the Hert: A Critical Edition with Introduction and Commentary*, Exeter: University of Exeter Press.

Williams, Megan (2006), *The Monk and the Book: Jerome and the Making of Christian Scholarship*, Chicago: University of Chicago Press.

Wikipedia (2021), "Aachen Cathedral." Available online: https://en.wikipedia.org/wiki/Aachen_Cathedral (accessed July 9, 2015).

Wilson, C. Anne (1991), "From Medieval Great Hall to Country House Dining Room: The Furniture and Setting of the Social Meal," in C. Anne Wilson (ed.), *"The Appetite and the Eye": Visual Aspects of Food and Its Presentation within Their Historical Context*, 28–55, Edinburgh: Edinburgh University Press.

Wilson, Christoper (1997), "Rulers, Artificers and Shoppers: Richard II's Remodeling of Westminster Hall 1393–99," in Dillian Gordon, Lisa Monnas, and Caroline Elam (eds.), *The Regal Image of Richard II and the Wilton Diptych*, 22–60, London: Harvey Miller.

Wilson, Christopher (2009), "The Architecture and Ornament of the Westminster Retable as Evidence of Dating and Origin," in Paul Binski and Ann Massing (eds.), *The Westminster Retable: History, Technique, Conservation*, 79–98, Cambridge: The Hamilton Kerr Institute and University of Cambridge.

Wilson, Katherine Anne (2015), "The Household Inventory as Urban 'Theatre' in Late Medieval Burgundy," *Social History*, 40 (3): 335–59.

Wilson, Katherine Anne (2016), "'In the chamber, in the garderobe, in the chapel, in a chest': The Possession and Uses of Luxury Textiles; The Case of Later Medieval Dijon," in Katherine Anne Wilson and Bart Lambert (eds.), *Europe's Rich Fabric: The Consumption, Commercialisation and Production of Luxury Textiles in Italy, the Low Countries and Neighbouring Territories (14th–16th Centuries)*, 11–34, Burlington, VT: Ashgate.

Windisch-Grätz, Franz (1982), *Mobel Europas Romanik-Gotik*, Munich: Klinkhardt and Biermann.

Witthoft, Brucia (1982), "Marriage Rituals and Marriage Chests in Quattrocento Florence," *Artibus et Historiae*, 5 (3): 43–59.

Wixom, William D., ed. (1999), *Mirror of the Medieval World*, New York: The Metropolitan Museum of Art.

Wolfthal, Diane (2010), *In and Out of the Marital Bed: Seeing Sex in Renaissance Europe*, New Haven, CT: Yale University Press.

Woods, Kim W. (2007), *Imported Images: Netherlandish Late Gothic Sculpture in England, c. 1400–c. 1550*, Donington, UK: Shaun Tyas.

Woolgar, Christopher M. (1999), *The Great Household in Late-Medieval England*, New Haven, CT: Yale University Press.

Wright, A.C. (1976), *Medieval Furniture*, Southend-on-Sea, UK: Borough Museums Service.

Wright, David H. (2001), *The Roman Vergil and the Origins of Medieval Book Design*, Toronto: University of Toronto.

Youngs, Deborah and Simon Harris (2003), "Demonizing the Night in Medieval Europe: A Temporal Monstrosity?," in Bettina Bildhauer and Robert Mills (eds.), *The Monstrous Middle Ages*, 134–54, Toronto: University of Toronto Press.

Zerner, Henri (2003), *Renaissance Art in France: The Invention of Classicism*, Paris: Flammarion.

Online Resources

Belgian Art Links and Tools (BALaT) (n.d.), "All Databases." Available online: http://balat.kikirpa.be/search_all.php (accessed April 22, 2021).

BILDINDEX (2021). Available online: http://www.bildindex.de (accessed April 22, 2021).

DRBO.org (2001–21), "Douay-Rheims Bible" and Challoner Notes. Available online: www.drbo.org (accessed April 22, 2021).

Kringla (n.d.). Available online: http://www.kringla.nu/kringla/ (accessed April 22, 2021).

Laboratoire d'Expertise du Bois et de Datation par Dendrochronologie (n.d.),
    "Mobilier." Available online: http://www.dendro.fr/mobilier.html (accessed April
    22, 2021).

The Metropolitan Museum of Art (2000–21), "The Met Collection." Available online:
    http://www.metmuseum.org/collection/the-collection-online (accessed April 22,
    2021).

Musée de Cluny (n.d.-a), "Coffre de Poissy." Available online: http://www.musee-
    moyenage.fr/collection/oeuvre/coffre-de-poissy.html (accessed April 22, 2021).

Musée de Cluny (n.d.-b), "Collection." Available online: https://www.musee-
    moyenage.fr/collection/http://www.musee-moyenage.fr/collection/oeuvre (accessed
    April 22, 2021).

Musée de Cluny (n.d.-c), "Table Pliante." Available online: http://www.musee-
    moyenage.fr/collection/oeuvre/table-pliante.html (accessed April 22, 2021).

Musée national de la Renaissance (n.d.), "Collections." Available online: http://musee-
    renaissance.fr/collections (accessed April 22, 2021).

National Trust (n.d.), "Collections." Available online: http://www.
    nationaltrustcollections.org.uk/ (accessed April 22, 2021).

POP: la plateforme ouverte du patrimoine (n.d.). Available online: https://www.pop.
    culture.gouv.fr/http://www.culture.gouv.fr/public/mistral/palsri_fr (accessed April
    22, 2021).

Rijksmuseum (n.d.). Available online: https://www.rijksmuseum.nl/en (accessed April
    22, 2021).

Swiss National Museum (2021), "Collection." Available online: http://www.
    nationalmuseum.ch/sammlung_online/ (accessed April 22, 2021).

Victoria & Albert Museum (2021), "Collections." Available online: http://collections.
    vam.ac.uk/ (accessed April 22, 2021).

INDEX